MW00584051

IN THEIR OWN WORDS:

AUGUSTA AND AIKEN AREA VETERANS REMEMBER WORLD WAR II

James Garvey, Douglas Higbee, and Hubert van Tuyll, editors

Augusta Richmond County Historical Society

www.thearchs.org

Augusta, GA

Cover design: Sarah Pacetti.

"In Their Own Words: Augusta and Aiken Area Veterans Remember World War II." Edited by James Garvey, Douglas Higbee, and Hubert van Tuyll.

ISBN 978-0937044-04-9.

Published 2017 by the Augusta Richmond County Historical Society, Inc. Augusta, Georgia. ©2017 Augusta Richmond County Historical Society, Inc.

To those thousands of citizens from the greater Augusta-Aiken area who served our nation during the tumultuous years of World War II, we extend sincere thanks for your personal dedication and sacrifice that have led to the preservation of the freedoms we enjoy today.

"And I saw that with my own eyes. And what I'm telling you I saw. There's maybe a lot of other things happened, but I'm telling you what I saw."

James Wisenbaker

Praise for *In Their Own Words*

"War is Hell" is attributed to Union Gen. William T. Sherman. He'd find no arguments from the men and women whose narratives fill this important historical book.

– Bill Baab, Outdoor Editor (Retired), *Augusta Chronicle*

These gripping, first-hand World War II recollections, painstakingly recorded by Fred Gehle and his team of interviewers and skillfully organized by the editors, will be read and appreciated by historians, researchers and local residents of the greater Augusta area for generations to come.

– Russell K. Brown, Ph.D., Augusta Richmond County Historian and Author

In their Own Words brings World War II up close and personal with the deft interweaving of the history of the period with the experiences of local men and women in their own voices. From a glimpse at the area before the war, stories in every theater of combat, to the efforts to rebuild normal lives after victory, this work documents the war and its impact through the eyes of our own veterans. A fascinating read.

– LeeAnn Caldwell, Ph.D., Director of the Center for the Study of Georgia History, Augusta University

Every soldier, sailor, airman, and marine has a story. This book captures tons of extraordinary stories shared intimately by those who lived them. They will inform, inspire, make you smile and break your heart. But patriotism is alive and well. Genuine thanks to the monumental efforts of Fred Gehle and those who spent thousands of hours producing a lasting tribute to what service to our nation is all about.

– Jeff Foley, Brig. Gen., U.S. Army (Retired)

This book is the culmination of a 10-year race against time by Fred Gehle and numerous volunteers from the Augusta Richmond County Historical Society and affiliated historical, government, and civic organizations to capture and collect WWII veteran's memories before they passed away. The soldiers, sailors, airmen, and marines, men and women of all races, and their families understood the importance of contributing their stories, thus adding their piece of the puzzle, no matter how small, to the larger picture known as WWII. Time did steal many pieces of the story, but in the end the race was won and you hold in your hands the evidence of that victory.

– Steven J. Rauch, Signal Corps Branch Historian, Fort Gordon, Georgia.

This remarkable narrative is skillfully distilled from the voices of real people who, abandoning the typical reticence of their generation, give us their eyewitness accounts of our nation's greatest effort to defeat tyranny and to plant democracy. The memories of these citizen soldiers are a taste of their genuine efforts, seasoned with a generous dose of heart and soul.

– Thomas Heard Robertson, Jr., author of *Resisting Sherman*

"What did you do in the war, Daddy?" *This question was answered by over 800 men and women of the Central Savannah River Area in an interview process orchestrated by Fred Gehle and sponsored by the Augusta Richmond County Historical Society. From these hundreds of interviews the best have been selected and are presented in chronological order with clarifying and informative background comments.*

– Tom Sutherland, Past President, Augusta Richmond County Historical Society

TABLE OF CONTENTS

Foreword

Welcome, dear readers, to a remarkable book, *In Their Own Words: Augusta and Aiken Area Veterans Remember World War II*, lovingly written and edited by Dr. James Garvey, Dr. Douglas Higbee and Dr. Hubert van Tuyll. It consists of fascinating vignettes from those noble patriots from the Central Savannah River Area of East Georgia and Western South Carolina who served America at the time of its greatest danger.

I am honored and humbled to have been asked to write this foreword. Although not a veteran of World War II and not a native Augustan, my recollections of World War II are quite vivid. My father was in the military and he had been stationed in Hawaii since the summer of 1940. On the morning of 7 December, 1941, my sister and I were in the back of an Army truck on the way to Sunday School from our small home in Honolulu. We did not make it. When we arrived at the front gate of Fort Derussy, the Japanese attack was underway. The truck turned around and the trip back home was very fast and quite frightening—I was six years old at that time. Having witnessed that famous attack at age six, I have had a lifelong interest in many aspects of America's World War II experience. This book has refreshed and reinforced this fundamental curiosity. I trust you will also find the book both fascinating and uplifting.

Are you interested in what it was like to come across Omaha Beach on D-Day, to fight in the Battle of the Bulge in the harsh winter of 1944, to enter a German concentration camp just after its liberation, or to watch two kamikaze aircraft crash explosively into your ship? You have come to the right place.

Patriotic Americans from Augusta, Aiken, Edgefield, North Augusta, Thomson, Waynesboro and many other local communities tell their stories. As you might expect, these men and women, all in their 80s and 90s when they shared their memories, pull no punches. What is truly remarkable is how vivid their recollections were and how willingly they told their stories.

What you are about to read are the vivid recollections of those who participated in some of the most important events of the 20th century. At the start of each chapter, the editors establish historical context. These editors then turn the narrative over to the World War II veterans themselves.

The context relates to life during the Great Depression, the build-up to the war, and recruitment. The narrative then moves to the training, to the deployments overseas, and, most importantly, to the combat experiences in every theater of war. The final chapters cover the redeployments back to America and how these veterans were integrated back into the life of postwar America. Hence, this is a complete book covering those years and events. The editors have chosen the vignettes carefully. Some of these veterans did not hear the sound of guns, yet every story in this book is well worth telling.

Here are some short highlights.

1. Leroy Robinson, a Navy fighter pilot, became an ace by age 19. Shooting down five Japanese aircraft could not compare with the mission where he was flying so low that he got hit by a large torpedo dropped from an enemy aircraft. He not only saved an American ship from being sunk, he managed to fly his damaged aircraft back to safety. Quite a story.

2. Chuck Ballas, who was wounded in France, went AWOL from the hospital so he could return to his unit. Ballas tells a wild story of getting lost, entering a bar outside of Paris and finding it full of German soldiers. You can read the rest of the story.

3. Chester McCoy fought with the 4th Marine Division in the Pacific in 1944. He served in the 24th Marine Regiment during the invasion of Roi-Namur in the Marshall Islands. In that same regiment was the son of Harry Hopkins, President Roosevelt's closest advisor, and the battalion commander of the 1st Battalion, Lieutenant Colonel A. J. Dyess, an Augusta native. Both Hopkins and Dyess were killed on the island of Roi-Namur. Wounded on Saipan, McCoy also fought on Iwo Jima.

4. Don Donner tells stories of being captured and surviving as a prisoner of war. He was liberated not by the Americans but by the Russians.

Much of the motivation of the soldiers, sailors, Marines, airmen, Coast Guardsmen and merchant mariners during World War II was based fundamentally on altruism. At no other time in American history did this nation operate at such a high level of personal and national unselfishness.

In the wisdom of more than seventy years of hindsight, it is clear that liberal democracy now flourishes in Japan, Germany and Italy as a direct result of two factors. First, the total military defeat of these three fascist empires. Second, the careful nurturing of democratic institutions in these three countries in the years immediately after World War II. The American military not only won the war but they stayed overseas long enough to win the peace.

There are those who would argue that World War II, like all wars, accomplished nothing of any long-term value. I strongly disagree with this point of view. The world today has a higher percentage of people living in working democracies than at any time in history. Japan, Germany and Italy have successfully operated as robust democracies for more than two generations.

These three nations have joined the United States, Great Britain, France, Canada, Australia and many other states in providing democratic role models for other nations to emulate. Hence, it is no exaggeration to state that the heroism of those in this book and the millions of others who fought for the Allies in World War II accomplished more of lasting value than any group of combatants in world history.

The veterans of World War II and the families who supported them during those desperate years of the early 1940s deserve the respect and appreciation of the billions of people who have benefited, directly or indirectly, from their sacrifices. I would like to rephrase the famous quote from Winston Churchill when he praised the pilots of the Royal Air Force immediately after the 1940 Battle of Britain. Churchill said in the House of Commons, "Never in the field of human conflict was so much owed by so many to so few." If Churchill were alive today, I trust he would forgive me for saying about the Marines, sailors, soldiers and airmen of the grand alliance, "Never in human history have so many people owed so much to a single group of warriors — those who fought in World War II to destroy fascism and to expand democracy."

It may be useful at this point to remind ourselves of the enormous efforts made by Americans in the early 1940s. 16.1 million men and 342,000 women served in our military. Of these, 6.4 million volunteered and 10 million were drafted; 406,000 men and 217 women were killed in action and 671,000 others were wounded. The victory does not belong to any one group, region or class; this was a triumph of the entire nation. It belongs to everyone.

I was ten years old when VJ Day was announced — at last the war was over and victory was won. I can remember the sense of relief, joy and satisfaction that permeated my school, my neighborhood and my family. One of the war's great emotional legacies is the prominence of shared responsibility, obligation and reward. This great war reminds us of who we can be when we are at our best. World War II did not eliminate differences of income and wealth, but it did emphasize equality of duty and patriotic commitment.

One of the great speeches of the twentieth century was delivered by President Ronald Reagan on June 6, 1984, at Normandy. The occasion was the fortieth anniversary of the D-Day invasion of France. Directly in front of him were many warriors who had come across Omaha beach that fateful morning. The following are excerpts from his speech.

The air is soft, but 40 years ago at this moment, the air was dense with smoke and the cries of men, and the air was filled with the crack of rifle fire and the roar of cannon.

Forty summers have passed since the battle that you fought here …you were hardly more than boys, with the deepest joys of life before you. Yet, you risked everything here. Why? Why did you do it? What impelled you to put aside the instinct for self-preservation and risk your lives… What inspired all the men of the armies that met here? We look at you, and somehow we know the answer. It was faith and belief; it was loyalty and love.

The men of Normandy had faith that what they were doing was right, faith that they fought for all humanity, faith that a just God would grant them mercy on this beachhead or on the next. It was the deep knowledge — and pray God we have not lost it — that there is a profound, moral difference between the use of force for liberation and the use of force for conquest. You were here to liberate, not to conquer, and so you and those others did not doubt your cause. And you were right not to doubt.

You all knew that some things are worth dying for. One's country is worth dying for, and democracy is worth dying for, because it's the most deeply honorable form of government ever devised by man. All of you loved liberty. All of you were willing to fight tyranny.

The Americans who fought here that morning knew word of the invasion was spreading through the darkness back home. They fought — or felt in their hearts, though they couldn't know in fact, that in Georgia they were filling the churches at 4 a.m., in Kansas they were kneeling on their porches and praying, and in Philadelphia they were ringing the Liberty Bell.

Something else helped the men of D-day: their rock-hard belief that Providence would have a great hand in the events that would unfold here; that God was an ally in this great cause.

For those interested in a deeper understanding of World War II, two books are recommended. 1. *Why the Allies Won.* This is probably the best one-volume history of the war. Rather than examine the major battles, the author develops a brilliant strategic analysis of the great strengths of the Allies. *2. Courage, Compassion, Marine: The Unique Story of Jimmie Dyess*. This biography, published in 2015, describes life in Augusta during the 1930s. It covers Marine training from 1936 through 1943 and the battle for the Marshalls where Dyess was killed. Dyess is the only person to earn America's two highest awards for heroism, the Medal of Honor and the Carnegie Medal.

As I close this foreword, I would be remiss if I did not highlight the remarkable efforts of our friend, neighbor and fellow Augustan, Fred Gehle. His commitment and persistence in reaching out to World War II veterans, raising funds, encouraging and supporting volunteers and coordinating three very complex projects was "above and beyond."

Fred played a major role in the filming and production of the individual videos, of the production of the *War Stories* video and of the research, writing and production of this book. Over the course of nine years, Fred made more than 25,000 phone calls relating to his role as Coordinator, Veterans History Project for the Augusta Richmond County Historical Society. His dining room table was unusable for these nine years since it was totally covered with documents relating to these projects. This book is the capstone to Fred's life of service to his community.

Perry M. Smith, PhD
Major General, US Air Force Ret.

Preface

I grew up before Pearl Harbor and remember the surprise Japanese attack on December 7, 1941, as an eight year old. As a young boy in my early formative years, I followed news of the war closely even though, unlike today, television did not exist. Instead, I relied on newspaper reports, radio and newsreels to keep informed about the momentous events of those years. These memories have led to my life-long interest in World War II history which continues to this day.

When my wife Jane and I first visited the National World War II Museum in New Orleans for a one-week conference on the war in the summer of 2006, we learned of the national Veterans History Project.

Approved unanimously by the U. S. Congress in October 2000, the Project involves collecting stories and experiences from living veterans of all wars as part of a nation-wide program tied to the Library of Congress in Washington, D. C. When the Veterans History Project was brought to their attention, board members of the Augusta Richmond County Historical Society (ARCHS) unanimously approved participation in the project, limited initially to World War II veterans living in the Central Savannah River Area (CSRA).

A few years earlier and unaware at the time of ARCHS' subsequent decision, Mark Albertin of Scrapbook Video Productions had been contacted by the Brandon Wilde Retirement Community in Augusta to interview on video approximately 20 of their residents with World War II experiences following the initial guidelines established by the national Veterans History Project. Mark provided ARCHS with guidance and advice which proved most helpful in the early start-up phase of our project.

Publicity in local area media—principally newspapers, television and radio—brought in early responses from World War II veterans as well as volunteers interested in conducting interviews. In addition, local veterans organizations such as the American Legion and VFW were contacted as well as numerous civic organizations to invite members of their groups who served in World War II to participate in the Project. Initial telephone contacts with each veteran were made for basic background information: branch of military, dates of service, theater of operations, most important wartime experience, and post-war employment.

After initial orientation of volunteers regarding interview procedures, two principal sites were established for interviews: Augusta University and Aiken Technical College; veterans with health or other problems would be interviewed at home or at a healthcare facility, if necessary. ARCHS provided funds for purchase of video cameras to be used by volunteer camera operators.

In addition to a Background Data Form and Veteran's Release Form, the Library of Congress required that each veteran video interview be at a minimum length of thirty minutes and have a Video Recording Log of significant topics discussed during the interview session in order to be accepted into their national database in Washington.

Over nine years, from 2007 to 2016, well over 800 individuals were interviewed on their wartime experience, with DVDs produced of each interview. Volunteer interviewers totaled exactly 75; each conducted one or more interviews, with three individuals conducting just over 100 separate video interviews each!

Four copies of each interview on DVD were produced—one given to the participating veteran; one sent to the Library of Congress, along with required documents; and two copies for current and future reference deposited at the Special Collections Library at Augusta University.

When a decision was made to develop a book highlighting area veterans with interesting or significant stories, all DVDs were reviewed in sets of five by experienced volunteers on a double-assessment system. As a result, approximately 150 veterans were initially qualified on the rating system for possible inclusion in the book. A transcription service in Atlanta then transcribed the sections which the editors had selected for developing the book.

The book emphasizes CSRA veterans; unfortunately, many who had significant and noteworthy experiences could not be included because of growing up and living elsewhere or having minimum post-war ties to the greater Augusta area.

Finally, it should be noted that ARCHS contracted Mark Albertin early in the project to produce a video entitled *War Stories: Augusta—Area Veterans Remember World War II*. The 70-minute video, completed in 2010, includes comments from 23 area veterans from all of the primary military services—Army, Navy, Air Force, Marines, and Coast Guard. In 2011, the video won an Archives Award from the Georgia Historical Records Advisory Board. Copies are available for purchase from the Society.

In conclusion, ARCHS has agreed to continue the Project to recognize both the Korea and Vietnam era war veterans and those in the conflicts that followed to recognize their service to our nation. If you served our country during those times and have not already been contacted, consider participating in this extension of the national

Veterans History Project that will recognize those who have served our nation in the past in preserving the freedoms that we all enjoy today.

Frederick P. Gehle
Project Coordinator
Veterans History Project - World War II
Augusta Richmond County Historical Society

Introduction

This book wasn't exactly meant to be. When Fred Gehle and his crew started their work a decade ago, there wasn't a plan for a book, just a video record of the experiences of hundreds of Georgia and South Carolina veterans of World War II. But as their work proceeded, and the rich results of that work became increasingly apparent, we felt the need to present this material in a format that would be both more accessible and more permanent.

Fred and a small group of reviewers selected what they thought were the most clear and complete interviews for compilation into a book. After months of meetings, they whittled down the hundreds of extant interviews to about 150. With the help of grants and contributions, these interviews were transcribed into hundreds of pages of text. From this raw material we selected the most personally compelling and historically significant passages into a working manuscript organized chronologically into chapters tracing interviewees' lives from their upbringing, training, and time in combat theater, to their return home, and postwar careers.

As our title suggests, this book is a work of oral history. We've left veterans' wording alone, preserving idiosyncratic grammar and syntax, only pruning redundancies and inserting an occasional word or phrase in brackets to preserve clarity, since these accounts were meant not to be read, but heard—with tone of voice, facial expression, and gesture all contributing to the meaning. We've written sections of historical narrative in order to contextualize the events and experiences recounted by the veterans, often situating their reminiscences with brief introductions. Our principle throughout, however, has been to get out of the way as much as possible and let the veterans tell their stories.

This is not history as it would be presented in a scholarly text, but as it was lived and remembered by ordinary men and women. At the time of these interviews, the veterans were in their 80s or 90s, recounting things they experienced 70 years before, when most of them were barely out of their teens. (Memories that old play tricks.) We have watched for obvious inaccuracies, either editing out such statements or calling attention to them in the text. Words or phrases inserted by the editors into memories are indicated with brackets ([ ]) and where part of the reminiscence has been removed, we have placed ellipses (...). However, readers should be aware that this is a book made up not of facts, but of memories, as time and life experiences have shaped them.

In organizing the book, we decided not to tell veterans' complete stories one at a time. Instead, we organized the accounts thematically and chronologically, so that a veteran may appear in multiple places – for instance, in the chapter describing life before the war, then later in the basic training chapter, still later describing campaigns in Europe or on Pacific islands, coming home, etc. Some veterans will be found in multiple chapters, some in only one. As individuals reappear in the book we have briefly re-introduced them. But for easy reference, we have included thumbnail biographical sketches, along with photos, of all the participants in an alphabetical listing in the Appendix. While we have tried to present a consistent narrative voice as editors, some differences in our styles — in introducing quoted passages, for instance — may be evident, particularly in the combat chapters. (Garvey was primarily responsible for chapters 1, 3, and 4; Higbee for 2, 5, and 6.)

Among the 800-plus interviews completed for ARCHS' Veterans History Project were many powerful and moving narratives not included here. We have limited the scope of the book to veterans who either grew up in the Central Savannah River Area (CSRA) and adjoining counties, or who lived here for a significant portion of their adult lives. This organizational principle necessarily excluded dozens of excellent interviews, but left the 147 you see excerpted here. Should you wish to view any of the 800+ interviews, DVDs are available at Augusta University's Reese Library.

Almost all the veterans whose memories fill this book are gone now. Fred Gehle's determined effort to find veterans of World War II and record their stories came in the nick of time. Sadly, it came too late for hundreds of area veterans who had already died and whose stories passed with them. Undoubtedly, many other area survivors were unaware of our efforts to find them and record their memories; others declined to be interviewed; and some could no longer remember or talk about the things they experienced so long ago.

Nevertheless, we are fortunate to have the vivid stories of the survivors represented in this book, and even more fortunate to have inherited the gift of freedom which their sacrifices preserved for us.

James Garvey

Douglas Higbee

Chapter 1
The Beginning

Life before the war

In 1941, Augusta was the commercial center of a rural district of dairy farms and played-out cotton fields. Almost 66,000 people lived within the city limits; another 16,000 lived in the rural parts of Richmond County. The population of Columbia County, which had been falling for decades, was down to 9,400. Aiken County had about 50,000 people, Edgefield County 18,000. Locals and country people from surrounding counties came into Augusta to shop and bank and eat and visit on Broad Street. President Roosevelt's New Deal had spent $10 million on Augusta, underwriting a little construction boom, building Olmstead and Sunset Homes, the William Bell Auditorium, a lock and dam near Bush Field; WPA funds repaired the levee, painted schools, paved Wrightsboro Road and Walton Way, created parks, and expanded the Academy of Richmond County on Baker Avenue. Though these developments helped, the region had not yet fully emerged from the Depression.

Things were tough everywhere, but especially in the country. Farming demanded hard physical labor from all members of the family and, in many cases, returned only a bare subsistence for all that work. Charles Carroll grew up on a farm just south of Hephzibah in Richmond County growing cotton and corn for market and vegetables for the table. His father farmed with mules, and his sons learned early how to plow:

> He had as many mules as he had boys big enough to plow, and when it came my turn to be that size, I was one of the plowhands, which was about 9 years old I started plowing.
>
> I started school when I was, I think, 5 years old . . . We had to walk a mile to catch the school bus, barefooted. And we usually got a pair of shoes in November, and that pair of shoes lasted us all year. Usually they were worn out by February, and by that time it would be getting warm enough to go barefooted. And until I was in high school, I went to school barefooted, because all the shoes we had were worn out by then. I remember up until the time I was 14 years old I went to church barefooted. We were poor farmers. Actually it was a matter of being subsistence farmers, and that's just about what it was.

Hundreds of boys and girls like Carroll grew up on farms still using 19th-century technology, without tractors or electricity or running water:

> We didn't know what electricity was. We used water from the spring that was a couple hundred yards from the house, and we took the water in two-gallon buckets from the spring to the house. And I can remember in the wintertime, your hand would get so cold you'd have to stop and set the bucket down and unpeel your fingers from the pail to put them in your pocket to warm them up so you could carry the water another 100 yards to the house.

The diet was pretty limited:

> If it hadn't been for buttermilk and cornbread, I wouldn't be here today, because that was our supper every night – I mean every night. I cannot remember ever eating anything at suppertime but buttermilk and cornbread. I still love buttermilk and cornbread.

Trips to Augusta were few -- Augusta was a lot farther away from Hephzibah back in the '20s than it is now.

> To get to Augusta, we had to go up to Hephzibah-McBean Road from where we lived to Hephzibah with a two-horse wagon and from Hephzibah on Highway 88 to Augusta. It was quite a ride. It was a one-day trip. My dad usually had a watermelon patch and he would load the wagon and leave the farm out there at 2 o'clock in the morning, loaded with watermelons, headed to Augusta.

But in 1927 Carroll's dad bought a Model T Ford truck and it didn't take a day to get to Augusta any more.

School had to take a back seat to young Carroll's responsibilities on the farm.

> I went to Hephzibah School. In those days it was 11 grades, from first through 11th, to graduate. Unfortunately, it took me 14 years to do the 11 grades, because when springtime came and after I was big enough to plow, I had two brothers that went into the CC [Civilian Conservation] Camp and I was the oldest one at home, and I was the plowboy from January until school was out, so I'd have to go and repeat that grade. In the fall, we picked

cotton . . . August through September, and we picked cotton until November, when cotton picking usually was over. And in those years where I spent two to four months working on the farm, those grades had to be repeated, so it took me 14 years to do my 11 grades. I graduated in 1940, after attending that school for 14 years.

Carroll's limited education limited his opportunities to build a life away from the farm. Enlisting in the Navy turned out to be his best option. The Navy had trade schools, so he could continue his education; and with war going on in Europe, everyone assumed the United States would eventually be in it. By joining in 1940, Carroll could make rank before the war began.

Well, the week after I graduated [from high school], I was in the field in the afternoon plowing. . . And a thunderstorm came up, and I took the mule to the house and put her to stay with my mother. She said, "Oh, you got a letter from the Navy this morning."

. . . So I opened it up and they were telling me to report to the post office in Augusta the next morning at 8 o'clock to go to boot camp, so I didn't waste any time. I was perfectly happy to leave and go to boot camp the next morning.

Carroll would become a hospital corpsman in the Navy, serving in the Mediterranean and the Pacific.

Farm life over on the South Carolina side of the river was no easier than on the Georgia side, and folks who left their farms found that jobs at the textile mills or anywhere else were few. John Taylor was pretty typical. He grew up on a farm about seven miles out of Aiken on Highway 215. He was the oldest boy of 10 children.

My main job I guess in life was keeping the farm going, the plowing, the hoeing, the raking, the milking, slopping, and cutting wood. I was the handyman, I guarantee you. The girls kept the house clean, but I kept the yard and the farm going.

When he was 13 the family left the farm and moved into Aiken.

My mother had died when I was very young — and so the older sisters raised us and it was ten of those, but one of them jumped off and got married at the very beginning, so that left nine including myself in the family. So the second to oldest children left their schooling and went to work in the textile mill to make ends meet, this was in the Depression.

Taylor went to school from seventh to eleventh grade.

> I went to school from early in the morning to about 3 o'clock in the afternoon and I left school and went home, got a quick bath and got something to eat and then went to work. I was employed at a Graniteville company in the Hickman division in Graniteville, South Carolina, and I worked there from about age 15 'til 17. . . It was a job they called a doffer, it was taking these spindles off the machines and putting them in a deal where all these threads together made cloth. No air conditioning. Cotton fibers just flying everywhere. It was hard times but we made it.

After tenth grade, Taylor left Aiken to join one of his sisters in Panama City, Florida. There he worked in a shipyard, earning triple what the cotton mill paid.

George Watkins lived in Augusta, but like those who lived in the country, he also had to work as a child.

> The times were tough and my mother and father divorced and I lived with my mother and we had three brothers and mama took care of us and we had to learn to work when we were children really. Mama made the crochet and she cooked the donuts and my youngest brother and I saw the older two brothers had to get out and go to work and so we sold donuts and we sold crochet, we sold quilts that mama and an aunt had made and it was a tough childhood, but we learned a lot from it. And we sold papers – my youngest brother and I sold papers on Broad Street and when I got a chance I got a job at the Western Union as a messenger. I was 15.

Eventually Watkins attended the Academy of Richmond County for two years, and found the ROTC training there useful once he went into the Army.

> It gave us a little bit of an insight about what it would be like later. . . I was only there two years, but I did enjoy the time that I was in there, I enjoyed the parades and the practice to get ready

to learn something later and I wish I'd been able to stay on and continue in it, but as things worked out we needed help otherwise.

Emerald (Bill) Williams had to quit school after seventh grade to get a job and help his family. He worked at Davison's Auto Service in Augusta, and Mr. Davison treated the 15-year-old well.

I really felt like he was my father because he'd taken me in and I had never worked in a place in my life and I worked for him for about two months and he came in one day and he said, "I'm not going to call you Emerald, I'm going to call you Elmer." So I got another name from him. So he says, "And I want you to take over the service station part of it." He had an auto repair shop in the back and then a filling station right on Greene Street and he says, "I want you to take over the business and run the filling station for me." And I said, "Mr. Davison, I'm a right young." And he said, "You can handle it. If you have any problems just call me, I'll take care of it, but I want you to run this service station."

Well, to start off with, I didn't know whether I was going to be able to handle it or not. But then I had a man working there and he was African-American and he'd take me over and that man taught me everything I knew about work. He taught me how to drive an automobile, he taught me how to drive a truck, he taught me how to drive a bus, he taught me how to run the filling station, . . . and his name was Virgil McCloud and I will never forget him as long as I live.

Lou Brissie's dad was a mechanic in Ware Shoals, South Carolina. Brissie learned about toughness watching his dad and growing up during the Depression.

My father was a mechanic. He owned a motorcycle shop. He was also a trick rider and also involved in a lot of the air and thrill shows during the '30s. He would take a car and roll it several times. But the thing to remember is that they did this with a football helmet – no seat belt, no protective anything, just a regular stock automobile that you would buy, and that's what they would roll. They also ran two automobiles together running 50 miles an hour. They did that without seat belts, just football helmets, the old type football helmet. And then also some of the air things and motorcycle, a bit and all of that. I was indoctrinated into that early. My mother didn't particularly like it, and I think that's the reason my dad eventually got out of it. But it was during the Depression, and everybody was doing everything they could find to do to make a dollar so they could survive. There wasn't any work, and it was very tough times. I think a lot of us in World War II really had good examples of toughing it out from our parents during that Depression, and it made a big difference to us in what we had to face up to in World War II.

Brissie got rheumatic fever as a child, and his Depression-era therapy required plenty of toughness on his part.

Back then it was no exercise and very limited in what you could do. And when I had that, my arms became stiff, my elbow, and I couldn't bend my elbows, and my dad gave me two one-gallon buckets full of sand and he says, "When you walk around the yard, carry these buckets with you." When I went to school in September, I had to take my buckets to school with me and set them out. He had talked to the school people and set them in the classroom. But he made me carry those things, and they eventually straightened my arms out.

Brissie loved playing baseball and he was an extraordinarily gifted player. But he had to overcome the effects of the rheumatic fever and his own family's resistance. One of his teachers got him back onto the field.

He's the one who talked me into start playing and I told him, "Well, they won't let me play. I've had rheumatic fever and I can't run." And he says, "Well, I'll tell you what, you play right field. You won't have to run because not many people hit a ball out there anyway." And that's the way it started, and he eventually talked to my parents and got them to let me continue to play, and that's kind of how I got back into it. A lot of my family were ballplayers. My mother's mother had five brothers who all played on one team at one time in the Greenville Textile Leagues, so when I was small, growing up, I was always going to a ballgame with one of them and following the Textile Leagues in Greenville, which was a big part of our weekends.

Brissie played in the Textile Leagues himself, where he caught the eye of Connie Mack, manager of the Philadelphia Athletics. Brissie's parents insisted he go on to college. He played ball at Presbyterian College until he went off to join the Army. Mack didn't forget him, even after Brissie was seriously wounded in Italy. With his toughness, Brissie would overcome his injuries and go on to play major league ball for Mack after the war.

Large families were common before the war. Leland (Roy) Raborn grew up in Greenwood, South Carolina, the youngest of 15 children.

> When I was born my father said, "Well, at least I found what caused it," so I was the last one. Well, I had a nice, pleasant life with my family. My mother lost a good many of her children. In 1918 I lost my father with a heart attack and also a sister in the flu epidemic. I had a brother and sister that was married, but we had in the family two brothers and two sisters and, of course, my mother.

> And my father, he was in the grocery business and he lost that through conditions and when he lost his daughter, that's when he died. Well, we didn't have a lot of money, so we would all have to pitch in to help. My oldest brother, he had to quit going to school and go to work. We had to do what we could. I pulled grass and did things for a dime or quarter, I never got more than a quarter. But we managed, had a good home. We managed to live good, not handsome, but we lived good as a family. And I went to the grammar school in Greenwood and then the high school, Greenwood High School. And then, later on in the '20s, things got rough, we had a real depression, nobody had jobs, you couldn't get a job and I finished school about 1931, and I went to a business college and I went there for two years or a year, but couldn't find any work. I worked at a place that sold donuts, that was the worst thing in the world, and then another they had was Upton Soap coupons. We got a dollar a day to do that. We had to go out and give out Upton Soap coupons to the people and explain to them what it was. But that was wonderful, that was a dollar a day.

Many in Augusta and nearby towns worked in textile mills and lived in mill villages. Ed Prater described growing up in nearby Batesburg, South Carolina.

We lived in a house that was furnished by the mill company and we had no rent so to speak. Most of the time my daddy and my mamma worked in the mill. Our rent, if you want to call it rent, for the house and so forth was based on how much they made. If they didn't make much we didn't pay much. So we had a roof and the mill company kept the house up so we didn't have that problem.

We had a garden spot. The mill company had a pasture back behind the mill village. You could have one cow and one hog per family. So every year we did. We'd butcher the hog. We used it. We had the garden. And we had the cow. My daddy was a real good hunter. He would buy three shotgun shells, go hunting, and he said out of the three shells if he didn't bring back four rabbits he was hurting. Usually one of those rabbits came out without being shot. But that was the way we survived. He loved to hunt, so it was a case of him doing what he liked to do and at the same time us survive.

John (Bob) Leopard grew up in the mill village in Ninety-Six, South Carolina, the third of nine children. He and his siblings wore clothes their mother made out of flour sacks until he was old enough to go to school. His dad worked in the textile mill, hunting and fishing to supplement the meager pay and diet.

Everybody raised a few chickens and had a cow, well, that was half your living. And my job, by the time I got big enough to milk the cow, I sat on a stool. That was my job, milk the cow. So I got up every morning before we went to school and milked the cow and after you milked the cow, you had to carry her so far to put her in the pasture and come back and wash up and dress and have breakfast and walk to school, every morning. I went to school 'til the 10th grade.

"My mother and father was real good people to me," but Leopard and three friends decided to leave the mill town behind and join the Army—with fake papers at 15. Eventually his father located him, proved he was underage, and Leopard returned home to Ninety-Six. When war broke out, he joined the Navy.

For Ferrell Holley of Aiken, a summer program offering military training without military obligation provided a welcome alternative to the dismal job market.

10

By the time I was 17, I graduated from high school. My friends and I had heard of a program called CMTC, Citizens Military Training Camp. We were interested in it and signed up for it, not because we wanted the infantry training, but because we wanted the $30 they were going to pay us. In 1937 that was a lot of money.

Gould Hagler grew up on McDowell Street in Augusta's upper-middle class Summerville area. Even for the relatively well to do, life was primitive by today's standards.

We didn't have a refrigerator, we had a telephone without a dial, we got ice from an iceman that drove a wagon pulled by a horse up and down the street. And since we had no air conditioning we could hear him in the summertime and he would yell, "Iceman!" and we would tell him to let us have ten pounds, which probably cost a dime.

And in my childhood we had streetcars in Augusta, going up and down Broad Street, Central Avenue, Monte Sano and going out to Turpin Hill, you could ride a streetcar all day for a nickel. My young sister – we had a maid once a week and they would get on the streetcar and ride all afternoon for a nickel. And all of my relatives lived, most of them, within about a three-block area and we had maybe 12 Hagler children and Barrett children, which were our first cousins. And we played as all children do, we used to hopscotch on the sand sidewalk. We did have some paved streets, but some not. And what else we did, we played street hockey on roller-skates, and as we got older, we played football and baseball on dirt streets or vacant lots. I went to St. Mary's Church, was about two blocks from us and the school was about three blocks. And then when I got high school age, we went to the Academy of Richmond County, we just called it The Academy. It was a public military school, military was compulsory. We wore uniforms and drilled an hour every day and I got to be a PFC once and then I was busted back to private.

Some area boys experienced the effects of the war even before Pearl Harbor. William (Sam) Carter, a farm boy from Cope, South Carolina, near Bamberg, had taken vocational courses in high school and worked at the Charleston Navy Yard in June 1941, where he witnessed the effects of the war in the Atlantic.

> Well, going to work one morning, I noticed there was a cruiser, a big British ship had come in. And in about three hours the welders had cut a hole in the side of that ship, up where they had patched it and brought out [the bodies of] about three dozen British sailors.

After that, much of his work at the Navy Yard was assembling LSTs. After being drafted, he would go off to fight in the Pacific.

Every morning *The Augusta Chronicle* and every evening *The Augusta Herald* reported news from Europe that grew more ominous by the day. France had fallen to the Nazis. England was being bombed by the Luftwaffe every night. You could try to forget it all at Augusta's grand new Miller Theater on Broad Street. Here a double feature cost 39 cents in the afternoon, 44 cents after 6:30; the Modjeska just a block up Broad was cheaper though, still only a quarter.

War was beginning to feel inevitable. By 1940, preparations for that possibility were underway in Augusta: 2,000 men and 100 planes were assigned to Daniel Field, now a military airfield; the Arsenal on the Hill was expanded with construction of 10 warehouses and new and modernized shops for manufacturing bomb sights and lens instruments. It employed 1,800 people in 111 buildings at the Walton Way site. And starting in 1940, all men between 21 and 45 had to register for the draft. (After Pearl Harbor, the age range was extended from 18 to 64.) Camp Gordon was approved for reconstruction in July 1941.

In June 1941 Jay Pearlstein and two buddies decided to face the inevitable and enlist rather than wait to be drafted. It didn't quite turn out the way they had hoped.

> We thought that if we enlisted that possibly we could stay together. So we went to the draft board and we asked the question, "If we enlist can we stay together as a unit?" And they said, "Of course." And so we enlisted. That was in June of 1941. And then we were assigned to leave on that date to go to Fort McPherson in Atlanta, Georgia, to be inducted. . . . And as it developed, when we got to Atlanta at Fort Mac the three of us stayed together for one day. The following day, I was transferred to Camp Wolters in Texas and the other friend was transferred somewhere in Wyoming and the third friend was transferred to Oklahoma. So it meant that we stayed together for just one day.

Richmond Academy, the county's principal high school for boys, had a long, proud history as a military school. ROTC and military science classes were mandatory. The class of 1941 had 150 graduates. In that year's *Rainbow* (the yearbook shared by the Academy and the Junior College of Augusta, which also shared the Baker Avenue facility), Sears, Roebuck & Co., located at the Confederate monument on Broad Street, sent its best wishes:

> Class of 1941, We offer you our heartfelt congratulations. Your life has just begun. Many of you will seek higher educational advantages, while others of you will begin your life work immediately. Yet, no matter where you are, or what type of work you are engaged in, all of you are sure to have a home some day. Therefore, whether home to you will mean an apartment for two, or simply 'a room with a view,' we urge you to start the practice early in life, of shopping and saving on all personal and home needs at Sears, Roebuck & Co., 'Your family store in Augusta.'

Pearl Harbor

On December 7, 1941, everything changed. For most of the current and past graduates of the Academy and other high schools, that apartment for two or room with a view became a barracks, a pup tent, or a porthole. And for dozens, within the next four years that life just begun would end on a battlefield in Europe or a jungle on a Pacific island, in a plane falling from the sky or a ship sinking under the waves.

Quentin Shivers, a Marine assigned to the *USS Pennsylvania*, was up early that Sunday morning. It was his 21st birthday, and he was spending it in paradise. He was sitting in the Bachelors' Officers Quarters (BOQ) at Pearl Harbor.

> I think I went on duty at 7:30 and I had what they called 8 to 12 shift and went to the BOQ and . . . I was fixing to write a letter home, it was my birthday and well I guess it was about a few minutes to 8 o'clock and the submarines were tied up right down underneath the administration building. And BOQ is kind of a B-shaped building and one end is glass from top to bottom where you can look out over the harbor, and they had a big conference table there, and they had some cots set up from some new ensigns that just came in to join Admiral Kimmel's staff, and

13

they were sleeping up there until they found room for them, and I was down at the end of the hall where our desk was and Admiral Kimmel's quarters was a few feet away.

I remember sitting there starting to write a letter and I heard a couple rumbles and then all of a sudden these ensigns down there in this open corner of the building started hollering and yelling and you hear these rumbles in the background and I walked down there real fast and you could look right out over the harbor and the first thing I saw was an airplane way up high just on fire – just spiraling down on fire, just like you'd see in a movie. Then, I went back to my desk and there was a window right beside the desk just overlooking the harbor and about that time a torpedo plane, I guess about a hundred yards away, it was getting down low to drop the torpedo towards the battleships and it got a direct hit and the full front end exploded and the front end torpedo came loose and it hung down, it didn't drop, it just held down the pilot, he was enveloped in flames. And I remembered a guy in the back, the rear gunner, had the canopy open and he was about half out, he was trying to get out, but the plane was about treetop level and it was fixing to crash, there's no way, he was going one way or another, he couldn't jump and the plane was burning up. Then I kind of looked back at a line of torpedo planes coming right by the window in the BOQ.

I went up on top of the building. I didn't even have a rifle, my rifle was over in our quarters in the rifle rack and so all I could do is watch. And it was me and a Navy chief, he got up there, and all the officers had went down to the administration building at that time and I just observed the raid, I mean I didn't have a gun and I couldn't leave my post and I just watched the Arizona blow up and watched everything go to hell.

Bruce Wright, who had joined the Navy in 1939, was serving on the destroyer *USS Selfridge*, which had just pulled into Pearl Harbor after a 30-day cruise.

We come in on Saturday, on December 6. We come in port. They let part of us go ashore and the next morning, of course — I always took my dungarees off and buttoned them up on my bunk chains so I'd have them ready. Well, about 15 minutes to 8, the general alarm sounded and I run out the top, went out on the deck. Now I saw those Japs, big red emblems on the wings, I knew who it was. So about that time our guns began firing. The guys must have been up on deck and they fired at them Japs, so our engine room was just right up there, I run and jumped down the engine room right fast and so they went across Ford Island. Well, they sunk the old *Utah*, they thought it was in service, you know. And they sunk it. They went across Ford Island, just shot every plane up so they couldn't take off. I think you'd had one plane that could take off. So then they hit the big battleships, they called it Battleship Row over there. And it was a terrible time.

When radio reported the attack back in Augusta and the surrounding area, some boys didn't understand at first why a far-away place called Pearl Harbor was important. Emerald (Bill) Williams, working at Davison's Auto Service in Augusta, was one of them.

Well, at that time it was really startling, I would say. It was really – I couldn't comprehend why at that time if they kept talking about America was bombed and Pearl Harbor was way somewhere else, it was not on where I considered to be America and then it dawned on me later on that Pearl Harbor was part of our country.

Williams would soon trade his mechanic's clothes for a Navy uniform.

Charles Bowen was eight years old, living at the corner of Winter Street and Kings Way in Augusta. He was playing with toy soldiers out in the yard.

I think my mother was outside doing something, and Dad came to the door and he called to her, he says, "Alice, you've got to come inside, now, and listen to this newscast." Well, we could tell by the urgency in their voices something was happening, so we kids trailed in behind them and we sat around that radio and listened to the news breaking almost every 15 minutes by that time in the day. And it made a great impression on us because at a young age you think there are going to be Japs on the sidewalk, and finally I think mom understood that it was concerning us a little bit, so she took out a map, spread that out and she showed us where we were, where Hawaii was, and where Japan was. So that eased the tensions a little bit — we'd get at least one good night's sleep before the Japs got there. But a lot of telephoning, a lot of neighbors visiting and talking because there was no way for the United States to remain out of the war and people were already thinking about their sons that would be going into service, and even on that day, that was part of the conversation. It was a pretty sober day. Of course, the next day we were in the backyard fighting the Japs, we had the war on two fronts, one at one end of the brick wall and one at the other end of the brick wall. We had to call more kids in with more soldiers so we could take care of it.

Down in a Florida movie theater, 17-year-old J. Stedman (Ted) Holladay couldn't understand why Pearl Harbor was significant. Like a lot of other young men, he was not thrilled by the prospect of fighting a war.

I was sitting in the movies in Florida. It's hot and there was no air conditioning in 1941-1942, so we used to go to the movies. And this was on a Sunday afternoon. And they came on and just made a brief—Pearl Harbor's been bombed. I didn't know what Pearl Harbor was, I didn't know where Hawaii is. I'd seen the movies with Dorothy Lamour and all that. But it didn't register, it's so far away. The whole war in Europe at that time, we weren't in it, and it wasn't personal. Well, I got back home and people were excited about this thing. I said, "Why?"

Well, as the days went on, the emergency draft board was called and war was declared. And then it became painfully obvious that you're going to be part of this thing, and I didn't want to be part of it.

Georgia Tech student Jack Kendall was another who wasn't ready to be a part of it yet. He heard the news of Pearl Harbor in a restaurant.

December 7, I was in the little town of Lexington, Georgia, and that Sunday morning we got up sort of late, went to breakfast and it came on the air that Pearl Harbor had been attacked. And I never will forget the guy that ran the restaurant said, "If I was one of you boys, I'd go right down and enlist." I was 17 years old. And we didn't go right down and enlist. I went on back to Tech.

16

After he finished school in 1943, he joined the Army Air Force, following in the footsteps of his brother.

George Watkins, married and working after two years at Richmond Academy, heard the news in the car.

> My wife and I had just been married a short while and we were at her mother's house eating Sunday dinner. My mother-in-law had a maid and we were going to take the maid home, so we got in the car and had the radio on and they interrupted to say that Pearl Harbor had just been bombed, and from there it just seemed like an explosion in my mind to understand how in the world all of the sudden the United States would be at war, but that was the way my wife and I learned that the war was underway as far as we were concerned. But of course the war in Europe was going on like that anyway and – but we had to learn about Pearl Harbor. It just seemed like an impossibility at that time. And it was hard to believe, and we kept our eyes on the newspapers and listened to the radio for every bit of news we could get. Mother and father-in-law didn't know it until we got back home and they didn't want to believe it either so we turned on the radio and started listening and everything was still Pearl Harbor on the stations we were listening to.

Up in Greenwood, Leland (Roy) Raborn was preparing to go down to the clothing store where he worked.

> December 6 was on Saturday and I had sold this customer of mine a big bill of gifts and I said, "Well, now, I'll wrap that tomorrow for you and you can pick them up Monday." So, that Sunday I was listening to the radio, and I was listening to Wayne King, his beautiful music, but I was listening for the news that was going to come on at 1:30 because all of us knew that something was going to happen — everybody but the President and the Secretary of the State, they didn't know that something was going to happen. And I never will forget, I ran back there to listen to the news before I was going to go down to the store and wrap those packages and the man came on and said, "We interrupt this program to bring you the following news," and then he stated that Pearl Harbor has been attacked. I listened to that for a while and then I went down to the store and did my duty.

17

A few years later, Raborn's duty would mean landing on Omaha Beach on D-Day.

Herman Boland was a 15-year-old kid when he heard the news as he left a movie theater on Broad Street in Augusta.

> In 1941, December 7, I went to Augusta, Georgia, with less than 50 cents in my pocket and I saw the movie *Sergeant York*. Now, Sergeant York was an American soldier who had won the Congressional Medal of Honor and was my ideal as of what to be. But I saw that movie, and when I went and came out about 5 o'clock, there was a boy outside selling newspapers, "Extra, Extra. Read all about it, Japanese bomb Pearl Harbor." Where in the world is Pearl Harbor? I said to myself, never heard of such a thing as that Pearl Harbor... Well, being 15 years old it didn't interest – I didn't really know what the story was... But as time went on I decided I want to see more of the world. I wanted to enlist in the Marines. I wasn't old enough. My father said, "I will not tell a lie for you to go in. Not going." So I ran away from home.

Bill Menger, who graduated from Richmond Academy in 1938, was building a career as a salesman at J. B. White's. But with the coming of war, he threw all that away.

> I was gonna continue to do that and I worked up to be manager of the men's furnishings, and then the war started and I got in as soon as I could. . . I never had thought about joining the service before then, but I couldn't wait to get in then, I don't know why I – just like a lot of boys.

Men already in the service got news of Pearl Harbor and orders to return to their bases. Wyndham Manning was visiting his parents in Stateburg, South Carolina, near Fort Jackson, on a weekend pass.

> My parents loved wildflowers, so we went out looking for wildflowers after dinner. Went then and picked wildflowers for an hour or so and got back in the car, my parents had turned the radio on driving back to our house and a gentleman by the name of H. V. Kaltenborn broke into the Philharmonic orchestra... to notify everybody that the Japanese had attacked both Pearl Harbor and Dutch Harbor [actually, Dutch harbor was not attacked until 1942]. I did not know where Dutch Harbor was.

18

Of course I knew where Pearl Harbor was. ... Then a few minutes later, Mr. Kaltenborn broke back in on the radio and said President Roosevelt had ordered all troops, all enlisted personnel, or military personnel, to report back to their bases as soon as possible. So my father very nicely told me to go upstairs and get my baggage and he would see to it I got back to Camp Jackson. But anyway, my father drove me about four miles to the nearest paved road to Columbia, Fort Jackson, Camp Jackson. And he said to me, he said, "Now get out on the side of the road, get a ride to Camp Jackson. I'm sure somebody will pick you up," which happened very quickly.

Willard Blankenship was a sergeant at Fort Jackson. He was on a weekend pass too and nursing a hangover when he learned of Pearl Harbor.

I was on pass. Me and two other sergeants, we went in a drug store to get us a beer because we were kind of hung over on Sunday morning. And the lady knew us, we'd run around that part of town for a couple of years, and she said, "Sergeant Blankenship, you supposed to be in Fort Jackson." I said, "Nah, I ain't supposed to be there, I'm on pass." She said, "The Japanese bombed Pearl Harbor." I said, "I don't give a damn what the Japanese bombed, I'm on pass. They didn't bomb me." So when I come back, everything was in a big turmoil.

Joining up

At Richmond Academy and most other area high schools, many boys enlisted as soon as they were 17. Enrollment plummeted at the Academy despite faculty advice that students stay in school instead of joining up. Students were told "they would be doing more than their share if they trained themselves now for those post-war years of rehabilitation where trained young men would be needed badly by their country," according to Academy historian Alethia Bigbie. But 15 Academy faculty had themselves left their teaching jobs to join the service, so it could be no surprise that so many of the older students followed their example. Ironically, as a result of the mass exodus to the Army, the Academy lost its rank as an Army honor school because it now had too few experienced cadet officers. Principal Eric Hardy said, "Our fifteen and sixteen year olds have enthusiasm, but they lack the training of the older cadets, most of which have entered the service."

Gould Hagler was one of those Richmond Academy students.

> Well, I turned 18 December 21, 1942. I had a friend who turned 18 sometime before that and another friend, Arthur, who turned 18 and we all wanted to go – by that time I knew where Pearl Harbor was, and we all wanted to go in the Army and beat the Germans. I don't think we must have thought of the Japanese, but I'm sure we did because they started it. But we wanted to go in and rather than wait to be drafted, and I don't know why we didn't sign up for the Marines or something, but just volunteered to be drafted. So, in January we'd notified the draft board that we were ready. We were all going to be pilots, everybody wanted to be a pilot in those days, a fighter pilot, and being color blind I knew I couldn't be a pilot and I knew carrots wouldn't get over your color blindness, but I ate some raw carrots anyway, just hoping.

Carrots didn't work. Hagler ended up in the infantry.

Gail (Gene) Casey grew up in Enoree, South Carolina, near Greenville, where virtually everyone was employed in the town's one cotton mill. His dad worked at the mill. The Caseys didn't own a car. Gene was the oldest of eight children. He went to work in the mill as a doffer, changing bobbins, after he graduated from high school. Getting drafted gave him one of his first opportunities of seeing anything beyond Enoree. It also got him some health care and new clothes.

> They fixed my teeth. I had a whole bunch of teeth that needed filling and they fixed those and they told me to send my civilian clothes back home and they gave me Army clothes. They took a measurement and they fit.

Minimum enlistment age was 18, but with a parent's permission you could get in at 17. Birth records were not readily available, so boys who looked a bit older than their years could lie and get in. Roy Howard lied not only about his age, but also about his place of residence.

> I told my brother, I said, "Well, I'm going to have to get in somewhere and do something, I'm going to get in trouble." So I said, "I'm thinking about the Navy." And he said, "Why don't you?" He was in the service. He says, "You know you're a little too young, but...," and I said, "Well, that's all right." But anyway, I went into the Atlanta Post Office and I went into the

Navy and they said, "Well, son," he says, "where do you live?" And I said, "I live in Alabama." And he says, "Well," he says, "you have to go to Birmingham to enlist."

Howard asked why he couldn't enlist in Georgia.

And he says, "You have to be living in Georgia two years before you can enlist in Georgia." So I said, "Oh, is that right?" So anyway, I went across the hall to the Army Recruiting Office and they said, "Where you live?" I said, "Atlanta, Georgia." They said, "How long you lived here?" I said, "Two years." And they said, "How old are you?" And I said, "17."

That was the start of Howard's 30-year career in the Army.

Herman Parker, an African-American from Georgetown, South Carolina, convinced his father to lie for him when he was only 14.

I was born in Georgetown, South Carolina, March the 15th, 1928. I had a pretty good childhood. My father was a fisherman and he was a cook. He cooked for some of the biggest people there were. He cooked for John Vanderbilt, he cooked for Bernard Baruch. And as I grew older – I guess I was around eight years old – my father would go with Mr. Baruch and them on hunting trips and he would take me, and I got to the place where I would serve them. I was just a kid, but they liked me. And they used to go fishing on the weekend. They had big boats, I mean big. These were very wealthy people and they had ships instead of boats, and the ships would take up practically a block, just about that long. And we would go fishing on Saturdays, Saturday evening, and they'd come back Sunday evening, and I loved it because I used to have so much money when I come back it wasn't even funny. They never used to count their money. They used to just take a handful of money and give it to you. And so all of that went to my father, so I guess he gave me what he wanted me to have when he wanted me to have it.

My mother was a Cherokee Indian, my father was an African, and my mother was wonderful. My mother was the greatest mother in the world, and the reason why I say that, she never used to beat you like other mothers would beat you. She'd never smack you around, she never did nothing like that, because I had a father with a Ph.D. degree in whipping, so when he come home, she would tell him, say, "Herman did such and such a thing today," and Lord have mercy.

Well, to be honest with you, my brother was in it, it was a war. I was saying to myself at the time, I sure don't want those Japanese and the Germans to come over here and hurt my mother and father, so I said, let's go. So my father said to me, "You must be kidding." He said, "You're not going into no service." I said, "Yeah, I'm going to the service and I'm not going back to school." He said, "What?" I said, "Yeah." I said, "And guess what?" He said, "What?" I said, "They say you're going to have to sign for me." So we went to Charleston and he say, "Okay," he says, "You're determined not to go back to school, let's go." So we went to Charleston to the Citadel and he signed me up. He signed me up saying that I was 17 when I was 14. But it was all on account of me, because I was determined and I wanted to go to war. And so I haven't regretted it, I haven't regretted it. I never lost one night's sleep over it.

Like the South itself, the armed forces were segregated. Nevertheless, many thousands of young black men lined up to enlist. Before the war, only 4,000 African-Americans served in the armed forces. By the end of World War II, about 1.2 million would be in uniform. Racial restrictions limited most of them to non-combat roles, though that changed late in the war and there are famous exceptions, such as the Tuskegee Airmen. Roosevelt Brooks was one of many thousands of African-Americans who enlisted, spurred partly by patriotism and partly by the lack of any other meaningful options in the South.

Well, to be frank with you, I wasn't doing anything. I had no, what I considered, important job . . . and I had seen in the papers where all these guys had volunteered for the service, but at that time they had to stop the volunteering and you had to wait until you were drafted. So I volunteered to be drafted. Prior to that, I was in the State Guard for a while . . . and went to camp with them and trained and all that.

Brooks and his brother went to enlist together.

So I went there and I went before my brother and—they call your name, they stamp Army, Navy, Marine. They stamped mine— where I had this Army training, so they stamped mine "Army."

They said "Congratulations and good luck." My brother came behind me and they stamp his "Navy" and he said, "Oh, no. I ain't going to no Navy, I'm going with my brother." They said, "Keep moving, get out of here." And he said, "I ain't going nowhere. I'm going in the Army with my brother." So they had to change it and stamp his "Army."

Enlistees like Brooks and his brother who volunteered for the draft were given at least the possibility of choosing the branch of service they wished to enter, and the boys enlisting made those choices for all kinds of reasons. W. Broadus Carter requested Army because he didn't think he'd look good in bellbottoms.

When I turned 18 on November 14, 1943, I went to the local draft board and enlisted for military service. Sometime later in early February they sent a bus down from Fort McPherson in Atlanta to bring the men up to be examined for the military. I knew that I wouldn't be accepted because I was 6 feet tall, I weighed 129 pounds and my left eye was 20/70 and my right eye was 20/50. So we went through the examining line and the officer at the end of the line said, "Army or Navy?" I said, "Sir?" He said, "You passed your physical, which do you want to be in? The Army or the Navy?" Well, all I could think about was those big old bell bottom trousers that the Navy men wore and me on a little skinny frame, I said, "That ain't going to work." So I said, "Army."

Robert (Pat) Roberts couldn't swim, so he chose Marines rather than Navy.

I had my physical examination at Fort McPherson. The doctor told me I was as healthy as a horse. He said, "You don't have anything wrong with you except you have flat feet." Well, when the colonel at the 10 Forsyth Street building in Atlanta was to swear me in, he tried to persuade me to go in the Navy. And I told him I didn't want to go in the Navy. He said, "Well, you better go in the Navy. When you get in the Marines with that heavy pack on your back and all the cartridge belts and canteens . . . that you have to carry and walking 15-20 miles, your feet are going to give out on you." And we argued a little and finally I told the colonel, I said, "Well, Colonel, I can walk a lot farther than I can swim." And I didn't go in the Navy.

Hal Beman just went along with a friend's suggestion that they join the Coast Guard.

> Well, a fellow . . . said, "Let's go and join the Coast Guard." I said, "Why?" He said, "Because they just guard the coast." So I said, "All right, I'll go with you." Well he was proved wrong later on.

Beman was to end up far from the American coast on an LST for the invasions of Iwo Jima and Okinawa. Beman continued,

> I went to Charleston, South Carolina, where they have a recruiting station and on the way down I made the mistake of drinking a Coca-Cola. Well, I got in there, everything went fine until they gave me a little physical.

Beman flunked the physical because of his high blood sugar.

> I said, "What do I do now?" He said, "Go back home. Next Saturday come back down here and do not drink Coca-Cola on the way down." And I did and I was sworn in at the Coast Guard station down there. . . I told the old fella, "I got a summons from the Army to show up Monday." This was on Saturday, show up Monday for the Army. He said, "Don't worry about it, everything's all right. You belong to us now." And that's true, I did.

Deferments from military service were given to those whose work—on a farm, for instance, or in a defense industry — was essential to the war effort. Some boys gave up their deferments, however, preferring to take their chances in the service. J. Stedman (Ted) Holladay just came to hate building airplanes 60 hours a week:

> I was going to reach my 18th birthday about two weeks after I graduated, and I went ahead and enlisted and enrolled in the technical school in Miami, Florida, to do aircraft design. And I went to the school and I spent about four months at the school learning to do this particular thing to work in the industry, and I went to work with Curtiss-Wright building airplanes. I had a deferment. I did a job. We were building a plywood airplane called a C-47 or something like that. And I stayed on there for

13 months and we were working 60, sometimes 65 hours a week and never saw the sunshine – maybe on Sunday morning. We didn't work on Sunday but we regularly worked 60 hours a week. I was making 72 cents an hour. I couldn't even pay for my room and board. I thought to myself, there must be something better in life than this. I'll go out and let the Japs shoot at me before I'm going to do this anymore. So I turned the deferment down. I could have stayed out this whole time if I'd have wanted to. But my brothers were all joining, my oldest sister and my oldest brother and my second oldest brother, sister-in-law, and I felt this great compulsion to be part of this thing and to do something, and so I volunteered.

R. Wayne Jolley gave up his deferment to escape from being labeled a draft dodger:

My family had arranged a farm draft exemption for me without consulting me and I grew uncomfortable with it because there was another farmer in the community who had two children that he knew would be drafted without an exemption, but when I worked in the family business, probably at about age 14, customers were referring to that man as a draft dodger and I knew that I didn't want to come back to that community and live the rest of my life and be called a draft dodger. So in the fall, I went to Gaffney and signed it away myself, without consulting them like they didn't consult me, but I had to go through the draft system. I was 18 in May and I went in December the 20th.

It wasn't long before Augusta, with its Arsenal and Daniel Field on the Hill and with Camp Gordon and Bush Field nearby, was transformed by the war. Charles Bowen's preteen memories are of a city full of soldiers, military planes roaring overhead, scrap metal drives, rubber drives, victory gardens, and even the rumble of tanks in the street.

Some type of work was being done at the Arsenal on tanks and armored trucks and they would bring those in – maybe from Camp Gordon, maybe from other sources and let them off on the rail lines to the south of city and then bring them into the city. One of the most direct routes to the Arsenal was Kings Way, which was the street that we lived on. And this is close to where Number 7 Firehouse is, right at the intersection of Central

Avenue and Kings Way, and they would cross right there at that Troupe Street crossing.

Well, we might be in the backyard and you could feel the ground before you could hear anything and we knew what that meant, it was a matter of taking off to the front yard to get a look and they would be turning about that time and you would hear those engines coming up the hill. And I saw many a tank pass right in front of my house and there would be two, three, four of them at a time and sometimes armor carriers or other vehicles that had cannons on them or machine guns or other type of armament that needed to be serviced in some way, and they would come up there. Of course, we would beg those soldiers to let us climb on those tanks and ride them and – "No, no, no, no, no." He'd be standing up that top turret going up there, they'd wave at you, but they didn't want you on the tank. And they fortunately used the different tread when they were in the cities, they used the tread that was softer, not the metal pleat, but they were so heavy that for years after, the imprints on Kings Way were in the asphalt and I used to smile, even in the 1950s or 1960s, those imprints, before they started repaving, were still visible.

It was an interesting thing for a kid to grow up in, you really got into it. The airport [Daniel Field] being so close by was another thing that could wake you up or put you to sleep, a lot of training going on up there, we saw a lot of BT-13s, which were basic trainer aircraft, and then as a time went on the AT-6s, which were a little a bit more advanced trainer, we see a lot of those around at the airshows today, it was what they trained in or moved up to just prior to going into something like a P-40 or P-47 or more high powered aircraft. So, we would see those all over the place, they would fly in formation over our homes at tree level because we were that close to the airport, they were on landing approach and we knew there would be a few dozen, sometimes, coming in at one time, it would take them a long time to get back down on the runways. We'd hit the bicycles and we were at the airport, we wanted to see the airshow. And the military prescribed landings in certain ways, you circled the fields and you peeled off one a time and the others came around and they peeled off, so we would see an airshow, and when it was over with, the MPs would let us go out and sit in the aircraft.

Banners with blue stars, one for each family member serving in the armed forces, appeared in windows all over the area. But before long, the gold stars—signifying those killed—would begin appearing too. There would be more than 400 of them in the windows of Richmond and surrounding Georgia counties, more than 150 in the five area counties on the South Carolina side of the Savannah River.

Chapter 2
Training and Deployment Overseas

Building a military

After the key contribution of over 4 million Americans in World War I, the U.S. military downsized dramatically. The tradition since the Revolutionary War had been that armies are for wartime, not peacetime. So when World War II began with the German invasion of Poland in September, 1939, there were only 330,000 men in the American military. Even with the German conquest of Europe and the Japanese occupation of major sections of Asia, the United States stayed aloof from the conflict, while slowly increasing its military readiness. By the time of Japanese attack on Pearl Harbor on December 7, 1941, the Army alone had more than a million men in its ranks – but far more would be needed to be capable of contending with the Axis powers.

This herculean effort created a military of over 12 million men by war's end, plus approximately 300,000 women in auxiliary roles. Key in this effort was the Selective Service Act, passed by Congress in September 1940, which when amended after the declaration of war greatly increased the government's ability to conscript its citizens. For while plenty of Americans voluntarily joined the military, over 60% of those who served during World War II were drafted—in the month of December 1942, for instance, 500,000 men received draft notices. Even though drafted men received a summons from Uncle Sam, the message was delivered to them by their neighbors: draft boards were made up of local citizens, usually local businessmen and professionals, many of whom were veterans themselves. Many received draft deferments, including farm workers, fathers, and those under 21. Still, the draft age was lowered to 18 in 1942, and with the intensification of the war in 1944, deferments were removed for many. While in 1943 fathers were only 6% of those drafted, by April 1944 they were 50%.

At the very beginning of their military experience, men were inducted at one of the scores of reception centers scattered across the country. They were physically examined in assembly-line fashion—about 25 men per hour, the ID tags around their necks the only article of clothing permitted. Charlie Fiveash describes the typically unceremonious medical inspection:

> You walk around a half day buck naked following the blue line on the floor. As you walk through one door somebody will hit you on this arm with a needle and somebody on that side will hit

you in this arm with a needle and then you go through and one guy would test your left eye and the other one would test your right eye and then you turn your head and cough, you know, you had to go through it all the way. Then they threw a uniform at you and it was extra-large, everybody got an extra-large, it didn't make a difference, you get an extra-large and that's what I wore for the next three or four days.

Recruits were then given tests to determine their aptitude for various jobs in the military. In the Army, the test consisted of multiple- choice arithmetic and vocabulary questions—the higher the score, the more likely the recruit would be selected for a more technical position and the less likely he would be assigned to the infantry. After several days, recruits were shipped off to basic training.

Spartan conditions

By the summer of 1942 approximately 14,000 men per day were arriving at the hundreds of training centers operating across the country. Most of these were hurriedly constructed camps, or reactivated holdovers from the World War I era. An average training camp required ample space for troop quarters, drill fields, and firing ranges, as well as a plentiful supply of water, good roads, and rail facilities. Many of these camps were opened in the Southeast—land was relatively cheap and weather permitted year-round training. Camp Gordon, just outside of Augusta, and Fort Jackson, in Columbia, South Carolina, as well as several others in the southeastern United States, such as Camp Croft, near Spartanburg, South Carolina, were in heavy use during the war.

Conditions at most training camps were simple at best. Ray Hitt from south Georgia remembers Camp Shelby, Mississippi, well:

The barracks were deplorable. I think it must have been built for the World War I veterans. It was a wooden structure, had no windows, no air, and it was heated with a coal stove, and we had approximately 60 soldiers in that one building.

Mabel Crawford, training to be a Navy codebreaker in Washington, D.C., remembers the rough conditions as well:

We got in the barracks and you had to stand in line to shower, you had to stand in line to go to the bathroom. The buildings had nothing but asbestos. Every one of us got asthma. At the time, we didn't know. Some of the girls got to the point where they couldn't breathe, but all we had as medication to take was APC tablets, pink stomach medicine and calamine lotion. That was all, and Epsom salts. You got cured of anything that was wrong with you.

Weather was a key factor in a new recruit's life. Future officer John Kristensen recalls arriving at Camp McClellan in northern Alabama in winter:

The first few days in the sunny south brought us several inches of snow, five or six to a tent and freezing. None of us city boys had known anything but steam heat up from the basement. We stuffed a potbelly stove with coal, opened the draft and went to bed and woke up in the middle of the night with a potbellied stove red and it's a wonder we didn't burn down the whole camp. And for the first time I was drinking a big mug of coffee at each meal and my bladder was complaining at night. Of course, the latrine was a hundred yards away in the snow and you could get shot for peeing al fresco.

The cold also got to Georgia native Richard Warren, who took his basic training at Fort Custer, Michigan:

We lived in a two-story barracks. They heated it with a furnace that was fired from downstairs and they had ductwork that was operated on a draft, on a gravity system. It didn't have the blowers on it. But it was fairly comfortable inside the barracks. When we went on the firing range with the M1 rifle, I remember my hands were so cold. I had to take my other hand to pull the trigger on the firing range. We stayed there six weeks and we drilled, we marched, paraded, did calisthenics in the snow.

James Wisenbaker, from Valdosta, Georgia, was not impressed with the food at Fort Jackson. Assigned to the Army's 106th Division, which would later earn a Distinguished Unit Citation for its contribution to the Ardennes campaign in 1944-45, he recalls that

They initially called it the Golden Lion Division. We called it the bagged lunch division. It seemed like every morning after breakfast they'd give us a bag that had two sandwiches in it and that was your lunch.

Not all new soldiers found the conditions challenging; some even found them a step up. In 1940, one in three American homes did not have running water or central heat, and Army food, though often monotonous, was more plentiful than what many recruits were used to. Warren himself admits that:

> When I went in the Army, I weighed 174 pounds. After six weeks of doing what Uncle Sam said, doing exercise, drilling, learning how to operate the rifle and the pistols and all, I had gained to 215 pounds. Growing boy.

Of course, the purpose of basic training was not to introduce recruits to a comfortable and interesting new life. It was to turn civilians into soldiers who could serve as functioning units in a massive military machine. As historian John Ellis puts it, World War II "was fought almost entirely by non-professionals, by men conscripted from civilian life and thrown into battle after only 3 months or so of training." For most servicemen, basic training lasted from 8 to 12 weeks, depending on the military's need for soldiers at a given time during the war.

Disciplines of the War

Though the regimen in the various services (Army, Marines, Navy, Army Air Corps, Coast Guard) differed somewhat, the primary purpose of military training for all servicemen, as John Ellis relates, is to rid the new soldier of civilian preconceptions about his "rights" and freedom. Such training was usually provided by men of the regular forces, and they didn't make it easy for the new recruits. The Marines are famous for their strict insistence on discipline, as Chester McCoy discovered at the Marine Recruit Depot at San Diego:

> One thing you learn in boot camp in the Marine Corps is the discipline. When you're a private in there, you're a nothing. You have to salute a corporal, "yes sir" and "no sir" to PFCs. In fact, you have to say "yes sir" and "no sir" to everybody. Boot camp is rough, but one thing I learned was discipline and to take orders. And to me, growing up in a family of eight where order wasn't always that good, it was something to behold, the way people could learn to participate and take orders and carry them

out. I've always admired the Marine Corps since then for it, and it has taught me a lesson through even my children growing up.

Though McCoy learned this lesson the hard way:

> In the Marine Corps, you can't just receive a package from home and take it. You have to go through the DI and he checks it out, and you're not allowed any candy or sweets, chewing gum and so forth. I was standing in line to take a box up to the sergeant and I opened it up. I knew what it was supposed to be. There was a pack of chewing gum in there, so I reached in and put it in my pocket. A couple days later, the sergeant called us out to assemble and I was chewing gum, and naturally he caught me. So he said, go to the PX and get me a toothbrush. Well, I knew then what I was going to have to do. I'd seen some of the others do it. I went to the PX and bought the longest toothbrush I could find and I carried it back and gave it to him. The first thing he did is take his pocket knife out and cut it in half. He gave me a bucket of sand, a bucket of water and half a toothbrush and put me in an 8x10 hut. He said, "I want you to clean this floor." So I worked up until about 2:30 in the morning and he come in and told me to go to bed.

Fellow Marine Rufus Belding was given an even harsher lesson in discipline: "I remember one day I didn't shave. They put sand and water on me and had somebody shave me. I mean it was rough."

The Navy had its share of ritualistic indoctrination as well. Jack Sloan recalls becoming a sailor with pride, his commander less so:

> We got baths and fresh clothing and a uniform of the United States Navy and I was real proud. A Mr. Franks was my company commander, Company 60, and this was a glad day for me and I thought the world of him. Now, he had a little habit that annoyed me, though. You get out of step, he'd hit you in the rear with his saber. It didn't hurt, it was just the humiliation.

An aviation cadet in the Army Air Force, Oscar Barney had plenty of opportunity to take military discipline but eventually got a chance to dish it out:

> That's where you learned to say "yes sir" and "no sir" and wear your uniforms and shine your shoes. All the cadet officers

bugged you all the time and you learned the cadet prayer. You'd be sitting down eating your dinner and one of the cadet officers would come up and say, "Cadet Barney," and you said, "Yes sir," and then he went into his spiel. Of course you had to repeat the cadet prayer and then he'd harass you a little bit and finally let you go. You never saw what you were eating, but it was always a square meal. So we didn't really know what we ate. And during the cadet training I was Cadet 1st Sergeant, so I had my turn with the new cadets that came in later on in harassing them a little bit.

As a new member of the Air Force, Ralph McLain was in a hurry to get in a plane at his training center in Michigan but ended up spending plenty of extra time pushing a broom:

I was told to report down to the hanger. I walked in and the Sergeant there says, "So you're the new radio operator." "Yes sir, I don't see no radios around here, where are they?" And he says, "Right out there." And he pointed through a window and there was a C47 [a transport plane, modeled on the DC-3]. I say "I'm going out and look at that." "Oh, no you're not," he says. "If you do, you know what." Well, I thought to myself, 17 years old and I come in here and they're already telling me I can't do what I want to do. I want to see one of those airplanes. Well, I spotted a gentleman over in the hangar where they had a coffee pot going. He was in a pair of flying coveralls and I walked up to him and said, "Oh, are you a pilot? Man, I joined to go for an airplane ride, when you going to take me for a ride man?" And he reared back and said, "Where are you from soldier?" I says, "I'm from the South, I mean Swampeast, I mean Southeast Missouri." And he backed off and says, "Well, can't take you today." About three days later they had me out sweeping the hangar. I was new on the scene and so I got real indoctrinated to the broom. I never had to clean the latrines or anything like that. I was a good floor sweeper though. Anyway, [the pilot] walks through the hanger and comes up to me and says, "Well, you ready to go for that airplane ride? I said, "Yes sir. Let me hide this broom." Well, I hid the broom. And he said, "Well, right outside the parachutes on the wing of the airplane, I'll be right out there."

I got out there and he fitted me with this parachute and gave me instructions how to operate that parachute. He took me for an airplane ride [in] a training aircraft, an old PT13 [a biplane], and he done everything that he knew how with that airplane. I knew what he was trying to do later on, I didn't realize it then, but he was trying to get me sick. I had a headset with a microphone on and I could talk to him on the interphone and he kept asking me, "Everything okay? You all right?" And finally I said, "How come you're asking me whether everything's all right or not?" Well, about that time he puts that thing in a dive and we pull out over water and he says, "You sure you're all right?" I said, "Well, you better pull it up a little bit, I'm about to get my feet wet." I look up and lo and behold, we just went under a bridge. And I said, "Well, you better hurry back to the base 'cause I might have to go to the bathroom."

Well, we're taxiing in and he says, "Uh-oh, staff car. Now whatever side that staff car pulls up on, you get out on the other side and take that parachute into the hangar and turn it in to personal equipment." I opened the door to the hangar and I took about two steps and that Sergeant says, "I told you not to get in an airplane didn't I?" I think he kicked me for every step I took across that hangar.

The Army was no slouch in teaching attention to detail, as Ray Hitt learned early on from his drill sergeant:

I think he was the meanest man God ever made because he was tough, but he knew his business. So we had what they called dubbing. You were supposed to dub your shoes to waterproof your boots. Well, I didn't like that dubbing because it was greasy and messy, so I didn't do it, but that mean sergeant found out about that. So he took a small piece of cardboard, put a string through it and wrote on there "I will dub my boots at least once every two weeks." And where did he put that other than around my neck, and I wore it for a long time. Needless to say, my boots was dubbed every two weeks.

Often such exacting discipline would cause bitterness between the new recruits and their Regular Army masters, as was the case when Olander (Jack) Barrett was denied a weekend pass:

34

We were camping out one night and there come a flash flood and we all got soaking wet. We were in little pup tents, all of our rifles got wet and had a little, light, thin film of rust on them, you could just barely see it but it was there. Early next morning we broke camp and went on back to headquarters and the captain inspected three rifles, mine was one of them. He gigged all three of us.

We got mighty hot about it and I was sure enough hot. I passed the captain on the company street about an hour later and I wouldn't salute him and he sent the sergeant. I went back in my tent and I wanted a pass to go to Mexico with some of the other boys to watch a bull fight, get some steak. I was gigged [and] I couldn't go. The sergeant came up into my tent, I was laying down there crying. "The captain wants to see you." I went in the captain's tent, I didn't salute him, I just walked up front to the desk and he goes, "Why are you crying?" I said, "Sir, when I get so mad at somebody I would love to jump over the table and choke them to death and I can't do it." And I said, "I cry." I never would salute him. I told him, "I'm not going to salute you anymore." He said, "As long you are under my command you'll always be a buck private." And we both kept our word. I stayed buck private longer than anybody and I never saluted him again. So that was the deal with the captain.

Veterans have a word for such discipline, and as with much military vocabulary it is not a polite word: *chickenshit*. Noted author and World War II infantry veteran Lt. Paul Fussell, an expert on such matters, defines chickenshit as "behavior that makes military life worse than it need be: petty harassment of the weak by the strong; open scrimmage for power and authority and prestige; sadism thinly disguised as necessary discipline; a constant 'paying off' of old scores; and insistence on the letter rather than the spirit of ordinances . . . chickenshit can be recognized instantly because it never has anything to do with winning the war." Even if one might think that Ray Hitt should have dubbed his boots or that Jack Barrett should have cleaned his rifle sooner, few would find merit in the treatment meted out to Reeves Parish by his drill sergeant:

I got kicked out of the company I took basic [training] with. There was a man that had to make the Sarge's bed every morning and sweep and mop around the bunk. Well, this man left for some reason and he asked me about moving – taking this empty bunk. I said, "Sergeant, all you want is somebody to make your bunk up for you and sweep around your bed, and I'm not going to do it." Well, it was only just a very few days after that this squad leader asked, "Who do we need to get rid of?" And I was the first one on his list to get rid of.

Parish was promptly transferred to the 35th Infantry Division and was eventually promoted to first sergeant.

Chuck Ballas literally took matters into his own hands when he found he didn't like the Army unit he was training with:

> I just didn't like the outfit. To me it was a chicken outfit and I wanted to get out of it. I did everything that I could, including hitting my CO. I was promptly put 15 days in the brig and then I was shipped out to an infantry outfit. It was a blessing, it was the best thing to happen to me because that's where I wanted to be and I wound up in Company A of the 110th Infantry Regiment of the 28th Division.

For all new recruits the day began before dawn with hurried dressing, washing, and breakfast, then long hours marching or drilling, physical conditioning, learning to handle their rifles and other weapons, listening to lectures on topics ranging from military protocol to hygiene, and various maintenance duties. After dinner at the mess hall, the men had a few minutes to write letters and prepare for bed before lights out in a barracks full of dozens of other exhausted, snoring men. Guard duty, KP, or night exercises would often disrupt needed sleep.

Men like Albert Shaw took training in stride, notwithstanding its rigors:

> I had a little buck sergeant that had already been in service and he'd been wounded and he was back. I think he took it out on all of us because having been in service [earlier] he was a tough little nut. We were being punished at one time for not doing the things we should have been doing and progressing like we should, so he made us do pushups with him. I made up my mind and [thought], you tough little devil, I'm going to do one more than you do if it kills me. He dropped at 150 and I did 151. And when we got up, under his breath he said, "You're one tough son of a gun." I said, "Sergeant, you ain't so bad yourself."

Jack Barrett remembers being kidded because of his southern accent, but his performance on a training march put that to rest:

> The heel came off one of my boots. The lieutenant told me to sit down and wait and a jeep would come by and pick me up and take me on back to camp. We had just started on the first stage of this march and a couple of Yankees [were in our group]. One of them told the other one, "He probably pulled that heel off so he wouldn't have to make the march." That got my dander up and I said, "Lieutenant, I want to take these boots off, I want to finish the march barefooted." He said, "No, you can't do that, it'll ruin your feet." I said, "It'll not hurt my feet. Please believe me, I can do it." He finally consented. And it was a piece of cake, real easy, because my feet were tough. I been going barefooted at home a lot. Those Yankees couldn't believe it. We got back to camp and I took a kitchen match and struck it on the heel of my foot. They wrote home about it. There was a write-up in the company paper and I was kind of a tough there from then on. The Yankees didn't make fun of my talking anymore.

Marches were, of course, a common feature of basic training, and they could occur at any time, day or night. Cliff Cherry recalls, with good humor, a night march that caught his platoon by surprise:

> The last day we were there we did training all day long and then we had night training until 12 o'clock. They brought us in to give us a cup of coffee and a piece of cake and then announced we're going to march back to the barracks, 26 miles away. And it was real funny, you'd be walking along, you'd see people just walk in a ditch and fall – I mean they'd go to sleep walking. We got back Saturday about noon and they had a pass waiting for us, a weekend pass. Of course nobody went anywhere, they went to bed, they were gone. It was real funny, really.

In addition to disciplining raw civilians into capable soldiers through exhausting and repetitive exercises and activities, basic training familiarized men with the weapons they would use and attempted to provide them some sense of the noise and confusion of actual combat. Men in the Army and Marines became well-acquainted with the rifle, though some like Jack Barrett had experience with guns growing up in the South:

You had a few boys that were familiar with guns, but most of them were not. They issued us the M1 rifle, the Garand, and it still had cosmoline on it, which is a protective coating. We had to clean these guns and learn how to put them together and take them apart. There was a boy from Detroit in our outfit, he had never had his hands on a gun before in his life. I took him under my wing and told him about the stock and the trigger and the barrel and the bullets, when you pull the trigger the firing pin hit the base of the cartridge and set off a cap that set off the powder and the gun shot and the bullet went out and spun like a football, and then told him about the front sight and the rear sight and how to aim. When I got through telling him, he had his mouth open the whole time just sitting there looking and listening. He said he figured I was the smartest fella he had ever run into in his whole life.

For others like Charlie Fiveash, rifle training was a bit more casual:
We would dismantle a rifle and put it back together, but it wasn't a modern rifle, it was [the kind] that Teddy Roosevelt used, the Enfield, and that's what we qualified with for sharpshooter. Everybody passed. I mean if the dirt flew you still got a bull's-eye. Everybody was going to qualify, no worry about that, you [were] guaranteed to qualify.

Together with its complement of riflemen, each infantry platoon had at least one man armed with the Browning Automatic Rifle (BAR), sometimes without much training before shipping overseas. As Reeves Parish recalls, "I was in Tennessee for three months, we went to West Virginia for a month and shortly after that somebody shipped out and then they made me the BAR man. They just gave me the BAR and said, 'This is it.'"

By and large, though, each new recruit was thoroughly trained on his primary weapon, and some, like Marine Pat Roberts, did so well they were made into snipers:

After boot camp we went through a camp near San Diego called Camp Elliot. We trained at the rifle range there and qualifying day I had a 319 bull's-eye count out of 340 rounds. The rifle range instructor said that they gave me the red flag seven or eight times for misses, which he said he didn't think possible because I was shooting too good. He said the bullets were going through the same hole. I had the highest score in the platoon and I understand it was a record when I left there. After that I went back to San Diego and they wanted me to go to scout sniper school. We trained there and we did all kind of camouflage, shooting at different ranges with scopes. We were trained long days on what they call hand signals because in that type of warfare you use hand signals a lot like assemble, skirmish right, skirmish left, hit the deck. What we would do is hit on the butt of our M1 to break our fall. One time when I started down there was a big rattlesnake right there, great big one and how I got up in the air and went over him I don't know, but I killed him. He had ten rattles and a button, big job.

World War II required the training of millions of men in such a short time that inevitable problems of organization would occur. Training centers would be short of weapons to train with, and units would be shipped overseas too quickly during combat emergencies (such as in late 1944, during the Battle of the Bulge). When James Wisenbaker was sent with his unit to Camp Atterbury, Indiana, on maneuvers, he learned the meaning behind the Army cliché "hurry up and wait":

> If you're an Army man you know this can happen. We got to Camp Atterbury, they said they didn't know we was coming. So we were standing out on the street out there for hours. They finally took care of us, but can you imagine a division of troops going from somewhere and nobody knew they was coming.

Bennie Thompson was drafted and completed basic training at Camp Wheeler, Georgia, after which he was selected for mountain training: "They sent me to Camp Swift, Texas, but there ain't no mountains in Texas. That's the way the Army would mess up all the way through. But they sent us out there. We stayed out there five or six weeks."

Sergeant Leonard Lifsey had enlisted in the Army before Pearl Harbor and was assigned to a military police unit in charge of guarding enemy prisoners at Camp Wheeler, Georgia, in 1943:

> We were getting in 2,000 German prisoners. We spent about three months training for them, speaking German. Everything had to be done in German. Everything we would order and eat in the mess hall had to be in German. So we just took German class, took German class, took German. We could speak it a little bit, enough to get by. And then when we got the prisoners in,

there was no Germans among them – typical Army. They was all 2,000 Italians, eight abreast, came marching up the street.

Here Lifsey describes the routines of the camp and the behavior of the Italian prisoners. Perhaps American trainees would have recognized some similarities between their lives and the Italians':

> We had [the Italians] set up in companies, 250 each, and each one had a supply house just like the Army, had a mess hall. We gave them the food of their country and they had plenty. They did their own cooking. They had a mess hall and they would designate whoever the cooks were. I had what I called my first sergeant, and he would call roll every morning and I'd stand there and observe. During the day we would [tell] them to go out and work. The farmers would call in and say I need 20, I need 10, I need 40, whatever he needed, and we'd send them out with guards, though there really was no point in it. They didn't want to go home. They really were good people.

> They would get 90 cents a day and we'd pay them at the end of the month, and the ones that did not work got 10 cents a day. And we had a regular PX. They could go in and buy anything except weapons and things like that. They would pay [with] these coupons that we would issue them, depending on how much they had coming, whether it would be 10 cents or 90 cents a day.

> The Italians, they'd tell you a story, a war story, and we'd say, "Where did you get that?" "We got it by wire." I said, "What do you mean by wire?" And they'd touch the fence that they had in the compound. They said, by the wire. That was their answer where they got that story at.

But once in a while the winds of war could create lucky occasions, as Ray Hitt recalls:

> I was in the chow line for our evening meal and I had not met anybody yet. But it happened to be there was four soldiers ahead of me all from Georgia, and since I was from Georgia, that was five of us, so we immediately got the name of the five Georgia boys. We bonded right away and we became friends. We stayed at Hattiesburg, Mississippi, for our training, we went overseas

together, we fought together, we stayed together, and we returned home together all safe and sound.

Advanced training

After basic, men were transferred for advanced training in order to prepare them to work as riflemen, airmen, and sailors, as well as members of a unit. Though trained as a radar operator, Bill Britton was transferred to the infantry and wound up at Fort Benning, where he was quite impressed by one particular instructor:

> I was told that I would go to Australia soon to help set up another radar school. However, my name got on a list of officers to be detailed to the infantry even though I had a critical MOS [military occupation specialty]. We're not supposed to be touched by anything. I was put on that list. And when I found out about it I went down and talked to the chief of staff of the post and he couldn't believe it. "You got no business going anywhere. They spent thousands and thousands of dollars on your training and now you're going to throw it all away." He was a full colonel. He called generals and everybody trying to get me off the list, but it seems that General Devens, who was chief of all Armed Forces in the United States, training forces, had signed an order and nobody wanted to move anybody that had already been assigned. So they said no. You're going to Fort Benning whether you like it or not. I said all right. So then I had to destroy all my secret stuff that I had and soon shipped out to Fort Benning where I went through the officer's training course.

> Benning was the most outstanding military school I ever saw in my life. It was head and shoulders above everything else I've ever seen. And they could brainwash you. By the time you got through, you were gung-ho for the infantry. You looked down on everybody else. If they wasn't in the queen of battles, they didn't amount to anything. They really did build up your morale, your spirits. And the training was tremendous. One thing that I remember was right funny. This ranger came in to give us some ranger training. He came in and he put this silhouette on this tree. We were out in the woods. He picked up a .30 caliber machinegun and started firing at this target. Then he set the machinegun down and got a submachine gun and fired that. Then he set that down and took an M1 Garand rifle and fired

that. Then he fired a carbine. Then he pulled his pistol out and fired that. Then he pulled his knife out and he threw that down and stuck it in there. Then he went down and bit a hole in it. And he turned around and says "Anybody want to start anything?" We sat there with our mouth open. That big sucker, he tore that target all to pieces.

After Benning, Britton went on to serve in the 90th Infantry Division as an instructor at Fort Hood, Texas, and appreciated the dedication of Japanese-American soldiers, many of whom would later serve in the highly-decorated 442nd Infantry Regiment:

> Training was rough. You worked almost a seven-day week in those days. War was on. They didn't care if you ever left the post. Once in a while you'd have Sunday off. A lot of times on Saturdays you went on a 20 mile march and things like that. You couldn't complain. They were training people to go give their life up if necessary and it was important that they were physically and mentally trained the best you could train them. And in bayonet fighting and all this, we really got into it with them and really got them to believe that they could do it. And some of the best trainees I had were Japanese-Americans from Honolulu. They're the ones that went to Italy, did such a marvelous job over there. They won more medals, their units did, than any other unit.

> But they were never complaining. You'd have to make them take their shoes off on a march because they'd walk with blood in their shoes before they would tell you that something was wrong with their feet. We'd have to check their feet to keep them from hurting their own self. They were that good of soldiers that they would just go the extra mile. Anyhow, that was very rewarding to me to see people that had the determination and had the desire to become good soldiers and to prove Japanese-Americans could be Americans and they had no alliance with the Mother Country. And they didn't. They were terrific soldiers.

Like the other branches of the military, before the war the Army Air Corps had a small number of men in its service—only 24,000 as of September 1939. And like the other branches, the Air Corps underwent a massive expansion in the months following Pearl Harbor. By the end of the war the Air Corps, renamed the Army Air Forces, had over 2.4

million members, 31% of the U.S. Army as a whole. Basic training in the Air Forces was often shorter than in the other branches and emphasized technical subjects; during basic the men were given aptitude and psychological tests to determine their suitability for pilot and other types of air crew training. Those selected for pilot, navigator, or bombardier training then embarked on a phase of their preparation that would take many months, often a year or longer. Initial training was done on slow, light aircraft emphasizing basic aerial maneuvers, which Jim Wetzel recalls as thoroughly enjoyable:

> Part of our training was 10 hours in a Cub. It was fun. We did things I guess you couldn't do these days, it wouldn't be allowed. We stalled out, did spins, had to count the number of turns, pull out and two and a half turns and then climb back up and let's do it again, that kind of thing. At the end of 10 hours, I soloed, so I was satisfied with that experience. That was very pleasant, that was fun.

Fairfield Goodale's first flight experience was in a Steerman bi-plane, which had an open cockpit. Here he describes being hazed mid-flight by his instructor:

> It was not uncommon for the instructor, who sat in the front seat, to turn the plane over and see if your seatbelt was tight enough to hold you in. He would cut the motor and scare the devil out of you because you thought, "My God, I'm on my back, the motor was quit, what am I going to do?" And then you'd look in the mirror and see him laughing and then you'd stop being quite so worried.

Goodale's attempts at revenge on other instructors did not go as planned:

> One of our instructors was good, but he had a dreadful stutter and one day he was late for class and I was up in front of the class imitating him and he walked in. I was caught red-handed and spent hours walking with a rifle around the compound.

> We used to shoot skeet in order to learn how to anticipate how to shoot at airplanes and our instructor was cordially hated by all of us and I used to mock him a little bit. He put me in the room from which you threw the little clay skeets out. And when he came to shoot his gun I would punch a hole in the skeet and it

would go out and fly irregularly and he would miss. And he learned sooner or later what I was doing and I'm sure that didn't help my later commission status.

Not surprisingly, most men selected for aircrew training wanted to be pilots; those who didn't make the cut were often trained as navigators and bombardiers—while a total of 193,000 pilots graduated from basic Army Air Corps/Forces schools during the war, a majority of these men "washed out" of advanced flight training. James Kauffmann remembers the competitive atmosphere of pilot training and the often arbitrary way some men were rejected:

> I went to Maxwell Air Base in Montgomery, Alabama, for preflight [training] and that was about six weeks. At preflight you didn't even know what an aircraft looked like. They crowded you with all kinds of schooling, navigation, astronomy and everything. We had to study that while we were there and of course the one thing that I was not very good at was mathematics but I sure did have some good friends and some good people to help me get through that and I did survive. But a lot of the kids that were there washed out. It could be that one of the instructors saw you in a hall or came into your living quarters and didn't like the way you had made up your bed or your shoes wasn't shined, your hair wasn't combed, a lot of things. Of course, after it's all over with you'd realize what they're trying to do. They're trying to weed out those that couldn't follow instructions or wouldn't. They were not good officer material.

Still, bombardier and navigator training was no easy task to complete, with such tools as the Norden bombsight and celestial navigation to master, and training for each of these positions would take as long as that for pilots. Jim Murry explains the importance of the Norden bombsight:

> The Norden bombsight was far ahead of its time in delivering bombs where you wanted them to go, and by taking the information that you had in the air – your air speed, your drift, your wind direction, your altitude – and feeding all of this information into the bombsight, it would give you a reading to give you tangents of dropping angles, to compensate for wind drift and that sort of thing. And we had something known as E6-B computers at that time. Well, it wasn't anything like

computers today. It was simply something that you could take and put information in and it would give you figures and so on, which I then would put into the bombsight and use that to calculate dropping angles and when we should turn the bombs loose and so on. But anyhow, it was highly secretive. The Germans didn't have anything like it and the Japanese didn't, and theoretically it was supposed to make us better. We think it did.

After basic training, Oscar Barney was selected for navigator training at Maxwell Air Base and remembers the complexity of learning celestial navigation and the special help he received while learning it:

I think one of the most interesting things in navigation school, celestial, was the most difficult part of it. We were out at night with little sextants and taking sight of some of the stars and everything. We had a class beside us that were black airmen and I mean they were sharp with the celestial navigation and I spent some time with them and probably learned as much from them as I did in class.

In addition to pilots, navigators, and bombardiers, there were of course other members of aircrews such as flight engineers and gunners. Tom Jackson was sent to March Field, California, for air gunnery training when he was selected for one of the more difficult jobs—ball turret gunner. Ball turrets were small, spherical, rotating plexiglass gun stations outfitted with twin .50 caliber machine guns and placed under the belly of B-17 and B-24 aircraft:

When I got to March Field they said you've got to be in the ball turret. They put me in a turret and I said, "I'm too big." They said, well, when you get with a crew and go overseas, you probably can swap. They said, get in there, and they put me in there, and it was 42 inches, I think, in diameter. The normal thing was, you put your elbows on your knees, and they've got two different things that turn the turret around, and on the top you shoot the gun with two buttons.

Air Force training was the most dangerous in the entire military— over 7,100 aircraft and 15,000 men were lost during training during the war in the continental U.S. Chuck Tarver survived two crashes during his training as a navigator/bombardier:

I crashed the first one in Jacksonville, Florida. The pilot was doing a stick back stall and it cut off the engine and he couldn't start it. He says, "Are you going to jump?" And I said, "Without a parachute?" We went in on a beach. It was a cub plane. The Coast Guard saw us coming in and they were rushing toward [us] and picked us up. The next one was in Newfoundland. I crashed—we were going to England, and we were going to land at a place in Newfoundland for refueling. It was snowing, and the guy flying the plane was a full colonel. He was commander of the refueling squadron and this was one of his planes. But the co-pilot was a base commander and he wasn't checked out [for] the plane. And I heard Colonel Rodell tell him, "Don't touch the feather, I'll do all of that." We made a perfect approach but we were going to overshoot, so they shot up a red flare, and as Colonel Rodell pushed the throttle to go around, that idiot feathered the plane and just brought it down, and that was one less B-24. We all got out, but all that was left was the tail.

Tarver would later pilot five B-24 missions over Ploesti, Romania.

Robert Jones was on a training flight outside of Houston, Texas, when nature presented him with an unusual obstacle:

I was flying co-pilot with another guy, we called him Andy Hardy. Anyway, we were flying [over] the river rather low and we went under some wires, when up in front of us a whole flock of ducks took off. Andy pulled up and I ducked and one came right through the windshield, took the radio that was out behind my head and put it in the back of the airplane. Another one hit the engine. We struggled back and swore we'd never been under 1500 feet.

David Davis was on his first training flight with the 401st Glider Infantry Regiment (part of the Army's 101st Airborne Division) at Camp Mackall, North Carolina, when something went wrong:

Something happened to the tow rope. We were supposed to go up and then they were supposed to drop the tow rope and we were supposed to glide around and come back down to the airfield. Well, the tow rope broke and we were released ahead of time and the only place to go was in a cornfield. In the cornfield there was one tree and unfortunately we hit the tree, and that was my orientation flight. It didn't hurt us at all, except it did break the wing off when we landed the glider.

Carl Sanders of Augusta, who was on a football scholarship at the University of Georgia, left his undergraduate studies in 1943 to sign up for the Army Air Corps at Daniel Field. Sanders trained at various bases, planning to fly the P-38 fighter. But the Army's needs shifted while he was in training, and now it was bomber pilots they needed. Sanders found himself shipped to Hobbs, New Mexico, to train on the B-17 bomber. By the time he neared the end of his training in Tennessee, the war in Europe ended and Sanders was discharged and returned to college.

Sanders' most exciting war experience was, perhaps, the bombing of Humboldt, Tennessee. On a practice bombing run, Sanders' bombardier misread the Norden bomb sight and dropped the dummy bombs a mile-and-a-half away from the target:

> When I got back to the base and taxied the aircraft over to the area where we supposed to leave it, I saw a civilian automobile and my colonel. And he said, "Lieutenant, come over here, I want you to meet somebody." And I went over and he introduced me to the mayor of Humboldt, Tennessee, and I said "Mr. Mayor, I'm glad to know you" and the Colonel said, "I want you to know that you bombed Humboldt, Tennessee." I said, "We did what?" He said, "You dropped some practice bombs on Humboldt, Tennessee." And that's when I found out that the bombardier had screwed up and had the bombsight wrong. I thought, man, we'll get court-martialed. Well, we didn't, but that was quite an experience because I doubt seriously if the Germans would have a chance to bomb Humboldt, Tennessee, but I did.

After pilots, navigators, bombardiers, and gunners were thoroughly trained in their individual specialties, they had to be trained to work as members of an air crew, and as an air crew they had to be trained to work in sync with other crews in their squadron as well as with ground units. Often such advanced training took place in-theater. Jack Kendall was in the 13th Air Force training as a B-24 navigator in the Pacific theater when he learned some of the less technical aspects of survival in combat:

> They had some Australians that taught us how to survive in the jungle if a plane went down. They called themselves the Nadzab boy scouts [Nadzab is a town in New Guinea]. We went out in

the woods and they showed us what we could eat if we went down. The tops of palm trees, you could cut some of the palm material out and eat that. Also they showed us worms and grasshoppers and different things we could eat, which wasn't too appealing.

Small world

Military training was difficult and exacting, and fairly strange to the vast majority of new recruits. But by and large it was quite successful in transforming civilians into servicemen. As the men learned more about themselves, and what it would take to become effective soldiers, sailors, Marines, and airmen, they learned more about the world outside of their hometowns—while training they became familiar with parts of the country previously unknown, and became acquainted with people they would never have come across otherwise. Southerners learned to get along with northerners, city boys got to know country boys, and new recruits learned from old soldiers. Thus for many men the war provided a broadening of horizons that lasted a lifetime.

Sometimes men in training would run across people who were well known or who would become well known in the future. John Clements was training with the 2nd Armored Division when he came into contact with its famous and controversial commander, George Patton:

> We were dry running for the North African invasion up in Virginia and we had been put on a small LCI [Landing Craft, Infantry] with an M8 [Armored] Car. We didn't carry the ammunition in the vehicle, we carried it in the trailer and we had to unhook the trailer and turn it sideways to get it on the LCI. So when we came back to unload, I had to get out and hook the trailer back up to the M8 vehicle so we could pull it off and I couldn't get the darn thing hooked up. Patton along with his staff was standing out on the beach, and he finally waded out [to] about a foot deep or more into the ocean and the other guy, a fella named Satterfield, got out and helped me and we finally got the trailer hooked up. But Patton stopped us, I got down in the M8, hid down there. He chewed Satterfield out good. But I admired Patton really. I think Patton was the right man at the right time for our unit.

Bill Prout trained with a PT boat squadron on the coast of Rhode Island before service in the New Guinea and Okinawa campaigns. He

48

recalls being introduced to people quite different from those he was used to while growing up in Appalachia, one of whom would go on to command PT-109 in the Pacific:

> President Kennedy was one of our teachers there, and we thought he was a good one. Kennedy and all of the people [who] were getting to be officers at that time were coming out of colleges. They were sent to a midshipman school and they became 90-day wonders, and then ensigns. And he wanted into our squadron, and I have to tell you why. The various squadrons usually had special people in them. The squadron [that] trained after us were all professional football players. In our squadron we had athletes and people who raced boats. We had Alfred Gwynne Vanderbilt and George Vanderbilt. They raced everything under the sun. And the radio man on our PT boat 191 was named James Fraser, and his father owned the New England Mutual Life Insurance Company. And just think, I didn't have a dime and came out of the hills of Kentucky.

John Kristensen was introduced to Army life at Camp Upton, New York, in 1942 by a tough sergeant when he came across the toughest man in the world at that time:

> My first night I was put on KP and worked in a mess hall for 11 hours. When I returned to the barracks around 6 a.m., a kind sergeant tapped me for KP duty. When I explained that I had just completed 11 hours of same, he said, "That's what they all say," and I went back on for 12 more hours. I ate very well my first 23 hours in the service. I was a little excited when I saw a corporal with a familiar face marching a squad along, heavy-weight champion Joe Louis. You may be sure they obeyed his commands.

Of course, during World War II the United States military was still firmly segregated—even Joe Louis, whose first round victory over Max Schmeling in 1938 helped disprove Nazi theories of racial superiority, served in a segregated unit in Kansas. Roosevelt Brooks trained with an all-black unit with white officers and recalls being willing to serve in a combat unit in order to prove that African-Americans were worthy counterparts to their white countrymen. As he puts it, "That's why I volunteered for it." Brooks would go on to serve bravely as a combat medic with the Army's 92nd Division in Italy.

While in Marine boot camp Chester McCoy came across another American celebrity doing his duty like anyone else:

> Tyrone Power had just finished making a picture with Maureen O'Hara [*The Black Swan*] where at the end of the picture he told her you have to kiss me three times or something like that. He was in the third or fourth platoon ahead of me. That means he graduated four weeks before I did. Some of the guys around there was kidding him, always hollering at him, kiss me, something like that, and they got in a little fight – not much before the sergeants got in there and stopped it. But Tyrone Power went through as everyone else.

While undergoing their rigorous training programs, men had opportunities to relax on leave. Many took full advantage, unwinding with drink or getting to know the locals. Reeves Parish remembers some fun times with his comrades while training with the 35th Division in West Virginia:

> Bootleggers all over the place. Men would slip off at night, find a bootlegger's house. In the barracks we did a lot of singing, this man would lay on [one] side of the bunk on the floor, this man would lay on [the other] side of the bunk and we would kick – kick the other one and see which one could make the other one get up and run. Just such foolish, childish things as that.

Herman Boland sailed with the Merchant Marine in the Caribbean in 1942 before later serving with the Marines in the Pacific. Here he recalls the trips to Cuba dodging enemy submarines and the pleasures of shore leave:

> I loved shore leaves. [One] time we went to Havana, Cuba. We always sailed alone. They'd have German submarines on that coast; of course they didn't know we were hauling [just molasses]. I got to liking Havana, I loved their music, I just loved everything about the city. I remember two girl orchestras, each one about trying to outplay the other one.

New Yorker John Kristensen recalls getting a taste of Southern hospitality while on a weekend pass from Camp Anniston, Alabama:

We were granted a Sunday pass to go to church, where kind Annistonians would take us home for a good old southern home-cooked meal. I was lucky enough to be one of the two drafted by a 90-year old couple who quickly stopped our salivating by announcing that they were vegetarians. We enjoyed those veggies. A couple of weeks later we did better with a fine meal with a great couple with a gorgeous daughter, had a nice home in Gadsden nearby.

Carl Schutte was an officer training with the 66th Infantry Division at Fort McClellan, Alabama, when he met a special girl while on a weekend pass:

I had gotten a leave for Fourth of July on a three-day pass. I went up to Troy and met a girl. She was a USO and we started corresponding and I went up there as often as possible and we decided that we would get engaged so I bought her a diamond ring in Montgomery, Alabama. I didn't intend to get married. I was going to get married after the war if I got back, and no guarantee of that. But she said, "No, I want something to hold onto and I want you. I want to get married." So sure enough on October 15, 1944, at the First Baptist Church at Troy, Alabama, we were married. My folks came down from Washington, D.C., and they were part of the ceremony.

Once in a while, time spent on leave with the opposite sex could have less storybook consequences. Jesse Scott's natural inclinations got the better of his attempts to be gentlemanly with a young woman before embarking on his duties on a Liberty ship in the Navy:

I goofed up. Her parents trusted me with her. They wouldn't let me sleep with her, but they thought a lot of me because I didn't drink and smoke and cut up like most of them do. I was doing good with her. She had a buddy and she's an older lady and that older lady let us go to bed down at her house. And boy, that goofed me up, she got pregnant and I never did write her again.

But no matter how enticing or diverting time off duty was for the men, most wanted nothing more than to spend more time back home. Before John Taylor would commence arduous duty in Europe as an infantry lieutenant, while on leave from training at Camp Blanding, Florida, he made it all the way home to Aiken for Christmas:

We only had a 50 mile radius pass, but I kind of broke the rule there. This other fella was from my hometown too and we got to discussing old friends at home and all, got kind of homesick, so we decided we wanted to go home for the Christmas Day.

We went around to the bus station and they didn't have anything going towards South Carolina, so we went around to the train station, this was about 12 o'clock at night and the conductor said, "Soldiers, where are you going?" We told him we're going to Augusta, we figured he knew Augusta better than Aiken. So he says, "Well, I'm not going there, going about halfway, but if you want to get in this coach right here, I'll carry you about halfway, but then I gotta turn left and we're gonna let you out and maybe you can get a ride on into Augusta." So we said, "We'll take you up on it." He said, "I know you don't have any tickets, you don't need any, you're in the service." So we got on, the whole coach was filled with ladies – war brides or war fiancés.

We [got] about midway between Jacksonville and Augusta, [and] we got off there about 6 o'clock in the morning. We went out to Highway 1, the highway that we knew went to Augusta and we thumbed a ride. Two ladies drove by in an old Ford pickup truck and stopped. One said, "Soldier, where are you going?" We told her Augusta. She said, "Well, I'm going to Augusta, you're lucky. This lady here traveling with me says she lives about 20 miles up the road, if you all want to ride in the back, about 20 miles from now she gets out and both of y'all [can] get up front."

She got out 20 miles out and I was the first one to the truck door. She had a big old long pistol in her lap and she said, "Get in," and I said, "Well, I'm kind of afraid to get in with that pistol," she said, "Look here, I'm not dangerous, I just want to make certain y'all are not." So she carried us all the way to the Valley Coach Terminal on Greene Street in Augusta. We got a bus there and rode the other 20 miles to Aiken and we got there in time for lunch.

Men like Taylor had joined up for a variety of reasons. But by the end of their long, rigorous training all of them had left their civilian lives behind and would serve their country in battle. But before they reached far off places like Normandy or Iwo Jima these men had to make the often arduous journey overseas.

Going over There

Old soldiers have sharp memories of the trip overseas. After months of training and waiting, they were finally leaving their home country and sailing halfway across the world to an unknown destination and an unknown fate. As the United States' involvement in the war picked up, and more and more men were being trained for war, so too did the pace of troops headed overseas. While in the month after Pearl Harbor only 4,000 men landed in Europe, by the end of 1942 nearly a million had done so. At the height of the war in 1944, 3 million troops sailed overseas, along with vast amounts of weapons and supplies. The transition from training to fighting was a monumental undertaking.

Before embarking, troops stayed in port areas about two weeks, tuning up their training, getting last minute vaccinations, practicing abandon-ship drills, and of course waiting. Mabel Crawford, in Washington, D.C. training as a Navy code-breaker, recalls coming across lonely troops about to go overseas:

> That was the most pitiful thing. They was fixing to go over. They'd take all their dress clothes away from them and put on fatigues. And they'd come out and you couldn't get a park bench to sit on. You had to keep walking. They'd even buy a paper and lay on the grass in front of the White House. They wasn't going back to the barracks and go to bed, because they were going over, they didn't know if they were coming back. They'd even meet you on the street and beg you to get married due to the fact they wanted somebody, they'd say, to come back home to. And we always had our words to tell them, that we wasn't going to get married, you know. We never did mistreat them, but it was right pitiful. They were young and they hated it so bad because they didn't know if they were coming back. A lot of them didn't.

The last day or two before sailing the men were put under "blackout"—because the secrecy of troop movements was essential, no one was allowed off post, visitors were forbidden, and no phone calls or telegrams were permitted. Coast Guard Seaman 1st Class Carroll Scott worked the mounted shore patrol at Seaside Heights, New Jersey, in the anxious days of early 1942, watching for German submarines, saboteurs, and spies. Here he describes the blackout restrictions on automobiles and the routines of patrol:

> I was patrolling the beaches there for a couple of miles. That's back in the days [when] all cars had to paint the top half of [their headlights] black to eliminate the glare. German subs [were out] there and that was the law, you just had paint all the headlights along the ocean. Half of it kept the glare out of the sky and kept the beam on the road.

> You had your beach [to patrol] and you had some length of time to make the patrol from this [station] to that one. [At] the end of your beat another horse patrolman from the same stables [came up]. If you were a little late [reporting], probably a chief petty officer would know and they would report it from theswitchboard to the headquarters back at Seaside Heights. If you were 20 minutes late he'd park that Coast Guard truck waiting for you to get back on that horse or find out where you were. See, we did have spies landing on the beach or coast of the United States.

Finally, when the time came, as each man approached the ship his last name was called, and he was required to answer with his first name and middle initial—this process provided another layer of security. Troops made their way up the gangplank with full packs plus helmet, rifle, cartridge belt, bayonet, canteen, gas mask, and duffel bag. Once on board, the men were directed to their berths, usually well below deck, and each man received a letter of encouragement from President Roosevelt.

The vessels used to carry troops to overseas theaters varied immensely in size and speed. At the large end of the spectrum were luxury ocean liners such as the *Queen Elizabeth* and the *Queen Mary*. These ships were retrofitted to allow for more "passengers"—compared to a peacetime capacity of 2,200 civilians, during the war they were able to hold upwards of 15,000 men (together the two *Queens* would carry a million men overseas during the war). Instead of first class cabins and stately dining rooms, troops were offered crowded sleeping quarters and hot mess halls. Charlie Fiveash was impressed both with the size of the *Elizabeth* and its crowded accommodations:

> We saw the *Queen Elizabeth* and it was a huge thing. I worked in the shipyard as a kid and in high school building Liberty ships,

but this thing was eight, ten times as large and they put 17,000 of us on that boat, so they squeezed you together in there. If you stayed in the chow line 24 hours a day you'd get fed twice a day because it took you a half a day to get around the ship three or four times to get back to the kitchen.

On the plus side, these ships were the fastest in the fleet, and could make the Atlantic crossing in 5 days—fast enough that they could do without the escort and convoy system the U.S. established to stymie German submarines. At the smaller end of the spectrum were the Liberty ships—2,700 of which were built during the war. Whereas liners like the *Queen Elizabeth* measured over 1,000 feet in length and displaced over 80,000 tons, Liberty ships were less than half as long, displaced 14,000 tons, and had a carrying capacity of about 550 troops. Liberty ships were also much slower than the liners—2 weeks to cross the Atlantic was about average—and because they were comparatively small vessels, they offered a much less smooth ride. The Army Transportation Corps even admitted that transport aboard a Liberty ship lowered morale. Roosevelt Brooks, a medic in the Army's 92nd Division, crossed the Atlantic as part of a convoy and had a rough time on one of the smaller kinds of troop transports epitomized by the Liberty ship:

> I got seasickness for 3 days, 3 nights. I used to go [to] New York to a dock in town and I'd see these big ships and I'd say, "Boy, that's a big boat." I looked out at the end and look at these other [ships]—they look like match sticks. And the waves were like a mountain. Roughest weather I've seen in my life. I'd never been on the ocean before at that time. I thought about these ships like the Mayflower and that stuff, I said, "Them people were either crazy or they had a whole lot of nerve."

For the vast majority of men heading overseas, whether aboard a large or small ship, the accommodations were strikingly similar. Sleeping quarters were well below deck, often in converted holds that were poorly ventilated—beds were canvas and metal-frame bunks, 6 feet long and 2 feet wide, suspended by chains and stacked one over the other, as many as 6 high, with 2 feet between bunks. Some vessels were so crowded that men slept in shifts. Showers and washbasins used seawater. Don Lundquist was with the 8th Armored Division on board an ocean liner en route to Scotland. He remembers the difficult conditions onboard not only for himself but for a group of nurses:

We went over on the *New Amsterdam*, which was a Dutch liner somewhat comparable to the *Queen Elizabeth* ships of that day. I have no idea how many people were aboard that ship, but it was crowded. There were 16 of us in one room that was probably 12 ft. by 12 ft. with bunks going up and down. I was the luckiest one in the whole cabin because there was one of the little air jets like you have on an airplane, and one of those jets was at my nose. The odors were not very good with all the people that were seasick and so forth, but I managed to stay healthy and no seasickness. We were fed twice a day, boiled eggs and slabs of pork. The thing that was terrible to see, there were several hospital units on that ship and the nurses – it was pathetic, we couldn't get on the same deck the nurses were on, but we could see the nurses on the deck and they would be crawling around on their hands and knees just terribly seasick, it was a shame to watch.

Al Tewkesbury was in the 1st Marine Division headed for the Pacific:

> They had stripped out probably three of the holds of the ship itself that in peacetime they would have put luggage and things in and put up these chain cots. They would hang five cots from one part of the ceiling and that's where you slept and the worst part about it is if you were my size you were alright, but if you were a little bit heavy it was hell to be above somebody and below somebody and all you could smell was B.O., all morning and all night.

Lou Brissie, who would become an American League All-Star pitcher after the war, crossed the Atlantic on a ship carrying 3,000 troops. Fresh out of Presbyterian College in Clinton, South Carolina, he and a football-playing buddy from Presbyterian just couldn't sleep on bunks stacked five or six high. Brissie was 6-4. He was assigned the highest bunk, his nose pressed against the bulkhead deep in the ship, just above the engine room. There was no room to roll over or sleep on his side. He had to be slid into his slot of a bunk by hands from beneath:

> So we decided we would sleep topside. We wrapped up and curled up in a cot on the topside. They had the gun turrets— protection around a little higher than [one's] waist, so we'd get back in behind that and they couldn't see us.

The two friends avoided detection for a couple of nights. But then a petty officer discovered them.

> "What are you guys doing?"
> "Well, we've been sleeping here. We're big and they got us on the top bunk and won't anybody swap with us and we can't sleep, and when we get in there, that bulkhead's right against our nose."

The petty officer agreed not to report them, and they slept on deck until they landed in Naples two weeks later.

Henry Burch, a member of the 80th Infantry Division, sailed across the Atlantic to Scotland on the *Queen Mary* and remembers the food well:

> We had a British troop crew and British food, which was a little different from ours. I commented to the fellas that I was watching them loading supplies on the ship and I was surprised at all the meat they were putting on [board]. This British sailor says "That isn't meat, that's goat." Well, we had it about twice a day and goat stew for breakfast was quite a challenge.

Jim Robbins was a member of an Army anti-aircraft battalion headed to the Pacific theater; he recalls both the food and the sleeping quarters during the 18-day trip:

> You were in racks or bunks in the cargo holds and we got a lot of frozen fish to eat. It was preserved in salt and they soaked the salt out and fed them to us. We'd go to the mess hall and get as many boiled eggs as we wanted just about any time of the day we wanted them. The showers was saltwater. The facilities for the bathroom was kind of crude. There were troughs that took the waste away. The odor gradually grew in the hold of the ship so they had to put those air scuffles on the decks to funnel air down into the hold of the ship.

Aside from trying to eat and sleep, there was not much for a man to do during the crossing. Harry Kemp and his twin brother, Larry, got lucky. The 14th Armored Division concert band was aboard the ship. Many of the band's members were professional musicians from big bands playing the music of Tommy and Jimmy Dorsey, Harry James, and Benny Goodman. Kemp, who was 18, had played piano in his own band in high school. He loved the music the division band played on the deck as they crossed the Atlantic:

> It was just terrific music. They had a guy, an Irishman, Sergeant O'Brien. And he played trumpet, but he'd also do parodies. He'd take a song like "Begin the Beguine" and here's the wording he put to it: "When I began to clean the latrine, it brings back some thoughts that are easy to remember. The Paramount Theater that smells so perfumey, the men's room at Roseland that was also roomy." And so forth and we were just—we were howling. And we're miles out at sea and there's guys over on the bulkhead and they're throwing dice and big money is exchanging. A lot of them were professional dice throwers and some guys just had big wads of money in their hands and stuff. But I wasn't interested in any of that. I wanted to listen to that dance band. So that was a great experience. And the band would come on deck every day and we had beautiful, beautiful music.

But most troops had nothing to entertain them on their crossing. During daylight, troops usually went up on deck for fresh air; at nightfall the PA system would direct them back below deck. Men wrote letters home, though these were censored for intelligence by their officers. And there was plenty of time for the rumor mill to operate—Where are we headed? Who would we fight? For Ted Holladay, a quartermaster aboard the *USS Abele*, a net-laying ship headed to the Pacific theater, the long trip overseas was interrupted by a broadcast by the notorious Tokyo Rose:

> Well, we were on the radio and they tuned it [to] *Tokyo Rose*. We were probably two and a half hours out of port. She came on and said, "All you sailors leaving Honolulu today, we know where you're going, but we'll be waiting for you on Iwo Jima. Don't you really want to turn around and go back to your wives and sweethearts? All we want is peace." Well, of course, we didn't know where we were going. Two hours later, when we joined up with the fleet, they had given us a guarded mail packet with a ribbon on it. We cut it and she was right.

Tokyo Rose was later identified as Iva Toguri, an American of Japanese ancestry who had been born in California and graduated from UCLA. After the war Toguri was convicted of treason and served seven years in prison. In 1977, she was granted a presidential pardon.

58

Joe Rucker was with the 9th Infantry Division headed across the Atlantic aboard the *St. Elena*, a captured German transport, when his commander finally told his troops of their destination: "Old Patton told us when we got way out there in the ocean. He said, 'I see you using your compasses, I'm going to do better than that, I'm going to tell you where you're going. You're going to North Africa.'" Rucker and his division arrived in Oran, Algeria, after a 24-day trip.

Albert Shaw found other things to do with his time:

> I got into a card game onboard the ship and I was not a gambler at heart, really – done very little of it. But I ended up taking everything onboard the ship that anybody would play with, ended up shooting craps. I won $900. At that time, that was quite a bit of money. I said to myself that with so many ducks onboard this ship with you, [someone] would put you away in a heartbeat for $900. So I got myself up to the captain's quarters and I begged him [to] please wire this money home for me. And he said, "Well, you're a damn smart soldier because you're right, there's someone here that would dump you overboard in a heartbeat for $900."

Shaw avoided such a fate and went on to fight in the Battle of the Bulge.

Other men escaped the tedium in unorthodox ways. Hugh Bedingfield, an ensign on the *USS California*, a World War I-era battleship previously damaged in the Pearl Harbor attack, was introduced to an old Navy ritual after he crossed the equator for the first time in 1944:

> On August the 21st the ship crossed the equator going south and, as most of the larger ships do, we had the usual ceremony for crossing the equator. The persons who had never crossed or couldn't prove they had crossed were referred to as pollywogs and the persons who could prove that they had crossed the equator were shellbacks. This was a ceremony to convert whatever pollywogs we had aboard to shellbacks. I had learned that if you sort of took part in the thing and played along that you got along a lot better than if you resisted. We all got nice haircuts where they just cut a little bit here, a little bit there. Eventually you had to go to the barber shop and get it all cut away.

Unfortunately for the crew of the *California*, shortly after crossing the equator it collided with another American naval vessel, the *USS Tennessee*:

> On August 23rd, just shortly before daybreak, the *Tennessee*, our sister ship, rammed into our bow, making a tremendous hole, killing and injuring some people. We were in such state that we had to have major repairs. We headed for Espiritu Santo [one of the Solomon Islands] and there was a floating dry dock, able to accommodate a ship as large as the *California*. We stayed [there] for several weeks until the damage could be cut away and replaced.

For Bill Williams, a boatswain's mate aboard the *USS Refuge*, a hospital ship, the equator ceremony involved less hair loss but more anxiety:

> Well, I was pollywog before I went south of the equator. The day before we went through, the shellbacks was trying to catch all the pollywogs and put us in jail, it was just a big game that was going on. As we crossed the equator one of the great things was that they had this tank filled with water and we had to walk the plank. They would blindfold you and tie your hands behind and you had to walk out on this plank and when you get to the end they would push you off in that water. You didn't know how deep the water was, but there's always somebody in there that hid until you went in and then came out to make sure you didn't get hurt.

While for most men the trip overseas marked a lull between the rigors of training and the dangers of combat, for some the journey was the beginning of their acquaintance with mortal danger, whether from nature or man. John Roland Waters, a seaman aboard the icebreaker the *Southwind*, got a taste of Mother Nature's power:

> We had word that a hurricane was brewing and was getting near. We were at anchor in port in Portland, Maine, but we were ordered to move out to sea, there were too many ships in the harbor. I guess we really got a sense of the sea worthiness of the *Southwind* because during the storm it almost seemed like sometimes the ship would capsize. We were told we had 90 foot swells during that storm and I can believe that because it seemed

like sometimes you were on top of a mountain and then the sea would rush out from under and you would fall down into the sea and the whole ship would be covered up with waves.

Bill Church was with the 3rd Infantry Division en route to Europe when his ship narrowly escaped an attack by the Germans. Unfortunately, a tanker in the same convoy was not so lucky:

> The ship we was on was loaded down with tanks and trucks and jeeps and it's 500 of us on there and 50 officers. And we had a round with a German submarine in that trip too. And a German plane – they come in a V formation one evening and they couldn't go over the barrage that the ships had, so they swung around one way and some the other way. One of their bombs hit the tanker right over from us and it was something, didn't a sole sailor get off of it at all, [it] sunk in a minute and a half.

Carl Schutte was in the English Channel en route to France with the 66th Division on December 24, 1944, when he saw the troop transport *SS Leopoldville*, itself carrying members of the 66th Division, struck by a German submarine's torpedo:

> It was getting dusk and we could see the other ship off to one side. It [was] hit right at the back of a troop compartment and two troop compartments, apparently, were blown just to smithereens and the ship started going down. All the lights went on. We could see the lights of Cherbourg Harbor in the distance and we thought maybe that they were going to be saved. But it finally sank. We didn't see it sink, but we saw it at an extreme angle before we pulled out. We weren't picking up survivors. We knew that three destroyers had come and we could see lights of other ships coming out to pick up survivors, so we thought most of them will be picked up. It turned out that wasn't true. It turned out that there were 278 bodies identified; 517 listed as missing and that was almost a third of our regiment and so we didn't know anything about that until the next morning.

Of the over 2,000 American soldiers on board the *Leopoldville*, official records indicate 763 died in the sinking.

Jim Murry, an Army Air Force bombardier, headed to the Pacific theater by way of Hawaii on his B-24 bomber but ran into engine trouble:

61

It was a rather interesting trip, one that I would not care to repeat. We left Sacramento at 8 o'clock in the evening with this same crew that I had picked up in Charleston, and we were going to John Rodgers Field at Honolulu. Obviously it was dark, [we] flew about four hours, and then there's nothing to do on about a 10- or 11-hour trip. Now, bear in mind that these planes in those days didn't fly 600 miles an hour like they do today. We puttered along [at] about 155 miles an hour. Since there's not a lot to do, we slept.

As we were sleeping, they had something on board that was a bell, and it had to do with safety. It had three rings to it. If you heard the bell ring, you knew that something was amiss. If you heard it ring the second time, we'd get ready to bail out. If you heard it ring the third time, you bailed out. Well, I was sleeping in the nose of the plane and the first thing I heard was a bell. Well, coming out of a deep sleep, you didn't know whether it was the first, the second or the third bell, so you didn't know whether you were going to jump or not. In any event, I came awake, took my chest power chute, hooked it onto my harness, and instead of remembering that I could go out through the doors on the nose, I panicked. I wanted to get back to the bomb bay because I knew there was a lot of room I could jump out there if I had to, so with the power chute on I went through this small companionway back to the bomb bay doors. Well, as all of this was going on, it had all come about because the flight engineer had let the bomb bay tanks get too low on gasoline, and vapor lock had set into engines 2, 3 and 4. And the airplane was built like a boxcar. Well, it fell like a boxcar when you lost that power. So as we were going down – we fell about 5,000 feet.

They were trying to get the booster pumps on, switch to main engines and get power back on and pull out, which they did at about 3,000 feet. The pilot was on the radio talking to the crew that had left about 30 minutes ahead of us, and the last thing that our pilot said to him was, we're going in. In any event, they pulled the plane out. The pilot decided to turn around and go back to Sacramento. They didn't do a thing in the world but to gas us the plane up again and say take off, so we did.

Having endured, and survived, the trip overseas, the men entered the combat zone, not knowing when, or whether, they would return.

Chapter 3
War in Europe, I: The Mediterranean Theater

Overview

The war that would cost perhaps 75 million lives began on September 1, 1939, when Adolf Hitler's Nazi Germany invaded Poland. Within days Britain and France honored their alliance with Poland and declared war, but it would be almost six years before Hitler and his allies were crushed.

After World War I, Americans fervently hoped to remain outside of any future European war. Many Americans (and Europeans) believed that this was not possible once Hitler came to power in 1933. Supported by Fascist dictators like Italy's Benito Mussolini, Hitler embarked on a series of prewar expansions which Britain and France were ill prepared to prevent. Lacking Russian or American support, and with little public appetite for war, the British and French governments were not successful in heading off Hitler's moves.

Many Americans still hoped to remain uninvolved and the America First movement, which preached isolationism, was powerful. President Franklin D. Roosevelt did not want war – in either Europe or the Pacific – but he feared it, and launched military preparations almost immediately. Roosevelt called for the construction of 50,000 military aircraft per year, promoted the draft, and created a centralized military command.

Roosevelt hoped that Hitler would be forced into a long, drawn-out war, which the United States could enter late (if at all) and create a framework for postwar peace. Nazi Germany's stunning defeat of the Anglo-French armies in May of 1940 was a huge shock. Hitler now controlled almost all of Europe; only Britain remained free. Roosevelt began giving aid to Britain. When it became clear that something more was necessary, the U.S. government launched the Lend-Lease program, under which the President could furnish supplies and weapons to any country resisting aggression. In today's dollars, about $300 billion would be spent on this aid. This phase of the war would see the first American lives lost. The destroyers *Kearney* and *Reuben James* were torpedoed by German submarines in the Atlantic in October of 1941, and the more than 100 sailors who were lost represented the beginning of the American human toll of the war. During the war, when American ships were fair game, serving in the U.S. Merchant Marine would be more dangerous than serving in the military; a higher percentage of civilian sailors died on duty than did military personnel.

Two momentous events in 1941 changed the course of the war. On June 22, more than 3 million Nazi troops rolled into the Soviet Union, leading to a phase of the war that may have been responsible for at least half of the death total of the entire war. Second, of course, Japan attacked Pearl Harbor on December 7. Japan's allies, Germany and Italy, subsequently declared war on the United States, so that Americans were now at war on both sides of the planet.

Nazi Germany was viewed as by far the stronger and therefore the more dangerous adversary. Young Americans would now be sent to fight in places they had barely heard of – Tunisia, Sicily, Anzio, Normandy, the Ardennes Forest – not to mention in the air over Europe and at sea, principally in the Atlantic, against German submarines.

Striking Nazi Germany would be difficult. The British and American militaries opted for strategic bombing. Although the ultimate results were disappointing, there was really no other way to take the war to the German heartland. The 8th Air Force's raids beginning in the summer of 1942 were the first attacks by Americans on Hitler's Reich. The American air force, or USAAF, opted for a campaign of daylight bombing, expecting better accuracy (while the British bombed at night) and hoped that heavily armed bombers such as the B-17 Flying Fortress and B-24 Liberator could defend themselves against enemy fighters. On some raids, the losses were enormous (up to a third of the attacking aircraft) as it was not until late in the war that fighter escorts such as the P-51 Mustang could reach the Nazi heartland.

The war, therefore, would have to be won the old fashioned way: on the ground. But while the American army was much readier for war now than it had been in World War I, the preparations and training were so demanding that it would not be until November of 1942 that American troops were ready to enter the war against the Axis, in North Africa. American forces landed in northwestern Africa with an initial goal of driving toward Tunisia. In February of 1943, however, Americans suffered one of their worst defeats of the war at Kasserine Pass in Tunisia. The poorly led and deployed U. S. II Corps suffered heavy losses, leading to the removal of its commander and his replacement by George Patton. Fortunately the Germans could not exploit their early success and the allied armies eventually crushed Axis forces in North Africa in May of 1943.

With strong British support and encouragement, the Allies next crossed the Mediterranean and invaded the Italian island of Sicily in July of 1943. Following the conquest of the island, the Allies then landed on the Italian mainland in September at Salerno. Italy was militarily far weaker than Germany and the Allies expected Italy to be the "soft underbelly" of Europe. Try telling that to any American veteran of this campaign! Yes, the Italian dictator Mussolini was indeed overthrown on July 23, and Italy surrendered on September 8 – but the Germans quickly occupied the peninsula and allied forces found themselves again and again being forced to attack through mountainous terrain. An attempt by American forces to outflank the Germans with an amphibious landing at Anzio in January of 1944 nearly turned into disaster. Northern Italy, long seen as a potential base for bombers, was not reached until January 1945.

North Africa

Seaman James (Fritz) Huiet of Trenton, South Carolina, remembered the first casualty of the war he saw while en route to the Mediterranean in 1942:

> But while we was out in the ocean, the water was rough and this baker had a mess cook, he was standing right beside him, and the ship made a pitch and pitched him with a knife in his hand and it buried it into his leg. And we had a doctor aboard and they removed the boy's leg up to his knee. And they sawed the leg half in two, and gangrene had set in and green was all the way around that bone, and some of us saw it.

On November 12, 1942, Charles Carroll was a hospital corpsman aboard the *USS Bliss*, a transport ship. Having carried troops to Morocco for the invasion of North Africa in Operation Torch, the *Bliss* was at anchor in Fedhala Bay. A German U-Boat slipped past Navy defenses, fired five torpedoes, and sank the *Bliss* and two other transports. Of the 235 men on board the *Bliss*, 31 were killed in the attack.

> I was at my quarters, which was at the bottom of the ship, and they started at general quarters, which meant that everybody went to their battle stations. Well, my battle station happened to be in the mess hall because, being medical, they used the mess tables for operating tables if they had to. And so that was my battle station, and I put my helmet on and rushed there, and just as they got there and I was buckling my helmet, we were torpedoed, and I was hit with a blast like a blowtorch. I had on a short-sleeved shirt and it burned all the skin off of me on both arms up to here and totally off my face. And I think it knocked

me unconscious, because I remember coming to crawling on the deck, and I found my way out. It stank. You couldn't see two inches in front of you.

Carroll found his way up to the deck by feel.

> Well, if I was in a passageway, I knew it was this wide, and then I climbed up the stairway on the ladder we called them. And my hands, being burned like they were, were not strong enough to [open] the hatch, so I went back down and back to the mess hall. Well, my best friend, my buddy, was at his battle station, too. Well, when I got back to the mess hall, nobody had come out. When the torpedo hit, all you could hear was just people screaming and…I almost screamed myself, but I says—I thought I'd had it. And I said, well, I made the course, but I said, I will not die screaming – and I think that's probably why I kept presence of mind enough to find my way out.

The *Bliss* sank slowly over many hours.

> It was laying over sort of on its side and it was in a sinking position. It just took it most of the night to sink. But I got topside through that ladder, and there was a doctor there that I worked with aboard ship named Dr. Broad. I had a lifebelt around me and I couldn't blow it up. I couldn't get any force on my lips. They were burned. The skin was hanging off my chin, my face, off my arms. I grabbed a piece of skin here and unwound it and pulled a fingernail off. When I got topside, I said, "Doctor Broad, I can't blow my lifebelt up," so he took it and blew it up. And so I went over the side. There was a debarkation net there, and I climbed down it, and as I got to the bottom of it, I was afraid—I had not re-adjusted my life belt, and it stayed down around my hips, and I was afraid if I jumped in, I'd come up tail-first and drown. So I climbed down that net and jumped in, and some guy jumped in the water right behind me, and the boats from the other ships were lined up out 100 yards from us. I don't know why they didn't come closer, because the ship wouldn't suck them down or anything. But at any rate, I had to swim about 100 yards with no skin, and I remember that burning some.

Carroll made it aboard the rescue ship.

There was a doctor there from my ship and I recognized him and I called his name. He says, "Who is that?" and I told him, "This is Carroll." And he said, "Carroll, do you drink?" And I says, "No, sir, not much." And, in fact, I didn't drink in those days, because all the money I made, I sent home. I didn't have money to spend on liquor. So he handed me a little bottle of medicinal brandy. And I said, "No, sir, not much," but I downed it in one gulp.

After his burns healed, Carroll returned to duty, eventually being sent to the Pacific.

Rufus Cockrell served on a Navy transport ship in Fedhala Bay. His ship, too, was torpedoed.

We was getting our troops and stuff off the ship with the landing barges when all hell broke loose. Some submarine got in there someway and all he had to do was shoot because they was lined up, 850 ships in this convoy, pretty good-size bunch. And later on you didn't see convoys like that, they split them up. All he had to do – it didn't make no difference which way he was shooting, he was going to hit something. Some of them had phones on the ships, like the old telephones, everybody could hear what everybody was saying and somebody on the bow would say, "Torpedo, track," and one would say, "Yeah, one just passed the stern. Another ship got hit over there." Well, then it cooled down that first night, and the next night it started again and I was on the generator flat and I wanted to go up and see what was going on. And I went up there and seen two get hit while I was up there and I sure hated to go back to that engine room, but I said I better get back down there.

And I didn't get down there but about 10 minutes before we got it. The lights went out and must have been about 30 minutes in there before we could leave out of there, we had to secure all the stuff down, the steam lines, keep them from blowing up. You had to do your job, and then the officer was down there and he'd tell you when you'd abandon the engine room, you didn't leave until he told you. Plus, you've got a .45 sitting beside him. I was regular Navy.

And when I got topside it was already jumping over the side and cutting life rafts loose and I didn't know which way to go. In fact, when I jumped off the ship, I thought I jumped off on the wrong side because they taught us in boot camp to always jump off on the opposite side and I jumped off on the side that got hit on and I felt like I was being pulled back in there. But I was swimming for all I was worth and I looked back, I must have been a half a mile from that ship. Anyway, we must have been in the water about an hour and our boats was coming by, picking us up, and finally one picked me up and carried me over on the beach and I stayed over there about five days and then went to Casablanca, caught a ship back to the United States.

Cockrell's life was saved as a result of a casual conversation he'd had a few days before.

The reason I reckon I'm here today is shooting the breeze. I was working on firing a boiler, number one boiler in the number one fire room on the ship that was sunk. And we was talking one day and one of those old boys says, "Just like the Navy, I went to a water tender school and I'm on a generator flat," and I said, "Well, I went to electricians school and I'm firing a boiler," so the chief let us swap. Wasn't about a day or week – a week at the most — and that's where the torpedo hit, killed every one of them in there. . . . I can't even remember his name.

"Fritz" Huiet also experienced the German attacks on the American ships.

Our general quarters alarm went off and when we got topside to man our gun, we were lit up just like the eternal street lights. They [the Germans] had dropped flares over the whole convoy and I might say this – at that time was one of the largest convoys that ever crossed the Atlantic. And we were attacked by submarines and dive bombers at the same time. How many ships we lost, of course, we don't know. They don't tell you those kind of things.

Even a year later, the Mediterranean was still a dangerous place for Allied convoys. John (Bob) Leopard served on troop transports, crossing the Atlantic 14 times in the course of the war. It was the Mediterranean that almost did him in, in November 1943.

In the Mediterranean we had the worst time we had had because the submarines lay down beside the Spanish-Moroccan coast and go on into the Rock of Gibraltar into the Mediterranean Sea. You had to pull the convoy down to two lines and go in and they would sit at each end and it was just like sitting ducks. And we had a pretty rough time getting in down there. Every night at sundown we stand dusk patrol, every morning at daylight it was dawn patrol, everybody was on their gun turret. And so we were in our gun turrets and it looked like everything Italy had, Germany had and everything else, low-level bombers, strafers, fighter planes came in first and low-level bombers came in second and then high-level bombers came in and torpedo planes. And a torpedo plane came in and one of the boys opened fire on him with the 20 millimeter, but he never did hit him and he had already dropped his torpedo and it hit us mid-ship – 21-inch torpedo hit us mid-ship. And just about the time he got over the ship, and he pulled up to get out of the way, and the boy on the right – starboard side of the bridge shot him down. We lost our ship, but we was always proud of the fact that we got the one that got us.

The ship didn't really start to sink until it was rammed by an out-of-control Norwegian ship that had also been hit. The ship sank slowly, so the 8,000 troops on board were able to get to safety. As a member of the gun crew, Leopard was not permitted to leave his post. With the ship now about to go down, he got a crazy idea.

It had took on a 45 degree angle, stern was going down first. And I was laying the gun to – another boy laying the gun to the side of me and I had bought a tailor-made uniform, blue-black gabardine uniform. Every sailor don't like the Navy uniform. He throws it away if he can. It just don't fit. So I had given $90 in New York for a blue-black gabardine uniform and had 21-inch bellbottoms on it. If you want to look like a sailor, and I was very proud of the fact that I was a sailor and I wanted to look good and all the girls said I did look good.

Leopard couldn't get the tailor-made uniform off his mind, and he told the sailor he was manning the gun with that he was going below in the sinking ship to retrieve it.

I had to go down about 25 foot, go down through the hatch and down one more deck and go out about 10 foot and go in through the right to get to the foc'sle.

He grabbed a suitcase and shoved the uniform in, hauled it back up on deck, dropped it on the boat deck, and abandoned ship in a lifeboat, forgetting the suitcase he'd risked his life to retrieve. Some instinct told him the lifeboat wasn't safe, so he jumped into the water, swimming on his back, just as the mast of the ship came crashing down on the lifeboat. The ship sank beneath the waves and suddenly, with a loud "phoof!" a huge vent which had broken loose came at him like a harpoon, but by then he was far enough away to escape. Soon he and 51 others who had gone over the side with him were picked up by tugboats and taken to a British hospital ship. He and his buddies were soaking wet, of course.

And all of the sudden I heard my name called and I said, "Well, now, I don't know who would be calling my name," and there was a fellow coming down the passageway and he had my suitcase in his hand and believe it or not, my suitcase was not even wet. So I had my clothes to put on then and I was the only one that had a change of clothes.

Traylor Tiller, a country boy from then-rural Evans, Georgia, sailed to North Africa via Iceland aboard the *U.S.S. New York*, an old World War I era battleship.

We carried ten 14-inch guns. You could crawl down through the barrel of them, some people could. And they had to fire all ten of them at the same time [as a test] and that's called a broadside. And they told us to go to the next deck below it because the turrets are on the top deck. The next deck down below it was where the 5-inch guns were. And they told us go down there and we could look out the gun port and we could see the shells going through the air. And when they fired, the concussion could knock you way back and it knocked the lockers down. It chipped paint off of bulkheads.

We went to Iceland at the first of the war to dig slit trenches up there for either the soldiers or Marines. They were kind of afraid that Germans might invade it 'cause they're fairly close. Iceland was a real important base. And we went back to Iceland again and went to Scotland a couple of times, taking convoys is what we were doing.

One day, Tiller was with a group of sailors who had to wade out into the icy water to free a motor launch.

> And we got back to the ship we got our feet, you know, wet up maybe our knees or something like that and in that icy water. And they took the ones that had done that and took them to sickbay in a line, and they gave us a bottle of whiskey. And some of the others found out what that line was for and they were trying to get in that same line, you know. They hadn't been in the water. But they could tell because our clothes was wet that we had been in there.

Then it was on to North Africa, where the Vichy French, allied to Nazi Germany, occupied much of the territory.

> When we went to North Africa, on invasion we had three battleships. We had the *New York* was the oldest, the *Texas* was next. It was *New York* was BB34, *Texas* was BB35, and then we had battleship *Massachusetts*, and I don't know what number it was. And we took our position. We were invading there fairly easy. The big guns were firing because we was out of range for the 5-inch guns to fire. And the big guns could hit a target in 18 miles, you know, if we could get our spotter plane up and all that to tell us whether our shells were fired too hot, over or under. After we had taken the beach and they went on to take pictures of where our shells had landed, it was a French pillbox and one of our shells had come in and just plowed a path right up to that pillbox. It stopped about maybe 10 foot before it got to the pillbox. And it wasn't an explosive shell. It was penetrating shell, solid. A solid shot, what we call it. And it just plowed a furrow right up to them, but I don't know what about them Frenchmen in there.

> We was sent from Safi, North Africa, and went on up to Casablanca. And the *Massachusetts*, the battleship, had fired all the shells it could afford to fire. So it went back and they sent us in to close the range on the French battleship named *Jean Bart* and we were to close the range on it and the *Augusta* was firing at it, a heavy cruiser built back in the early '30s. Roosevelt used it a lot to travel and all. And it was firing at the *Jean Bart* and *Jean Bart* had four guns to the turret, 15-inch guns. And the *Jean*

Bart would fire a salvo at the *Augusta* and two shells caught it astraddle. Two shells landed on the starboard side and two on the port side. And the *Augusta* [named for Augusta, Georgia] was carrying the admiral and the admiral pulled that ship out fast to get away from them. And then they sent the *New York* in and we were getting our range, but instead of going straight in like that, you go in a circle. And each circle you make you get closer and closer. And before we could start, the Army captured that *Jean Bart* at the dock. The first time that ever happened, you know.

For a foot soldier, even one from South Carolina such as Joseph Rucker of the 9th Infantry Division, North Africa was brutally hot.

It was 130 in the shade. Only shade we had was a stack of rocks and throw our jacket over us, had a little shade over it. But they'd bring water out to us to keep us from passing out. And at night, you'd have to have a blanket, it was cold as you know what at night.

We were up on a mountain, up on a green hill and places like that. See, when we got to North Africa them trucks come and picked us up at the foot of the mountain and we had to work ourselves up so far 'til daylight to where we were up there and dig a foxhole. It was hard if you hit rocks, it was a rocky place. They'd give us TNT to start the hole, said, "Don't put one – half of one."

The local Arab population took what advantage they could of the well-equipped foreign troops in their midst.

They'd steal everything they could get their hands on. We were on a train going to somewhere, and you'd take your shoes off to sleep at night, them son of a guns would steal your shoes.

Hank DeLorme landed in Safi, Morocco, November 8, 1942, on a most unconventional landing craft, a stripped-down World War I destroyer.

Well, they thought they had set up stuff ahead of time, fellas supposed to come from a submarine and go on little rubber boats and make it so we could actually find the right place to land. But, as in any battle, confusion and mistakes happen and they couldn't get that, they couldn't find where we could slip right in. So, the captain of the destroyer says, "Well, I've got to get you onshore," so he ran the destroyer right up on the beach and there we're stuck, a good target for anybody who wanted to shoot and our ship was shooting, so we all had to get off there real fast. So they lowered the cargo nets and we, with all the equipment we had going down the ramp, and if you fell down on the rocks there, you were gone, especially with the equipment and everything you carried. So we did land, and the French did put up some resistance, they had old World War tanks they were using and, luckily, they were nothing like the Germans, which we saw later.

Fortunately, the landing was made during the night, so the troops were able to get off the beach. DeLorme said, "If it was daylight, I think we would have probably all been killed at the time." Resistance lasted only until November 11.

Winter rains slowed the fighting. In February 1943, DeLorme's 9th Division crossed Kasserine Pass, where badly led green American troops had just been defeated in their first encounter with the Germans.

Well, we knew that the 1st Armored Division was in Kasserine and the Germans slaughtered them. It was terrible. And we went through the whole battlefield with our trucks, and when we saw it was terrible, abandoned equipment and wrecked guns and all – you could see somebody took a beating and it was us, and it meant one of our generals lost his position as a result. Because – from what I heard about it later — we didn't take precautions. We camped in the wrong areas. The Germans were already waiting in certain places for us to come and we had no reconnaissance, nobody going out ahead to find out what's beyond that hill, and the Germans must have been laughing their heads off. And finally, when we started out – even when the battle where I got wounded, there was the big valley and we heard "Go through there" and nobody checked out to see what was waiting for us.

DeLorme's unit was part of Patton's push on El Guettar, a battle which would result in the first American success against Axis forces. It was Sunday, March 28.

My unit had the habit of starting all sorts of maneuvers on Sunday, I don't know why. We couldn't go to church or have any church services, Sunday morning they liked to attack. And we were doing the same thing that fateful morning on March 28, when I got hit. Sunday morning, we're going there, it's peaceful. And everything looks fine, not an enemy in sight. They're far away but within artillery range, and then all of the sudden it starts and the artillery comes into there and you look around and you wonder who's going to get hit next, because I was the squad leader at the time and all of the sudden I realized that I've been hit. But it didn't knock me out or anything, but I was on the ground and I said, "I can't go any further this way," and I had my own sulfa drugs either to drink with the canteen water or to put on the wounds.

I'm thinking to myself, "What do I do next? Where am I going to go?" Because you're all scattered out in this field, nobody right next to you or anything, and each squad or each platoon would have a medical aid man and when somebody got hit you'd yell, "Help, help!" and he'd come, but nobody came this morning when I was there, so I just did what I had to do, and the units keep moving on and you stay behind. So you can't go further.

You do what you can. But there was a lot of blood there and I had a field jacket on it and that was all bloody too, so I still didn't want to leave it there because it was cold, it was still cold because this was in March, early morning. And I kept looking around, "Where can I go that I'll be sort of safe for a while?" So what they have over there, when it does rain, it rains crazy and it makes what they call a wadi, and that's like a big ditch and that can extend for hundreds of yards or feet, and so I worked my way there.

Because the units keep moving, they don't just stop the war because you got shot for anybody, so they just keep on going. And they find out later that this battle in El Guettar was one of the worst battles, one of the leading generals said, "As far as the amount of men that got hit and killed," said, "it was a very bad battle," and the Germans were very strong right at that point and I think it went on a few days before it ended.

Well, right then, you try to stay alive because you can't show yourself above that top of the ditch and the only hope you have is nightfall to come. So, there was no food or water, the only water you had you carried on your equipment, so they just waited there and naturally you get tired and hungry and the effects of being shot hit you, too. So, finally, when it did get dark, one of the fellas that could move around, he went scouting around and in the distance he saw some lights, so he managed to find out that it was an American aid station, so he said, "Ah, we're going to be saved, get some help." So, he says, "I'm going out there," so then the fellas that are with me decided to do the same thing, but by that time I couldn't move anymore, I was so beat, so I said, "Tell the officers up there that I'm down there and if you can get me up there somehow." So, eventually, they sent a stretcher, a couple of guys down and they took me up there and they look at you and figure out what they can do quick and that's it for the night. Then, by the next morning, it was safe, there was no enemy at that particular point, so they send you to another place, further back, and eventually you wind up going back further, further, further and by the time I hit the last hospital I was in Algeria, over there – that was the last hospital I was in and they did an operation when I was there.

Well, when you're wounded in those days, they have two classifications, one was EK and that stood for "English Kindling," and the other one, which every soldier wanted, was ZI, Zone of Interior, that meant you were wounded enough that you had to go back to the U.S., but the only way you could go back was by ship and there were no ships around. I was in that hospital and I looked out at the harbor, there was not a ship, and the doctors at the hospital said, "Well, you may not go anywhere right now, because we've got officers going around and they check everybody who's been wounded, and if they can keep them in this field of war, they're not going to send them back to the States," so I said, "Yep, that's my luck, I'll probably be stuck here." So day by day we waited and this was March 28 when I got wounded and it was April and it took 'til almost the middle of May before I finally wound up back to the U.S. But that was a tough thing because you waited and each day if any visiting officers came, you could have your classification change and you'd be going back to England temporarily.

We were in the hospital in Oran and, as I said, there were no ships, and then one morning word came to the hospital, "There's a ship, a ship has arrived," and we knew that meant possibly getting home. So, everybody was sent down to the dock in minutes, and we stayed there, loaded up, 'til nightfall, and then they said, "We're not going to move this ship out of here until night because it's too dangerous." So, finally, night came and we slipped out of the harbor and sailed across to Gibraltar, out in the Atlantic, and we made the whole trip back to New York with no escort, and the ship was full of wounded men, some of them in body casts and I said, "If we ever get hit, they're dead." So then we got home and they were waiting for us there and went to a hospital in Pennsylvania, a new hospital.

After he had recuperated, DeLorme was assigned to the 106th Infantry training in Tennessee. Before the unit was sent overseas, he was examined by a doctor who had been in Africa himself. He arranged to admit DeLorme to the hospital so he would not be deployed.

I had to appear before a military board and they were trying to see if they could squeeze out some more of the fellas in the hospital back to duty. So here I appear and a bunch of fresh doctors and they look at you and they says, "Tell me what happened," and I told them and he had my record right there, but you had to tell them and then he finally looks at you and he says, "Soldier, why do you want to get out of the Army when we haven't won the war yet?" That was a tough one. I thought, "What can I tell him?" And my brains were spinning around and I'm thinking, "Gee, he has the power to make me stay." So then I said, "Sir, if the Army can fix me up to where I was before I got shot, I'm willing to stay." And he glances back at the papers and you could see that wasn't the answer he wanted, so he says – at that time, if you were going to get out of the service, you had to see the Red Cross, even though the Army's doing the paperwork — so he said, "Go and see the Red Cross," and dismissed me and that was it. So then I did finally get out, September.

Like DeLorme, Lewis (Pop) Newman, who would become mayor of Augusta in 1973, saw most of his combat early in the war in North Africa. He flew missions out of Oran in the B-17 he piloted.

76

We fly in formation and that's one of the things that you have to learn is not to run into the people on each side of you. But we would have anywhere from 12 to 36 B-17s on the mission that we were on. The lead plane basically would find the target and give the word and all you do is open those bomb doors and let them go when the time comes, and then head for home as fast as you could.

Well, there are 36 in a group at that time. Twelve in a squadron. We had three squadrons. A B-17 had a 10-man crew. You had a pilot, copilot, bombardier, navigator, and the rest – I guess the rest were gunners. We had one crew chief. We didn't call him a gunner, but he'd get on a gun if you wanted him to. But a B-17 had a lot of firepower. We had .50 caliber, about 10 of them I think, from the front to the tail gunner, to the side gunners. And the German pilots were very aware of B-17s and they were very careful with them. And they knew they were dangerous, so they'd rather attack B-24s to tell you the truth and other planes than a 17. But they would, of course, attack them. But what you do is you try to keep in as close a formation as you can so you have the most guns you can aimed so he'll stay away. And that's what they would do. They'd get way out and they'd try to whip through your nose. And they weren't very accurate when they did that. But my plane got hit a couple times, but just very minor. We lost about three planes in the whole time I was there out of my group and I think most of them were captured as prisoners, so I don't think we had too many that got killed. They bailed out.

And, you know, when you're bombing from 20,000 to 25,000 feet, you're not really accurate, although we had the good bombsight. But you just try to keep it steady while we're dropping the bombs or even keep it steady when you're being attacked because the closer you had your formation and the more planes you had, the farther away those fighters would stay because if they knew it was dangerous to come in with, you know, 30 or 40 guns aiming at them and stuff instead of just one plane.

It gets cold up there, and we didn't have much heat either. Of course, North Africa is not a cold country, but at 20,000 to 25,000 feet it gets cold. And you have to open those doors for the gunners, you know, when you're on a mission, and so you can't keep it closed up. But we had heavy garments. We had full-lined leather jackets and pants and hats for the high altitude stuff.

After completing 50 missions, Newman was sent to Louisiana, where he spent the rest of the war training pilots. On the ship to the States, he remembered everyone was happy—and no one more so than the Italian POWs.

> I guess we had about 700 or 800 Americans coming home who had done their missions or whatever. We had some that'd been wounded, this, that, and the other, but we had about 1200-1400 Italian prisoners on the ship and you're talking about a happy bunch to be coming to the United States. They were tickled to death to be getting out of that war and coming home.

President Roosevelt, British Prime Minister Winston Churchill, and the Free French Army's General Charles De Gaulle met at the Casablanca Conference in January 1943 to plan the next stage of the war. John Clements was to see plenty of action later as a Sergeant First Class in armored reconnaissance in Sicily, France, and Germany, but he always treasured his role at the conference:

> We were picked as the Honor Guard for President Roosevelt and 'til this time I feel like that was one of my highlights in the war, was I stood there saluting President Roosevelt when they were there and unconditional surrender was decided at that meeting. But Roosevelt came by and we were picked as the Honor Guard and he ate lunch with us and ate out of one of our regular old mess kits and one of the men in the company got the mess kit he ate out of. But he was there and we felt honored that they picked our unit – our company, it was C Company of the 82nd Recon that he picked.

Sicily and Italy

The Allies achieved victory in North Africa in May 1943. Now they turned their attention across the Mediterranean Sea to Sicily and, beyond it, the Italian boot.

Joseph Rucker's 9th Infantry Division landed at Palermo in Sicily in July. German artillery had the Americans pinned down. The Americans knew the Germans must have had forward observers in a church steeple.

We know that somebody was sending in information about artillery and it kept on, just kept on, nobody didn't get hurt – we were behind that wall. And we wait 'til it got dark, I think it was a couple of us, sneaked up to that church and there was three of them and I had to kill them boys up there. There wasn't no more artillery, we didn't have more trouble.

George Busbee got to Africa at the end of the campaign, then participated in the invasion of Sicily. In Gela, Sicily, his artillery unit joined the 1st Division of Patton's 7th Army. They would set up the guns, fire, then move as the troops ahead moved. During the campaign, Busbee had his first encounter with Patton and experienced Patton's rivalry with British Field Marshal Montgomery. Busbee was driving a 2.5 ton GMC truck. With him in the truck that day was war correspondent Ernie Pyle.

He was a real concerned person. I thought the world of him. And he would talk to us just like one of the guys. He was just the nicest person as he could be.

We stopped and word come back to us that we couldn't go through because the British was stopped in the road having tea. And Patton come by and wanted to know what was wrong. And he took off up front and they said he went up and found Montgomery up there and told him if he didn't move them off the road he was gonna push 'em off. Patton wouldn't let us support Montgomery in Sicily. And he told us to start with, that Montgomery was supposed to be in Messina when we got there; that he was gonna be there a day ahead.

The Americans did beat Montgomery's troops to Messina, the last stage of the Sicily campaign, "and they said that [Patton] was out in the street waiting to welcome Montgomery into the city."

When we got there, he requested that we set up one gun ready to fire across the Straits of Messina into Italy. He wanted to fire the first shell from Sicily into Italy. The Straits is two miles across there. That was no problem. And we got set up and they let him know that we was ready. He came up and there was no photographer or no news personnel and he wouldn't do it. He got in his jeep and said "Get 'em up here and then I'll come back." They finally got him back and he wrote something on the projectile that they fired over. I don't know what he wrote on it, but he wrote something on it. I was there watching him and they loaded it and fired it across the Straits into Italy.

The men in Busbee's unit did not care for Patton. "I wouldn't say he wasn't a good general. But he was not liked by the troops." Two slapping incidents made Patton highly controversial and probably damaged his career.

> We had a part of an antiaircraft outfit attached to our outfit to protect our guns and all from the German aircraft. And this was the one that the young man was in that had to go to the hospital. He kind of lost it and they put him in the hospital. And this is the man that Patton slapped that time.

Busbee next participated in the invasion of Salerno on the Italian mainland in September 1943.

> It was rough when we first went in on the beach. I think they let our big guns go in too quick because we couldn't get far enough up in there to get 'em camouflaged and off of the beach, but we finally got it. It wasn't more than a day or two. We had naval ships was out on the beach and they were firing, giving the troops support with their guns. And I told them, I said, "Well, if I could walk on the water, I'd walk back out there to the ship."

After Salerno it was on to Naples, Rome, and the long, bitterly fought slog in northern Italy. Wounded later at Monte Cassino, Busbee returned to the fight. One day some green replacement troops asked him and other combat veterans a question.

> They were asking some of us about being up in the front lines and wanted to know how long it would take to get where you weren't scared. And I told him, I said I hadn't been long enough, 'cause I was scared every time I got there. We got under heavy fire, I was scared.

Also at Salerno was Billy Coleman, a naval officer commanding several Higgins landing craft. After the war he would practice law beyond age 90, the oldest lawyer in South Carolina. While aboard a transport ship to the Italian coast, Coleman played cards with some Army boys. One of them was seasick.

80

I can't remember his name, but he'd get seasick and he'd laugh or we'd laugh at him, make fun of him, and he'd have to run to the side, throw up. Come back and play. And he did that just about every day. He kept saying he would be so glad when he got off of that ship. He didn't like getting seasick or he wanted to get on solid ground. He kept saying that. And finally, we pulled out one afternoon and during the night, we didn't know where we were going, but when they dropped the anchor the next morning about 5 o'clock, it was black dark, and it happened to be at Salerno. And, of course, the first thing that was done, I sent my three boats over the side and dropped the cargo net. And then they sent a vehicle, a weapons carrier, into each boat, and then an 18-man crew came down the nets and got in each weapons carrier. And then my boat crew came down, five Navy boys, to take charge of each boat. I came down and then the Army officer, and that was what we carried to the beach on the first trip.

The night landing seemed to take the Germans by surprise, and the first wave made it to the beach unopposed.

Apparently they didn't know we were there. I didn't hear a thing and see a soul. We got back and this old buddy of mine that played bridge with me, he was on the next trip. Same outfit, three boat crews, 18 men to each crew, three weapons carriers. Oh, he asked me a thousand questions, and what did I see, what did I hear, and I kept telling him nothing. So he kept saying he'd be so glad he'd be on solid ground. Well, we made it in on the second go round, and of course by the time we did that, it was about the crack of dawn.

There were 300 or 400 other boats and every one of them doing the same thing that our flotilla was doing. And the beach was crowded with not only personnel, but vehicles and trucks and vital supplies and everything. And so, my card-playing buddy, he was tickled to death to be on solid ground. And he came around and he was thanking me and telling me goodbye. We were wishing each other good luck in the future, shaking hands, and looked up and there's four German planes coming down the beach strafing.

They were right on the beach, right on top of all of us, and one right behind the other. You see the fire coming out of the wings of each ship, and they were up not too far ahead. So we, of course, both fell to the ground and they went woom, woom, woom, woom, like that. I know everybody felt just like I did, scared to death. And I realized that I had men hit. I was okay. But my buddy, he was killed.

In September 1943, Italy surrendered to the Allies. However, this surrender merely shifted full military defense of Italy to the Germans, who had no intention of giving up the Italian peninsula without a fierce fight. Bennie Thompson of the 34th Infantry Division learned that the Italians themselves couldn't be trusted:

> Italy made out like they were for us. But until the Germans left out, they made like they were for them, too, because we were warned about that before we got into the town, to be careful of being too outspoken with them, tell them about our planes coming when they were shot down. Those Italians would get out there with those guns and shoot our boys that were coming down on parachutes. That's just part of it, but the Italians were for whoever was in charge. After we took Italy and we did go back to Rome, all those places back then, they treated us just like we was home folks. I guess they didn't know who were their friends because the Germans had went in there claiming they were. But I think Mussolini and Hitler were big buddies anyhow. I don't know, that's just what we thought.

The Salerno invasion in September had gone relatively well. But the landing at Anzio in January 1944 was a near disaster. The Americans were trapped for weeks by strong German defenses. Thompson almost didn't make it to the beach.

> We finally got to where they said we were going to land at, and that's when we went to Anzio. And some of the landing party was kind of like on Sicily, they dropped the gate too quick and you jump off in the water, you're over your head in the water.

Loaded down with steel helmet, rifle, and pack, Thompson dropped like a rock into the deep water. But despite the load pulling him down, he managed to swim into shallow water. "But you know," he said, "when you're scared you can do a lot of things."

Bill Church of the 3rd Division also almost drowned at Anzio:

There were two sandbars and they said the ship might drag on the first one, but it's supposed to go and hit the second one and let us off in water around our knees. Well, he stopped the ship on the first sandbar and me and Fred Chandler was the two first ones off of that ship and we never did hit the bottom of that water. And he couldn't swim and I was trying to help him and we lost our rifles and our helmets and I helped him because waves was coming in from them other ships too, you know, bad and it's carrying us back out in the water. I told him, I said, "I'm giving out, Fred." He says, "Turn me loose." He says, "I'll mash this little belt [life preserver] we have on." But it didn't do a bit of good. I think it flipped him overhead and I never heard nothing more from him, so.

It was just carrying me back out by that ship, the waves were, and I don't know why he done it, but this sailor had a little pontoon back in the back of the ship he just threw it in the water, and jumped in it and grabbed me. Started pulling me out and he asked me if I could hold on. I told him, "Yeah." He says, "Can't you get in?" I told him, "No." I was too give out. And he paddle dragged me out to the edge of the water and he told me, he says, "You take one swallow of water, wash your mouth out good, don't swallow it. Then take you another swallow, just one swallow, and swallow it. Don't drink no more." He got back in that boat and he went back out to the ship ...

After the Anzio landing, Allied forces were pinned down for a month by German defenders in the hills surrounding the beachhead. To help the Allies break out, the 12th Air Force flew bombing missions. B-26 pilot Stan Woodhurst remembered:

The principal mission was to keep down the communications and transportation for the German troops down in Italy, and so our mission there was to bomb out bridges and tunnels and overpasses and underpasses to prevent the train traffic down through there. Our other mission was to help the ground troops get out of the Anzio beachhead, but they were having a hard time getting out and making an advance. So we were flying primarily anti-personnel missions to try to kill off as many German troops as we could with fragmentation bombs.

We flew a mission every day, and I would say it was a dozen or so that we flew over Anzio beachhead. And then after they broke out, they still had a hard time getting up to Italy. And then our mission that was all along was to help them advance, and it was our anti-personnel missions.

After being trapped on the beachhead for weeks, the Americans finally fought their way inland across the rocky, mountainous terrain where the Germans had fortified themselves. Bill Church of the 3rd Division witnessed an act of extraordinary courage by Sergeant Sammy, a half-Indian, in savage fighting by the Volturno River:

We was going across the Volturno River and there was three tanks sitting on the other side, shooting right down that river. And man, they just slaughtered a bunch of American soldiers there on that river, boy, that – awful sight. Well, they had to pull back a whole battalion of companies. And the captain and the major come up to our 3rd platoon. I asked the lieutenant, "You think Sergeant here could take a couple of men and go down the river and cross it and go around and come back up on the other side of that hill and knock them tanks out?" The lieutenant said, "Well, Sergeant, how about it? You think it could be done?" He says, "If it can be done, we can do it." So he told me and another boy, I forget where he's from now, but he said, "You two boys come and go with me."

We went down there and we got across that river, up around our neck, had to hold our rifles up. And we got up around on the other side and come up on that ridge, we come down that – pretty good rocky place, little old shrubby trees, not too big a trees. And them tanks was backed up on that river, one right behind the other, and we got down in there and we was within, shoot, less than 50 yards from them and then a big old rock. Sammy said, "Church, I want you to take aim on that second tank." And whatever his name was, "I want you to get an aim on that third tank. And if anybody sticks their head out that turret," he says, "shoot it off." I said, "Well, what are you going to get the first tank?" He says, "I'm going down there to knock him out."

That sergeant slipped down there and he crawled a little bit and he slipped a little closer and then finally got down there to the tank, on the side of it, and the turret was open on top and he had

84

that big old tank grenade and, you know, if he hit him on the side of the track it'd knock the thing off. Well, he put that thing in that doggone tank and set that [grenade down the] turret. And shut it and he started running back up where we was. He got up there about where we was at and that thing went off and man, it just blowed the whole thing all to pieces. And them guys in there – when it went off it ignited all that ammunition in there and it just jarred the whole place.

About that time guys started out them back two tanks and this boy shot at one of them, that back tank, and one started out the center tank and I shot at him, but I didn't hit him. So next thing, they had two white flags coming out and they gave up – all of them in them two tanks gave up.

The three men's actions cleared the way for the division to cross the river. Weeks later, the sergeant was presented with a Silver Star for valor. As General O'Daniel presented the medal, the sergeant said, "Them two boys, right down there," he says, "they need a medal of some kind. Because if it hadn't been for them, I could've never done it." But Church and his buddy were never recognized.

The countryside was dotted with churches and monasteries that were supposed to be off-limits, but provided tempting cover and lookout possibilities. Bennie Thompson's 34th Infantry Division experienced deadly fire from a monastery.

Every one of our men who tried to go over that wall, there were machine gun nests in there and I don't know how many men we lost there. But I wasn't in on the group that went over, went up the wall. It was a fellow, Henry, who was from down in Thomasville, Georgia, with me, we was dug in together. And I got a little wound, flesh wound, and I was sent back to first aid. And they say that the shell hit directly in the hole with him after I'd been left there ten minutes that blew everything all to pieces.

While fighting in the mountains, Thompson's squad got separated from the rest of the company and, surrounded by Germans, hid overnight in a cave.

So we found this cave, and we went down in this cave. And the next morning, we finally started coming out, but we're coming out shooting. But anyway, when we got out, we didn't see anybody. They [the Germans] wasn't out there then. What they were doing, they had moved around to the side and had us cut off either way we would go. And so we had to go back down in the cave and they started throwing grenades in there. And we thought they were live grenades, but they were smoke grenades. And so we knew we had to get out of there. When we came out, they closed in on us. There were a few shots fired back and forth, but anyway, that's when we were captured.

There was a fellow from New Jersey, an American boy with me that could speak German. And that probably saved our lives because I think one or two of them had got killed in the scramble that we'd had that morning. But when he started talking with him, that boy and they communicated back and forth a little bit. And they told us to lay our rifles down, we laid them down, and that's when they took us back about two miles from there down the mountain to another big cave and put us in that cave. But what was in that cave was the Germans that had been wounded, and they were keeping them in that cave. And they put us in there with those wounded ones, so that wasn't too good a feeling. But anyway, that's what happened.

Eventually Thompson and the other captured Americans were transported to a POW camp near Munich, where they lived in barns.

It was fenced in with, I think, about a ten-foot fence around. They must have had six or eight of these buildings. They had hay in there on the floor and they had a latrine and they had running water. So that's where we stayed at night. And in the daytime, they'd get us up at 4:00 and put us on trains and send us into Munich and we worked in Munich every day until it got dark. And when it got dark, after dark they'd bring us back.

The most famous of all the monasteries, 900-year-old Monte Cassino, stood atop a mountain, from which the Germans repulsed three Allied assaults starting in January 1944. George Busbee was wounded in one of those assaults on March 28.

Well, it was a religious building and they would not let us fire on them. And every time they tried to take this hill they couldn't take it. They had tunnels under the building and they'd come out and even come in behind some of our troops. And they still wouldn't let us fire on it. I got wounded with shell fragment in the leg and also in my back.

They took me in a jeep back to the tent field hospital. And I've often said that they didn't give the nurses over there the credit that they deserved. They waited on us hand and foot and done everything they possibly could to make everybody comfortable. And they had to wade from tent to tent in half knee-deep mud to get to the tent. Then they took me out and they flew me back to the 73rd Station Hospital, which was back in one of the little towns. I don't remember the name of it. And that's where they took the shrapnel and the shell fragments out of my leg and all. And in a couple weeks' time I was ready to go back.

Bill Church fought at Monte Cassino, too, part of the force that finally took it in May after bombs reduced it to rubble.

Yeah, we'd have to climb them rocks and pull ourselves up by little shrubby trees and bushes and stuff like that to get to the top of it up there and it was kind of valleys in the top of it and we run the Germans off of the top, back down on the other side going down towards that Cassino. The Cassino was on top of the mountain – just right across, on top of the mountain from us. Now we could see it real good, but those Germans every morning would come up in the fog and we'd hear them coming, talking. They'd get up there and they'd get within all 50 yards of us and that fog would rise up off of them, oh man, we had a battle going on. Throwing hand grenades – we'd get the best of the Germans though, and they'd go back down – and they'd done that for about three or four more mornings. And finally the top officials tried to get the Germans to move out of that Cassino and they would not and no matter, so they told me to go out and bomb it to get the Germans out. So we pulled off of that mountain – back down and went over there and waited. The Germans, they wouldn't get out, so they started bombing that thing and they tore that beautiful building down to where it was just a, I don't know, just a mess. Very little standing. A few Germans was left in it, we went up the mountain, took them and it was rough getting there, fighting them.

Rain, mud, and disease dogged American forces in Italy. George Sabine knew them well.

Yeah. It was the water, it was the wet. And we didn't have typical Army equipment, you know, they're always a day late and a dollar short on it. All we had was the regular G.I. boots and shoes and, you know, they'd get wet and stay wet instead of having something that was, you know, rubber boots or something to go in – all my toes were black, the ends of them, and everybody was the same way, and a lot of the malaria, I think – you don't know where you got the malaria, whether I got it in North Africa or in Sicily or in lower Italy or what, but I had bad bouts of malaria for a long time. Even when I came home, I go so long, maybe have one or two more beers than I should have and that damn malaria would come back on you.

The war in Italy was fought at very close range, with American and German troops often infiltrating each other's lines. Bill Church described many such close encounters:

Sergeant asked me, "Who wants to stand guard the first two hour?" And I said, "Well, I'll take it." He said, "I better let this new guy stand guard first." "Okay," I says, "I'll take the last then." And we was hungry and we got us some C-Rations and I had eaten one can and fixing to throw it outside, it was getting pretty well dark, and at that time I was carrying an M1 rifle and also one of them tommy guns, we'd call them. So, before I threw that can out, I turned around, I heard the racket behind us. [A German] boy was walking back and forth behind us. I looked up there and I looked back, about three or four all ganged up right real tight. And I thought something was wrong, I reached down and I got one of my hand grenades and I hollered at them [Germans]. I didn't get nothing.

And Sergeant up there, he hollered at them and he didn't get nothing, and both of us hollered at the same time and heard nothing and we both threw these hand grenades and they killed two of them and the other two started down my way and I just opened that tommy gun up and I hit one of them, he hit the ground and he crawled down to that gully. So a little later them Germans come up through that gully and we could hear them coming, there's daylight where you could see them coming through the sagebrush had grown up and dried. And so me and the other guys gather – well, we just shooting, all we could do.

We hit one or two once in a while and they'd holler, though they kept coming. There was only two of us left in that squad. Wood, a boy from Rapids, Virginia, I never will forget him, he got up there, was shooting at one German going from the building down to the gully and one of those bullets hit him in that helmet, went through his steel helmet and ricocheted off his inner liner and out the top, and there were three prongs at the top of that steel helmet. And he says, "I ain't sticking my head up no more."

Church was hit by machine gun fire.

Yeah. I've got the two bullets hit this shoulder here and come out my back, and the other one hit me in the top of the shoulder and broke my collar bone. But there was blood running everywhere, but still – we was still fighting.

Despite his wounds, he took prisoners for interrogation:

After that, we took the two prisoners on down there and it's getting late at night, and the captain wanted us to take them on over across the street on the corner, a little creek runs down through there, the interrogations over there, turn them over to them, come back and he says, "I'll have you a pot of coffee made." Well, we took them over there and one of them, he decided he wanted to get into the reeds and hedges at the branch. Took off across the street and I hollered at him two or three times and he didn't stop and just as he got over there to the other side of the road, I had one of these big old battalion guns on me. I wasn't supposed to have it though.

Now I just pulled that thing out and I shot at him and tore one of his legs about off. And you've never heard such a racket, here come the major and the captain, all of them out down to there and one went, "What in the world happened?" I said, "Well, that German tried to get away and I stopped him." And they had the medical boys go over and get him and his leg was just dangling. So the major says, "What kind of a damn gun did you shoot him with?" I pull that thing out and showed it to him. He said, " I ain't never heard such a racket in my life. I thought it was a cannon going off."

Later in the war, Church was captured. He spent about five weeks as a POW. As a prisoner, his only fear was of SS troops:

> I'd hear a few little stories about those SS troops, and we got a little taste of them. They come through a couple of times and they just wanted somebody to bat an eye at them so they'd kill them. They wanted to kill us all anyway rather than try to get enough food to feed us. Somehow the top – the guys in charge of us I reckon they just stopped them, told them they couldn't do that. The Germans treated us as we would treat theirs. They didn't do no favors for us, nothing like that. But those SS troops, man, they didn't want us – they didn't want them to feed us nothing.

In those weeks of captivity, Church's weight fell from 170 to 110 pounds.

Charles Estes was a replacement with the 34th Division in northern Italy.

> And we started up this hill on the 23rd of October, 1944, and it was a beautiful day, the sun was shining, the morning air was crisp and you felt just fresh all over. Of course, the shells were going overhead, the old saying, they sounded like boxcars and you were not afraid of the ones you heard, it was the ones you didn't hear are the ones that got you. We started up the hill and the Germans began shelling us with 88s, I guess, which I think is probably the best weapon that came out of World War II, not taking anything away from the Americans. But anyway, a lot of trees and some of the shells came close by, burst, my squad fell into a little ditch and I started with my shovel. Anyway, you can imagine us trying to dig a hole in the side of a mountain and get in a foxhole because there's nothing but rock there. And suddenly a shell burst in the tree and the fragments, they're just like an umbrella, they come down, and fortunately I only suffered a superficial wound, shell shrapnel went in both my hands, it didn't go completely through, it just skimmed across and cut all the tendons and layers and whatever in my hands and I couldn't use them, just useless. The guy next to me, whose name was Chum – I never did find out his last name — he was our platoon medic and he suffered a severe injury to the left arm, it was almost blown off and the guy behind me, he had a wound to his right leg. But the shelling stopped and we got up and I got

on one side of the guy with the bad leg and Chum got on the other side and we ambled on down to the first aid station and from there we went to the battalion aid station. And I'll always remember the night that I got there, I couldn't hold anything to drink, couldn't use my hands in any manner whatsoever. A medic came up and says, "I've got a cup of coffee. I know you're not supposed to have any coffee, but I'm going to give it to you anyways," so he held up a cup of coffee while I drank it.

Lou Brissie was fighting in northern Italy with the 88th Infantry Division. On December 2, 1944, he had a good breakfast: scrambled eggs, sausage, hotcakes with butter, and all the syrup he wanted. Then Brissie's unit was trucked up to the front. The convoy came under German artillery fire.

I had gotten out of the truck and was headed for a creek bank to get up against something to try to get some protection. But the next [shell] hit right at my feet. It was a 170-millimeter shell. Those things happen—you're not really conscious that they happen, but you're there and then it's over with. And I raised up on my elbows and I could see blood running off my face, and then I realized that I couldn't move my legs too well. And so I started crawling for the creek bed and I crawled into the creek, which was partially frozen over, and I got about halfway out the other side. And I got about halfway out and I turned over. I didn't think I was going to make it, and I turned over on my back and looked down at my feet and I could see my right boot sticking up out of the water with a hole in it and blood coming out of that. But I could not see my left foot, and I thought my leg had been blown off. Well, the bone in the lower leg had been shattered into over 30 pieces, five and a half inches of the shin bone, and the leg had flopped over. And that's about all I remember.

The medics picked me up eventually and put me on the hood of a jeep, to try to get me back to an aid station. And on the way back, they started throwing airbursts in, and either one of those shells hit near that jeep or the driver swerved to miss a shell, a hole or something, and it flipped the stretcher off of the jeep and I went into the bank and hit a bank on the back of my head. It took them a while to get me loaded up again, I guess, so it took me about five hours or six hours to get to an aid station eventually.

Now, I don't know how long the shelling went on after I passed out. But we lost eight men that day. We ended up with one officer left in the company.

When Brissie came to in the hospital, he begged the doctor not to amputate his leg. "I'm going to play ball," he explained, "and I need my leg."

> When I woke up the next afternoon, I remember looking down, and when I saw both those toes sticking up at the bottom of that bed, I don't think I ever worried about it again.

Over the next two years, Brissie had 23 operations on his leg. Finally, with a metal brace still on his leg, he was signed by Connie Mack's Philadelphia A's in 1946. He pitched in the majors until 1953. While with the Cleveland Indians, he was selected for the All-Star Game, and was on the pitching staff with Bob Feller.

Medical care, rough as it was in the field, saved the lives of Brissie and thousands of others. Roosevelt Brooks was a raw replacement, a medic in the 92nd Division of "Buffalo Soldiers," an all-black unit. He arrived in Italy in September 1944. For him, warfare wasn't about bravery: it was just doing your job.

> Well, when you say bravery—all you're doing is what you're supposed to do. If anybody wasn't scared, they're either lying or they're a fool. If you see somebody get hit, you do what you can for them. You do what you're supposed to do. So I can't say I was brave or anybody was brave out there, you were there, you had to be there. Like one time, one of these white soldiers from the 473rd, he got hit in the leg and I got to him, he was—the blood was just squirting out. I said to myself, "This guy won't live another five minutes." So I put a tourniquet on him, stopped the bleeding and got a couple more guys with the stretcher and we took him to the aid station. On the way there, with the tourniquet on, sometimes he'd be hurting so bad he'd scream, I had to loosen it up a bit. But I had to put it back on as soon as I can because he would have bled to death. I don't know whether he lived or died, but we got him to the aid station.

Trained as an infantryman, Kasper Fulghum found himself assigned as a combat engineer when he arrived in Florence, Italy. He learned engineering on the job and under fire.

> That's how we learned it, I mean, clearing minefields, putting up Bailey bridges [prefabricated bridges designed by the British, assembled in sections] … with other engineering units and just observed and worked with them and that's where we got our training. We gained a lot of experience and gained it fast, we had to. We broke all kinds of records putting bridges up to try to get the heavy armor up to the front.
>
> The armor would be backed up behind us waiting to get across maybe a river, maybe a big blowout. The Germans were great at going up a highway and a railroad tunnel would run under a highway, and they'd blow it and leave a great big hole there, and we'd have to put bridges across those sometime. A lot of times we'd just take a bulldozer and doze dirt in there until and go out that way, but sometimes we'd have to put a bridge across. Quite often under fire.
>
> The German air force was out of it by this time. But we had a lot of German artillery and we had our artillery here lobbing shells on the German artillery over there and we'd be in between them, in the shells back and forth. We had a lot of that, a lot of mortar fire. Also, Germans always had the high ground, when they were retreating they always took the high ground and we had to come up the valley and they would sit up there with mortars and drop mortars – just put them in your hip pocket almost if they wanted to. They were amazing, I mean, the Germans were amazing soldiers.

The German army in Italy was led by Field Marshal Albert Kesselring, a brilliant tactician. Fulghum said he was respected by the Allies and loved by his troops.

> He was a master at retreat. And he would drop back and form a line, all on high ground, things would get too hot for him, he'd drop back another 20 miles, form another line, and he did that all the way up Italy, created a lot of trouble.

With the D-Day invasion, both German and American forces in Italy were depleted. Fulghum noticed a difference in the makeup of the enemy.

> Towards the end of the war we saw a lot of old men and young men in the German army, they started drawing them out to take them into Europe and all that, after the invasion. [The American Army brass] took most of our stuff out of Italy too, several divisions out of Italy and a lot of the equipment and everything else and sent it to England for the cross-Channel invasion, which left us almost naked down there. But then by that time we still had three or four German divisions tied up down there that they couldn't pull out and send to fight the invasion folks. We kept them occupied down there.

One of those German divisions was made up of the elite SS forces. When it came time for them to surrender, they demanded special arrangements.

> There was a lieutenant general in command of this SS division and he would not surrender to anything less than a lieutenant general. So we had to get on the radio, get back to Allied Military Headquarters and tell them we needed a lieutenant general for this general to surrender his division to. So they told us where to tell him to go – I mean, nicely, told him – actually directed to where he was to take the division. He had to go back about another 20 miles, back behind where we were to surrender his troops to this lieutenant general. [The American general] wouldn't come up there for them to surrender, they had to go to him, so they did. He took his division back there and surrendered them. It was a complete total SS division, which would have created a lot of damage had they gotten over to the invasion in France.

The brutal war in Italy would drag on for months. But the main battlefront had long since shifted to France where, on June 6, 1944, the Allies landed in Normandy.

Chapter 4
War in Europe, II: Normandy to Germany

Overview

Since late 1943 American and Allied troops had been battling their way up the Italian peninsula. The Anzio landings in January 1944 had failed to speed up the advance. But slowly and inexorably the Nazis were pushed northwards, until in June, the Allies entered Rome.

But by then the American effort had shifted elsewhere. On June 6, 1944, American and Allied troops landed on the beaches of Normandy. Supported by airborne paratroopers, our ground forces were able to gain a foothold. This landing by 156,000 American, British, and Canadian troops was the largest amphibious invasion in history. But it would take a month of heavy fighting in Normandy before the Allies broke out. Allied troops then surged across France. By the end of the summer of 1944 it looked like the war was about to end. The Allied advance benefitted significantly from the simultaneous Soviet offensives from the east. The Soviets, who would face three quarters of the Nazi army throughout the war, had thrown more than 2 million soldiers into a costly but successful strike that all but destroyed Germany's eastern defenses.

The quick end was not to be. In September of 1944 the Allies attempted an airborne and ground assault through Holland to get around the main German defensive lines, but this ended in failure. Then Hitler decided to throw what he had left in a massive assault which we know now as the Battle of the Bulge. Surprise was complete; one American division lost two-thirds of its men in the first day of the battle. Eventually the offensive ground to a halt, slowed by strong American defensive stands at St.-Vith and Bastogne, and a rapid counteroffensive by American forces from the south.

Nazi Germany now no longer had the capacity to wage war effectively. There was plenty of hard fighting left on the drive into Germany, but by the spring German troop morale began to crumble and mass surrenders occurred. Germany's strongest fight was for its capital city, Berlin, where the opposing Soviet and Nazi forces together lost about 175,000 men killed. Germany finally surrendered on May 7, 1945, to the British and the Americans, and a day later to the Soviets. Hitler was not around to see it, having committed suicide the week before in his bunker in Berlin.

More than 162,000 Americans died in combat in the European theater. Without their ultimate sacrifice – which led to the eventual

German defeat – Europe today would be a different, and much worse, place.

Normandy: D-Day and beyond

The D-Day invasion of June 6, 1944 involved the massing of some 5,000 ships and 150,000 troops on the south coast of England, just across the English Channel from Normandy, for the largest amphibious invasion in history. The Germans had long expected an invasion on the coast, but they could not agree on where it would happen, nor on the operational method to repel it. Field Marshal Rommel had prepared troops and fortifications along the coast from Norway to Spain. To keep the Germans guessing, the Allies kept their moves a secret, massing real and dummy armies in various places along the English North Sea coast. Rommel and Hitler believed Calais, only 21 miles from England, would be the probable point of invasion.

The landings in Normandy were only part of a massive Allied operation that included over a million troops to attack from Britain while the Red Army massed two million troops to attack from the east. The Allies benefitted from the complicated German defenses; armored German forces, for example, were controlled from Berlin, not by local German commanders. Even so, the fighting was fierce; some 9,000 of those who landed were killed.

In the hours before the invasion by sea, the Allies dropped paratroopers behind the German lines. Gerald Paulk, a paratrooper with the 101st Airborne, jumped from 300 feet above Sainte Croix du Mont at 1:30 a.m.

> So you got to open your chute and then you got to land. And I had a 30 pound radio strapped on my leg and I landed in what I thought was the English Channel, but it must have been an irrigation ditch that was just a little bit over my head and I had all this equipment on and I could kick myself up and get some air and come back down. I got rid of the radio, I got rid of a lot of other stuff, and then I made a left turn, about two steps when I hit the bank, so when I got out of it I was in kind of a swampy area and it was pitch black dark.
>
> We had two things, we had a compass and then we had a cricket for identification. See, the compass had gotten full of water – everything had gotten full of water and our jumpsuits were gas-impregnated and that made them waterproof, so without

realizing my pants filled up with water I kept walking, I kept getting tired, I said, "I don't know why I'm so tired, I'm in pretty good shape." And then when I finally sat down – water sloshed.

Those clickers were like you used to get in your popcorn; if you challenge the man with one click, he's supposed to give you two clicks. When I finally came up on a hedgerow and I got a click, I reached up in to get my cricket and it was – it had disappeared in that canal, didn't have it. So I heard some fella say, "He didn't click back, shoot him," and I used a few choice words on him and he said, "Well, he must be a GI if he'd talk like that." So they said come on through the hedgerow and we went through the hedgerow and there was about 30 troopers over there, I suppose, several different companies …

There was one officer, Lt. Col. Ewell. I walked to the colonel – of course I was a buck sergeant – and I said, "Colonel, I'm reporting." He said, "Well, you know, we got some Germans in front of us and we got some over here and we got some over there. You said you saw a couple coming that way, but we're not surrounded." And I said, "Colonel, if you don't mind telling me where you come from," and he said, "Jacksonville, Florida," and I said, "Well, where I come from, they said when you got people on all four sides you're surrounded." He said, "I don't believe that."

In the confused scene on the ground, paratroopers from different companies joined up in makeshift units.

But it works to our advantage because every time the Germans turned around or ran into paratroopers, they thought we had about five times more than we had there, they were as confused as we were. Probably helped us out a lot.

Among the Canadian paratroops who jumped behind the German lines was 17-year-old Dennis Trudeau, who, years later, would become mayor of Grovetown, Georgia. For him it was to be a very bad night:

Well, prior to our jump into Normandy, of course, we received so much training and briefing. We knew what the battalion's objective was, what the company's objective was, what the platoon, what the squad, what the individual person was. We had maps, we had little sand outlays where they showed us the streets, the buildings, everything. So we knew just about everything in that landing zone what we were going to do. And then we knew the invasion was at hand and that finally one day they said, on the 4th of June, they said we're ready to go, but a storm came up that particular day and they delayed it 'til the next day.

So the next day they said was a go, so we packed all our gear, repacked it, packed it again, we repacked it, got our ammunition, got our grenades and our weapons and everything, live ammunition, loaded that up and then I had additional equipment because I was a radio operator and I carried a little radio with a couple of batteries, weighed about 15, 20 pounds, along with my other gear, and it was all packed in a little like a sack, a gondola we called it, and strapped to my leg when you jumped. And we loaded on the planes, we got down to the airport about 9:00 that night I guess it was and got our parachutes on and just laid on the tarmac there waiting for the pilots to come and for us to get on the plane.

Finally about 10:30 they loaded us up and we managed to get on that plane, they were C47s, and waited, and then finally about 11:00, 10:30 they took off and then I guess they flew around getting themselves in formations. And we started off for the shores of France.

And I was a number-two man that time and I could look out the door and I could see nothing, nothing but planes. I mean we looked like our wingtips were touching each other we were so close to another. And you'd look down on the ocean in the Channel there, you could see the contrails of the ships down there. And you'd look like you could walk across and so many ships down there. And we were all joking and laughing, but once we got in the planes and started taking off and knew this was it, a lot of us did a lot of praying, did a lot of praying. And I would wonder if I was going to see the next day or not, next sunset or not. Didn't know, you know.

Finally when we seen the shores of France appear, that the way it was when you put your foot out on the ledge of the plane's door, you'd count 1,000, 2,000 and 3,000. If the light did come on to tell you to jump, you jumped. Well, as we were going across, the red light came on, which meant we all stood up, hooked up our parachutes to the static line, got into the door and the first man was a lieutenant. He was our squad leader, our platoon leader and he was to go first.

Suddenly the sky lit up with anti-aircraft fire, the plane lurched, and everything started to go wrong.

Well, what happened, as they crossed the French shores, everything exploded. It looked like the 4th of July left over. And our planes were rolling over to side, and the young lieutenant fell off in the back and hit the wall on the other side and by that time the green light came on and we were so trained so much, when that green light came on, I shot out the door. And my Griswold container that I had on, my equipment and my radios, my rifle and a few clothes, food, I was supposed to let it down on a rope, well, it just took off and I lost it. I don't know if it got shot out or not, but I never did find it. And we were only jumping from 300 feet, so you didn't have much time. And of course, we only had one chute. You never had reserves. And my chute opened, I looked around, I could see fire going all over, see planes falling on fire and I said to myself, "My God, this is for real." I could feel in my heart, I knew it was going to come out of my chest because it was pounding like all get-out.

And finally I hit the ground and got into water about up to my waist. And I looked around, nobody was there. I was "where's the rest of the stake?" Nobody was there. And I'd lost everything. I lost my weapons, I lost my radio and here I was in France with nothing but a little old parachute knife and a bandolier around my belly with nine millimeter ammunition in it. And I said, "what am I to do?" And they told us at the briefing that the planes were flying in a certain direction. If you got confused, wait 'til the next wave of planes came over and then if they were coming this way, you knew you have to go to the right. So I waited 'til the next wave was almost right on top of us, and then the next thing you know, there were planes going left and right, north, south, east and west. So I just worked my way to the edge of the field, where it was kind of dry and shook my water out of my boots and everything.

I met another soldier there and he was from an altogether a different regiment and he didn't know where he was and I didn't know where we were. None of it was recognizable of what they showed us in our briefing. And so we kind of looked at each other and said, "What are we going to do?" And so we just started walking down the road and another soldier would show up, another soldier would show up, and finally a captain showed up from the adjoining regiment from our left flank. And he had a map and we got to kind of a road, and a French farmer came up and told us to disregard the way they had the signs on the roads because the Germans had switched them around so that you couldn't go by those signs. But he told us how to get to our DZ [Drop Zone].

So we walked along this road. We got about oh, I guess about four or five miles and we were told in the briefing that the Air Force was going to bomb those areas after everybody had jumped. Well, this was I guess about 3 in the morning. And everybody's supposed to have been landed by then.

And here comes these bombs and British and American bombers and they just pattern-bombed the entire area, and when the bombs started whistling coming down, we all jumped into the ditches and there was quite a few of the members got killed. That's the time when I got shrapnel in both my legs and my back, but it wasn't bad enough to lay me out or anything like that. I could still walk, although it was hurting pretty bad. And we finally – I guess about 5:00, 4:00 - we got into our DZ. Our objective was to secure the DZ, to blow up a radio transmitter and to seize a bridge and plant explosive on it ready to blow up.

There was only four of us there. And one of the boys said, "Well, I can work my way across the bridge and let them know that you're over here and then you can come across." He started across and the people on the other side didn't know who it was, so they started shooting at him and eventually he got hit and fell into the river. Apparently he drowned, I don't know. And so the rest of us, the three of us stayed until it was daylight so they could see us.

Well, when the daylight came along, the Germans were, I guess, having a counterattack on the bridge and that's when we got

100

captured. I was taken then with the other two to a battalion headquarters which, whatever weapons I had or anything else, they took my belt, they took my watch, they took my shoes and put us in a little farmhouse that night. Well, the next morning I could hardly walk because the shrapnel I had in my leg really bothered me and so they put me in a truck and a couple other wounded soldiers in the truck and they moved us to a place called Rennes and there were put in a hospital.

It took us about two days, I guess, to go from where we were at to the hospital in Rennes. We only traveled during the nighttime, didn't travel during the daytime at all. At night they'd park us in amongst the trees and bushes and go in barns or something like that. And we got into Rennes and went into a hospital there and they operated on me, took the shrapnel in my legs and out of my back. And the doctor gave me a piece of the shrapnel. He says, "Here, keep this for a souvenir." He says, "That's an American shrapnel." He said, "That isn't German."

As part of the airborne assault, hundreds of CG4A gliders, each carrying two pilots and up to 12 soldiers and equipment, landed at dawn or in the pre-dawn darkness. The Germans had prepared for such an assault by seeding the French fields with "Rommel's asparagus," 10-foot stakes wired together and holding explosives. Glider pilots could barely see the fields they were landing in, let alone the stakes, and many gliders were shredded in landing. Charles Beason, a medic with the 4th Infantry Division, treated many of the casualties of those crash landings.

Well, let me tell you, we met up with the Airborne and the glider boys. Now, the gliders, the Airbornes, they really put us to work because they had casualties all over the place. The fields that the farmers had, they'd pick up the stones in the field and they'd pile them around the fence rows and then the bushes would grow up in the fence rows and you'd have a wide open field. It's all pretty good-sized fields where they could have landed a glider or something in, but the Germans – they're smart people — they went in there and they put poles, like telephone poles, about 8 or 10 foot up in the air and when they'd come in they'd hit them poles and scatter them all over the place.

The aerial landings were a fiasco – but ironically, they worked. As the paratroopers were dropped all over Normandy by accident, the

German defenses were completely confused about Allied intentions. They could not interpret what "plan" lay behind the drop locations – because there no longer was one.

Charlie Fiveash of the 4th Infantry Division was one of the thousands of soldiers who knew the invasion was coming, but not when or where. When he heard the planes taking off on the night of June 5, he knew it was happening. Soon it would be time to board the boat that would carry him across the Channel:

> We all knew something was going—when, we didn't know, where we were going, or where we were going to land. So that night the planes fly over and the gliders and the C-47s with the paratroopers in it, they would pass over our head and we knew then that we would start leaving in the morning.

The crossing to France was miserable:

> It took us about 24 hours to cross the Channel and I don't even know what kind of boat it was, but we all sat there and we all scrunched up like that so we had to collapse, you couldn't stand up for 24 hours, so when you went down, you had somebody's feet in your lap and your head was just somewhere else and it was just a mess. And they gave everybody three craft bags, about eight pound bags, and these were to be used for any personal needs you had: you could puke in them, you could go to the bathroom in them or whatever and they would pass them from one to the other – they'd leak too, it'd be all over you, you got so darn filthy.

In fact, the time in the boat was so miserable, that Fiveash couldn't wait to hit the beach. "I got up front of the darn boat and I wanted to get off, I was going to be prepared to be the first one off." Temporarily attached to the 4th Infantry Division, Fiveash's boat was headed for Utah Beach on D-Day plus 1.

> And then they opened the boat and this time they backed up and I was dunked in eight foot of water with about 115 pounds on my back, sank like a rock. But I remembered which way the beach was, so I was able to walk about 30 yards and get my nose above water and I was on up there. I was beat then, but I was able to get to the shore, and first thing I did was throw an M-3

away, which was a small .45 caliber shooting gun and it was made out of pressed parts except for the barrel. And I threw that away and picked up a Garand and I carried that for the rest of the war. And at the same time I threw away everything I had, my gas mask, blankets were gone, everything was wet so I filled it up with nothing but ammo and something to eat.

On the beach, all was chaos.

We didn't know what the hell was going on, just go on, just get off the beach. Get off the beach was the word that we had. Don't stay on the beach and the poor guys down at Omaha was just getting beat to death. We ran into some machine gun fire, but we mostly had 88 artillery landed on the beach and it wasn't nearly as bad as it was down at Omaha. I'm glad I went to Utah.

Well, everybody was milling around and messing up, nobody seemed to know what they were doing. This was an individual war and I really think it was the individuals and selfs in the service won the war, because they would get together and decide what to do and go do it. So I'm sure that there was plenty of direction from the Army high command, but at the same time I got to give a lot of credit to the individual initiatives that was being made by individual people. We walked down towards Utah Beach about two miles and we got where we was supposed to go and we found out that this point that the Germans had dammed up a little bit of stream, I don't know what the name of the thing was, but it ran from about St.- Lo down to the beach and that flooded the whole area. So I had to walk about five miles through the swamp and we cut pieces of shrubs to hold up and walk in front of you – we were trying to move slow so nobody would notice it was a moving bush.

Understandably, Eisenhower was pessimistic about the landings; had the Germans been able to build stronger defenses, disaster might have occurred. The losses were actually lower than expected, but it was little succor for the soldiers who experienced the bloodshed.

Richard Warren, of Milledgeville, landed on Omaha Beach with the 29th Division:

A lot of boys drowned in deep water because the big ships couldn't get to the beach. But this little boat – well, it was a ship - this little ship we was on, them Englishmen were very efficient. They put that thing up to the beach and run it up on the beach and on each side they had ladders or steps. They shot them things out to where they hit the dirt.

The water was discolored. It wasn't red. It was deep orange with blood from those soldiers that got killed coming in on the beach. Well, we landed and the shelling was pretty strong, the artillery. Right where we landed at that moment there wasn't small arms fire facing us. But we got off and went. There was a large hill that you had to get up to get out away from the beach. On the way up I passed a pillbox, that there was a German soldier about three feet from the entrance of it that looked like a hot dog, looked like a wiener. He had been roasted. When they went by they put a flamethrower on him and, of course, he come out. He was on fire, but he died before he got just seven steps from there. We went up the top of that hill and bivouacked for the night.

Leland (Roy) Raborn was part of the information team charged with reporting on the progress of the invasion from divisions and corps headquarters to General Bradley at Army headquarters. The information team, loaded with jeeps, radio equipment and cans of gasoline and water, was to go ashore in two amphibious trucks called "ducks."

We had started out on the 5th and the weather was rough, it was raining, wind was blowing, it was miserable. But anyhow, it was a vast sea of ships, line after line of ships. I laid down that night, but I didn't sleep. Now about 1 or 2 o'clock we were called, "Time to go," so we got up and they gave us some C-rations, some K-rations. They gave us a little breakfast and then we boarded the duck. This was one thing that had worried from the word go, was how we were going to leave the LST because we had heard through different sources that in Italy the ducks had a time getting off of the LSTs in there and they would go to the bottom. So I was a little leery. Well, they opened up the LST, they lowered the ramp. At first, the water just came gushing in like everything, Well, they closed it up and they took the LST and they turned it all the way around where we were facing England coming out and it was better.

The ramp was about 60 degrees and you can imagine the duck being overweighted. There we were, we had all the personnel on it, all of the equipment and on the sides we had to carry gas for 24 hours. . . Well, anyhow, we came out of that all right. Thank goodness we had a good pump on our duck and the water that we took, it got rid of it. So, anyhow, we got out of that fine and then we started our slow procedure to the beach. I don't know how far it was, I thought it was ten miles or five miles.

But anyhow, we went into operation and the operation included Colonel [Benjamin B.] Talley, who kept General [Leonard T.] Gerow informed as to the waves, first wave, second wave, third wave. They knew what included in each one of the waves and they had certain sections of Omaha Beach designated for certain waves and things. Colonel Talley's duty was to inform them what waves and what sections were on there. About the second or third wave, we sent the message, "Colonel Talley recommends that you discontinue waves until further notice due to the congestion on the beach." I thought then, "Well, things are not going as planned."

We were supposed to land at each hour, plus one, so he told the driver to proceed to the beach. Well, we got within I guess about 50 yards or 100 yards to the beach and this machine gun opened up on us, but we were a little bit out of range because the bullets were about 50 yards short of us and of course immediately we'd turn and the rest of the time that we were on the ocean we maneuvered up and down Omaha Beach, going in and out. And we, from a security standpoint, go off the air a little bit in case the Germans was trying to triangulate us in, but they were more interested in the big ships and in the infantry LCIs.

And then down the beach, this duck was bringing in a field gun with the personnel and ammunition and all, and one of those 88 shells hit it and it went up like an explosion – all of those people, all the soldiers on there I guess were killed in that.

But anyhow, finally, we sent the message that soldiers were up on the hill. It was a big hill and they had taken all everything. Well, what that meant, we were relieved of all small machine guns and things like that. The only thing we had to worry with was the 88s, and they did not have a way of spotting anything.

They was just shooting at random. But that went on all day there, and about 7 o'clock that night Colonel Talley went to see General Gerow and I was with him and he said that we were going to have to operate on through the night. So we did, we kept communication and operation through the night. The next morning we were relieved.

Now, that was the end of D-Day for me. I was awarded a Silver Star and the French Croix de Guerre for my work on D-Day, along with two or three of the others. My life in the Army settled to more or less a routine.

Truck driver Marvin Coursey of the 30th Infantry Division made the night crossing to Omaha Beach in an LST.

Well, that night we went to sleep best we could sleep; of course I slept in the cab of that truck most of the time. But woke up the next morning and we could see all the ships that had been sunk and make an artificial harbor. And the nearer we got to the beach, some trigger happy German was shooting artillery shells over the landing facilities and we didn't know what that was. Artillery round come in, we could hear "fhoom" and we could see the water splash over there. So about the third time that come over we knew what it was.

Jay Pearlstein landed on Utah Beach with the 4th Division. Like so many other soldiers in the assault on the beach, he experienced a botched landing.

When we rendezvoused to go in, on either side of us were Yankee skippers. They hit the beach and dropped their ramps right on the beach. Well, this British skipper who I was with, he dropped his ramp. I thought it was in mid-ocean. And the first two jeeps that went off sank. We lost equipment, maps, cameras, whatever it may be on the jeeps and he was screaming at me to get off his boat. And we were receiving incoming fire from artillery and from machine gun fire. But I refused to get off. Even though I was in command of the troops, as the skipper of the boat, he was the commander of me and everybody else on the boat. But he finally lifted up and started sounding and moving in closer. And he finally dropped his ramp again and I took off and we hit the beach.

On the beach it was just mass confusion. This was Utah Beach. And I was assigned to rendezvous with the company at a predetermined location but all the landmarks that I had memorized from the sand tables were all obliterated because from the artillery fire from the naval ships and from the bombarding from the Air Force, all of our landmarks were obliterated. They were gone. And when I hit the beach, there were MPs on the beach and I asked an MP about direction and he said, "Ask that man." And I looked down. It was a decapitated man.

But we eventually met with the company. It was about dusk. And we were told at that time to remain perfectly quiet and even though it was June and it was cold. The paratroopers, 82nd Airborne and 101st Airborne, had dropped right in front of us, and the paratroopers when they took off their parachutes, they just laid them on the ground. And that night, I wrapped up in a silk parachute to stay warm and wouldn't move, even though there were foxholes that were dug in the ground by the Germans who had occupied this area before. We had been warned about these foxholes might be mined, to be careful.

Charles Beasley was a combat engineer. When he hit the beach on D-Day, bullets flying everywhere, he looked for a place to take cover:

I mean we hit the beach. They were bombing and all of the artillery and machine guns and all of this stuff and they had an aircraft with their tracers going up, all that was happening, and they were still bombing and so forth, and so the only place that I could see…whether it was protection from the shrapnel and all, was under a trailer that was hooked onto our trucks. Well, I headed for that trailer and went underneath the trailer. I noticed no one else came with me and when it was over, I looked around then and they told me, he says, "Boy," says, "do you realize what that trailer contained?" And I said, "No, not really, not when I went there," but it was loaded with ammunition and the Bangalore torpedoes, all kinds of explosives. Well, to make a joke of it…and I said, "Well, if I had to go, I wanted to go big." But I had no idea that was weapons on that trailer, ammunition and Bangalore torpedoes and things, when I went.

The troops on the beaches had to fight with very little support from the air. Overcast skies rendered the Allies' air superiority virtually useless. Pilot Wes Chitty of the 9th Air Force was able to harass the Germans farther inland.

> The main thing I remember, the weather was terrible. And when we crossed the Channel I've never seen so many boats and ships in one location in my life. It was really crowded. And we had to go in under an overcast and climb back up through it . . . And then as we broke out between there and Paris, and our mission was a highway from Paris to the D-Day landing site, was trying to find any convoys or anything that was trying to get supplies from Paris area to the landing site. And we was strafing and bombing convoys and whatever we could see that was moving.

The crew of Jack Connell's B-26 Marauder had already flown enough missions from their base in England to go home, but they wanted to be part of the invasion.

> We had flown probably 65 to 70 missions when we were given orders to come back to the US, and as a crew we voted unanimously to fly a few more missions so that we could help towards ending the war and protecting the invasion forces that were crossing the English Channel into France.

> Our squadron had two missions scheduled, one was at 6:25 on D-Day to bomb the French coast to help the invasion forces. The second mission was that afternoon and there was a coastal battery of German long-range guns on the east coast of Normandy, and our job was to lead a squadron of B-26s, and we were given orders by bomber command that it was such an important mission that we had to find a way to get in, though the weather was bad. And normally our regular flight schedule was at 12,000 feet above France – France, Belgium and Holland— and we went in as a lead ship of the whole squadron at 4,000 feet, went by the coast – the French coast on D-Day — and our target was about one to two miles inland, and we went right across a battleship a quarter of a mile off the coast. We were at 4,000 feet and we were lucky that they didn't try to shoot us down, but they didn't. And we made a very successful bombing of the coastal batteries.

108

Even a week later, troops landing on the Normandy beaches entered a horrific scene of wreckage and rotting corpses. Johnny Ware, a Signal Corpsman, landed on Omaha on D+8:

> I remember I went around one building there and as I went around the corner there was one that was just sitting there and of course he'd been there I reckon from the first part of it, but anyway he was all swelled and all and his button was just – looked like they was going to pop open. But that kind of stuff and just cows and chickens, everything, whatever had been bombed laying around dead because they hadn't had the chance to clean it up. And then of course we're advancing every day and then later on they start cleaning it up, but a lot of people thought, you know, the loved ones sent back home, no way the way things we're going you know, they'd taken their dog tags and they had bulldozers dig out a big hole and put them in it and cover them.

Having landed on Omaha Beach, Richard Warren's unit had made it successfully off the beach. And the next day, in the hedgerows, he was hungry.

> During the wee hours of the morning the sergeant come up, "Warren, get a detail and go to guard." So we put the guard out. That was always a normal process to have guard out wherever you were. So the next morning, before day, we got orders to go in the 29th Infantry Division, and we did. Well, most of the fellows that wasn't on guard had already gone by and drawn their rations for breakfast and dinner, K-rations. And me and my squad, the ones that was on guard, we hadn't drawn ours. As we walked away going with our first section to the 29th Infantry Division, we got us some K-rations. As we was going up, there was dead Germans on one side of the hedgerow, the dead Americans on the other side of the hedgerow, and I'm eating K-rations. And the lieutenant chose to chew me out, and I chose to not let the lieutenant chew me out under them conditions. And he and I got along real good after that.

Medic Charles Beason of the 4th Infantry Division and a buddy named Brown needed to bed down after the nonstop frenzy and horror of D-Day.

We was going along this little farm road and a big field on the left. I said, "Brown, let's go in here and dig us a hole get a night's sleep if we can." He said, "Okay, let's go over there and dig in at that hedgerow." I said, "Nah, we don't want to do that, we'll dig in out there in the field because if they start throwing artillery in there and it starts hitting them trees in that hedgerow, it'll blow them up before they hit the ground, shrapnel will come in that foxhole."

So we started up inside that field and all of the sudden I stopped and he said, "Why'd you stop?" and I said, "Look up to your left." A German was sitting up there in a foxhole with their rifle pointed right straight down at us. Never did pull the trigger, just stood there for a minute and directly I said something to him in German. He didn't answer me and I said something else and Brown said, "What are we going to do?" I said, "There's something wrong with that guy." And he didn't move, nothing, and I checked him over and he'd been shot. A shell hit that guy in the back of the neck, right in between his shoulders and froze him right where he was.

Beason and Brown dug their foxhole. They watched tracer bullets flying back and forth over their heads. Beason wasn't afraid of getting hit by the bullets, but what if a German dropped a hand grenade into their foxhole?

And I didn't have to say no more, but he got to shaking, and I said, "Brown, are you cold?" He said, "No, I'm just scared. If you had any damn sense you'd be scared too." I said, "Man, I'm scared. I'll tell you what though, you sit at that end of the hole and I'll sit in this end. If they toss something in here, we'll toss it back out." But you know, I often thought about that thing — if they would have tossed something in there, we'd have probably got blown up trying to throw it out, both of us.

Repercussions of the D-Day landings were felt back in Georgia where, at Fort Benning, 19-year-old Army nurse Marie Murray was making her rounds in the hospital when someone called her.

I heard a voice say, "Lieutenant, you have orders." And I looked around. I thought it was a doctor. And he said, "You are to leave Fort Benning by noon and go to the port of embarkation as soon

110

as you can get there. They have an emergency. They need more medical people units in the Battle of Normandy."

And so we had three hours to pack. And when I went back to B12 where I lived, my roommate was packing and we laughed and cried. And I said, "How am I going to get in touch with my boyfriend?" One of the nurses took care of that and we said a tearful good-bye.

Sixteen hours later she arrived in Brooklyn, and soon after that was aboard the *Aquitania* and crossing the Atlantic. Days later, a barge carried Murray and the other nurses onto Utah Beach.

The infantry division went over first. We couldn't talk to them. We were not allowed to talk with the infantry. And we climbed over the ropes and into the water and I said, "I can't swim." But anyway, we had help up on those barges, and it was raining and bullets were flying. And finally we could see trucks, open G.I. trucks waiting for us. They didn't know where to take us because our advance party was in England.

We had no place set up. So we went all night long on the truck. Next morning we ended up in the 57th Field Hospital, and they put us up, too. We were wet. And they fed us a little bit and we got dry and we had to set up the field hospital. And that was not far from the 57th. It was 15 miles outside Cherbourg, France. So then we immediately started getting wounded soldiers. It was at the time the paratroopers had gone in and blown up that area in Sainte-Mere-Eglise where the parachute was on the church. Wounded patients, so many that we couldn't – we never had any time off. They had to go right into surgery.

My first assignment, as soon as it was set up in a cow pasture, it was to night duty. I had five wards. And the mines were around there, snipers. And each night when I made rounds everybody got a shot of penicillin. I had a patient on each side of me and I'd sit on the bed and say, "You're going home." Some did and some didn't. They were screaming and hollering. And we had very little time to sleep and no water to take baths with. About two cups of water a day. But the hours were long. And we made our own supplies. We had to do our own supplies; cotton balls, roll them, and fold gauze.

111

I was there a year, just about almost a year. But I was thrown from a jeep going into Cherbourg to get uniforms. A mine hit the front of that jeep and I was thrown out and down the embankment. And we didn't have specialty then, only medicine, internal medicine and surgeons, surgeons mainly. So they didn't diagnose me. I had the eighth cranial nerve hit, knocked that ear out, and back injuries. However, that didn't stop me from doing my duty. I was in bed about two weeks.

After allied troops fought their way up off the beaches at Normandy, they had to fight across France, through the deadly hedgerows where the Germans were entrenched. Finally, on July 3, they reached Saint-Lo. Fighting around the town was fierce. Roy Howard served on a tank destroyer with the 35th Division.

The first shot I fired in Saint-Lo, just as soon as I fired it, I saw a soldier, American soldier, walking in front of my sights. He didn't know his arm was missing. Now to this day, I don't know whether I did it or whether the shelling come in and did it. It's in me, but it was just – I've always thought did I do it, because we were firing direct. And he could have ran into it, but I could have done it, we don't know. But I thought about that all my life, really.

Friendly fire was a regular occurrence, and there were far more such incidents than were actually reported. The "hedgerow" country around Normandy was peculiarly favorable for defense by the Germans. Visibility was poor and the superior firepower of the U.S. and British armies was partially nullified. Germany was running out of many materials and essentials, but the German army had better tanks, superb tactics, and the terrifying "88" guns which devastated Allied armor throughout the war.

John Clements of the 82nd Armored Reconnaissance Division was also haunted by something that happened just beyond Saint-Lo:

Something that bothered me for years was we had a fella killed there, and back in those days in all your units with the enlisted you always had somebody in your company you called "preacher." He was always reminding us, "Don't say this and don't do that." And he was one of the first men killed in France; and for years that hurt my Christian belief that how in the world

– his name was Doc Savage – how in the world did he end up almost being the first man in France that was killed?

The Air Force was called in to soften up Saint-Lo for the ground assault. To aid the bombers' targeting, colored smoke was set out to demarcate American and German lines. But before the bombers arrived, the wind shifted, putting some American troops inside the smoke line that denoted the enemy. Charles (Chuck) Ballas was there with the 28th Division:

> We wound up in Saint-Lo when the U.S. Air Force went over and wanted to soften up Saint-Lo for the attack that was to take place there and we were sitting right there with them and a lot of the bombs were dropped on our people as well as the 29th Division because of the smoke that they put off to let the bombardiers know where they're dropping. The wind had shifted and was blowing back and we received quite a few casualties from that, in our unit as well as the 29th. The 29th got hit worse than we did. Of course you don't find stuff like that on records because they don't want to talk about hitting their own people.

Ballas was wounded himself.

> I think I was somewhere I shouldn't've been, probably. I was standing where I shouldn't have been standing and I took some shrapnel—shell fragments in my legs and everybody said that's a blessing because now you can go get away from here and I was put in the hospital, I was taken care of and everything else and nine days later I left the hospital on my own, went looking for my outfit and I finally picked them up again.

Ballas actually went AWOL from the hospital. "Well, they just wanted to keep me there for a while and everything else and I said, 'I got told I had to get back.'" He walked and hitched rides with anyone heading toward the front for two-and-a-half days until he caught up with his outfit.

Charlie Fiveash of the 4th Division also experienced the bombing at Saint-Lo, the falling bombs passing right over his head:

We saw the big air raid that came at the breakthrough of Saint-Lo, which was a real spectacular thing to see. It was about 3,000 bombers and I'd never seen that many airplanes before in my life. And they would be over here and they'd let out the bombs and the Germans were over here and it worried the hell of me until with the momentum of the airplane going and the speed that it had took them over your head – except for one thing. The blue smoke that the artillery men had put out that marked the line of where Germans were and where we were – the wind came up and they started blowing the blue smoke down towards us and we started getting bombed. We were laying all in our slit trenches, but when one of them landed on top of you the slit trench didn't do much good. But you could really see the individual bombs being dropped and it was quite a sight to have them go flying over your head.

Wes Chitty was flying his A-20 Havoc light bomber on one of those missions.

They were trying to break through the German lines around the Saint-Lo/Caen area. And our mission was to strafe and frag-bomb the German troops behind the enemy lines. And we were going in pretty low level and got hit in the right engine. The right engine caught on fire and it was burning so close to the right wing tank until I was expecting the explosion most any time. So I pulled up and got back over friendly lines and bailed my two gunners out. And I was going to bail out, and I look down and there was so much stuff under me, just tents and trucks and everything you could think of down there, and so I headed the airplane back toward German lines. And once I was sure I was clear of everything on the ground, I bailed out. And landed and really didn't know where I was. I got completely turned around, disoriented. And I looked over in one direction and I could see some tanks over there firing. I looked back the other direction, I could see some tanks firing. But I wasn't sure who was who. So I kind of stayed where I was until two tanks got to me and luckily they were from the 2nd Armored Division, the Hell on Wheels outfit. And I rode with them for about two days.

One night the company commander came in the tent and said, "You wanna take a ride with me?" And I said, "Where we going?" He said, "Well, there's a little village up here that we

114

want to go through." So I got in there and they had a .30 caliber mounted on the hood, the driver and the captain and myself. And I was riding in the back seat. And we rode down the road a little bit and came to this village. And it was like a tomb. There was not a sound. You could not see anything moving or hear a sound or anything. I was getting the hairs picking up on the back of my neck. And this captain finally turned around and he says, "I don't like the way this feels. Let's get outta here." So we turned around and went back. They started to move us through the next day and had to fight their way through it. The Germans were all holed up in the village, but they weren't gonna give away their position shooting at one jeep, thank goodness.

Once he was flying missions again, Chitty would encounter lots more danger in the sky.

We were on the bomb run and I was flying right wing on the lead ship. And the first thing I knew was I got hit and my left engine cut out and I hit the feathering button to feather the prop and it wouldn't feather. So I managed to get up enough power to get back in formation and stayed in formation until we were able to drop our bombs. And just by the time we released the bombs we got hit again. And we found out later that what we got hit with was something we'd never seen before. It was 150mm. antiaircraft guns. And when they exploded, it would almost put your plane on your back. It just almost flipped you. But the next burst that I got was on top and I had several holes in the windshield, several holes in the canopy. I was covered with – looked like powdered sugar because all the Plexiglas had been powdered. I was not hit, not seriously. Was hit on the right arm and hands and the left arm. And came off the target and our gunner called and said he had smoke in the gunner's compartment. So I slid a little bit out of formation and told him to see if he could get a fire extinguisher and put it out. And he called me back and said it was burning too bad and he couldn't put it out. And I said, can you tell what it is? And he, well, it's in the top of the bomb bay is all I know.

So anyway, we started back home and I started playing with the left engine and realized my fuel pressure was about zero, so I flipped on high boost and the engine sputtered a few times and caught up. And I could get about half power out of it, and from then on back home I thought about it. Said, well, maybe we should bail out. By that time we were back on our side of the lines. But I think if that bomb bay tank was going to blow, it would've already blown up because I kept it full of gas. But apparently what had happened, the burst that hit on top of us had cut wires running from the top turret cockpit to the top turret back at the gunner's position and it was the wires that had sparked fumes coming out of that bomb bay. And it was burning and it burned probably about 40-45 minutes until we got back home.

Every once in a while a bomb would hang up during a bombing mission; it was scary landing with a live bomb on board.

You never knew what a bomb was gonna do. I came back with one, 500 pounder, one time hung up in the bomb bay. We couldn't get it loose. The gunner, he was trying to pluck it out and it just would not come out. So I flew home with it. Landed. And, of course, when you land you always open your bomb bay doors. When I opened the bomb bay doors the bomb fell out on the ground. All you could see of my crew chief and assistant crew chief was buttholes and heels. It was a composition B bomb and a composition B almost had to have a real hard impact to set it off. It rolled around for a while and didn't do anything.

Reeves Parish of the 35th Division hadn't seen any action before reaching the vicinity of Saint-Lo. He was green but confident and hot to fight.

We walked a short distance, just back of the frontline, and we were told we were going to attack the next morning. I was in 3rd Platoon, they said, "The 1st and 2nd Platoon's going to lead the fight, 3rd Platoon is going to be in reserve." We thought – or rather I thought – like I said, the young bucks like me, we were on fire to fight, we were the best and we wanted to get on the front and when they told us we were going to be in reserve, we said, "We've got the dumbest, sorriest officers in this Army." Here is this platoon, the best we've got, and they putting us in reserve, putting those two second-rate platoons up front. If you said something about our outfit or I said something about your outfit, somebody is gonna get some knots on his head. If this platoon said something about my platoon, we fought.

The *esprit de corps,* the unit's pride and solidarity, which Parish reveals here, was central to soldiers' experience. Soldiers of all armies ultimately claimed to be fighting for their buddies in the unit.

> The company went in to attack that first day and we were just hanging around back of the road, leaning upside of a ditch, bank, or something, and a man would come along back trying to find the aid station, had been wounded, something – some extent. And he'd say so and so has been killed, so and so has been killed, so and so is dead, so and so is cut off out front, we can hear him hollering, he's down, but can't nobody get to him. And they just kept coming through like that, and the medics would come through, they had litter bearers bringing them through. And I thought, "You know, they hadn't made such a bad mistake after all."

> Let me say this, to start off with – each one of us thought we were the best men in the United States Army, to start off with. I was the sorriest . . . I wasn't worth . . . I was the biggest coward in the Army. For the week, 10 days, some period of time like that, I hit the ground. When the firing started I hit the ground, I froze, I didn't move, I didn't get up, I had to get up and follow the squad. I did absolutely nothing. I was petrified. And it came to me one day, "You know this war is going to last a long time, you're going home only one of three ways, with a hole knocked in you, or you're going home in a mattress cover, or the war's going to end and you just go home with everybody else. But this is a long war, there's a long time 'til peacetime," and I just said, "To hell with it." And I settled down and became the soldier that I should have been.

South of Saint-Lo, while fighting in the hedgerows near Rennes in Brittany in July and August, Robert "Sarge" Carstarphen experienced the savagery of close combat on the ground:

> Early the next morning, the Germans attacked us about daylight and attacked one of our squads, which we wasn't no shoulder to shoulder, but extended up and down the line in trees and farms and locations like that. And the Germans came up about daylight and attacked our men in the tents and bayoneted them in the tents, drug them out of the tents and put them in haystacks and set them on fire and some of our soldiers came up in time to pull

them out. And some of them was throwing [bodies] down wells to poison the wells. The Germans that attacked us—well, they just was extremely mean and bad. We didn't expect anything like that and we never received any type of training that would prepare us for what happened and what went on, we just wasn't prepared for anything like that.

Carstarphen received the Bronze Star for his action there.

I was in a combat reconnaissance platoon, but only six men had gone out on the patrol, myself and two other men went all the way behind the German lines. We actually went behind the German lines, and we heard the Germans talking and found evidence of German positions back there and we left. And as we were leaving and backing up . . . behind this hedge row as we was leaving, the Germans opened up on us with three machine guns at one time. I silenced them all within a minute or two.

Later, while on a patrol in pitch darkness, Carstarphen was briefly captured by two German soldiers. He didn't stay captured long.

They were two young German soldiers, one of them was the first hippie I ever saw in my life. He had long blond hair down below his shoulders. He was the main one, and he had a German rifle and he put it my stomach and pulled the trigger on it twice, and thank God and my guardian angel, it jammed on him. And the other man that was with him, young boy, he never had a weapon on him.

But when this German soldier put his gun in my stomach and pulled the trigger on it twice, at that time I didn't know what was going on, but I noticed that he threw his rifle on the sidewalk, which was in the area of where there was a big, long apartment building, block long and it was two stories high. And he was trying to get inside this apartment building. The doors was locked and he couldn't get in there and I remembered I had a .45 pistol under my Army jacket and I took the one soldier that was standing there with me, and I put the .45 pistol against his head. I wasn't going to kill him, but he didn't know that, and I told him in German, "I want you to call your comrade to come in and surrender himself to me. If he don't, I'm going to kill you." I wasn't, but he didn't know that. And the other man, which tried to kill me, he came up and walked up on me sheepishly and I kicked with my boots until it injured him where he wouldn't be able to injure me. It was two to one, two German soldiers against me, and I hurt him pretty bad when I kicked him with my heavy boots, but I didn't want to kill him.

In the aftermath of the Normandy invasion, the Germans reached into their arsenal and began launching V-1 rocket bombs at England. Their pulse-jet engines gave them a buzzing sound, and the British called them buzz bombs. Doug Barnard, who would eventually spend 25 years with the Georgia Railroad Bank and serve four terms as Congressman for the 10th District, was a 21-year-old soldier assigned to the Army's finance disbursement section in southern England. When he arrived in London by train, he had his first experience with the frightening German weapon.

As soon as we got off the train, they alerted us to get into a ditch and we got into this ditch and we heard these buzz bombs, tut-tut-tut-tut-tut-tut-tut, and they said as long as you hear that noise it's fine, but when that noise shuts off, better be aware because it's going to fall someplace. It was operated by gasoline and it was, of course, full of ammunition, dynamite and stuff like – but, it was a bomb – a bomb that was delivered by propeller, motorized propeller, and of course the idea was when you gave out of gas, it fell and did its destruction. They were primarily aimed at London and that area, but occasionally it would get off course, but we learned quickly the sound of that tut-tut-tut-tut-tut-tut ...

On August 26, American troops marched in triumph through a liberated Paris. Thousands and thousands of Parisians, many weeping for joy, cheered the battle-weary troops. The soldiers gloried in that moment, knowing they would soon be back in combat where no one would be cheering. Charles Beason of the 4th Infantry Division remembered:

I've never seen anything like it before. The people were lined up on each side of the street, five and six deep, I mean from the middle of the street where we was going through. I mean, we just had to almost crowd our way through there and they was so happy to see us. But we went in and we really enjoyed Paris. We only got to stay there one day and night, then we moved on out.

Chuck Ballas, having fought at Saint-Lo, been wounded, gone AWOL from the hospital to rejoin his unit, then fought across France to Paris, was filmed in the iconic newsreel of the American troops marching through the liberated city. The triumphant march was a very brief respite.

> We marched through the Arc de Triomphe, and when we got to the other side of it we were almost back in combat again. And from there the next combat we really went into was clearing the suburbs of Paris and entering St. Denis. And that's where my company commander got it right next to me. We're standing on a hill, overlooking the river that ran through it and I was behind a building and he came up wanting to know why we were waiting, and I told him they had a machine gun nest across the way and we're kind of waiting 'til we get a mortar there so we could get rid of it. And he said, "Well, let me look and see." And I said, "Don't do it, don't put your head out back there." And he did and unfortunately he was killed at that point, Captain Ludwick. He's a great, great, great friend, but nothing you could do. This was war and these things you expected to have happen.

Soon afterwards, Ballas found himself in the middle of a German drinking party.

> And one of the funniest stories was right after we had gotten out of Paris – I call it funny now – but we were being transported at night and I was riding in the front of the cab with the driver and somehow or other when the rest of the convoy went to the right we went to the left and we wound up in the town of Chantilly. And of course there were no cars in front of us and I told the driver, I said, "Why don't you stop here and let me go in here and find out if anybody had been through here?"

> And Nick Juris and I, who was my constant companion, we get out of the cab and went into a bar and we opened the door and started walking in and realized that this place was full of Germans. And walked right up to the bar, just didn't pay no attention to them or tried not to and asked the bartender where we were and if any of the troops had come through, and he told us no they hadn't. We turned around and I tell what, I don't know who was more startled, whether it was the Germans or whether it was us. But we got back out in that truck and had him flipping around and we were heading back down a road 90 miles an hour

120

until we finally caught up to where we were supposed to be. A lot of funny things happen in a war, but there's a lot of serious ones too. That's one I'll never forget.

Tom Riley, who would teach at Augusta College years later, was a lieutenant in the 29th Division. He had a terrifying experience while fighting alongside British units around Brest:

> The British had a big heavy tank called the Churchill tank and it had a flamethrower attached to it, and with that thing they could fling them out 50 or 150, 200 feet. On one occasion we were attacking a fort that had been pretty well reduced. There was no more fire coming from it, little small arms stuff. So the tanks were going up to flame the thing and just finish it off. So my platoon happened to be assigned to follow the tank.

Engineers had already combed through the area with mine detectors, laying down tape to mark the path where there were no mines.

> So I was walking ahead of the platoon, probably 150 feet behind this tank, and suddenly the tank just disintegrated, just an enormous explosion, blew it all to pieces. And it just made no sense, because there was nothing that could shoot it anywhere around, so it just terrified us. . . . I couldn't speak. It was only after the war that I found out what happened. The Germans had buried a 500-pound airplane bomb 10 or 15 feet below the surface, and it took the pressure of that tank going over it and just completely destroyed the tank.

Now Riley and his men were en route to Paris. They were to have a three-hour break in Dreux before getting back on the train.

> The boys hopped off and run around. After they'd been gone about a half an hour, an hour, word came down we're leaving in one half an hour. Well, here I was with my 45 men scattered all over the city. I thought, well, now, where would they be? So I go into the station, talk to the station manager, said "How about lending me your jeep and driver, and tell me where the nearest cat house is," cat house being a brothel. So we get into the station manager's jeep and the driver and we go to this house. And, of course, I was still in combat gear, helmet on and camouflage and that business. So I went into the front door and there's my whole

outfit, dead drunk. And a gal said, "My God, we're being arrested," screaming and running. One old GI laid back and said, "Lieutenant, who are you going to shoot?" So anyway, we got them back on the train and went on our way.

Doug Barnard had been transferred from England and was now attached to a finance office in Chartres and sometimes served as driver for his commanding officer.

Paris had not been completely liberated, but Lt. Col. Bowden was sort of an audacious fella, and fact is, he was a brother-in-law of Senator Russell [Richard Russell of Georgia] and he was quite an individual. He took a liking to me and he drew up his own orders, he didn't wait for anybody else to do them. He prepared his own orders, including me, and several times we went to Paris and I was the driver. And Colonel Bowden, he was not inhibited about taking a drink if he felt the need to have one. So one day, as we were leaving to go to Paris with orders that he had written, he says, "Doug, I got this policy: every time we cross a bridge I get to take a drink of scotch." I said, "Yes, sir." And so here we go, we'd be riding down the road, and all of the sudden he'd say, "Stop, stop, we just passed a bridge," and he'd have a drink of scotch, and I'd look around, damn if I saw a bridge. But it was a lot of fun to be with him, but the first time we got to Paris, it wasn't fun at all because snipers were still in all of the towers around Paris and you could hear shots from time to time, but we'd stay a couple of days and then we'd go back to Chartres. I wasn't drinking, I was just counting the bridges.

While we were stationed in Chartres and our wonderful troops were moving east, they had surrounded Marseille and taken it over and in doing it, they had confiscated all of the wineries in Marseille. And we got word that all of this wine and champagne was available, so we commissioned a big truck, big truck, and so we took off to Marseille. And we went to the caves that this was stored in and we filled up that truck with wine — white wine, red wine, champagne — filled it up completely. And so we lived off of that wine for about six months.

One of the men in our unit lived on a farm in Illinois, and his parents would kill a beef or a cow every now and then. And they would cook the meat and then can it and he would get a shipment of canned beef approximately every three or four weeks, and naturally he shared with us, and we would canvas the countryside in France and buy eggs and our most delicious meals were a serving of canned beef, warmed of course, and scrambled eggs. And I'll tell you what, that was heaven, absolutely heaven.

After leaving Paris, Reeves Parish and the 35th Infantry Division were soon fighting again. His squad got left behind one morning, and when they caught up with the rest of the company, Parish's unit caught hell from the company commander. He decided to punish them.

So he said, "Some Germans have got across a road up here and we gotta knock them off and you are going to take the lead."

So we took the lead to get the Germans off of the road and there was a low spot and it was a lot of bushes in there, and we get all mixed in with those Germans down there – in those bushes. We're crawling around in those bushes and nobody has any control over us, we just get mixed in just like that with the Germans. This German crawls around this way and I come around the bush this way and me and the German butt heads. And well, I had my rifle in the right position and I fire and I cut a hole through his head just about like this. There's some tanks up here on the road, so the squad leader runs up that bank to tell the tanks to put some fire down there, but when he clears that bank somebody's up here in the house and they killed him.

And we keep on and we get the better of the Germans there, so we go off and sit down and the company just stops for the rest of the day and I and about three more say, "You know, we need to go down there and go through those Germans' pockets and see what we can find." We loved to go through the dead men's pockets to see what you could find, and I said, "No, no, no, let's wait 'til after dinner. They about half dead, some of them got fever, half crazy, let's wait 'til after dinner and give them all a chance to die, then we'll go down there," they said, "That's good thinking, that's good thinking. That's how come they made you a PFC and we still a private." I made $4 a month being a PFC.

So we go down there and they're all dead and we go through their pockets and they have a bunch of cigars on them and this one that I had shot through the head, his head has swollen out and it turned in, it just looked like a chocolate doughnut and his head was a purple – just the color of a light chocolate, and he's stiff as a board and we prop him up and we hit rocks – we got sick or were chunking rocks through that hole in his head and I went on the cigars and I was a confirmed smoker of cigars ever since.

Parish was a "BAR" man, an expert on the Browning Automatic Rifle, an air-cooled machinegun. For one firefight in France he was awarded the Bronze Star for his courage. Parish attributed his actions not to courage, however, but to wine.

> I became good on the BAR. I know one time we ran into the Germans up there in the woods and they drove us back to the edge of those woods and it was a pretty hot fight. And we just about cancelled one of them out, but the Germans flanked us on our right side and then – we going to get killed up here in a heart's beat. And this man got shot through the belly, said, "Georgia boy, pray for me." I told him, "You know God's not going to hear my prayers, not the life I've been living, he's not gonna," He said, "Yeah, but he'll hear yours before any the rest of us."

Then something like a miracle happened.

> So I gave him this great big, lofty prayer. In about two minutes, the heaviest, thickest fog you have seen fell down on us, a London fog would blush beside that fog that fell. And we got back out of that position – back in that fog, and we took up positions in that ditch. Well, they put me with the BAR and several men inside the barn to protect our left flank. There was a big window up top of that barn, oh I guess four by four, something like that, and I get up – climb up on a ladder to watch if anybody was coming then I'd come down. And we found wine underneath the trough covered up with straw and the Germans are shelling and the shells are bursting in those trees alongside that ditch out there and the men are getting covered up with tree limbs and they're dying by the handfuls out there and we inside drinking the wine.

So there was a pole embedded in the barn that protruded out and I'm up there looking out the window and the Germans come down a ditch and start coming up underneath a bridge. Well, I can't get a shot at them, the angle is wrong to get a good shot at them and I'm scared to death of heights, but I'm well-fortified with wine and I climb out on the pole and I start the attack and they hand me clips to my BAR and I flip them back the empty one and they're loading it for me, I stopped the attack. And they tell me what a hero I am and they gave me the Bronze Star, but I don't deserve a tin star - I had been drinking all that wine, no way in the world I crawled out on that pole, no way I'd've done that.

But that battle changed Parish. His assistant BAR gunner, a man named Torrez, was killed in that fight.

He was coming to me to back the BAR up when he got shot through the belly and I was never the same after that. I got careless, my mind would just – look like would just drift off and I did things that I knew not to do. I don't know what I had, but I just I didn't have it anymore and we were up in this wooded area, the place was full of snipers and I got up one morning and there was a sniper that shot me through the ankle and I got a $1 million wound and came home.

Getting wounded didn't always get you sent home, of course, and confinement in a hospital had its share of misery. Tom Riley was wounded in October 1944 and evacuated to England where he was a bed patient for four months.

I was still a bed patient, had a big cast on my leg, couldn't get out of bed. And this particular ward I was in, it was an officers' ward and we had a bunch of A-men in there who were real hillbillies and they had every hillbilly record in the world – "Way Down in Fort Worth Jailhouse" and that sort of stuff – and they played those damn records day and night.

When I finally was relieved from that and I got up on crutches and made it over to the officers' club, got good and drunk, fell down two or three times, broke the cast all to pieces. But anyway, got hauled back in a wheelchair back to this ward. And I said, "Well, I've had enough of those records." So I had a little coal stove sitting in there, broke up the records, put them in the coal stove, set them on fire, burned up all the records and, for good measure, beat the panel out of the wooden door. Of course, half an hour later, the adjutant was in the office taking depositions. I wound up in a colonel's office [with him] saying, "Son, I'm going to make an example out of you," and he damn sure did.

Still, for many GIs, a wound which got you pulled off the front lines was worth a million dollars. Some went so far as to take fate into their own hands, shooting themselves. When such wounds were discovered to be self-inflicted, the soldiers faced court martial. Late in the war, Jay Pearlstein, though not a lawyer, was assigned to hear such cases:

> The court martialed were men that had just come out of combat, who were pretty much embittered. They were very stern and very tough. And during this court martialing, I only had one acquittal, which was an individual that I knew was guilty but as the circumstances were, this particular individual in one morning when they were going into combat had decided he'd had enough and he pulled his rifle and shot his foot. And the moment he shot the gun, he started screaming for a medic. The medics ran up, took his shoe off. The guy had missed. And while the medic was holding his foot, he shot himself again and this time he shot his foot. And that was one of the individuals that I was court martialing.

The soldier was acquitted – the only acquittal Pearlstein observed —— because of a technicality. "And the court couldn't find him guilty and I knew this man was guilty and he was found innocent." Those who were not acquitted received harsh sentences.

> The verdicts were life, 50 years, death. But these had to be reviewed before the sentence was actually carried. And in the case of a death they had to be reviewed by the President. And I don't think any of them were ever really carried out. But it was something that I had to do.

Allied troops pushed eastward past Paris. By September 1944 they had reached Metz near the German border and a fierce three-month battle began there. The American Third Army took the city in November and proceeded into the industrial Saar Basin. That's where Weldon Page of

126

the 87th Division saw his first action on December 11, 1944. Hitler's Seigfried Line fortifications had been neglected for four years – but they were still a nasty challenge for the Americans.

> We got to this place where we set up our tents and the next morning it was snow all over the ground and that was December 11, the first day we went into combat. They called it the Saar Basin. The Germans had the pillboxes all along their border.

> All I remember is a railroad track, we had to cross it and a little hill in front of us and I couldn't imagine what in the world we'd be attacking because you couldn't see anybody to attack. But then when we got over there, every sergeant said "Dig in" and we did and the Germans started shelling then, artillery. It took out about half of our company. That was the first time I had seen a man that would go – I don't know what you'd call it, crazy or just lose his cool because he stood up and started running around firing in the air, one of our men. He was with our little group that had dug this big hole. And we had to get him and had to send him back to the rear.

Page's company learned from an error that had cost many men in a skirmish.

> The thing we had learned during that first little skirmish was don't stay close together, you walk ten feet apart, at least, to keep from getting everybody knocked off. So we went down in that canyon and all afternoon until dark. To my thinking and to some of the other boys, we were on a suicide mission because [the Germans] had tanks set up and all kinds of artillery around that town, and when we came up from that canyon into the road going into the town it was dark, so you couldn't see. Then the company commander had us all fire at one time, just run towards the town and fire your gun, no matter where you were, just fire in the air. And so we surprised them and they didn't get to fire a shot. The Germans were in the upside of the town where they could have knocked us all off and they just didn't hear us. I captured about 30 that was in the building there. Enjoying their meal.

Of course, units of both armies were always trying to surprise each other. In the nearby Vosges Mountains, Cliff Cherry of the 70th Division protected himself from surprise with tin cans.

> We had barbwire in front of our foxholes, we put tin cans on these barbwires. Put rocks in there and if anybody come across there it would shake those things and that's when I let a grenade go. I bet I threw 20 or 30 grenades out of my foxhole and I'm sure it wasn't anything but the wind blowing that around, but I couldn't take that chance.

In November, near Germany's border with Belgium, the Netherlands, and Luxembourg, Chuck Ballas's 28th Division was now facing day after bloody day of fighting in the Hürtgen Forest. This was another area where the outnumbered and outgunned Germans could take advantage of the terrain to nullify the American superiority.

> Well, at the time I had a company, because during the Hürtgen Forest Campaign in the little town of Kommerscheidt, I think is what it was, that we would attack it in the morning and take it, and at night the Germans would counterattack it and kick us out. And I watched my outfit go down to as low as seven men at one point and the next day we'd get replacements and go back at it again. Well, the average strength of a company was supposed to be about 170-180 people. We actually got down to about seven at one time on one of the advances that we went in there. By the time we come back out there weren't very many of us left and, like I said, I had an angel with me, looked after me.

Charles Beason, a medic with the 4th Infantry Division, saw what some desperate soldiers would do to escape the brutal Hürtgen combat.

> We got bogged down in the Hürtgen Forest, it was bad, bad. And it was so bad that the soldiers got to where they would stick their feet out of the foxhole, it was cold too, I mean bitter cold – they'd stick their feet out of the foxhole and let the cold freeze their feet, and that got so bad that they started general court martialing them if they come in with frozen feet.

Battle of the Bulge

After fighting in the Hürtgen Forest, Joe Good of the 28th Infantry Division had an early warning of the German counterattack which was to become the Battle of the Bulge.

> I was up there on the frontlines and went up in a house and in the trees and looked through the field glasses and I could see the German tanks forming, and I got on my phone and told them back in the back, I said, "The Germans are going to be here tomorrow, fellas. You better be ready." All these guys said, "Oh, you're crazy as hell," says, "The war is over, you're probably going home in a few days." I said, "You pay some attention to me, they're going to be here tomorrow," which they did. They come through the next day or the day after that in tanks.

Good thought he and his unit were safe in that house. They weren't.

> I was hit with a bullet up here on the head, glanced, place is still up there, and it almost knocked me out. And after that we stayed there 'til that night, I think, and then the Germans came through and they threw grenades in the place and one of the grenades went off and wounded me. And then the Germans come up, I think it was the next day, and I was the only one still alive and they led me down to put me in the company jeep and that's the only time I ever rode in the company jeep.

A German corporal captured Good.

> I got to know him. He was from Vienna, Austria, and I've done forgot his name and he had an American .45, I remember that, and I started to tell him, "Now look, if you get captured, the Americans will shoot you with that .45 just [like the Germans] would shoot us when we had a Luger." But I figured the least I said, the better off I was, so I didn't say no more.

Lt. Jay Pearlstein had also been fighting in the Hürtgen Forest, but now he and his men had been moved into a rest area outside of Luxembourg when all of a sudden one morning shells began to explode all around them.

> We woke up that morning and we were just being shelled. They threw everything but the kitchen sink at us. And I was in command of this platoon. We had our cannons there. And we

were in a farmhouse and in this farmhouse, next to it was a barn that had hay in it.

I went up into the attic, and looking through the eaves of the farmhouse I saw the Germans advancing and I called for artillery fire, which broke up that advance. And I kept observing through the eaves of the farmhouse and they were moving forward again with minesweepers. I called for artillery fire again but the artillery that was behind us had been overrun.

Pearlstein's actions held off a company of German soldiers. When the Germans set fire to the farmhouse, he was able to withdraw his troops to another position. He was later awarded a Bronze Star, the citation of which read, in part, "His heroic delaying action enabled his battalion to set up a powerful defense. Lt. Pearlstein's courage and initiative reflect great credit upon himself and the military service."

The Battle of the Bulge was Nazi Germany's "last hurrah" in the West. Although it was probably doomed to fail – Hitler's targets for the offensive were far too optimistic – it caught the Allied commands completely by surprise. One American division suffered 69% casualties on the first day of the offensive (16 December 1944). Untrained and unprepared troops were thrown into the breach, with disastrous results. Resistance by many individual units slowed the Germans until a counterattack could be organized and a change in the weather allowed air power to be used effectively.

Pearlstein, like the troops he commanded, fought bravely; but like the thousands of others who fought at the Bulge, he would look enviously at those whose wounds allowed them to leave the front.

We were moving a platoon and a half-ton truck and I was riding in the front seat with another lieutenant and the driver and we hit a mine and we lost several men that were riding in the body of the truck. After getting up off the ground and dusting myself off, I found I wasn't hit. I was perfectly fine. But the lieutenant mentioned that he couldn't move his arm. And the weather was bitter cold and we were in overcoats and long johns. I got his coat off, pulled his sleeve back up and a piece of shrapnel had gone up his sleeve and it wedged in his arm and that arm was turning purple. And when he saw that, he just had a broad smile on his face. He said, "Well," he said, "I'm leaving you." He said,

"I'm one of the walking wounded." And I looked at him and I looked at him with envy. I said, "Why couldn't that be me? Why couldn't I walk away from this?" And I'll never forget when he left.

In the midst of the terror of battle, the confusion, and the bitter cold, it was hard not to envy the walking wounded. W. Broadus Carter recalled:

From the time I saw that first soldier coming over the hill, holding his arm and the blood running down him, if you say you was not scared when you were over there, you lied. I done a lot of praying and it was terrible, it was cold, it was so cold. The cold – I feared the cold more than I did getting hit, but I said, "If I get hit, I'll get to go back to the hospital." I was wanting to get an arm or a leg – a hand or an arm, something wrong, minor, that would take me off the front because, yes, I was scared. And I guess I never did get to where I was not afraid.

For Clarence "Jack" Jackson of the 3rd Armored Division, the Bulge meant filth and cold, rumors and confusion.

Shells were bad enough, but the worst thing about it was, there were no facilities to brush your teeth, no bath, no nothing. You were filthy dirty. You were just plenty dirty, even though we were walking on snow and slush the whole time. And one of the worst things also was trying to dig a foxhole for the night. The ground was frozen. You couldn't dig down into the ground and our entrenching tools were terrible. The Germans' [tools] that we could pick up occasionally were much, much better. Then word came down the line, as rumors do, that if the Germans took you prisoner and they found a piece of German equipment on you, you would immediately be shot. Well, some of the guys had along the way picked up German intrenching tools that they'd find in a house that we had advanced toward. They threw all those away. There was no German equipment on us at all, because you certainly didn't want to immediately be shot.

Also, the rumor came down the line that Malmedy – where the Germans had just mowed down with machine gun fire—I guess it was a platoon of our soldiers, indicating they were not taking prisoners. Now, the word went down the line that we could take prisoners if we wanted to but we didn't have to, and we did take some prisoners, and I had the pleasure one time of taking prisoners back. Now, this was a real choice chore because maybe two guys would take back and cover them with M1s and you'd walk them back to an encampment area where barbed wire was around it. And this was choice because you could sort of slow down on the way. You didn't have to run right back to the front where the guys were. And we were trying to advance the whole time. We really didn't know whether we were advancing—and actually in the long run we're going backwards. We didn't know what in the world was going on.

As terrible as the German forces were, Jackson said they were not the ultimate enemy.

The enemy was the cold. The cold was horrible. So we were on top of a hill one day with about a fifth or sixth second lieutenant and I was standing near the radioman and the map, and he was looking at it. The poor guy didn't know any more about it than I did, and I knew very little about it. We did have map reading and training, but you were looking at something brand-new, and you were cold and you were miserable. And all we had to eat there for weeks on end were K-rations.

In the brutally cold weather the Americans were caught beyond their supply lines, and the snow and bad weather prevented any supplies from reaching them. Albert Shaw remembered:

They couldn't get ammunition and food supplies up to us, let alone clothing and anything else. So we sat there in the Bulge for about 11 days, 7 to 11 days, unable to move on. We didn't have ammunition, we didn't have gasoline for the tanks, and we were on one K-ration a day. And if anybody's ever eaten K-rations, that's not a whole lot of food, believe me.

To beat back the lice, the men sprinkled themselves with DDT powder. Despite the cold and hunger and filthy clothes, Shaw made sure he had clean socks.

I did carry an extra pair of socks. I'd wash them in my helmet and then pin them inside a jacket next to my body to dry the next day. A lot of guys didn't bother with that and a lot of them ended up with what they call trench foot, freezing of your feet.

That's what happened to W. Broadus Carter. After hours of forced march he fell asleep in his foxhole, too tired to change his socks.

And I was so tired, I was so tired and we kept warm socks next to our body under our shirts so that when your feet sweated you could take off your wet socks and put on the dry socks to keep your feet from freezing, and I was just too tired, I just couldn't make myself put them dry socks on. You would take the wet socks off and replace them under there where the dry socks were when you did this, but I didn't change my socks and the next morning I attempted to stand up, I couldn't, I just couldn't stand up, it felt like I was on two stumps, my feet were frozen. I never did like the word trench foot, so I said I had frozen feet.

So these officers came and looked at me and sent me back to the aid station and the aid station they cut my boots off. I couldn't get them off because my feet was swollen so, and they had purple streaks up and down in several places, the big toe, the heels, the little toes, just about I'd say 40 percent of each foot had purple stripes in it. So they loaded me in one of these square box type Army ambulances, and those ambulances hold four people, they got a litter up top on both sides and a litter on the bottom and there was three other soldiers in there and they carried back to the aid station. So that was December 23, '44.

To stay alive that terrible December in Belgium, you had to win the fight against the Germans and somehow keep from freezing. Unfortunately, as Albert Shaw discovered, the two could be mutually exclusive. He and a buddy, George, thought they had beaten the cold.

Well, he and I had built us a real fancy foxhole while we were doing nothing there and we covered the top of it with logs ... and then covered that with pine boughs, so it was a pretty nice little hut we had going. And we built a little stove out of ammunition cans and we had us a fire going there pretty good one night. It dried out the pine bough on top and caught fire, and of course the Germans were waiting for something like that. The 88s were coming and everybody was hollering, "Put that damn fire out! put the fire out!" I grabbed George's blanket and threw it over the fire. He grabbed my one canteen of water for the day, poured that on the fire. And when he finished he said, "You burned my blanket up, burned a big hole in my blanket." I said, "Well, George, you used my whole canteen of water for the week." We had to put the fire out. And all the rest of the troops were about ready to kill us by that time, 'cause we had started it to start with.

W. Broadus Carter remembered the German mortar fire, both in the Hürtgen Forest and the Bulge, with particular dread.

There was a lot of machine gun fire, rifle fire both ways and artillery coming in. But the most fearsome thing we had to contend with was mortar fire. We could hear the artillery coming, the 88s. They made a whistling sound and you would hear the explosion wherever it hit, sometimes close to you, sometimes a long ways away. But mortar fire you don't hear. It's there and you have no idea where it's coming from. It just doesn't make any sound at all and that was our most fearful thing. You'd be surprised how it just tore trees up. They'd break off halfway up or three-fourths of the way up, even as low as six foot off the ground, it looked like a logging crew had been in there and hadn't taken the logs out. It was just terrible. And it was cold, it was so cold, I don't know how we ever stayed out there without freezing to death, but we did, we made it through somehow.

We had C-rations to begin with and that's the canned stuff like corn beef and cabbage or something like that. We didn't like that very well, but later they had K-rations and this was good. It had a round of cheese in it, it had a round of meat in it, it had crackers in it, it had two cigarettes and we had plenty of those and if one wasn't enough, then we could open up another one, so we got by. But I can't remember what we did for drinking water, evidently we ate snow. I just can't remember that part of it, but this went on back and forth until December the 16th and that's when the Battle of the Bulge started.

Well, we could hear the machinery across the way of the Germans at night and in the daytime, we could hear all kind of machinery over there and we had no idea what it was, but they were preparing all of their tanks and artillery stuff to make this big last push. They was hoping to get to some seaport, I forget what it was. But that's when the Battle of the Bulge really began, on December 16, and the best words I can use is all hell broke loose. I hate to go into detail about the carnage I saw, but so many men were killed, so many men lost arms, they lost legs, it was just pitiful. And I was very fortunate. We had a buddy system — in my bay Richard Jay Hisch from Norwich, Connecticut, I'll never forget him. He got killed, and they reassigned me to another buddy, Si Franco. I don't know what happened to Si Franco, but he was there when I left because on December 22 we had a forced march at night and we must have walked for four or five hours and I don't know why we did this march because we came back and I got in my same foxhole that I had dug before we started this march, I never will understand that, I never will figure it out, no one ever told me why.

After that march Carter got trench foot and was hospitalized.

Now, the doctors wanted to amputate my feet and I begged and I cried and I begged and they said, "Okay, we'll try something else for a couple of days." And so I got penicillin shots and they had soldiers in there, privates I'm sure, they rubbed my feet continually, day and night, with some kind of salve, some kind of oil, just kept rubbing my feet to rub circulation back into them. I didn't put my feet on the floor for 63 days and finally I was able to get up and walk and finally toward my end of stay at the hospital I walked some, they marched us some and they got me in condition to where they said, "You are ready to go back to the front."

When Carter returned to his unit in May, it was no longer the unit he had known in December.

They sent me back to the front to my same outfit, but I didn't know anybody, all the men had been wounded or sent back or killed, I just didn't know anybody. The squad leader, Sergeant Teasight, he had a direct hit with a rifle bullet to the head they told me, our platoon sergeant was now 1st lieutenant, he made a battlefield commission, he's the only one that I really remember when I got back to my outfit. I was told that my company was replaced 300 percent. In other words, where 200 men went in, it took another 600 going in to bring 200 back out.

When replacements came in, the veterans kept their distance from the newcomers. Reeves Parish explained why.

> When those men would come up, you were friendly, you were nice, whatever you had you shared with them, but you put a wall between you and them. All your other friends had gotten killed or they're wounded and it hurt when those men that you had soldiered with, partied with and all that stuff – so you put a wall up, you were nice, you were friendly, you shared, but you didn't let them get too close to you. Because they were going to get killed and you hurt too bad if they were that close to you. You just about kept them at an arm's distance.

Corporal Richard Warren of the Military Police was awarded the Bronze Star when he was able to evacuate 19 German prisoners when German troops threatened to overrun his stockade. Afterwards, the building where he and his unit were sheltered at Camp Eisenborn was hit by a German shell.

> The shell hit within four feet of several of our guys, it was about eight feet from me, and we had to jump over plastered walls and all that it had knocked down to get out of the building. It had a basement like most of the buildings did . . . But I knew where there was a foxhole right on the outskirts of the building. Then I ran out to it and jumped in it. It was one that had logs on top of it and it was open on both ends. Well, Anderson jumped in that other end as I jumped in the closest end. And I looked up and he was barefooted. . . . Snow was on the ground. I said, "Anderson, aren't your feet cold?" He said, "Why?" I said, "You're barefooted." "I didn't know it." Anyway, we tried to find our tracks between that foxhole and the building and there wasn't any tracks. I don't know if both us flew or one of us flew, but honestly we could not find the track between that foxhole and the building when we started back.

After the Malmedy massacre, in which 80 captured American soldiers were machine gunned by SS Lt. Col. Joachim Peiper's men, Warren wouldn't be guarding any more German prisoners. "And after that we didn't have to guard any German prisoners because we didn't take any German prisoners. We left them laying in the woods."

136

Don Lundquist saw the grisly evidence at Malmedy a few days after the massacre.

> Of course I was not there to see the shooting or anything, but we did come by about, if I remember correctly, it was two days later, and the quartermaster boys were picking up the dead bodies. Of course, everyone was frozen solid by that time. They were just throwing them into big two and a half ton trucks and taking them away. That was a memory that I will never forget.

Both the Germans and the Americans did continue to take some prisoners, but while there were few other massacres, POWs were not treated gently. James Wisenbaker of the 106th Division learned that first hand. His unit on the front line was surrounded.

> We began to move back away from the front. I don't know who was directing the movement. Anyway, we ran into some places where they had a crossroad and they had people who seemed to be MPs with an American jeep and they would motion you to go one way — and they were Germans.

Disguised in American uniforms, the Germans directed the Americans into a wooded area, "and the next thing we knew 88s were zeroed in on us. . . . They were coming in there. And you had to give Germans the credit. That 88 gun they had was a good weapon and they used it well."

> I was about 10 feet from my battalion commander, Major Burris and I looked over to him. I heard a thud, crash. I looked over to him and I could see blood coming out in various places. And I don't know how I got back. But he died. I mean the war was on then. No doubt about it. You're in war. And finally the person in charge of all of our group said that we had to surrender and we didn't like it. But you don't know what to do. Them 88s was talking to us. But he sent a courier somewhere and met and our people agreed to surrender. And some of us, I didn't, but some cried. It's not fun. You feel like you're a failure in one way and you feel like you'll never get released and back home and it's just an awful feeling.

> When we got the word to surrender, we were told to dismantle our guns, which if you had a rifle, you took the bullet guide out

and buried it, making that rifle of no value. And if you had another gun, you'd take something out of it to disable it, and that we did. So then they came and got us and they took everything you had. If you had a ring they got that, a wristwatch or something they'd get that.

We walked day after day. And we started out and you just become exhausted and the food was very scant and different from anything we'd ever had, like black bread. If you got anything, a piece of black bread like that with blackstrap molasses. And that will upset your digestive system, but you'll eat it. But we were walking one day, maybe five in a row down the road, and since we only had that one uniform, when dysentery struck, this man went out to a ditch to relieve himself so he wouldn't just ruin his uniform. This SS officer came up riding a horse and saw him over there and shot him just because he was taking his pants down. And I saw that with my own eyes. And what I'm telling you I saw. There's maybe a lot of other things happened, but I'm telling you what I saw. And, of course, what could we do? We hollered at him and things like that but there wasn't anything that we could do.

Like so many others, John Clements of the 82nd Armored Recon Company remembered the combination of German artillery and the cold.

Now the thing that sticks in my mind about the Battle of the Bulge, is how when an artillery shell hit and that ground was frozen so bad that the shrapnel just spread everywhere. A 60mm mortar shell hit and didn't hardly make a hole in that ground because it was frozen so bad. And that is the place where I saw a number of German soldiers that were wounded, still alive, that was frozen and stiff as a board, they were completely frozen, and I also saw a few Americans that was in that condition. They checked my feet and said I had frostbite. It was cold, I don't know, I think it'd gone down to 20 below at times. I remember I made the mistake of putting my tongue on the ring mount of a .50 caliber and it stuck and pulled some skin off my tongue.

Wayne Jolley of the 30th Division had been wounded in France after D-Day, hospitalized, and returned to action. Now he was at the Bulge.

138

While we're lying out on the ground, pinned down by mortar and artillery fire both, you couldn't hear the mortars coming. It'd been real stressful and traumatic for me in Normandy because it was my first experience, but I grew up a lot while I was recovering in England. And I never will forget lying out there on the ground with all that heavy weapon stuff they were throwing and this whole right flank was just blowing up and I remember raising up on my elbows and I says, "I believe I'm going to be able to take this." I recognized that I'd grown up a lot. I was now all the way up to 19.

Against German tanks the Americans used some unusual—and, Jolley claims, illegal—weaponry. Jolley's unit had retreated back to an American reserve battalion.

They had two 90mm anti-aircraft guns, which we're not supposed to have leveled according to the Geneva Convention. Some of us, like myself, didn't know that we had special rules about how we should kill each other and it was on a 90 degree curve, I mean a sharp 90 degrees, and they let two Tiger tanks get around and hit them with two 90s and that's the way we stopped that division, and it was Hitler's number one Panzer division.

Gerald Paulk and the 101st Airborne were at Bastogne when the siege began there December 20. He wasn't in the room when the Germans presented General McAuliffe with their ultimatum to surrender or when the general made his famous reply of "Nuts!" One of the GIs said as the German delegation returned to their lines, "You poor bastards, you got us surrounded and you picked yourself a lot of trouble."

Radio communication was not working, so Paulk's company commander asked him to run some telephone lines so he could talk to the 1st Battalion.

There was splotches of trees here and then open land and then trees and I was running this wire. Me and Jones had been into those woods and they had dug foxholes and they had put logs on top, two or three logs, and they get really fortified. So, as I got in there, I guess an observer had seen, they started throwing 88s in there and they're chopping down trees and they kept chopping my telephone wire, and I'd have to go back when they quit and put them together. And I spent all afternoon in that clump of trees. [The Germans] kept cutting the line as soon as I jumped into one of those foxholes.

Paulk finally gave up in futility and returned to headquarters.
During the siege, with most of Bastogne leveled, there was no shelter. Paulk turned an extra large GI raincoat into a tent, "and I guess I had enough breath I guess to warm it up."

I didn't take my boots off the whole time, from the time we landed. We had lots of frostbite — guys getting their rest and they take off their boots and I think that's what caused a lot of it. But you should have seen those socks when I took them off.

Paulk was wounded by an artillery burst. The company medic gave him a shot of morphine. "They're supposed to put a tag on you when they give you the shot," Paulk explained, but there were no tags. So when Paulk was taken back to the battalion headquarters, the medics there, unaware he'd already received morphine, gave him a second shot. "I was floating, I was like – that was a little party." Paulk survived the overdose and was eventually evacuated to the 48th General Hospital in Paris.

Throughout the ordeal of the Bulge, the awful weather prevented any help from the air. Air crews were ready at bases back in England to provide air support for the beleaguered troops on the ground, but for several weeks there was never a break in the weather. Henry Gibson of the 8th Air Force remembered his frustration as he waited as pilot of a B-24.

During the Bulge days, we would go out every morning, sit in the plane, sometimes you'd sit there four or five hours and they'd tell you they couldn't get off. Weather during the Bulge was absolutely awful. Any break whatsoever, you were going. And a typical takeoff during that time was, as you got on the end of the runway, everything would be socked in, but if they thought it was going to be clear over the target, we went. And the co-pilot would sit on the side and look out the window at the runway and tell him left or right, left or right, knowing you were on the left side or the right side, and he set his radio compass right on that runway heading and he would fly that compass. Halfway down the runway, there was a jeep that would tell you halfway and you knew then what your speed and everything had to be. Then, when you got right at the end, as you started takeoff, there was a big floodlight on both sides that would light up the plane. You couldn't miss it because it lit everything up right quick and we knew then if you wasn't off the ground, cut the throttle, hit the brakes and pray.

Alerted to the German offensive at the Bulge, General Patton rushed his forces from the south overnight to Luxembourg to relieve the 101st Airborne at Bastogne. Anthony McAuliffe, its commander, and his troops believed they were winning the battle. Henry Burch's 80th division was part of Patton's Third Army.

> Patton said that he could be ready to be in Luxembourg the next morning. That was a 125-mile drive. We did that through the night with no lights, cat eyes on the jeeps, and we arrived there the next morning and dug in. Well, we assisted in taking Luxembourg because that was a viable city. And then Patton, along with the 4th Armored, started to Bastogne to relieve the 101st Airborne Division. And the Germans, we attacked them from the rear and they hadn't expected that. We really kept them off guard, too. The 101st, we heard later that they said they really didn't need any help. But they were glad to see us when we pushed in there.

On Christmas Eve, however, a German unit counterattacked. Burch was manning a water-cooled machinegun.

> Our machine gun was steaming if you fired it for any length of time, and I had lot of scares from artillery. That was a dead giveaway with that steam for the artillery. When it steamed, that was really something. The artillery spotters, was just tickled to death. And we had a lot of close calls, for the shells falling.

During the battle, a German soldier fell. Burch saw a German medic come out to help him, so Burch yelled "Cease fire!" However, a rifleman didn't hear Burch and he shot the medic. On Christmas morning, Burch was shot himself, and that rifleman's actions from the previous day had dire consequences: In retaliation for the treatment of their medic, the Germans fired on the American medics.

> Well, I was in my foxhole and then we had the counterattack and that's when I got shot in the left thigh. And I, of course, had to

have blood, but the enemy wouldn't let them evacuate me. Every time they would come down with a stretcher they would open up and I wasn't able to be evacuated until about two o'clock.

Though medics of all armies were protected by the Geneva Convention, they knew they were never safe. Both German and American medics often became targets of enemy troops. Medics were not supposed to carry weapons, and some painted crosses on their helmets. Charles Beason learned that the Red Cross on a helmet sometimes made an enticing target.

They taught us that we was not supposed to carry guns or anything like that in combat, that Germans wasn't supposed to shoot a medic, so some of the guys, they painted crosses on their helmets. One guy, Jack Lester, he had a red cross painted on the front, back and one on each side and a sniper shot him right through the middle one.

After that, like most medics, Beason carried a weapon and displayed no crosses on his helmet.

Eventually a brave medic was able to reach the wounded Henry Burch.

The medic jumped in the hole with me and gave me blood, which saved my life because actually that bullet nicked that femoral artery, that main artery into the leg, and I almost bled to death. They gave me, I think, three units of blood in there. And after the counterattack was stopped, I was moved into a First Aid Battalion and from there I went to Belgium for my surgery.

Tanks from Patton's 3rd Army relieved Bastogne on December 26, ending the siege. Gerald Paulk described the relief the Americans felt when "Blood and Guts" Patton's tanks roared into Bastogne on December 26.

I'll tell you what, I don't think there's any way to describe how good we felt. Some of the tank fellas, they said, "Yeah, yeah, 'Blood and Guts,' it's *our* blood and *his* guts!" He was riding onboard, rode on the front of a tank with his two pearl handles, sitting on front of his tank coming into town. He brought all his tanks right down through Bastogne. He was sitting right on the front. He was a showman.

I'll tell you one thing, he backed us up some in Normandy and every time they said the 3rd Army was coming, we expected them to get there. We felt like he'd be there when he said he would.

By mid January, the German offensive at the Bulge was over, at terrible cost for both the Germans and the Americans. Historian Stephen Ambrose estimated that "Of the 600,000 GIs involved, almost 20,000 were killed, another 20,000 were captured, and 40,000 were wounded." It was the costliest battle of the war for the U.S. Army. The Germans lost about 100,000 troops. They had delayed the Allies' invasion of Germany by a few weeks, but had lost their reserves, a sizeable part of the Luftwaffe, and much of their armor.

The American fighting force was so depleted that replacements had to be drawn from all over the Army. Negro troops, who had been restricted to non-combat functions, were now brought into the fight. And soldiers with support jobs in offices and warehouses found themselves yanked into the infantry. Doug Barnard, working in a finance office in France, had his future determined by the flip of a coin.

They had to do something to reinforce their troops, so everybody in my unit had to take a physical. I was 21 years old at the time, and unfortunately, me and another fella in my unit were the only ones that passed the physical. The average age in my unit was 36 years old. And, of course, I felt the consequences of being the youngest too. But anyway, it was shortly after that, that my commanding officer, Lt. Col. Bowden, called the two of us into the office and said, "Well, I've got some good news and bad news. The good news is that you passed the physical, the bad news is that you're going to be departing this unit and going into the infantry."

But only one of us was supposed to go immediately. And so he said, "So, I'm not going to choose which one's going, I'm not going to do that. I'd have that on my conscience the rest of my life." And I said, "Well, what are you going to do?" He said, "Well, I think I'll flip a coin." And so I had carried a silver dollar with me all the months that I had been in the service, so I said to him, "Colonel, if you're going to flip a coin, then we're going to flip an American coin," and he said, "Oh, that'll be fine." So, he flipped the coin and you will be surprised what happened: that coin hit the floor and rolled, rolled, rolled. It finally rolled up against the wall and stood straight up. I'm telling you, that was an omen, I didn't know what that omen was. So he flipped it again and I won, so the other fella had to leave immediately for the infantry, but that gave me another month or so to suffer the consequences of wondering where in the world I would go next.

War in the air

As miserable as life was for the infantry, the men who flew the bombers high above the mud and snow experienced their own danger and terror as they flew their missions over Germany. They were expected to fly 25 missions, but few survived past 10. Even after German fighters had been largely eliminated, anti-aircraft fire took a deadly toll. Two pre-war beliefs haunted the American airmen: that strategic bombing was sufficiently accurate to knock the enemy out of the war, and that well-armed bombers could effectively defend themselves against enemy fighters. Neither turned out to be correct. The Germans knew that level strategic bombing was inaccurate; consequently, they concentrated on dive-bombers, which gave their armies much better air support. (The inaccuracy of the large level bombers meant they were not very useful for attacking tactical targets.) But the Americans' focus on strategic bombing gave them the lead in the development of large airplanes. The *Luftwaffe's* superiority was eventually nullified by its inferior numbers and declining fuel stock.

George Waddell was a tail gunner on a B-24 Liberator in the 15th Air Force. He flew 18 missions, returning to base once with three of the four engines out. But the plane he was originally assigned to never made it back to its base in Italy.

> We had our name on the plane, *The Uninvited Guest*, with Eleanor Roosevelt's picture on it. And they gave the plane to another crew to fly the next day after we landed. And it got shot down on its first mission. That was a real blow to us.

Assigned to another plane, Waddell flew his first mission.

> Well, I was scared to death when we started, but after we got up there, it was a reasonably short mission. I didn't know at that

time it was short, but I found out later it was. It was probably six or seven hours. And we made it up there and back with not too much problems. And I thought well, I might get through this after all.

But things got much tougher in subsequent missions to bomb well defended rail yards in Germany. He remembered the toll that flak took once the enemy gunners on the ground got their range:

Anti-aircraft was hitting us pretty hard, but a lot of it was above us, exploding above us. We got to the target and the bombardier said, "Can't make it! Can't make it! Go around again!" So we circled and come in. And this time, the Germans had our speed and our altitude and everything figured. And they was hitting us hard. We finished that bomb run, and during that bomb run, we'd lost numerous planes. I don't know, it looked to me like everywhere I looked a plane either had a wing shot off or was exploding or something. And we made that run and they said "Bombs away!" and dropped the bombs, and by the time they said bombs away, we had got hit hard.

Julian Proctor was also a gunner on a B-24. in the 8th Air Force. It never got easy after a mission knowing you'd have to go up again.

Well, you didn't have a choice. A lot of times we might be in the barracks playing cards, and they'd come in for us to go on another mission. So we'd jump up and just have to go and go by the mess hall and get a snack and go on another mission, that was it. You're gonna do it anyways, but you would never know where you were going until your briefing just before you took off on a plane.

Always had a talk with the Lord just before I got off the ground and that was one of my things I had to do. You crawled into that B-24 from the bottom, there was a door under the bottom of it and you got up in there, and they had to wait on me, because I stood there and said my prayer before we got off the ground. Every mission.

It worked. Proctor survived 32 missions.

Tom Jarrell flew 38 bombing missions, most of them over Germany, piloting a B-26 Marauder, a medium bomber.

> [The Germans] had fighter planes when I first got there, but our fighters got rid of them and I didn't see any fighters, maybe 10 or 15 missions and we didn't have any fighter planes. But we had flak . . . it looks like a square box and they had flak for 2,000 feet, for 10,000 to 12,000 feet, and they shot flak up and you had to fly through it to bomb. Half the missions I was on we had damage to the airplane.

In one mission, his pitot tube, which measures the plane's airspeed, was shot off. To get back and land safely, he had to follow another plane and land right behind him. On another mission, flak knocked out his plane's hydraulic system, preventing him from dropping his bombs over the target.

> Everybody dropped the bombs but us, and the bomb bay doors are open. And we were too slow to keep up with the rest of the flight. We were on our own. About 15 minutes later and my bombardier called and we didn't have enough fuel to get back to base with the bomb bay doors open. And my engineer had a crank . . . they cranked the doors. Well, we had to get the bombs dropped, we dropped them in the field, and they cranked the doors closed and my bombardier called and got a field where we can land and get gas and like, we land there and we spent the night and gone back to our original base the next day.

To pilot a bomber was to fly a slow, lumbering cargo plane—whose cargo, of course, was bombs—and to deliver that cargo to a target far below. That target most often bristled with anti-aircraft defenses shooting into the sky, and the pilot avoided the flak and anti-aircraft fire as well as he could. When attacked by enemy fighters, the bomber's gunners fought back, but theirs was a defensive task, protecting their plane from much faster, more agile attackers.

The pilots of fighter planes had a whole different set of skills and experiences than the bomber pilots did. Fighter pilots liked taking the aggressive role, flew fast planes with acrobatic capabilities. Fairfield Goodale flew a P-51 Mustang. The Mustang was used to escort bombers on their missions, was excellent in dogfights, and could even carry

146

bombs itself. Goodale's mission was reconnaissance over Germany, but often the reconnaissance was merely an appetizer to the main course.

> The reconnaissance missions involved determining the location of enemy troops. It involved a lot of photography of enemy gun emplacements and these were all single snapshots from our cameras, which were big and we got very good pictures. And onto enemy troops, we radioed artillery and got them to aim at the troops, German troops, in various locations.

> Strafing was part of it. If there was not much flak, we in the P-51s would often bomb or strafe the German troops, but if there was any flak, we were not well armed against flak, but the P-47s were, and squadrons of P-47s often flew around, only to be called in for dive bombing and that was going to be better than artillery fire against the Germans. Patton's troops moved so rapidly and often detachments of American troops would go so fast they'd get lost away from their own base and we would have to find them, we would have to arrange protection for them until the other forces could join up with them.

Goodale learned on the job from his flight leader, Clyde East, who was already an ace, with nine planes shot down before Goodale became his wingman. Goodale would fly 23 missions with East.

> My first mission with him – not only my first mission, but my first combat because we broke unexpectedly into a group of German fighters. And Clyde shot one down. The chaos didn't last very long, but when it finished, I was completely lost, thoroughly scared and badly flustered and I couldn't see Clyde's P-51 anywhere. But he radioed and said, "I'll be on your wing in a minute and I want you to find our way home." And I was blessing him for finding me and cursing him for testing me so soon, but eventually I did find a way home, and the lesson I learned from him was that it is possible, indeed crucial, to learn how to think under pressure.

> And then I flew the next 23 missions with him. His one idea of fun was to get the reconnaissance out of the way as quickly as possible, which he did well and did rapidly. And then he would say, "Okay, Goodie, now we'll have a good time," and he would take off to the nearest German airfield and we'd burst in on it

and shot up as many planes as possible as they sat on the tarmac and it was like hitting with a baseball bat a big bee's nest and we'd come around for a second time and there'd be German planes in the air, and that was not my idea of fun, but that's what Clyde liked.

Fighting into Germany

While the Battle of the Bulge was winding down, some of the toughest fighting of the war was heating up in Alsace on the border between France and Germany. The 14th Armored Division faced German Panzer divisions, infantry, and parachute troops. Here twin brothers Larry and Harry Kemp faced battle for the first time, with both heroic and tragic results. The Kemps' unit was selected to test the nearby Siegfried Line on December 18. They found it to be fiercely defended. Harry Kemp described the scene.

It was cold that morning, about 18 degrees, heavy snow on the ground and you got a thousand men heading towards Germany and the Siegfried Line. And as we approached, the Germans had spotted us and they knew the Azimuth, they knew the range, they knew what artillery was most effective, armor piercing, whatever it took, they fired it. And of course, a dog-faced infantry soldier like me, he learns one thing first in combat, that as you hear an incoming shell, hit the ground.

There were lots of incoming shells. They were coming at us so fast and they were erupting and tearing up men and flesh and rifles and tanks and things were splintering left and right and I hit the ground, like any dog-face that wants to stay alive. We're talking about big concentrations of incoming German 88 millimeters. They are killing men, you can hear boys hollering, screaming, wounded. And we dug in.

There wasn't any attack on the Siegfried. The German engineers blew the bridge over the Our River and there was not going to be any breaching of the Siegfried there. So we dug in and stayed there for three hellish days and nights in that cold ground while they just threw artillery at us time and time again. Those foxholes that we dug there, mainly we had to dig into shell holes that would come in from German shells because the ground was frozen, and any infantry soldier knows quick that you better dig

148

where the ground has been broken open if you want any kind of a hole.

So those holes that many of the men in my battalion dug was not only their home for those next three days, it was their final resting place. They were killed there. And we had tremendous casualties: 30% of the battalion, 300 men were slaughtered and killed there. So yes, that was our welcome into Alsace-Lorraine and the German border.

That was like somebody coming up and smacking you in the face with their right hand and say, "Take that." That was my first taste of combat and I knew then that it wasn't going to be an easy war. Lots of casualties, lots of blood, lots of gore, lot of moaning and dying and wounded men. "Help me, help me." And you can't help, you can't even get out of the hole you're in. It's tragedy.

On January 11, the unit attacked the village of Rittershoffen.

Lt. Gosselin came over and said, "Which one of you Kemp boys has ever fired a Browning Automatic Rifle?" I said, "I have, sir." And he turned to my brother Larry. "How about you, Larry?" "No sir, I was never privileged to fire that Browning Automatic Rifle." So he said, "Well, we've got a new Browning Automatic Rifleman: his name is PFC Harry Kemp." And he hands a brand-new BAR to me. He says, "I'll take your M1 and turn it in to quartermaster. You're our new platoon BAR man. And guess what? You're going to get two ammunition bearers because you're going to be firing that thing an awful lot and you're going to need a lot of .30 caliber BAR ammunition." So I knew that I was going to see lots of action.

So the next day Lt. Gosselin says, "PFC Kemp, take your BAR team and knock out that machine gun nest right in front of us." I said "Yes sir. Could I get some smoke, sir, from our 60 millimeter mortars?" Well, this was the beginning of my trek from PFC to 2nd lieutenant. Lt. Gosselin kind of smiled, he says, "You're kind of a thinking kind of a fellow, aren't you?" I said, "I try, sir." He said, "That's a good idea." He says, "I'll get our 60 millimeter mortar squad to drop some white phosphorus in there and give you some smoke." And I said, "You give me the smoke, I'll knock out the German machine gun nest."

It went like clockwork. I could hear the 60 millimeters pop when they dropped down to, uuhm, and here they came over to right in front of the machine gun, boom. And big old white phosphorus clouds of smoke. And I'd already told my two ammunition bearers, I said, "Get two grenades out. On the first grenade, don't do anything, but hang the second grenade on your cartridge belt." I said, "Just as soon as Lt. Gosselin gives the signal and the mortar squad cease firing, dropping smoke on the machine gun squad, you pull the pins on your grenades, throw the pins away, don't worry about anything else, but that grenade." I said, "Go in with me under the smoke and get to the German machine guns that were firing out of an open window in a German farmhouse, get to that open window and all three of us throw our grenades right in there to where the Germans are firing their gun."

Of course when the white phosphorus started, this started the Germans firing even faster with their machine guns. But then when the smoke got so thick, they stopped firing for a moment and when I sensed that lull, I said "Now!" And we went charging across about 40 yards and I said, "Okay, throw!" And we threw our grenades. Well, you know, it takes five seconds after that handle flies up for that grenade to detonate and we all threw it right in there. I noticed the German machine guns had stopped firing and sure enough, five seconds later, here came three explosions, boom, boom, boom, just like that. And nothing but silence. And in about I must say 10 seconds, the door to the German farmhouse opened and here came two German soldiers out with their hands up and their word, if they want surrender is, "Komrade, komrade." So I said, "Holen Sie sich hier macht schnell." That means get over here fast. And we searched them, they didn't bring any weapons or nothing. I told the two ammunition bearers, I said "Take these two German soldiers back to Lt. Gosselin. He told me earlier that General Smith wants captured German soldiers for interrogation to determine their strength here in Rittershoffen."

The mission was accomplished, but now Kemp, fueled by adrenaline, took it to the next level.

I said, "I'm not going back. I'm going to go on further and I'm going to see if there aren't some more higher-ranking German officers back there that I can either capture or I can kill." And they looked at me like I was kind of a crazy boy. Well, I guess I was, but I was fighting mad.

I went on to the next house. Went running in there and went to the back wall. I had noticed that an artillery shell, either theirs or ours, had blown out a section about, just about eye high for a man standing up and I could see over that section and I looked and I could see a German soldier walking towards me. And I moved to the back door of the kitchen, and kicked open the door and stepped out with my BAR just like this. And I said, "Halt." Well, H-A-L-T, halt means halt in German and it means halt in English. And I meant every word of it. I had the safety off of my BAR. Well, he was a German lieutenant. He didn't think I meant business, so he went for the Luger on his hip. A tragic mistake for him. Before his hand could even touch the weapon, I just barely touched that BAR trigger and five rounds of .30 caliber ball ammunition went right into that man's chest and he was dead before he hit the ground. And I was running over there on top of him, pulling his gun belt off. I wanted that Luger as a war souvenir. And he was dead. I could tell he was dead.

So I went and I put his gun belt over mine, went running to the back or front door of that same house and I learned as a boy to whistle like this. Wheet! I could do it a lot louder those days, but getting old now, but you get the idea. You could hear that whistle a long way off, so I did like that and I gave two signals, which every infantryman knows is like this: assemble on me quick time, double time. So Lt. Gosselin saw it and he sent a squadron of soldiers up led by one of my favorite sergeants, Sergeant Richie Cedars of Sweetwater, Texas. And when he got up there he said, "What's up? What's up, Harry?" I said, "I've just killed a German lieutenant. It's my fairly good assumption that he is being observed or he will be followed by more German infantry." And he said, "Well, it looks like it's time for us to set up our positions and get ready to welcome them." I said, "That's my idea exactly, Sergeant."

And so we got positions in the windows of this house and started looking and there was a stone wall. The safeties were off of our weapons and we had everything from M1s to machine guns, to BARs. And this wall it was 35 yards out there, we see one helmet, German helmet, in two, in three, four, five, six, seven, eight, nine, a whole squad of Germans, about 10 of them were looking over that wall and some of the braver ones nodded to each other and they came over the wall, and then the rest came —10 Krauts headed right straight towards Cedars, and in his old Texas drawl he says, whispering, "Hold your fire, hold your fire." And they get closer, 20 yards, "Hold your fire." Well at 10 yards, he says, "Commence firing." And it sounded like all hell broke loose. Machine guns, pow, pow, pow. We killed every one of them, all 10 of them. Went back and told that story to Lt. Gosselin and he said, "I tell you what, Private Kemp, I'm sending you in for a medal, the Bronze Star for bravery up and above the call of duty." He said, "You went on and not only did your job by wiping out the machine gun nest."

Gosselin recommended Kemp for a battlefield commission to 2nd lieutenant. But whatever joy and pride Kemp felt was soon shattered.

Well, my twin brother, private 1st class Larry Kemp was killed in action January 15, 1945, about six months before the war ended in Europe. He was part of an attack on Rittershoffen. Anyway, being January, of course it was cold and we had been set on the attack into the town. It was a very intense battle. Well, I had laryngitis after all that cold weather. My brother, we fought the Germans all night and we were catching a little bit of sleep and my 1st Sergeant, through my Platoon Sergeant, came to me and said, "PFC Kemp, the medic tells me you're running a fever and we need to get you back to the battalion aid station to get that laryngitis cleared up." I could just whisper, ah, ah, ah. And my brother was asleep on the table over there. I said, "All right, sir, let me cover my brother up." So I put an Army wool blanket – he was laying on the table - I put a Army wool blanket over him. That was the last time I saw him alive.

And I got on an Army jeep and went back to the next small village and the medics started treating for my laryngitis. The next day an Army medical officer, a captain came to me and says, "private Kemp." I said, "Yes, sir." He said, "I have very serious news. Your twin brother, PFC Larry Kemp, was killed in action yesterday afternoon after you left him in

152

Rittershoffen." And my eyes already began filling up with tears and I said, "How was he killed, sir?" And he said, "A German sniper. He was on a tank infantry team attack to knock out the church steeple in Rittershoffen because the Germans were using it as an OP, observation post, to call in German fire on American troops here. And your brother volunteered for a tank infantry team to go in and knock out that church steeple. However, enroute, which is sometimes the way it happens in war, a German sniper killed your brother." And I said, "Where was he hit?" He said, "The sniper set the bullet right straight through his steel helmet through his temple and at that close range it pierced and went all the way through and your brother was dead before he hit the ground." I said, "Well, thank God he didn't suffer." And he said, "You're right about that." I said, "I've seen so many men suffer before they died, but thank God he didn't suffer."

And he said, "I'll tell you what I'm going to do, PFC Kemp. "You two boys were the only twins we had in the battalion," and he said, "Because you are twins, I'm going to get special permission from my commanding officer to take you to the grave where he is being buried. You're not going to go back into action until I send you back into action, but I'm going to take you to the grave where your brother is buried, Epinal American Military Cemetery."

So he got his jeep driver and we got on our overcoats and we got in the jeep and we drove the 50 or 60 miles, whatever it was, through the night, or through the morning by that time, to Epinal and we got to the grave registration officer and the captain, the medical officer said, "This is Private Kemp. His brother is being buried here." And I turned to the medical officer, I said, "Do you think you could request permission for me to see my brother one last time?" And I saw the two officers speak and one of them shook his head, well, I more or less read through the lines that I didn't want to carry that picture of his face for the rest of my life, so I will remember him as he was, as he looks in this picture right here: A handsome, virile, strong, young American soldier fighting for what he believed to be right. God bless his soul. Anyway, he refused permission. I said, "I can understand that sir." But he said, "However, after your brother is interred, you may visit the gravesite." I said, "Thank you, sir." So I waited until they buried him.

We didn't carry any caskets overseas. Men carried with them mattress covers. Men who were killed in action were put in those mattress covers and they couldn't build that many coffins, and some lime and sulfur and put that in there with it to delay the decay process. And so that's the way thousands and thousands and thousands of men who were killed in – they were buried the same way in mattress cover bags. But, because of war, many terrible things happen. Anyway, I paid a final salute, snapped to and gave a final salute to my brother and walked away with tears rolling down my face.

And so I went back to war, and then shortly after that I was called to division headquarters and got my battlefield commission and led my platoon.

By March, the Allies had reached the Rhine River. The German heartland lay beyond. Albert Shaw was at Remagen, where, to the Allies' surprise, the Germans had tried but failed to blow up the bridge across the Rhine.

We were guarding this bridge to keep the Germans primarily from coming back in and to blow it up. That was our mission. And we were lobbing these 81 mm. mortar shells across the river just beyond the bridge to keep them from coming back to blow it up. We were still shipping lots of troops across, tanks and artillery while we were guarding this bridge, but we were not lucky enough to go across it ourselves. The bridge fell and we had to go across in small rowboats, eight to a rowboat, with our mortars and everything, ammunition and everything onboard the little boat. It was about this high on each side, and you've got four soldiers rowing this boat that had probably never rowed a boat before in their life. And I don't swim, so let me tell you, that was one of the scariest moments of my life crossing that river, the Rhine River, in this little boat with eight other soldiers in there and all your supplies and things. But we made it across. And then, of course, once we got across, we had transportation and they moved us on to the next target. We lost a lot of people there, we sure did.

The capture of the bridge led to one of the most serious disagreements between Generals Eisenhower and Bradley. Ike at first was reluctant to rush reserves forward to exploit the capture of the bridge, and Bradley demanded to know whether he should blow the bridge up or simply give it back to the Germans.

Julian Haddock was with the 89th Division on the drive to cross the Rhine.

> We hit the frontlines on the Rhine River. We come up there and they shelled us and our artillery shelled them all night long. And then the next morning before daylight the first company made it across, but a lot of them got killed because they had machine guns sitting up on the other side. I was lucky enough. We wasn't the first one, but probably the third that crossed. Of course, there were different points that we crossed, it wasn't all in one spot. It was just becoming day, you could see a little bit, and we're loaded in boats and I think eight or ten to a boat and I don't know whether the engineers supplied them or not, I couldn't tell. I was just looking out for my hide there. And then, from there on, we were clean-up force. The Germans would leave behind 88s. The farmers at that time had just gotten to starting planting and plowing the fields up and every time you start across an open field, one of them 88s would open up on you and you would hit the ground as soon as you heard one coming. If you didn't hear it coming it was just about going to hit you. And oftentimes, when we'd get up, you could look four or five feet away and a big piece of shrapnel, just laying down on the ground. It wasn't there when you hit the ground. And of course as soon as it was over you got up and run as hard as you could 'til another shell come and you'd hit the ground again. And you'd come into these towns, you'd spend the night and we'd just go and pick the biggest house in town and tell the civilians they had about 30 minutes [to take] enough stuff out for the night, and we would spend the night in that house and we'd be gone in the morning. So that's the way it went.

American airmen did what they could to help the forces on the ground and paid a heavy price themselves. Henry Gibson, a B-24 pilot who volunteered for the mission, remembered the toll.

> We flew one low-altitude mission on the 24th of March. It was the only low-altitude mission we got to fly. It was a volunteer mission, dropping supplies to the paratroopers and the gliders,

they were crossing the Rhine, and they really took a beating getting on the ground, they did. And we had one of our heaviest losses there. There was 30 planes and we lost three —10 percent of the planes was shot down, that crashed and we lost, then we had several that didn't make it back, but their crews were not hurt.

Sgt. Ray Hitt moved to the Rhine and beyond with the 65th Division. In this last phase of the western front, German soldiers were surrendering spontaneously in large numbers, especially in the Ruhr, where Field Marshal Walther Model was effectively allowing his units to do so. But Allied soldiers such as Hitt never knew in advance whether the enemy unit to their front would surrender – or shoot.

We encountered a lot of Germans that had given up and we met them on the side of the road and they had white handkerchiefs and their hands over their head. They was going back to a prisoner of war camp. And our officers didn't make any effort in trying to stop them, because they knew where they were supposed to go.

Well, then we started walking. We walked and we walked and we walked, had no idea where we was going. Finally we came up on the Rhine River. But just before going to the Rhine River, we had an occasion to see General George Patton, who was the commander, and I never will forget what he told us. I saw him— he was noted for a shiny helmet, and it was shiny. So he told us one day, he said, "With your blood and my guts," he said, "we're going to win this war." Of course, we did. So then they put us in some type of a boat. There was about three groups of us.

Before that, we was in someplace in Germany and we had a 1st lieutenant that was young, smart and well-liked by the officers, and he was given the task of doing some scouting for the division. He wanted two jeeps to go with him. My jeep had a .30-caliber machine gun mounted on it and the other jeep was the rifleman. So we took out scouting. And we came over this hill. This is the closest, I guess, I could have been killed. We came over this hill and we saw two German Tiger Tanks, and luckily, the men, they were on the outside of the tank. So that's where the element of surprise came in effect, we immediately annihilated the German troops. And we got a little closer and

156

there was one of the German soldiers that was kind of hid back up underneath the tank and he had a pistol, and he aimed it at our lieutenant, and fortunately the gun misfired. So we had one guy—one of our soldiers, he was kind of a roughneck, and he got hold of a machine gun, and he riddled that soldier 'til his body was nothing but pieces. But had we not seen them—had they not been out of the tank, we probably would have likely got killed there.

But then we was doing some more scouting and we ran up on a few soldiers in a field with some woods, and I happened to see a German soldier that was setting up a machine gun. So, of course, I opened fire with our machine gun, because it had a range of about 720 yards. So we took care of him. I'm sorry that it was necessary to kill somebody, but I know that had he had time to set up his machine gun, that he would have probably shot us, that we might have gotten killed.

Then we were doing some more scouting and we ran up on some more German soldiers, and this was the first time we had any casualties whatsoever. One of the Germans shot, and the bullet hit our soldier's helmet, steel helmet, and the shrapnel got into his face and ears, but he was all right.

At that time, we had taken two prisoners, and this was the worst thing I've ever seen happen. We had the two prisoners and they was marching back to the designated area. They had their hands over their heads because they had given up. My machine gunner, he was armed with a .45 pistol. He was walking those two soldiers back and he asked me, he says, "Sergeant, what do you want to do with these prisoners?" I said, "I don't know." Then he asked me again, and I told him the same question. Then he took his .45 pistol, shot both of them in the back, and when they fell to the ground, he walked up to them and [shot] their heads. I don't know what happened to the soldiers, but I'm sure somebody came and got them. They tried to court martial this boy, and they should have, but we all lied and said that the German soldiers was running, trying to escape, and that's the reason he shot them. But I don't know whether that boy thinks about what he did to those soldiers. I know they was the enemy but they didn't have any reason to be killed, because they had given up. They had given completely up.

After months of deadly fighting, the depleted Army ranks were now filled with replacements, untested on the battlefield. Jack Barrett, a veteran infantryman in the 80th Division in Luxembourg pushing east into Germany, tried to look after a green replacement.

> We had a new man named Frank Longo, from New York, and I took Frank under my arm. When a new man would come in we'd put him with an old man to help him get caught up with things. And I had Frank and we were going out of the woods and going across a big field towards Dahl and bullets and shells were flying all around and a shell fell close to us and Frank fell down on the ground. And I thought he might have been hurt, but he wasn't. I realized he was just scared, shell shocked. I kicked him and woke him up. I said. "Get up!" And he stood about. I was shaking him and a bullet came right by my face and hit him right in the neck. Sniper was shooting at us, two of us standing still, that was a good target. Hit that boy right in the neck and he fell again and he stayed down that time. And we got on into Dahl and medics were around. I said, "Right over that hill there's a man laying down. He's shot, but I don't know whether he's dead or alive." And two of them took off running over there and he was still alive and they saved him. I'd like to know what happened to him after the war, I don't know. But he lived.

Another soldier he tried to save was a German soldier whom he had wounded.

> It was a little outhouse like, we were on the edge of this town and I'd shot that German and he had run in that building. I had knew he'd run in the building, but I threw a phosphorus grenade upstairs in the closet and caught it on fire and then I run downstairs threw another phosphorus grenade in a stack of hay, caught it on fire. The hay started moving and somebody started hollering and it was that wounded German, he had got under that hay and was hiding. But he was real weak. I drug him out of the building and drug him over to our building. He had defecated all over himself and his pants came off and I pulled his pants back up and fastened his belt and drug him on into the building where we were, and he lived for about an hour and then he bled to death.

158

Barrett's proudest achievement came when he ignored orders and saved a squad that was about to be ambushed.

We were on a small river, very small. And my outfit was in reserve. We were in a little village like, and right across the river was the Siegfried Line and we were supposed to go and take that Siegfried Line. We were in Luxemburg going into Germany. We had orders for us not to shoot, period, don't shoot. Well, we could look out and you could watch it, just like watching television, and there was a squad of men off a little bit to the right. I don't know whether it was a full squad or a part squad, but it was a squad of men, eight or ten or whatever. And they were going up this hill, they'd already crossed the creek or the river, and they were strung out, but they were all going up the hill. And over to the left of them there were two Germans run out of a pillbox with a machine gun and they set it up and they were going to wait until those squad of men go up there and got lined up, and they were going to work them over.

Well, I couldn't sit there and watch them men get shot. I put a tracer in my gun. And it was a long shot, probably 500 yards, and I shot and the tracer hit low, just a little bit. And I held up, used to be what they call "Kentucky windage," I held up just a little bit the shot and killed one of the Germans. The other one took off running, he run down the hill and dove in a little foxhole we didn't even know was there. But I saved that whole squad of men from getting annihilated. I figured that might have been the biggest thing I did the whole time I was over there. I don't know none of them, they didn't even know who I was. Didn't even know about me, didn't know I'd saved their lives, but I did.

One of Barrett's men was fascinated by the tracers. He soon learned, however, that they trace both ways.

Leo wanted to shoot a German so bad, but he had terrible eyes, he had thick glasses. He shouldn't even have been in the combat infantry. But I made that long shot with the tracer and he come up there wanting to know all about the tracers. He wanted to shoot a German and he got some tracer bullets and I was laying down behind a hedge row shooting, but I couldn't tell where I was hitting. And I wouldn't put a tracer in because that was too dangerous in that particular situation. He ran up there and

159

wanted to know where they were at. I said, "They're right over yonder." And he shot all them tracers out through there and they turned the machine gun loose on us. And the bullets went over us, they shot high. But he took off running and he lost his helmet and his rifle and he ran to a little building over there and dove through the door and slid right into a pile of fresh cow manure.

Thomas McCollum was a green replacement combat infantryman in Patton's 5th Infantry Division.

We finally went back into combat and the first day we went in I wasn't no more afraid than I am right now. I just had my gun across my arm about like that, going rabbit hunting or something. But it didn't take us too long to wake up to the fact that we were right there on the frontline. We walked across this huge pasture land, looked like something out west, it just kept on a going, and way over yonder on a hill were a clump of trees and bushes, and we were getting a little bit of machine gun fire from somewhere and they decided it might be coming out of those bushes. And they called the cannon company out; they lobbed a few big shells in those bushes and nothing happened, so we figured it was all clear and we started, and they hollered "Move out!"

You know how you go to a post to hold onto to get over a fence? I laid my hand up there on it and about the time I got straddled the fence, I have no idea how many bullets hit that post, it splintered it, flew everywhere. And I jumped back and hit the ground, and he was still shooting at me because there was cow tracks all along beside that fence and they were full of water because it just rained, but I laid down as flat as I could get and bullets were still coming and he was close enough to my head that it knocked the water out of the tracks into my face.

And at that very moment I saw the first man get killed. It was a man in our squad. He smoked a crooked stem pipe. He got hit right smack between the eyes with a bullet and he just sat down and then laid back holding onto that pipe. I'll never forget that.

We moved out then and went on, took a little town or two and finally we were getting a lot of machine gun fire and mortar from a little town just ahead of us, so they called in the 8th Air Force.

They sent some B-26s in and bombed the place. I'm telling you those bombs stir up something, see sides of building sailing off out there, it's something.

PFC McCollum was about to achieve an unbelievable victory almost without trying.

> We went on in and took the town and after we got everything secured the man in charge says, "I want this squad right here," and I was in it. There was a house right down the road maybe a quarter of mile or less, a big beautiful two-story building. "I want you to go down there and check that house out, see if there's any Germans in there." So we went down the road, just happy-go-lucky, and we got there, house had a pretty picket fence around the front of it, painted up, and the boy I was buddying with, he says, "I'll go up the back and come in from back there, you watch the front," I said, "Okay."

> Then the squad surrounded the whole house, and I said, "Okay, I'll watch it," so I opened the gate and went on in and walked up to the steps to go up on the porch, but I didn't go on the porch. I thought it was him coming through the house, I could hear steps, and pretty soon the front door opened and, I forget how many, it was six or eight SS troopers, the best thing that Hitler had, come walking out the door, each one of them had their automatic weapons and everything, and I knew it wouldn't do for one little PFC to start shooting at that crowd. So I just stood there and you know, those men came down the steps, pitched their rifles and automatic things over in the bushes and walked straight by me a-smiling and walked out the gate and got out there in the road and did left, right, left and straightened up to attention right there, all for one little old PFC.

McCollum, an anti-tank grenadier, toughened up fast on the battlefield, but he could still experience sympathy for the enemy.

> The grenade fit on the front end of the barrel on the M1, and I tell you what, I fired it one time from my shoulder, but I said that'd be the last time I'd ever do it, wasn't much left of me. When we was in combat, we was getting machine gun fire from a clump of bushes, wasn't too far away, maybe 300 feet or something, and somebody hollered and said, "Tom, lob one of

them anti-tank grenades in them bushes." So I was already laying down, I took the butt of that gun and got it embedded pretty good in that dirt, elevated about where I thought it ought to go and it went exactly to the spot, right in the middle of those bushes. All the firing stopped, and we went easing on up there and we didn't kill anybody, but they sure were dazed, I'm telling you, they just couldn't hardly stand up.

And there's one thing that's never left my mind: there was a young boy, blond-headed boy, sitting there with a picture in his hand. He was crying. I don't know who the picture was, whether it was his wife, his sweetheart, his mother or who. But he was really too young to be married, looked like, but we got him up from there and I think we gave him some C-rations or something to eat and they put them all on a truck and sent them on back for prisoners of war.

The Siegfried Line lay just across the Our River. In February, Jack Barrett's 80th Division prepared to cross the river and attack Germany's "West Wall."

We were going to cross the Our River and take the Siegfried Line. Boy, they built it all up, they said, "Man, you all are going to really do it." Anytime they did that, you could expect the worst. We got up there and layed down in the ditch. The engineers were supposed to have built a pontoon bridge that night, but every time they'd get it almost built the Germans would throw in a barrage and knock it out. They had it pinpointed and could tell what was going on down there. I don't remember whether the moon was shining or what, but they kept knocking it out and knocking it out. We went up there and layed down in the ditch and layed there a long time and a boy, right by me, a shell hit him dead center, it turned him into hamburger meat. Part of it splattered up against my face and I had to dig it off, but I didn't get a scratch in that.

But Barrett's good luck was about to take a terrible turn.

They gave us our orders to withdraw. Well, we started withdrawing and I had a squad of men and I had two men missing, couldn't find them. I went back looking for them, found out later that they had deserted. Well, after I couldn't find them

I was turned around and was coming back to regroup with my outfit and this big shell hit right behind me. Boy it got me, I mean it blew me up, 30 something shrapnel wounds. I went numb all over, I couldn't feel nothing, I was just lying there like a drunk man. And the first thing I could move around was my hand and the first thing I did was feel my privates to see if they were still there and they were, and I felt pretty good about that. I was making a splint out of my bayonet, I took my pills, I took all of them and I struck a big kitchen match to light a cigarette, and there was a jeep coming down the road, coming away from fighting part. I kind of think they saw that match, and the jeep slammed on brakes and there was four or five medics in it.

One of them lay down right by me and I was really getting weak from losing blood, but I could talk and I said, "I need some help, Cap, when they quit shooting." And he looked at me and he jumped in scaredom, he didn't know I was laying there. And they didn't throw them but about five or six shells and they hit all around and then it was over with and he hollered for his buddies. He said, "Come here! We got a casualty." And four of them loaded me on a stretcher and jogged with me a little ways to a little farmhouse that they'd made an aid station out of. And they had me in there on a cot, working on with two medics — and a shell hit. It hit in the windowsill, and the shrapnel went right over my body and killed one of the medics and wounded the other one. The reason I know it killed him, they come in there and examined him and they covered him up, and the other one was wounded and they started doctoring on him and I didn't get none of that.

In just a little while an ambulance backed up there and they picked me up and was toting me down the hall to put me in the ambulance and a shell got a direct hit on that ambulance. I don't know what happened to the driver, I don't know whether it killed him or wounded him or scared him or what. Another ambulance came in there and there was two of us and they loaded us up and boy, he got away from there, I mean he was scared, and he had a right to be.

Leading the Third Army across France, relieving Bastogne, and then thrusting into Nazi Germany, General George Patton had no patience with anything or anyone who stood in his way. George Watkins,

163

like many in the army, held him in awe. An assistant Sherman tank driver and machine gunner in the 8th Armored Division, Watkins was star-struck when he actually saw the man.

> That was like being near God. I didn't talk to him, I wasn't close enough to see him well, but I did see him. I felt like just seeing him was awesome, I'd heard so much about him. His name was always on the radio and "General Patton did this" and "General Patton did that." But it was like at last a movie star idol, and he was my movie star idol and it was an exciting experience. But he told us – he didn't tell us, he told our commanding officer— to get the hell out of that town we was in, I believe it was in France near the Swiss border. They were having a rest area and his men were in there and he didn't want us contaminating his men.

Watkins' commanding officer didn't like that one bit. "He said, 'I can't help it, he's the boss. He said out of this town.' So we moved on out."

Roy Howard, a gunner on a tank destroyer in the 35th Division, got to see how deeply Patton despised inaction. Having been given a week to put new tracks on their tanks in Belgium, Howard and the others completed the work in three days. Their officers told them to just enjoy the rest of the week. Then General Patton arrived.

> The next day somebody knocked on the door where my section was and I just had a pair of pants on and some lieutenant, he says, "Soldier...," he couldn't call me because he didn't know what I was. But he says, "Soldier, where's your CP?" I said, "Next door." He said, "Is your lieutenant there?" And I said, "Yes sir." He says, "Well, why don't you go and find him and you tell him that General Patton is out here. And he's hot." And I said, "Yes sir." So I jumped into some clothes and the snow was about that deep. And I made some prints and I got to them and I told the lieutenant. He come to the door with just shorts on. And I said, "Lieutenant, you better get out of bed that fast." I said, "Patton's sitting out there and he is hot about our tanks just sitting there." So man, I tell you, I made a dent in the snow. That lieutenant didn't make no dent at all. I bet he told that General Patton about 10 times, "Yes sir, yes sir, yes sir."

Having received a battlefield commission for his courage and initiative at Rittershoffen in January, 2nd Lt. Harry Kemp was now leading a platoon of the 68th Armored Battalion against the Siegfried Line at Steinfeld. On March 19, after a 17-minute artillery barrage prepared the way, Kemp and his men charged across the dragon's teeth defenses and captured two houses in Steinfeld.

I blew the whistle and gave the boys the let's go sign and I was right up front. As the platoon leader, I felt it was my job to lead the platoon. If you're not a platoon leader, you're sure not a platoon follower. I was 21 years old, I was strong and I did that 300 yards in less than 3 minutes. And my radio man was with me and he was gasping for breath. I says, "Come on son, come on, come on." So we got through the dragon's teeth and as I was threading my way through the dragon's teeth and clipping barbed wire so that my boys behind me could come on through, I thought to myself, what a place, the Germans had really missed out here. They should have planted shoe mines and blow our legs off, but no shoe mines went off, thank goodness. So we got through the Siegfried Line, I routed through the dragon's teeth on into the first house of Steinfeld, expecting to see German soldiers, but they're nothing. They were in their bunkers because why? that severe artillery concentration and that was the only way. They couldn't have survived in the houses. The houses were blown to pieces. So I got through, inside the house.

A young lieutenant, his name was Napier, and he had just graduated from West Point and this was his first combat. He had just come in as a replacement. I had the first platoon in B Company 68th Infantry, he had the second platoon. He replaced an officer that had been killed in previous combat. He came running up to me breathless. "Lt. Kemp, what do we do now?" I said, "lt. Napier, we hold what we've got and we outpost this and get that next house. Give me four of your best men and I'll get four of mine." And in that first house, there were only 23 men out of two platoons that were full strength of 90 men, 45 in each platoon, only 23 of us had gotten through – 15 from my platoon and 8 from lt. Napier's group.

So he gave me four of his men and I sent four of mine over with a staff sergeant in charge, to the next house, to set up machine guns and I'm sure glad I did because all afternoon and all night long [the enemy] tried to run us out of there, but we held our ground, and stayed there all night long.

About 4 in the morning, a code message came in on the radio and when I decoded it, it said, "Lt. Kemp and Lt. Napier, be prepared for an unidentified explosion in your area at 0600 hours this morning." It was already 4:00. I told the men, I says, "Stuff cotton in your ears, do whatever necessary because there's going to be one big blast going off." They didn't tell me what they were going to do, but I had figured something was up.

Well, the Army engineers sent a detail of men with CN2 putty. CN2 putty is nitroglycerin. Nitroglycerin explodes. They wrapped this nitroglycerin in the CN2 putty, wrapped the putty around the dragon's teeth, stick a fuse in it, back off 100 yards and set off an electric charge. And the Siegfried Line disappears. Boom, just like that. Well, that was – I'm here to tell you folks, when that explosion went off, I had my hands over my ears, I had cotton balls in my ears, but when I took the cotton balls out, my ears were ringing and they rang for a week after that explosion. The house I was in, the ground shook like an earthquake and the concussion came through like a hurricane wind. And it was the loudest noise I've ever heard in my life. But it did the job. It blew the dragon's teeth wide open and the engineers then laid a big steel track down over that big gigantic hole so that our tanks could come over it. We had breached the Siegfried, they could come and break out on through Steinfeld and clear the enemy out of there. So that's exactly what happened. The tanks came through and the 62nd came through and we liberated Steinfeld and we chased the Germans out of there. And they headed for the Rhine River. So we won the war, what can I say?

After being relieved, we were tired. We had been in action for over 24 hours without sleep. So our company commander told us to pull back to Kapsweyer and get some sack time. So we did that and then got our sleeping bags out and curled up and went to sleep. That was about 7:00 in the morning. We slept until about 10:00 that night and a soldier came up to me, "Sir, Lt. Kemp sir, Lt. Kemp sir?" And I was very mad. I almost slapped that young man. I said, "What is it, soldier? What is it?" He said, "The 62nd Infantry has run into big trouble in Steinfeld and the

68th has been ordered to go back in and relieve the 62nd." So I called my platoon sergeant, Dale Reagal. I said, "Dale, whatever men we've got left, form them. We're going back in." He said, "Yes sir." So we went back in and as Dale and I were going house to house with bazookas and machine guns and clearing out the Krauts and so forth, I stepped out into the road just a moment to get some idea of how much further we had to go before we had the town cleared and I heard a bullet go right by my head.

Well, a bullet going right by your head makes a cracking noise, so I knew I'd better get moving. And I headed for a shell hole in the ground and a bullet went through my leg just below the knee and all the way through the bone, the tibia, the fibula and blew a big hole through my leg. Of course I hit the ground, crawling for this foxhole or shell hole and I just tumbled over into the shell hole. If I hadn't, a Kraut would have killed me.

But my good old platoon sergeant, Dale Reagal, he saw that Kraut shooting at me and he had an Army grease gun. It did the same thing that a tommy gun would and it would fire just as fast, but it looked like what you'd grease a car with, a round cylinder on it and so forth. Well, he took that grease gun and he wiped out that German that was shooting at me. He saved my life. I'm obliged to him right now. So that ended my war right there for me. The war was over.

Once across the Rhine and the Siegfried Line, the American forces stormed eastward across Germany, more or less unstoppable. "Patton or somebody's theory," Charles Beason of the 4th Infantry Division remembered, "was if you keep pouring into them and keep them moving, they don't have time to shoot back at you. And once you get started to moving, just keep moving as long as you can before somebody runs way on out there and sets up a defense against you."

Prisoners and Liberation

As cities fell and territory was gained, the troops liberated concentration camps and POW camps. Jay Pearlstein, a Jew himself, helped liberate Jewish prisoners.

During the course of action leading a platoon of soldiers we liberated a concentration camp and the prisoners. Of course, we were combat soldiers and all we had with us was our K-rations, and we gave them what we had to eat. I remember that they were lining up to eat and their food was really boiling water with potatoes at the bottom. That was their potato soup that they were eating. And they were amazed that I was a platoon leader and I was of the Jewish faith and most of these guys there were Jewish people. But there were also Russian people there.

And that night, after we had given them everything we had, they asked me if they could play some music. But they didn't have the instruments. I said, "Where are you going to play music?" They said, "We know that there's a town close by that we can go get these instruments from the people who live in this town." And I said, "Go ahead." They went and brought back all sorts of saxophones, all sorts of instruments and that night they played music and they played a Jewish song that I knew of and they played it for me. I'll never forget that.

W. Millwee Owens, an infantryman with the 45th Division, saw Dachau concentration camp on May 1, 1945, the day after the Americans took Munich and liberated the camp.

The next day after it was liberated, the company commander said he wanted to send one officer and one enlisted man to Dachau to see what was going on. And so he sent me and he sent another. . . . The only thing I can remember, they gave me a little lunch in a brown bag. They gave me an apple and a sandwich. I remember that more than anything else.

Our sister battalion captured Dachau [the day before], they rounded up the guards and they pushed them in with the prisoners. And they – I don't know how many guards were involved, but the prisoners killed them. And I took a picture of two that had been killed and there were some more.

George Watkins also saw Dachau shortly after its liberation. He took pictures, too.

And then we went to Dachau – I have a lot of pictures, the gas chamber and the oven where they burned the bodies. I had it out

168

showing it to some friends a while back and they didn't believe things like that had happened. I saw it. We had a guy to guide us through Dachau. We got to the front gate and all unloaded and got out and we went in and saw things that only God had seen before us and it kind of gave you a funny feeling to see where so many people had died and know what went in that type of place. It kind of floors, it touches your heart a bit. It was an interesting experience, but a sad experience too, because you have to think how in the world do another human being that way? And on some of the areas the blood was still there where they had people. It was a terrible experience.

P-51 pilot Fairfield Goodale and a friend visited Buchenwald, and the experience changed the direction of his life.

The compound was huge, I don't know how many acres, filled with people in striped uniforms, often with different colored bands on their wrists, all of whom had tattooed numbers on their wrists. They all looked like skeletons walking around and indeed, in the camp, there were piles of skeletons in the dormitories, all well washed and all carefully stacked in high stacks. But these people, these prisoners walked at a very slow pace to maintain every bit of energy they had left.

Soon after our arrival we were shown into a hospital – so-called hospital area in which there were sick patients, all of whom were being experimented on with typhus, typhoid and other diseases, and one especially unpleasant area in which prisoners were being tested at various temperatures of very cold water to freezing water to find out how long they would live, so that the Germans would be better able to know how rapidly they would need to save any of their fliers who were downed in cold water. In this building there were lampshades, the covers of which were made of the prisoners' skin, many of which that were tattooed, and there were maybe a dozen of these.

After leaving the hospital, Goodale met a group of prisoners.

My friend and I had a chance to sit down with five or six of the prisoners who asked us to share a meal with them, lunch, and we tried to decline as politely as possible because they obviously didn't have much of anything to eat. They said, "No, please."

One of them spoke good English and had been a professor at some university and they had a tiny fire, and they were cooking things over the fire. They gave a little something off one of these sticks they had and we could hardly swallow them, they were something awful, we didn't know what it was.

I talked five or six hours with these people who impressed me enormously with their courage, their tolerance, and their ability to accept conditions and to live within the boundary of those terrible conditions that they were living under. They had enormous dignity. They discussed quite openly what kinds of lives they expected to have after they got out of this camp.

While we were there, the American troops liberated two of the German troops who had been captured – two of the German guards who had been captured and somehow, among the thousands and thousands of troops of prisoners there, a group of them surrounded these two released German guards and killed them. But the dormitories of which there were many, many – I don't know how many, probably thousands — each had bins for bunks and each bin would hold up to 20 or 25 people trying to sleep and in these dormitories there were these other piles of the bodies all stacked up neatly. The place had a smell all of its own, which I will never forget, compounded of God knows what, small fires, unwashed bodies, death in the form of burning in the furnaces, it was a smell which remained on my clothes for days and days afterwards.

Ray Lundquist, a navigator on a B-24 in the 15th Air Force, saw several labor camps.

> I did not see any of the real terrible concentration camps where half the people were dead when they walked in and the other half were dying. But we opened up the gates to several different labor camps. But they would labor these people practically to death. I mean, by the time we got there they were all skin and bones for the most part. Most of them that we could determine were Polish, but the medical teams around there told us not to even try to feed them because all we had was C-Rations and K-Rations and that was not the diet that they needed. They needed some soup and some very mild foods first to get their stomachs functioning.

Among the camps liberated in the closing days of the war were POW camps. James Wisenbaker, whose unit had been surrounded and captured during the Battle of the Bulge, was in the camp called Stalag 111-A in Luckenwalde, about 30 miles south of Berlin. But he had been in a string of camps before that. The Germans kept moving the prisoners to escape the approaching Russian army.

> One reason is the fronts kept changing and when we got closer to where the Russians were, we just had to keep moving because the Russians kept coming on. And we went to about four different stalags before I ended up in Luckenwalde.

> And we were at one time loaded in boxcars and sent somewhere. . . But the RAF bombed this train yard. And we were all locked in the boxcars and I'm telling you it was tough times back then. And someone happened to get out. I don't know how. But come along and unlocked the doors so you could get out. And we got out and got as far as we could from the rail yard. But there was nowhere for us to go. We didn't know where we were. So when they said get back in the cars, we had to get back in the cars. We went somewhere else.

At Luckenwalde, the prisoners were housed in tents, hundreds to a tent.

> We were three to five deep this way, foot to head, head to foot, and then right by each other like that, and no beds. It was straw and just an aisle down the middle. And they had one little water faucet out there that just had a very drizzle of water and you couldn't change it, make it faster. And there was somebody up every hour of the day down there trying to get water. There'd be a line because you just couldn't get all the water you wanted unless you went down there and got it.

However, the prisoners' guard was an old, kindly man.

> We had in our tent an old German – I forget what you call it, but it was the lowest class soldier they had. It was sort of a home guard type unit. He was up in the years. But he was our guard in the tent. But we learned to like him. He hated Hitler. He said, "because he had two of my sons killed." And that's unusual, but he was a good guy and if there was anything he had that he could bring, anything he had he could bring he would, even a little bit of something. He didn't have much himself. But we all appreciated the old gentleman and he was good to us. And we

really didn't try to escape all that much, not that we didn't want to, but what are you going to do? You don't know where you are. You don't have any help to tell you where to go.

Also at the camp, but kept in a different section than the Americans, were Polish POWs.

> We had it bad, but now we had it good compared to the Polish POWs. When you see a picture on television, you see these stripes around them like this, that's the way they were dressed. And they worked them to death. [The Germans] hated them, you see.

The western Allies held as POWs were comparatively fortunate. About 4 million Soviet soldiers who were prisoners of the Germans died in captivity.

The food the Americans ate was plain and barely adequate: barley soup and brown bread.. "Loaves about as big as a watermelon, black and heavy as could be. You'd eat it." Then one morning the German guards were gone. There was gunfire in the distance, and then Russian troops arrived and liberated the camp. Wisenbaker remembered them as "very friendly but undisciplined. When I say that, they moved over the land like fire ants and they mainly existed off of what they could find to eat. Whatever they wanted they'd get."

Wisenbaker had a strange encounter with one friendly Russian soldier on a bicycle.

> He was riding a bicycle and he motioned to me, come on, come on, like that. And I got on that bicycle, riding the handlebars, and as long as I live I'll always be able to remember him breathing heavy and panting behind my head riding that bicycle. And so, we went, oh probably a half a mile or a quarter of a mile down there to a house and he motioned come on in. And we got in there and there's German people there. And there was a big old console radio over there and he got on the floor and said, "New York, New York." So they went over there, tuned that thing in to New York, and as luck would have it, there was some opera singer or something. She was carrying it on for him. He let that go for a few minutes and he had got on the floor again and says, "Moscow." So they went over there and got Moscow and had some Russian music going, and he was enjoying this. And he

just thought he was doing me a great favor. He'd look at me and says he's just having a good time.

He looked over there on the stove and there was a pot with some baked potatoes in it and I don't know what else. So we had some of that and they had two loaves of bread. And he found a little wagon out there and put them two loaves of bread in that wagon and tied it behind his bicycle. And we started out. We was on some paved street in a town. I don't remember what the name of the town was, but he got off the bicycle and said, "Berlin, Berlin," meaning he was going to Berlin. And a German man, an old man, was riding down the street on a bicycle and he took his rifle by the barrel. He swung around and knocked that German off that bicycle, pretty as you ever saw. Took his bicycle, rode off, and told me to take that one. Now that's a fact.

So I went back to camp and shared the two loaves of bread with anybody that wanted it. But that's some experience. Just see a man take a rifle and knock an old man off a bicycle. But now they had reason to do it because they were rough on them Russians, the Germans were. They was rough. And they were scared of them, too. Once they got the upper hand they was afraid of the Russians. And they were headed for the American lines just as fast as they could go to turn themselves in because they didn't want to go in the hands of the Russians.

Very few German POWs ever returned from Soviet captivity.

A couple of days later, U. S. Army trucks came for the freed prisoners.

They come and cut the fence. We went down the road about a half a mile and I looked over there in the field, it was filled with Army trucks with a white star on the side. You talk about a pretty sight.

I think every one of us wanted to get in the first truck, but they said, "Hey, we've got plenty for you. Just take your time. Don't hurt yourself." So we rode in those trucks and they told us, oh a few hours. And we arrived at a big tin warehouse looking thing. Don't know what it was, but we unloaded from those trucks and we went inside and they stripped us and took our clothes and deloused them and give them back to us and give us a chance to go get a shower. And we was loaded with lice, if you've never seen these little old cream-colored things. And they didn't bite all that much, but when they moved they just aggravate you. And they'd crawl on you and just worried you to death. So they deloused our clothes and give them back to us.

When we left there we went to Camp Lucky Strike [in France] and we lived in some tents there and they had chow 24-hours a day. You could eat anytime of the day or night you wanted to. Now you couldn't eat much. If you ate too much you'd upchuck it. It didn't take many days before I could eat. And they told us we're going to be there a few days to get our paperwork in order and if we wanted to we could get a pass to go to Paris. I told them I didn't care about going to Paris. I was afraid they were going to call my name to leave and I didn't want to miss it.

Don Donner of the 103rd Infantry Division also experienced capture and life as a POW. His capture came in France where he and the squad he commanded were holed up in a farmhouse. At the time, he and his men were getting some shuteye on potato sacks when a German tank rumbled up.

And I jumped up real quick and grabbed my weapon and I went up there and by that time that tank was in firing range of the house. And you could the hear Germans talking and hollering and everything. We had some grenades, I don't how many we really tossed out the window, but the minute we tossed one out, well, then you got fire.

After I realized that they had hit one corner of the house, I knew I had to do something 'cause I just felt that house was going to be blown to pieces. So I run back downstairs and got the rest of the squad up and by this time they had completely surrounded us. Tank was a firing on us. I looked around to the fellas, I says, "Do you want to fight it to your death or do you want to give up?" I thought I'd give them a choice, and they all said they wanted to give up, of course.

Two of my men started up the stairway to the outside entrance because the Germans had reached the doors up out there and I was afraid they gonna throw one of them grenades down in there and then would have gotten every one of us. I was trying to save the lives of my men was what I was trying to do. At that time I was down to where I only had about seven men left in my squad. Some of them started up the entrance of the exit, the lead man got shot in the leg and the one behind him got shot in the arm, and so I got them back down and another man went by me and started up and he got shot, got killed. So then that's when I threw my weapon outside and hollered "Comrade!" I just didn't want – do no more of it and that was it. They took us out, pushed us around, of course, trying to search us for other weapons or anything. I had one hand grenade on my belt and they took that away from me.

The Americans were taken to a headquarters where later Donner underwent interrogation.

They asked me who my platoon leader was and I said, "I don't know." And that German, he looked at me kind of like, well, you a stupid person? And so I finally quoted, "I'm only told to give my name, rank and my serial number, that's all I'll give you." Then he says, "Well, I know your company commander's name, I know what division you're out of," and I was just sitting there doing that little dense, you know. And I guess he figured this guy, is he really stupid? I don't know what he thought. I didn't care.

He gave me the name of the company commander, which I can't tell you right now who it was. He said, "You're of the 103rd Infantry Division. You're out of one of the companies." And then he held up a picture, which was a picture of my wife. And I thought, "How in the world did they get that?" Then I remembered they had taken my billfold from me, so they took it out of the billfold. So he in the process threatened me that if I didn't answer any of their questions that they would see that my wife would get killed over there in the United States. And like I said, I just sat there dunce, I didn't ask anything and I didn't say anything.

While Donner was being held at an interrogation camp near a railroad yard in late December 1944, a stray RAF bomb hit the building housing American officers. It killed 67 of them.

I was selected to go up there on a detail then to dig up what parts of the bodies we could find, take them by wheel barrows or carry them or some wagon type things that they had us pull to bury the body parts. I remember distinctly, I'd seen this hand, I reached down to pull it out, figured I'd be pulling a body and all I brought was just an arm. And that got the best of me.

Donner agreed to join with a sergeant who was eager to escape.

We got through the hole in the fence. I remember getting hung up a little bit on some of that fence and he helped me get loose and we crawled on our stomach all the way into the woods. Then we got into the woods and we got up and we started walking and he said, "Let's go south to the Swiss border."

That was 50-100 miles away.

I remember we walked all night and it was just about daybreak when we come up on a river. It wasn't a big river – well, it was big to me because I had to swim it. He said, "We better not be close together swimming." I said, "Okay." So he says, "You go up about ten feet from me." So we slid down into that river. First thing that hit me was a block of ice, oh my gosh, and cold oh, "If I live through this I can do anything." We swam across the river fighting that ice and he stopped before I did because he got across before I did and he stopped. He said, "Are you all right?" And I said, "Yes." He says, "Well, let's get up and go." And at that time the German says, "Yes, c'mon."

They were standing right there waiting for us, and that end of that barrel looked as big as a cannon. And I didn't say anything, said, "Yes, comrade." He got up, started running and I thought, "Oh please, Sarge, Sarge," I hollered at him and about that time they lit fire on him, killed him. Took me back to the same camp, the only camp they could take me to, I reckon, I don't know. Just inside of the camp was a kind of masonry or concrete block building, had no windows to it and there was a little window at the door, put me in that. Solitary confinement.

But it wasn't long before Donner's camp, too, was liberated by the Russians.

176

Canadian paratrooper Dennis Trudeau had been captured in France on D-Day. While being transported by train to a POW camp, his train came under fire by Allied fighter planes.

> The Germans had supposedly POW written on top of the boxcars, but some of these pilots would disregard that and they'd strafe the train that time. One particular time they had let us out to go to the bathrooms, and we were outside just along the railroad track, and the planes came and they started strafing us up and down, and a bunch of us, we all got together in a crowd and waved our hands and one pilot came through and he waffled his wings, you know, and we said, "Oh, they know that we're prisoners."
>
> There was three planes. And the third plane come around and for some reason or other he let go with his machine guns and we all scattered. And I went and hid in a culvert down there and I stayed there for about, oh, I thought, I guess four or five hours. Figured that they'd move out. And what happened was another attack came and a German soldier come and hid in the same culvert I was. There was two of us in that culvert and of course that German was as surprised as we were and he took his little Luger, pointed at us and he says, "Raus!" I guess "Get out!" And we got out and got back in the train and we finally ended up in a place called Limburg, Germany. That was the first time that we were actually registered as prisoners of war.

Once in Stalag IV-B, a huge POW camp near Muhlberg, Trudeau was put to work.

> There were literally thousands of prisoners there. It was acres and acres and acres of buildings with prisoners in there. And me being a private, they let us go to work. We were called "Arbeit Commanders," working commanders. And we went to a place called Halle, Germany, right near the big old open pit coal mine. And we worked in this coal mine and it was kind of rough. We had to shovel coal. We had little gondola cars and there'd be two prisoners on each side of the car, and we'd start to work at 6 and we'd have to work until that gondola car was full, whether it took us 5 hours, 10 hours or 15 hours. They wouldn't let us leave until that car was filled. We usually worked 12, 15 hours a day.

We'd break for lunch for about a half an hour. But lunch was a cup of soup and a loaf of bread divided by five people. So we got a piece of bread about maybe three inches wide and then a bowl of soup, which was made out of mostly potato peelings. Sometimes we'd get cabbage, sometimes we'd have a little horse meat in there. And every day one of us would get the opportunity to lick the bowl where the soup came in. And let me tell you, we looked forward to that too. It was something else.

We worked six days a week. They wouldn't work on Sunday. Sometimes they would, but most of the time Sunday would be off. And Sunday they'd turn the water on during the day so we could get water, wash our clothes or do what we could to keep ourselves clean.

We didn't have no heat at all, no heat at all. In fact, the shoes I had was wooden shoes and of course, socks were long gone. And what they gave me for socks was a piece of cloth of a two foot square. And I'd wrap that around my feet and those wooden shoes and worked out in the snow and everything. Never got cold feet. It was surprising. I figured I would freeze my feet off, but I guess the rubbing on that wood kept your feet warm.

After they finished their work in the mine, back at the camp the POWs talked about the one thing that obsessed them:

We mostly told stories about how good our mothers cooked food. That's all we talked about. We didn't talk about the present, we talked about the past or the future. We all knew that we were going to be liberated by Christmas. There was no doubt about it.

And then the Bulge, Belgian Bulge came in and they got new prisoners. And they said, "Oh, the Germans run us over and the war is going to be extended another year or two years." Talk about a bunch of depressed people. We were really feeling bad. But the thing is, we kept dreaming about the future, about getting out of there and getting home. And if you let yourself go and just give up, a lot of the older folks, the oldest soldiers that were there, did that and they – they died. They just give up and die. And of course I was young and I was only 19 by the time that happened and thank God I was really in good top shape when I got captured.

We ate a lot of grass, we ate a lot of raw potatoes. The farmers, they were planting potatoes and we'd dig those potatoes up and bring them back in our clothes and we'd get home at night and then we'd eat them.

Trudeau and other POWs helped four of their comrades escape, and afterwards they suffered the consequences.

We all got around them and one of them got a pair of wire cutters and they went in the back of one of the barracks where the guards really couldn't see us most of the time, and when the guard would go by, he'd snip a wire. And then we'd play like we were doing something else and then when the guard come back, he'd snip another wire. And finally he snipped enough so he could push the wire aside and they got off.

Of course, when we had what they called muster, roll call some of us answered for them, but when they started counting, they were short and they kept counting and counting and counting and finally they told us no supper tonight. And we just told them we didn't know where they were. And of course they seen where the wire was cut and they give us a hard time for a while.

But then they got captured about, I guess about a week. And they came back to the same camp that we were. And this one particular man, he was an Australian, he went out to work with us and the guard that was supposed to be guarding him back at the camp, I guess he got reprimanded or something for it, and he told this one Australian something about he's going to keep him working, fill up the car by himself or something like that, and this Australian, I guess he said something to him and the German just pulled out his pistol and shot him and let him drop right there. We tried to get over there to him and he said, "You get over there, I'll shoot you too." So he just left him there and he died. And so we brought his body back and buried him best we could. The guy's name was Shallow Max. I'll never forget it. Never forget that name. They just cold-blooded shot him, just right there.

Cold-blooded murder like this was unusual, but many guards harassed their prisoners. Trudeau still carries a scar from one.

> We had some guards that came back from the Russian front and they were all shot up and wounded and that's what their duty was, guarding us, and they were pretty mean. They would give us some rifle butt every now and then, they'd poke us with their bayonets. In fact, I've got a cut in my side where one morning I just didn't want to get up. I felt bad, I didn't want to go to work or anything and he took his rifle and just poked at me in the bed and I jumped out of bed pretty fast. He was something else.

Captured air crews received better treatment in German POW camps than enlisted men such as Trudeau did. But first they were subject to intense and unsettling interrogation. Lt. Richard McDonald, a B-24 bombardier shot down on his twentieth mission, was even protected from violence by his German guards:

> I was never mistreated by any German person in the outlying sections of Germany, in the countryside. We were threatened in the Frankfurt railway station by a German gentleman who was very irate about the fact that we were killing hundreds of civilian people in the English night raids and our daytime raids against the manufacturing facilities. He was very irate, but our German guard advised him that they were there to protect us. We were put on a train and transported to the interrogation center in Frankfurt.

> They had an interrogation center there. You're put in a single cell with no access to cigarettes or other personnel. You stay in solitary confinement until the interrogator decides to call you in to be interrogated. He spoke English as well as I did. He had been in Chicago and had come to Germany to visit and was immediately taken into the German war machine, German military units, as an interrogator due to the fact that he spoke English so well. I was a 1st lieutenant. The plane I was riding in was a tail-end Charlie [a rear gunner]. I convinced him that the shortness of time in which I had been with the unit precluded me from having any knowledge whatsoever of the operation of the unit or anything that would be of value to him. After discussing my situation with him, convincing him I was not a spy and a saboteur, he then released me and I was transferred to Stalag Luft

180

3 about 30 miles from Berlin at a place called Sagan. There I joined the RAF and the camp under the command of the group commander, which is the equivalent of the colonel in our force.

McDonald was to spend nine months in captivity.

The Germans gave us one bowl of soup a day. We had our food parcels. The Canadians had their hockey sticks, their pucks, and we had quite a large athletic program. We had four companies of actors that put on the old English plays, *Arsenic and Old Lace*, *HMS Pinafore*, *The Importance of Being Earnest*, all these old plays. Costumes were purchased or rented from Berlin and paid for by Americans.

He witnessed what came to be called "The Great Escape" and its aftermath.

Escape activities were highly secret. You were invited to join if you wanted to escape. I had absolutely no desire to escape because I figured the war ought to be over any day – and it should have been. It was a senseless waste of German youth when the Germans can sit in their cities and see 800 to 1,000 bombers blowing the hell out of everything. We were not forced to do anything except follow the rules set down for us. The men escaped through that tunnel, 85 of them. Thirty-five were executed. There were posters in the camp that said if you are caught outside the confines of Stalag Luft 3 POW camp, you will be shot as a saboteur and spy. The Germans mean what they say. It was only after the Swiss got word that they were executing escaped prisoners that that brought it to a halt, and the remainder of the men were released back into the camp. But 35 of them were executed, and had the representatives not intervened, all of the escapees would have been killed.

James Wicker was captured in France on D-Day after his P-38 was shot down on a reconnaissance mission. He was well treated by his German captors, who protected him and other POWs from angry German crowds as they traveled across Germany. While being held temporarily in Chartres, he learned that the war felt very different on the ground than it did in the air.

There I realized what war was really like for an Air Force person who hadn't seen anything but flying at high altitudes. I was in with the D-Day people that had gotten shot up, paratroopers, all people wounded, all types of wounds. We were up in the second or third story of a school building and we saw the bombers coming and all of us were real happy, B-25 bombers, and we saw them coming across and we were all happy to see them bomb the Germans. Then the bomb bay doors opened and we were looking at that and we didn't get happy after that. That changed our idea. And they bombed an area, but they didn't hit where we were at. And that really woke me up to the real war. Army people in the infantry and the ground troops give us a hard time about this because —really being sincere about it — an Air Force person flying until he gets something happens to him, doesn't really know too much about the hazards of being on the ground.

He was interrogated by an officer whose detailed knowledge of Wicker's unit astonished him. Wicker provided only name, rank, and serial number. Then he was sent to the same POW camp where McDonald was held, Stalag Luft 3, near Sagan, Germany. There, unbelievably, he met a friend of his from his hometown.

When you go through the gate, all of them that's already in there come to see who the new people are coming in, and of all things, a fellow come to me right away and he was from my hometown of Monticello, Georgia, which is 2,000 population. After I graduated from flying school, I had heard he got shot down. He was in a B-17 bombardier and I talked to his wife in September of 1943, and she was telling me about him being shot down — and then to go and get shot down myself and go into POW camp and run into him, was something. And he immediately checked me out more or less on being a POW. He got me assigned to his cell. He identified me as a POW. You don't just go into where the young Americans [are] and get accepted because there again, they've got to make sure that you are authentic prisoner of war and not a German stooge that they put me in to get information. And so this made me get identified immediately because he knew me from home.

Food in the camp was scarce.

When I first got there, they got Red Cross packages once a week. They started off getting a whole package and by the time I got there we were only getting half, a package for two people, and as the war went on and got more critical, we got less and less of the packages. The Germans gave us some soup, barley soup and blood sausage and as hungry as I never got where I could eat blood sausage. So I never made that. Anyway, we did get these Red Cross packages and that was a savior for us because they had margarine in them, Spam, which we learned to eat. You could do all kinds of things with Spam and prunes, which were very good. And canned powdered milk. So those things were very good to cook with. And then this stove we got, you had a time. Each cell like I was in had a time to use the stove like 30 minutes, 15 minutes to use it. Life and that, they locked you up at about 10 I think at night, all, everything was out, and they had dogs that roamed around so you couldn't get out. By the way, to get to escape from this prison camp, you had to go before an escape committee that was well organized. And they had to think you had a fair chance of getting out and they would give you all the help then if you could, for example, speak German, and they would give you passes and things to help you.

We had a football team, a baseball team, we had a library, had a chapel. I mean and we did have a chaplain. That was a shock to me. A captain was in that who had been a – captain had been captured and he was our chaplain.

As Russian troops approached in January 1945, the Germans abandoned Stalag Luft 3 and marched the prisoners southward to other camps. Morale among the German guards was poor during this evacuation as their country's defeat appeared to be inevitable, but SS troops maintained their resistance to the approaching Allies. Richard McDonald said that one guard refused SS orders to resist the Allied assault. He was shot as an example.

But the other guards, to my knowledge, never fired a weapon. The SS troopers did put a machine gun unit into one of the steeples in one of the churches, and our 14th Armored personnel shot it up pretty good with their machine guns.

Wicker described the camp's evacuation:

But now come January the 28th, the Russians were approaching our prison camp from the east. The Germans were real concerned that they were going to come in and liberate us. And in this camp, we had roughly 10,000 officers. And the Germans did not want to let us go, and we feel like that they wanted us, to keep us for a bargaining tool. So they evacuated us out and we got notified the night of the 27th about 8:00 or 9:00, and then we were going to have to move, so we packed all we could carry with us and it was snowing outside and I think the temperature was somewhere below 20 degree and snowing. And at 4:30 in the morning we marched out and marched I think for 8 or 10 miles that day and in the snow and with what pack you could carry and what food you could carry. And I don't remember them giving us any food along the way, except what we had. And I was on this road for somewhere around six or eight days before we got in boxcars, and this was some rough times.

A. L. Williams, who had played catcher in high school at Richmond Academy and later rose to become the school's principal, was injured when he bailed out of his B-24, which had caught fire on a bombing run over Kiel, Germany. He was badly burned and injured his leg in his jump. Taken to Stalag 17-B on a freight train, he spent 17 months as a POW. To pass the time there, the men played a lot of cards. He teamed up with Al Volos, another member of his B-24's crew. Together Williams and Volos would play for Red Cross food parcels that contained a pound of powdered milk, corned beef, five packs of cigarettes, and candy. Al was a real gambler.

Yeah, he'd been a member of our crew and he was a good card player. And a group of soldiers came in and they were big braggarts, and… They'd brag about how much they could do around the track. He said he could run that track without stopping. And Volos called him a liar. He bet a parcel, two parcels that he couldn't run around the track. He said he could run around that many times.

The braggart, it turned out, wasn't lying. He ran the whole course without even breaking a sweat. Williams and Volos lost the bet, and Volos felt terrible about it.

We had a meeting and he said, "Willie, we're gonna break up partnerships. That was a bad bet I made." That was a big bet. But

184

I said, "No. Partners when we lose and partners when we win." So we stayed partners all the time we was there.

Williams said that as the end of the war approached, the Germans marched the prisoners to camps farther from the front.

> Well, the Germans didn't want the Russians to liberate us because they'd be captured themselves. They marched us across Austria to keep the Russians from liberating us. Of course my leg was still bothering me and if you couldn't walk, they'd stick a bayonet in you and leave you down on the side of the road to die. I was fortunate. They put me on the back of a wagon. They didn't stick a bayonet in me. I was lucky. And we were in a forest somewhere there in France when Army soldiers belonging to Patton liberated us.

Joe Good, captured during the Bulge, also spent the rest of the war as a POW. German citizens, infuriated by an air raid, nearly killed him.

> Well, life wasn't pleasant. We were hungry and the Germans didn't have anything to eat, and they didn't have anything to give us, so we starved, and at one time I weighed about 115 pounds. And they transported us all over Germany as POWs and I wound up in Poland. We were in a railroad car, pinned up in there. The Germans took off when the Americans raided, and it wasn't Americans, I found out later, that it was Canadian Air Force. And thank goodness they missed the railroad yard where we were locked up, so after the raid was over we got out and they hauled us through and we walked through this village that the bombs from the Canadian planes had actually hit, and I think they would have lynched us, but this lone German private, I guess he was — I was hit in the leg and couldn't keep up with the company column and they stopped, and I think if he hadn't've dropped back and sort of protected me, they would have probably shot me, the civilians would have.

> I ended up in a POW camp in Poland. When the war was over, the Russians come through and liberated the camp. We woke up one morning and the Russians had guards around the place. They wouldn't let us out. The Russians said, "No, we want you to go back by the Black Sea," and the Americans knew we were there and they were sending trucks up the roads to pick us up and [the

Russians] wouldn't let us out. But we knew that the Americans were sending trucks up there, so I went out to the fence and talked to the Russian guard with what Russian and German and what English he knew. He said, "I know about that," and I said, "We want to get out of here, the trucks are going to pick us up." He said, "There's a hole in the fence down there," he said. "Now, if I see you go through that hole, I'll have to shoot you. But when I turn around and walk up the hill and I can't see the hole, then go through the fence."

And that's what I done, got on the road and the truck picked me up. Got on an American truck that they sent by to pick us up and there was about four or five of us and one German. One English officer tried to take over and boss us and somebody told him, "Now look, sir, shut up, because you know we'll throw you out of the truck." He shut up.

Of course, German and Italian troops had been captured during the war as well, and some of them were held as POWs at Camp Gordon in Augusta. They became a familiar sight working on area farms and at the Arsenal. Charles Bowen, who was 8 years old when the war started, used to visit the Arsenal with his father in a jeep, accompanied by a soldier.

They left me in the jeep and I saw the German prisoners, with the POWs plainly on their white uniforms, blue stripes, the whole thing, and it was fascinating to me. And one German in particular looked up and he saw me sitting in that jeep, they were under armed guard – I mean, they had the MPs all around them, and he just watched me, and after a while that became unnerving because I didn't know his intentions. I later perceived that he might have been thinking about a family member back home, maybe a kid brother or somebody, but he finally winked and nodded his head and that took me out of the jeep to the back of the jeep and he just laughed and turned his head, walked off.

It was interesting about the German prisoners of war, they were doing menial labor and assistance at all facilities, Fort Gordon, the processing plant that I talked about, certainly at the Augusta Arsenal, and every now and then one of them would escape and we didn't know how vicious the Germans [would be] when they escaped, so it would alarm the community a little bit until they found them. But they were probably just as petrified as our guys were over there when they were captured.

Bowen remembered the capture of two escaped German prisoners by a member of the "Blue Rinse Club."

> Those were the dear old ladies that were getting the development at that time of putting the blue rinse in their gray hair and they were all in the beauty parlors – well, they were beauty parlors in those days, they weren't fancy salons and this type of thing. But that was the central nervous system, all the news spread – what wasn't in the *Augusta Chronicle* and the *Augusta Herald* was passed through the "Blue Rinse Club."

> But, there was one dear little lady that lived on Milledge Road and she woke up one morning and looked outside, and under one of those fir trees at the back she saw movement and recognized that at that hour in the morning in her backyard could possibly be the two German prisoners, and I think this was recorded in the *Augusta Chronicle*. But she was brave enough to put some donuts together and a couple of cups of coffee and go out that back door by herself and just stand there and offer it to those Germans. Now, they'd been out for two or three days and I imagine those donuts and coffee looked pretty good, and they just did like this and came out and followed her inside. The maid was coming to work about that time and she saw what was happening and went to pieces, but she just told her, she says, "Calm down and call the authorities, call the police and I'm going to keep them here in the kitchen." Well, they put up no resistance, they went with the authorities, but I think they were awfully glad to get the donuts and the coffee.

Victory in Europe

The end of the war in Europe was approaching. April 1, 1945 was Easter Sunday. Army transport pilot Jim Brennan went to Mass at Notre Dame in Paris. The city had been liberated since August, but the American troops had luxuries – like cash and cigarettes – that the Parisians were starved for. Collection plates were passed with an urgency Brennan wasn't used to.

They had the church baskets and they'd say, "S'il vous plait, s'il vous plait." And they got to me and I had about three more days over in Paris that I knew about, and I had a $20 piece of French currency in my pocket. I think it was a 1000-franc note. And they got in front of me and I was with a friend of mine – he was a navigator. I was with him at Mass, and they stood in front of me and banged the crosier and said, "S'il vous plait, s'il vous plait." And I said, "No francs, monsieur." He kind of turned around. He got back over in front of me again, "S'il vous plait, s'il vous plait." On the third time that he did it I reached out and my heavy flight jacket that I had, and I pulled out two packs of Chesterfield cigarettes and I put them in the church basket at Notre Dame Cathedral on Easter Sunday morning in 1945. And he said, "Merci beaucoup, merci beaucoup, merci beaucoup!" They'd cost $20 a pack over there on the black markets, and they got $40 instead of every penny I had in my pocket in cash.

American troops were marching across Germany from the West, the Russians from the East. Still, Hitler did not surrender. On April 12 the Americans received heartbreaking news. Fred Ashhurst remembered that day in a German village:

We went to a little square in the middle of this little small town and the church bells were ringing and the children were being marched to a school by the nuns. And these tiny steps, just like they'd been in a military academy, and the nun walks up to me and said, "Mr. American Sergeant, I wish to sympathize with you. Your president has just died." I looked over at my lieutenant, I told him what she said, "Oh, that's propaganda, don't believe it." Our colonel came down a few minutes later and said he just heard Roosevelt just died over the radio.

But of course the momentum of approaching Allied victory did not slow. German troops surrendered to the Americans, singly or in mass. Lt. Joe Watson of the 75th Division was settling his platoon into a commandeered house in Germany when three young men came by volunteering to help clean the place up.

These three young men came there and wanted to help us, and they were bragging to one of my men in my platoon that could speak French what number of languages they could speak. So they helped us clean up the house. But then, sometime during the night, my jeep driver who was on guard duty said, "Lieutenant, lieutenant," and I got up and went out there. And there were the three young boys in German uniforms, and they wanted to surrender. I asked them why they didn't surrender when we came into town and he said that he knew how nervous and excited people were when they first got in, so they wanted to wait 'til everybody calmed down a little bit.

German troops were desperate to avoid falling into the hands of the conquering Russians, from whom they could expect no mercy. Fred Ashhurst learned how deeply the Germans feared the Russians when he encountered a German officer near the pontoon bridge the Americans were crossing into Germany:

A [German] captain walks down; we were beginning to put Germans in three big prison pens and finally this captain walked down and so I went out to ask him, "You surrendering?" "Yes." So he gave me this dagger on the table. And he said, "I was a captain of JU88 and we bombed that old bridge way over there because we wanted you to get to Berlin before the Russians, so we didn't bomb you. But the SS officer standing back of me might have shot me because they are very strict. He didn't recognize what I was doing. I got by with it."

Such surrenders in face of the Russians' advance were happening not only on the ground. P-51 pilot Fairfield Goodale witnessed whole squadrons of German flyers looking for Americans to surrender to.

At the end of the war we did see columns of Russian troops on horseback riding into German territory, Russian troops with swords and it looked like World War I!

The German squadrons would fly around aimlessly, looking for American pilots to surrender to because the Russians were closing in on them and they did not want any part of surrendering to the Russians. These were squadrons of 20, 25, 30 and they'd waggle their wings when they saw an American pilot and then we'd bring them back to our own home bases and they would land and they'd often pull up their wheels and destroy their engines that way. They were by and large an arrogant lot of people that were not very attractive. Oh, they were frightened to death of the Russians.

189

The Americans were not fans of the Russian army, either. Henry Burch and his outfit had just "married up" with the Russians near Austria:

> We were on the border of the Enns River and the Russians were on the other side. And Patton had given instructions that were not, under any circumstances, to fraternize with the Russians. He didn't like the Russians at all.

In what turned out to be the last days of the war, W. Millwee Owens, a combat officer with the 45th Infantry Division, was given a map of Munich with a blue circle drawn around a building. He was told only, "This is your objective, and you take it."

> And that was it. So we started into Munich and we had some street fighting and nothing really alarming. I don't remember anybody being wounded or killed, and when we got down to this building which we were supposed to take, we took it, but we didn't know what it was. It was just a round blue circle on a map. So when we took it, they had a right good many guards, they were all dressed up and everything, but they didn't put up much resistance. I don't know whether maybe one of two of them got shot, but I didn't see them.

Once the building was secure, Owens had the surprise of his life.

> The building was Hitler's headquarters in Munich, just happened to be where he stayed when he was in Munich. We stayed there about a week until the big brass found out where we were and what we were getting up to, then they came and ran us off.

Owens even slept in Hitler's bed, and he took many "souvenirs" from the building: Hitler's stationery, a table cloth and silver service with Hitler's initials on them, a cigarette case. "I got a right good many things out of it that were his." Unfortunately, after the war, the artifacts, which he had donated, were stolen from a North Carolina museum.

John Taylor of the 106th Division found himself not in Hitler's old headquarters, but staying in the home of an old German couple.

190

They assigned us, me and three other guys, to an older couple's house that had two extra bedrooms and they told the couple that they would let them stay in the house and live their own lives if they let three or four of the military live in with them in the extra bedrooms and they said well, they would. And this couple, the old pop was about 80, I guess, and the mom was just about that old too, so whenever we moved into the bedrooms they more or less adopted us just like we was some of the family, and we had a nice time with them. They would give us little parties at night with beer and this kind of thing. And one night the mom come in just before dark and she said, "MP, MP," hitting her arm here like you're hitting an MP signal over there and, come to find out, Pop had gone to get us a keg of beer up in another village and she wanted us to go with her to locate Pops so the MPs wouldn't pick him up because his curfew time was over with. So we caught him up at a little pig path road coming through an apple orchard, he even had a big smile on his face, you never seen one like it. They was thankful that we saved him and we got back to the house and we had a big beer party that night.

Albert Shaw's unit was in Leipzig at the end. They had come into possession of intoxicating contraband:

While we were there, we ran across a big warehouse full of fine French champagne, so we unloaded two of our 6x6 trucks and loaded up with champagne. So when the war ended, we had one heck of a party, believe me. [My buddy] George and I were not drinkers. But we were celebrating this night, and the last thing I remember about this particular night was this dining room table was trying to spin, and George was holding on one side and I was holding on the other side and we couldn't stop it from spinning. To make a long story short, we were drunker than skunks.

In the days before and after Germany's surrender there was confusion, fighting, injuries, and death. Shaw himself was injured two days before the end of the war in Germany:

We were set up outside of Leipzig just lazing around, waiting for the Russians' advance, and I got hit. We had one shell come in all day, one ID 88, and a piece of shrapnel hit this left hand two days before the war ended. My captain told me, he says,

191

"Albert, you really need to turn that in and we'll put you in for a Purple Heart." I said, "Man, I don't want any Purple Heart now. This war's about to end and I don't want to leave my company and I ain't going nowhere except home."

So they sent me back to a field hospital and the doctor looked at this thing and said, "We're going to have to take this finger off." I said, "Doctor, you ain't about to cut that damn thing off. I can move it." I said, "There's nothing wrong with that finger that time and healing won't cure. Now, if you're going to cut it off, I'm going to get up and walk out of here and I'm going to find me a German doctor that will patch me up." So that's the way I ended the war there.

John Taylor came within inches of disaster:

There was a minefield and I was unlucky enough to walk through the darn thing one time, about six, seven days before the Germans surrendered. I was walking through just a field of grass and so I was stepping along and all the sudden I saw something sticking up about an inch and a half above the ground, looked like a big bolt. So I said, "Oh man, I know what that is." So I . . . moved my foot a little to the right to miss that and I did and I didn't know whether there was any more mines in there or what, but I walked through that thing and didn't another one touch me.

Wes Chitty learned of Germany's impending surrender while on a bombing mission.

The last mission that we went on we were recalled and we were given no reason for the recall. But when we got back we found out later that negotiations were going on for a surrender and that was probably the reason they called us back off the mission. So we all came back home with bomb loads, which we never liked to do.

When surrender was announced, all hell broke loose.

We had a report on May 7 that the war was over. I remember it was dangerous because I think every gunner on the base went out and fired up their .50 calibers and were shooting all up in the air. You'd see nothing but tracers all over the place.

192

Sgt. Lloyd Glisson didn't understand what he was hearing when a German woman told him the war was over.

> A lady came upside of the halftrack I was sitting and she kept talking. We were still fighting. She just came beside the halftrack where we were sitting, waiting on the side of the road there to get over the artillery fire and she said, "The war's over." I said, "I know, it's all over the damn world." "No," she said, "No, it's over." I said, "Well, it's over, it's over." But I hadn't realized that. You know, we were still fighting.

Even after Germany's surrender, some units in the German army did not know the war was over. John Clements was in charge of a unit near the concentration camp at Magdeburg:

> Some of the Germans did not know the war was over and we had an attack in our place in there. This is after the armistice is signed. And we killed two or three of the German soldiers. They thought the war was still going on. And the little village we were in, we went down and rounded up as many of the German civilians as we could find and brought them up and had them walk by and see [the concentration camp prisoners]. Now whether that was the right thing to do or not, I don't know. I also took over a Mercedes-Benz from a German doctor and kept it for a week or two. That upset him.

> There was some anti-aircraft weapons set up in that area and German girls was manning those German anti-aircraft weapons and we captured one of those locations and one of the German girls, after we captured her, wanted to go back and pick up a suitcase and I told her no, and I almost shot her because – suppose they had a hand grenade or something there, see. It turned out it that it was her sanitary napkin she wanted to carry with her.

Even after hostilities ceased, soldiers with time on their hands still found ways to get killed. Albert Shaw and a buddy just barely escaped disaster while taking a joyride in a P-40:

> While we were waiting around after I'd been transferred to this ordnance company, we had lots of time on our hands. And a

buddy of mine from home came by one day and asked me, he says, "Come on, we're going for a plane ride." And I said, "What are you talking about?" He said, "Well, I've got to get in some flying time." So he picked me up, we went out to the airport, and he had an old P-40 out there. And both of us got in this jewel and he was flying around. We had a merry old time, when it conked out on us. It just died on us. And he kept messing with it, trying to get going. He says, "We're going to have to bail out." I said, "Bail, hell." I said, "I've never jumped in my life." He said, "Well, you just stand up in that seat and I'm going to get you out." He said, "Count to five and then pull your cord."

Five never got there. The minute my feet left, I pulled the cord, and it's wonder that I didn't get tangled up in the tail of the thing. But we both landed safely, and the old plane went over and crashed in a beet field and burst into flame. He said, "This damn thing ain't worth trying to save, so we're just going to save ourselves and we're going to get out of here." So that's what we did, and a farmer picked us up and carried us back to town.

Everyone rejoiced that the war was over; but they all knew that it was over only in Europe. Soon many of the troops would be making their way to the Pacific for the inevitable invasion of Japan.

Clockwise from top:
Dennis Trudeau (front row, second from left), with
Canadian paratroopers before D-Day. Albert Shaw
(left), mortar specialist, European campaign. Fairfield
Goodale photographed these victims at the
Buchenwald concentration camp.

Clockwise from top right:
L.W. "Robbie" Robinson, Navy Hellcat pilot, who became an "ace" by shooting down five Japanese airplanes. Gould Hagler at the Joan of Arc statue, Orleans, France. Olander "Jack" Barrett, 80th Division. Charles Beason, 4th Infantry Division, Christmas 1944, Battle of the Bulge. Lewis "Pop" Newman (front row, center) with his B-17 crew. Photo by Bill Britton of released POWs, Omuta, Japan, September 1945.

Clockwise from top:
James E. Wicker (front row, left) with fellow
ex-POWs during repatriation from Germany. Photo
by Hugh Bedingfield of Kamikaze attack on
battleship USS California. Ray Lundquist (on right),
navigator on B-24 "Whoda Thunkit," Lecce, Italy,
June 1944.

Clockwise from top:
Future Georgia Governor Carl Sanders (second from right) with parents and members of his B-17 crew during a visit home, 1945. Lou Brissie, March 1944, at Montecatina, Italy. Robert "Sarge" Carstaphen, 94th Division, after knocking out three German machine gun nests in France.

Chapter 5
War in the Pacific, Part I: Midway to the Philippines

Overview

Fewer Americans died in combat in the Pacific than in the European theater—about 100,000 fewer—but the fight for each yard of territory was if anything more bitter than in Europe.

It is not hard to see why. The hostility between America and Japan was far deeper than between America and Germany. Racial difference was a longstanding factor. Americans had feared a Japanese attack as early as World War I. Japan and America were at loggerheads over dominance in East Asia, including the annexation of the Philippines by America in 1898 and the future of China. Japan annexed Chinese Manchuria in 1931 and began a campaign of conquest in 1937, which the United States opposed. Unlike Germany, Japan had launched a direct attack on the United States at Pearl Harbor. Once the war was joined, America found itself fighting against a foe who simply did not accept surrender—on either side.

Trying to deter further Japanese or "Jap" aggression, the United States moved its Pacific Fleet from the west coast to Pearl Harbor in 1941. Aggressive elements in Japan saw this as both a threat and an opportunity. Of Japan's four likely opponents in a major Pacific war, three (Soviet Russia, Britain, and France) were fully engaged in the war against Hitler. The American-controlled Philippine islands sat astride Japan's contemplated path of expansion, toward the oil-rich Dutch East Indies. Japanese engineers had just invented an improved torpedo which, among other factors, made the attack on Pearl Harbor possible.

The infamous surprise attack of December 7, 1941, killed some 2,500 Americans (including civilians) and disabled much of the Pacific Fleet and the Army Air Forces stationed in Hawaii. This enabled Japan to sweep southwards, overrunning the Philippines and British and Dutch territories in Malaya and the East Indies. However, Pearl Harbor was also a Japanese failure. The U.S. aircraft carriers were out to sea; the shallowness of the harbor meant that many warships could later be salvaged, and the port facilities were not destroyed. The U.S. lost only two capital ships permanently—the Arizona and the Oklahoma. This may explain why the flow of the war changed so dramatically within a year.

The United States launched a bombing raid on Tokyo in April 1942, as much to raise Allied morale as to inflict damage. As a response, Japan planned a naval operation to lure the Pacific Fleet into battle and destroy it. First, however, Japanese forces had to complete their conquest of the huge island of New Guinea, where they were fighting against Australian and (later) American ground forces. Japan opted for an amphibious landing at Port Moresby, Australia's main base on New Guinea, but the American navy intercepted the Japanese fleet at the Battle of the Coral Sea (May 1942), the first naval battle fought purely by aircraft. The battle was a draw, but it foiled Japan's plans for New Guinea and Australia.

The Imperial Japanese Navy then executed its massively complex plan to draw the Pacific Fleet into battle near the American-held central Pacific island of Midway (June 1942). A critical part of the Japanese plan was to attack Midway and then wait for the Pacific Fleet to counterattack. However, American naval intelligence had broken the Japanese naval code and the American carriers were already present. This seesaw battle ended with the loss of four Japanese carriers against one American, a disaster from which the Imperial Navy never completely recovered. Japan was now on the defensive.

Midway and the Solomons

Curby Smith served as a Boatswain's Mate 2nd Class on the *USS Hornet*, the aircraft carrier that carried Dolittle's raiders to Tokyo. He describes the stressful conditions on board during the three-day battle at Midway, including no rest and scant food:

> You didn't go eat. No, no. In the three days at Midway, you didn't go eat. [We had] a couple of sandwiches. And we ate all the potatoes and carrots—on the fantail, we ate all those raw. Raw potatoes are not very good unless you're hungry.

Smith also describes the kind of accident that was all too frequent on busy ships under battle conditions:

> Every plane had men on each side holding the lines tight to keep it from bouncing off the ship. And when [a sailor] took the line loose, we went into what we called—sailors call a trough. And it lunged and he reached out to catch something to keep from falling, and he stuck his arm right through the prop and it cut it off.

Once the United States gained the initiative against Japan, it set out to capture numerous Pacific islands. The so-called "island-hopping" campaign, which began at Guadalcanal in August 1942, was incredibly bloody. The islands were heavily manned and fortified. Many provided no shelter for attacking troops. There was no room for maneuver. Attacking units sometimes suffered casualty rates of 80%. Japanese soldiers rarely surrendered. Americans soon realized that if their own troops surrendered, they could expect no mercy from the Japanese. The only way to take the war closer to Japan was to attack Japanese commerce with submarines, but this was highly dangerous; one third of the American submarines that went into the western Pacific did not return.

New Guinea became a site for heavy fighting fairly early in the war. The bitterness of the fighting is demonstrated by the fact that the Japanese would lose over a hundred thousand troops, battling across the mountainous Kokoda Trail to drive the Australians off the island. American naval forces at the Battle of the Coral Sea blocked a seaborne Japanese invasion in May of 1942, which was followed by troops under Douglas MacArthur contesting for control of the northern coast of New Guinea.

The next phase was a series of landings in the Solomon Islands, starting with Guadalcanal in August of 1942. That island was not secured until February of 1943 when the Japanese finally evacuated their surviving forces.

Curby Smith was still aboard the *USS Hornet* when it engaged the Japanese navy in the Battle of the Santa Cruz Islands (October 26, 1942) during the Guadalcanal campaign. He describes the *Hornet* attempting to fend off Japanese fighter planes and dive bombers:

> [We heard] rumors that the Japs were liable to bomb us anytime. But from about 9 o'clock that morning through the rest of the day, I don't know what happened. I was all, you might say, in a daze. They came in and bombed the hell out of us and were gone for a couple of hours and came back.
>
> Torpedo planes are what did the damage. The only time in my six years in the Navy that I thought I was fixing to die … here was a torpedo plane coming down right into the gun gallery, he flew over my head, and he hit the flight deck on the other side.
>
> A bomb is what killed the men below deck, it killed some, but there was one that hit the flight deck. Then the bombs exploded. When the first one hit, we knew then we was hit, and that's what killed so many. And there was all the men, some of them blown off, their legs was blown off, it was terrible.

201

The *Hornet*, listing heavily and on fire, was in trouble. Though the *USS Northampton* attempted to tow her to safety, the Japanese strafing was too dangerous. Soon the *Hornet* began to sink. Smith describes the terrifying ordeal of abandoning ship:

> There was a lieutenant commander, the executive officer, second in command. He said, "Boys, she was a good ship, but let's get the hell off of her now," so in the water we went. It seemed like [we were out there] forever. My best friend said, "That sun's fixing to go down and I'll be damned if I want to spend a night out here."

Smith survived the sinking of the *Hornet*, but 140 sailors did not.

Navy Gunner's Mate 2nd Class Leonard Gunter served on LST 398 [Landing Ship, Tank], landing troops in various battles during the Solomons campaign in 1943. LST 398 barely missed being hit by a torpedo as it brought troops of the Army's 25th Infantry Division onto the beaches during the invasion of Vella Lavella in August 1943:

> [This] kid, would be younger than I was, must have lied to get in the Navy. He said what's that thing going yonder? I said, well, that's a torpedo one of them planes dropped. And it missed us. But anyway the [ship] next to us, it was further along than we were and it got hit. No troops got off of it, but seven or eight people I think got off the ship.

In November 1943 Gunter and LST 398 landed troops on Bougainville. Under fire from Japanese aircraft and mortars, LST 398 became immobilized near the beach until she was towed to safety. Gunter was slightly wounded:

> Well, there's a beautiful volcano up on the mountain on Bougainville. We didn't have no searchlights or nothing on us— we went in at daylight. But we had planes that [attacked] us, once we [were] trying to get the men down on the beach and we had mortars flying at us. There's planes coming in towards the fantail from some of them other islands after us. Not just the [boat] I was on, all of them. And I turned that 40-millimeter I was on. I told the boy to train that on the beach. I said that's when you can see that mortar when it's [firing]. We turned it on it. About that

time, I don't know who, somebody or else one of them LSTs knocked it out.

At this point in time you were a sitting duck, but [we] finally got a tow, they got us off that beach. [But then the Japanese] had strafers and dropped bombs [on] us. And we had wounded, too. When you got out in deeper water [we] cranked the door up and got some pumps to pump the water that [came] in and went back to Guadalcanal with the door open. Went all the way back to Guadalcanal like that.

I think there was seven of us killed, I might be wrong, and a good many casualties. Those fellows that got wounded on the gun, none died that was on that gun. There was shrapnel in all of them mostly. I got scratched across the head with a piece of shrapnel. I didn't know it. And a soldier said, "Well, you're hurt too." I said "No I ain't hurt." And he took his hands and he wiped and he looked at me and he says "I'll be damned. That thing done scratched you and went across your head. The skipper says you deserve [a Purple Heart], too." I says "Do I have to take it, because there ain't nothing wrong with me. There's something wrong with them fellows that was down on that floor."

Marine PFC Rufus Belding landed on Bougainville with the 21st Regiment of the 3rd Division, in November 1943. He recalls repelling nighttime "banzai" attacks:

We landed on Augustus Bay. We wasn't in the first wave, we was maybe two weeks later. The 17th Marines or something had already hit it and established a beachhead, a perimeter, and the CB [Seabees] was already building the airfield and we were to guard the perimeter for a while there.

I had a machine gun—water cooled .30 caliber. At night the Japs would try to make a break and come in and we just wrecked the whole field out there. But you didn't know whether you killed anybody or not. You just kept them at bay. They screamed, "Die, marine, die!" I was a young fella, it unnerved me. I didn't want to die, but still at the same time it was either kill or be killed.

A few weeks later into the Bougainville campaign, Belding and the 21st Marine Regiment took "Hellzapoppin Ridge." Belding recalls the

American artillery coming a bit too close for comfort, a fortuitous earthquake, and the aftermath of the attack:

> They were dug in on every hill there. And there was one called Hellzapoppin Ridge that we tried for days to take and every time we'd get half way up it they'd drive us back. And so one night they said they was going to shell it [with] 105mm howitzers from the beach and the 100 pound bombs was going to be dropped on it and hopefully we could take it the next morning. We had dug a foxhole and got into it because those 105 Howitzers, friendly Howitzers, [were] coming [in] from the beach. And one of them hit a tree just above where I was at and that whole tree came down on top of me and my buddy. I forget his name, but he got half his ankle blown off by shrapnel and I got my ears tore up. And I couldn't hear for two days, but he left and went back to somewhere else, I didn't see him again and my ears cleared up and I stayed.

> We took the hill. There was a volcano on the other side of the island and you could see it smoking every night. And that morning, just at daybreak we had an earthquake and didn't know what it was. Trees and everything was shaking and we realized when we looked over on the other side you could see the volcano and it was really blowing off. And intelligence tells us that [the Japanese] were superstitious about volcanos and earthquakes and they left. And by the time we pulled up to the top of the hill, Hellzapoppin Ridge, you could see them going in the woods over yonder about 700 yards. So they just went on back to the other side of the island I guess.

> We stayed there a while longer and mopped up. We found 1,200 Japs dead on that hill. I remember walking into them because you could see the holes where they had caves in there and arms sticking out and the legs sticking out and we'd pull them out. All of them had sake in there sack, whiskey.

> We didn't take prisoners. You don't ask the guy will he be a prisoner. You just shoot him. That was the roughest island I had ever seen, Guam was nothing but a picnic.

Boatswain's Mate 1st class Paul Harless was fending off Japanese planes aboard the destroyer *USS John Rodgers* during the naval Battle of Empress Augusta Bay (November 2, 1943) off the coast of Bougainville:

> That's where we had our first fight. It was a night fight. [We had] four destroyers and two cruisers. There was a [Japanese] plane that flew around us all afternoon. We knew it was a [scout] plane and we didn't have any air coverage. And we knew they were coming, so just before dark, why they did come. Torpedo bombers and dive bombers and we estimated between 35 and 40 of them. And we had quite a little excitement maneuvering and so forth, from about 6 in the evening until about 2 the next morning. We would dodge from one rain cloud to another and finally one of the cruisers got hit, and we had to slow down for them to make repairs, but that was the only one that [was hit]. That's when we shot down our first plane. We did get straddled by a bomb and a torpedo at the same time, [but] was fortunate they didn't touch us.

Lt. Clarence Smith served with the VP-81 patrol squadron as a Navigator on a PBY Catalina flying boat charged with reducing the remnants of Japanese resistance at the tail end of the Bougainville campaign, April 1944. Here he describes the sorry state of the Japanese troops and his squadron's tactics:

> In the one massive bombing mission that we were all on, there was one particular island and they had grown gardens, because the Japs were starving. We were isolating them. It was cruel, but that's what happens. The idea was to get rid of the gardens, so they called on us and some other airplanes. [We used] napalm so we pretty much left that devastated. That was on the other side of Bougainville.

Navy cook Clifford Dickey was on LCI-L-223 (Landing Craft Infantry, Large) in the Pacific. Here he describes his interesting interactions with the natives of the Solomon Islands—especially what they liked to eat:

> There was another interesting thing, the natives hung around the landing area and when they got ready to eat, they'd take a hand grenade—hand grenades were piled everywhere—and go out into shallow water and lob it as far as they could and the concussion would kill a lot of fish and they'd gather them up and come back with eight or ten fish and just run a sharp stick

through them, and hold them over the fire and roast them on both sides and then they'd peel off the skin and scales and ate [them], no salt, no pepper. That would be their meal and they was perfectly happy with that.

By the way, those islanders—the Solomon Islands I think— was under the protection of England prior to World War II, so [there were] English missionaries on some of them. Most of the [native islanders] were cannibals also and England had been working for some years trying to convert [them]. One of them could speak fairly good English that he had learned from missionaries and [one of our crew] asked him had he ever been a cannibal and he said, "Oh yeah, I eat men, a lot of times." And I said, "Did you ever eat a white man?" And he said, "Only one time, he's too bitter, I don't like white man." So I guess being white was an advantage down there.

Dickey was also a keen observer of social practices aboard his own ship:

Another little interesting story. We integrated long before Truman required the military to integrate. At first it was total segregation in all of the military and I guess when Truman become President he stopped all that, but that one lone black mess boy had separate quarters on the landing craft. Everybody liked him, we got along real well together, so he would eat and play poker with us, but it come time to go to bed he had to go his quarters. Collectively we went to the skipper and said, "You know, we got an empty bunk here in crew's quarters, why make him go over there?" He did dread going over there by himself because with the sounds at night by yourself [being on a ship] is kind of weird. So that was the happiest young black I've seen when we went to him and said, "Well, the skipper told us it's up to you fellas, if it suits y'all it suits me." So we said, "Go get your stuff and move in the bed down there." And that was the happiest one black boy I've ever known too when he moved into the crew's quarters with us. So we was ahead of Truman on that.

Dickey describes how he became a cook, and the importance of good food and ready coffee for the 188 men aboard:

They assigned me to this landing craft at 11 o'clock and I'd never cooked a breakfast or an evening meal, and I never even cooked a lunch. But fortunately the cook aboard that ship was so bad [that] the skipper told me to go down and tell him [to get] off the ship within the hour and I said, "How about letting him serve the lunch he's prepared?" He said, "Nope, I want him off now." [He] said he's about to create a mutiny on this ship and said he is so lousy and does such a poor job, said the crew is up in arms. So talking about being fortunate, following somebody that bad they thought I was good, and I didn't know much of anything. The beauty of doing it on a ship, if it doesn't come out, you throw over the side and you try again.

You had to have coffee in the Navy, always had to be a coffee pot on. [Everyone in the] Navy was allowed to take a ten minute break every hour for coffee, everywhere. Coffee had to be there the whole time.

Army PFC Jim Robbins, with the 951st Anti-Aircraft Battalion, spent over seven months on Bougainville in 1943. In addition to the dangers of combat, often the soldier's greatest enemy was the jungle environment:

There was green blow flies by the millions, billions everywhere. They brought our lunch in the canisters on the trucks. And we tried to eat and some of the guys were so disgusted with the flies they threw their lunch kit away. There's a lot of dirty, unpleasant circumstances that people don't even know about.

That environment often included bad weather. Robbins describes a trip aboard an LST between different islands in the Solomons:

We got into the storm between Guadalcanal and Bougainville. We lost our lifeboats. A cable broke loose on the ship, beat up against the ship, and beat the lifeboats up against the ship and knocked them all apart. [We] cut them loose and cut them adrift.

The LST is about 400 foot long. They're built like a bathtub. There was four guns on the deck of the LST lashed down with chains and locked in on the deck of the ship. That night during the storm when they come up on top of a ground swell both ends would be out of the water and when they dip off and go back down in the trough of the wave, when the propeller of it started digging back in, it would go fuff. It hit first and then you'd get all this vibration. Sound like the ship was going to fly apart. You're hanging onto anything—hanging on the side of a bunk or wherever you was at and try to make everything stay together. That's the most unpleasant morning I think I spent the whole time I was in the service.

China-Burma-India Theater

The "CBI" theater contained two widely separated regions connected tenuously by supply lines running through Burma. The Japanese attempt to conquer China had begun in 1937. After Japan expanded the war in December of 1941, Japanese forces invaded British possessions in Malaya and Burma and attempted to invade India as well. Most of the forces in this area were British, but there were a number of American participants, including the "Flying Tigers" (a volunteer American unit opposing the Japanese air force in China), the aerial units flying supplies across "the hump" of the Himalayas, and special units like "Merrill's Marauders" in Burma.

Army Technical Sgt. Willard Blankenship, a member of Merrill's Marauders (officially, the 5307th Composite Unit, a special operations force tasked with long-range missions behind enemy lines in the spring of 1944), describes the kind of odd moment that could occur in the unpredictable jungle fighting:

> I had five canteens and I went down to the stream to fill them damn things and I left my rifle and I walked down to fill my canteens and I looked over across the stream and a damn nip [was] sitting on the other side and he had his canteens. I looked at that son of a bitch and he looked at me. He got up and went up back to his side of the hill and I got up and went up back to my side of the hill. Those types of things could happen. The trail would grow up on you so quick, you'd go through it and it'd be gone the next day.

1st Lt. Wyndham Manning, B-24 pilot in the 14th Air Force, flew 99 missions in the CBI theater. Here he describes his plane's accidental downing of a P-51:

> One time we were pulled out of China and sent down to Calcutta [India]. We'd go on missions in Burma. I was breaking in a new crew. We went down to bomb that place and going over the bay before getting to Rangoon [Burma], the Japanese started coming

in and one plane came from the rear. I never saw the plane, the top-gunner told me, "Lieutenant, there's a zero at 12:00." I said, "Shoot him down." I still never saw him, but they claim he shot him down and it turned out to be a P-51—uh-oh. The Air Force got a PBY in that area, before we even got there. So they scooped down and picked up the pilot and he was home before we were.

Manning then describes a mission he'll never forget:

> We had a night mission in bad weather in Hong Kong. And our prime function was to lay magnetic mines in the Hong Kong harbor. We were flying a diversionary mission at 12,000 or 13,000 feet. The planes laying mines, of course, were down about 100 to 200 feet above the water.

Manning's plane hit a violent thunderstorm and got disoriented. The crew jettisoned their bombs and bailed out. Manning describes the scene:

> We bailed out at 2:30 in the morning. The navigator and the radio operator couldn't make their connections. We bailed out in a string of about five miles long.

> [The crew] were very calm about it, probably calmer than me. But there was one little gunner up there, I don't believe he could have been 14 years old, came apparently from Mexico and he was looking down at the clouds below us. The airplane lights kind of made the clouds below us shine up a little bit. And I said, "Son, you better jump." He said, "No sir, you jump first, Lieutenant, and then I'll follow." Well, he was frozen. So I just put my foot under his behind and pushed him on out and then I jumped. But I knew how he felt.

When Manning landed he hurt his left leg. He was alone, and only had his "side arm, a little package with some Chinese money, some sulfa dust for wounds, morphine." Luckily he landed in friendly territory. He quickly came across a group of Lolos, an ethnic Chinese minority. Manning spoke very little Chinese, and of course the Lolos spoke no English, but they were hospitable (to an extent) and helped him return to U.S. lines:

> Our first meal that morning, it was rather chilly because it was November, they threw a chicken in a big pot of scalding water

and left it in there for about 20 minutes and then pulled him out and said, "Just take the feathers off and just eat what you want to." I ate a chocolate bar that morning.

[The Chinese] went out and cut [some] bamboo, probably four inches in diameter, and they made a contraption like a sedan chair. And these little people, they just steady trot all day long, carried us up and down these mountains. I mean I couldn't even walk.

Manning's parents were at first notified that he was Missing in Action. Twelve days later they learned he was safe. Not all the men on the mission were so lucky:

There were 13 [planes on the mission] as I recall, four of us got disoriented and lost our way trying to get home. Two of the planes [landed] in Japanese territory and the crews were executed the next day. Two of us got out and walked home, like I did.

Manning also had an encounter with Major General Claire Chennault, commanding officer of the famous "Flying Tigers":

We had a baseball team that our colonel, commanding officer was on and they used to play the Air Force team which General Chennault played on. And I remember one time I was walking past the game, I didn't care for baseball, but my colonel called me over and said, "You are going to be the umpire for this game." It came time for General Chennault to get up to bat and he made three strikes and I called him out. And my colonel said, "Manning, you are through."

1st Lt. James Kauffmann, a B-24 pilot in the 10th Air Force, 8th Photo Reconnaissance Group, describes the important work of aerial mapping over the often treacherous mountainous terrain known as "the hump" of the CBI:

Well, mapping is taking pictures, and they had a way that they could actually tell you how high a tree was or a hill was or whatever. They would transpose this to a topographic map and those maps would be used if we had to invade or have people in that area. We did a lot of mapping of course on the Malay

Peninsula and in China of tides. You'd be surprised how often we made maps of tides. And of course, the time element was something else. The amount of tides with the moon phases, all of that was taken into consideration and they could see how high it came or how low it went. And the purpose of that was for [possible] invasion problems.

We had an F-7 [a B-24 adapted for photo reconnaissance] that had strobe lights in it used for night photography. It didn't make any difference what altitude; it was proficient at 20,000-25,000 feet. And when those lights went off, of course it was synchronized with the cameras. They would take pictures down below and it was used a lot for Japanese troop movement on the Burma Road and I flew quite a few missions with it.

When that thing went off, you could look out the cockpit or wherever you could see and just count the number of trucks or whatever was on the Burma Road. [We flew into] a gorge or river, followed the river pretty much all the way through there. The first time that I went across "the hump," you're flying alone and you're looking down. You're seeing mountains everywhere and you look over to the side and you look up and you see nothing but mountains. They're high.

PFC Galen Freeman was an Army Air Force mechanic stationed in the town of Changyi, southern China, and enjoyed getting to know the people there:

We'd go to Kunming once in a while. Also a little town, Changyi, very small, three or four restaurants, off limits, service people couldn't go in and get a good meal because it had to be inspected by Air Force authorities.

I was treated like a king over there, because I respected the people, they're hard working people and it's not the easiest thing in the world to make a good living at that time, in that area.

Marshall Islands and New Guinea

PFC Chester McCoy of the 4th Marine Division came ashore at Kwajalein Atoll on January 31, 1944, as part of the Marshall Islands campaign. He served in the same division as Medal of Honor recipient

Jimmy Dyess of Augusta, who was killed on Roi-Namur, just north of Kwajalein, on February 2. Actor Lee Marvin also served with the 4th Division (24th Regiment), earning the Purple Heart later at Saipan. McCoy was in the second wave of the invasion, and describes coming upon both American and Japanese dead and the prevalence of friendly-fire incidents:

> When I got there, there was bodies laying everywhere. Now, a lot of these bodies wasn't Marines, they were the enemy. [We] had bombarded several days before we got there. But the thing that I tried to get away from was the dead bodies and the smell, the stink. There's nothing to me that smells any worse than a dead body. It's something that you don't forget. But I didn't have that much trouble getting on [the beach], because I was in the second wave. The first wave had a good bit. The 24th Marines, they had the roughest part to land. That's where most of the fighting was. We fought that night. I would say half the wounded was from enemy fire. That was our first operation. Everybody was gun-happy. Anything that moved got shot. And that was our first night in operation, and there's no doubt in my mind that the enemy wasn't our main problem that night, it was friendly fire.

Outnumbered and out-supplied, the Japanese often resorted to desperate tactics, so the Marines could not afford to be careless.

> During the night, the Japanese, when you hemmed them up, would always call a banzai attack. That is when the Japanese think that's their last hope. They give it everything they've got— and if you could stand that banzai attack, then you've got it made. During the night they made a banzai attack, and we shot most of them. And no doubt in my mind, we shot some that shouldn't have been shot. There was a lot of natives on the island, and if they moved, they got shot. In the Marine Corps, one thing they taught you, you don't take any prisoners. We don't need prisoners.

McCoy's attempt to escape briefly the brutalities of combat was dangerous in itself:

> We got through the night and the next day. During the night it was so rough that you [couldn't] overcome the stink. But the next day you'd look around after [we] had the island secured. It

212

was sickening. I went down to this beach and took most of my clothes off and just got out into the water. I got caught in an undertow and I went out a little too far. That's when [my] Marine Corps training came in. I knew I couldn't make it back on my own, so I just floated. I just laid on my back and stroked my way back in. But that was one of the awful-est nights that I've ever spent in the Marine Corps.

Ensign Bill Prout, quartermaster on PT-191, a small but fast attack boat, participated in the invasion of New Guinea. Here he describes an action off the Huon peninsula, September 30, 1943, when his PT boat engaged the enemy on the shore and helped rescue another PT boat that had been stranded:

Let me tell you about what I thought was the greatest thing we'd ever done. We'd moved up to Dreger Harbor, and every place we went to, we went out and commandeered an island. We didn't dock at the base like everybody else. The PT-192 boat docked with us and the YMS [minesweeper] docked with us, and we would build a camp and sleep on the beach. There wasn't anybody else out there. And one night we were patrolling with the PT-68 boat which came out of the Philippines. It had a very poor turn radius on its propellers. We had about a 35-degree turn radius. Their engines weren't very big, either.

So we were out in the ocean. We see coming around the beach two barges. We take out after them, and we go around the cove where they're going in and we sink the first one. We swing around, we sink the second one. We swing around and there's another one sitting on a sandbar over there, which happens to be PT-68. Well, we started a fire on the beach—how, we don't know. But after a while we're trying to pull the PT-68 off the sandbar. We couldn't do it. We broke all our ropes. We were doing this for a long period of time, and all of a sudden [the Japanese] had probably a 37-millimeter and a caisson and they begin to shoot at us. The PT boat's here in the middle of this cove and we decided we've got to do something. So we backed that PT boat up, we turned the port gun over there to where that caisson is. We put the starboard engine forward, the port engine back, and we'd start to turn. All of our guns except one can fire over the starboard side, and we started [firing at] that beach all the way down and we wiped out a lot of Japanese on the beach.

We saw a fire over there. It wasn't ammunition. What it was, I have no idea. But we could see that fire over 35 miles away. It was something the Air Force had been looking for and couldn't find, and we stumbled onto it. And a lot of things like that happened in the war. I guess heroes usually stumble into trouble and get out of it, and that one happened.

On the morning of December 27, 1943, PT-191, along with PT-190, fought a battle with Japanese aircraft along the New Britain coast. Prout's boat was heavily damaged, many of the crew (including Prout himself) being wounded. With the help of PT-190, Prout and the rest of the PT-191 crew were towed back to base at New Guinea:

It's 9:30 in the morning. We looked up into the sky and she's filled with Japanese airplanes, and we estimate there's 38 or more of them up there. That's not counting the two-engine bombers. And they came down, started to bomb us, and didn't do very well. They dropped every bomb they had. They would glide in at a 45-degree angle and let those bombs drop at about 500 feet, and we would turn away from them. They blew a hole in our gas tank. They put a lot of bullet holes down the side of [the boat]. The fellow firing the 20-millimeter on the fantail, a bullet went in his helmet, went around, took both of his ears off. [Another sailor] who was loading the 20-millimeter magazine for him, a bullet hit that thing, blew it up in his face. He was just blood from here all the way down. Barton, who was firing the port gun, they got him, shot his gun belt off, and all it did was just bruise his belly. We also noticed there were several bullet holes in the 20-millimeter where Peterson was firing. I was up firing the [machine] gun and there was a string of bullets down beneath me, and I didn't get hurt.

The skipper who was in the cockpit got hurt. A bullet went right through [him], pushed his liver aside, and came out the back. Fred Calhoun, the assistant, got shot in the rear end. At this point, I'm firing the forward twin 50 and instinct says, go to the cockpit. So I go back there and I'm steering the boat. [Captain] Ewing, he kept saying, "Give me a drink of water." I said, "Skipper, you're not getting your drink of water. You're shot in the stomach." And that was it.

214

Then we limped all the way home to New Guinea on one engine, and we had some assistance from the 190 boat that was also with us. So they took the wounded off and we sat on the bow of the PT boat, reminiscing what was happening so far. And as we're doing that and saying, well, we think they're all going to live, the Japanese raid the air strip at Dreger Harbour, and all of the people on the base want us to go into the dugouts. We wouldn't go. So I went down to the medicine cabinet and I broke the lock on it, and for medicinal purposes, there were little bottles of alcohol and everybody got one. And I, being a teetotaler, I still drank that thing, so don't tell all my children about that. [Then] we went to Australia, Brisbane, and I had to go to a doctor. He took a piece of steel out of my eye, and I didn't get a Purple Heart for that. He said it's not bleeding.

Army nurse Evelyn Landreth was working in the 60th General Hospital on New Guinea. Her commanding officer's duties apparently included protecting the morals of the nurses in his unit:

The enlisted men had built a hut for a recreation room and they wanted to have an opening party, so Colonel Todd, our CO, allowed the enlisted men to invite the nurses and I was one of them that went, [we] had a wonderful time. But a day or two later the wrath of the base commander came down on Colonel Todd, and relieved him of his command because he had allowed the nurses to come to their opening party. And everybody felt real bad about it.

Chief signalman Jack Sloan, aboard the destroyer *USS Swanson*, was in action near the Admiralty Islands in March 1944 as part of the New Guinea campaign. Here he describes the leadership ability of Lt. John Lindsay, gunnery officer on the *Swanson* and future mayor of New York City:

MacArthur had been told in the Admiralty Islands that the Japanese had evacuated their 5,000 troops and they were no longer there. MacArthur ordered 12 of us destroyers to take 200 men up to the Admiralty Islands. They did get some landing craft there and so we let them ashore and we were directing gunfire because the Japanese hadn't evacuated, they just hid in the bushes. And MacArthur ordered 1,000 troops in, 1st Calvary Division dismounted and 5,000 Japs were there attacking our

215

troops and we were shooting every 5-inch .38 around the clock, 24 hours a day. John Lindsay volunteered to go ashore and be with the troops and direct our gunfire and when he came back after a week there he stunk to high heaven. I met him down on the main deck when he came aboard and he said, "I want to see the captain." I said, "You ought to take a bath first." He said, "I'll see the captain."

Sloan was later made an officer for work on LORAN, the Navy's new long-range radio navigation system, which stayed in use until the late 20th century.

The Marianas: Saipan to Peleliu

By the summer of 1944, however, the net was closing. Japan was hopelessly overstretched, fighting the Americans in the Pacific, the British in the Indian Ocean theater, and the Chinese on the mainland. In June of 1944 American forces began their assault on Saipan in the Mariana Islands, which the Japanese regarded as their outer defensive perimeter. Saipan fell after extremely heavy fighting—the Americans suffered nearly 14,000 casualties. More importantly, perhaps, was that the Japanese navy launched a massive attack which failed completely, costing it some 420 aircraft and virtually crippling Japanese naval air power. General Hideki Tojo, who had led Japan into war, was forced to resign.

Chester McCoy, a Marine veteran of the February 1944 battle for Kwajalein, and now a corporal, was in the first wave of troops landing on Saipan, a battle that lasted from June 15 to July 9, 1944. He describes the intensity of the fighting and being wounded:

> We went in and there was dead bodies everywhere. And this wasn't the enemy, this was the Marines.

> [On] the first wave, we really get knocked off. We did get in far enough to dig in, to fight. And I remember laying there, though, and [our] planes was still bombing. We put flags out as far as we could advance, and the planes were [bombing] beyond the flags we put out. But in the meantime, the enemy planes came, and they was warning me to lay there in that foxhole. I always remember the little P-38s knocking the enemy planes out. We advanced a little each day. And again, we shot everything that

moved, and I'm sure that we shot some native people that actually shouldn't have been shot.

When I was wounded on the third day [of the battle], I was jammed up behind a brick outhouse, and I still got hurt. I leaned against it and I got it in the hip. I had five pieces of shrapnel, so that was the last of my time on the island. I was knocked out temporarily. The corpsman got to me and they put me on a stretcher and carried me back to headquarters, where I stayed until they'd taken it onto the beach.

They showed me the pictures of my wound where it went in, it just knocked a big hole. And they didn't take the shrapnel out, they told me it would never bother me, it would work its way out. There was one large piece. The rest of them were really small. When I got out, I used to fly a good bit, and every time I'd go they'd say, you know you've got shrapnel. And I said, yep. But it's worked its way out.

Corporal Pat Roberts earned three Purple Hearts during his service with the 2nd Marine Division. He describes landing on Saipan, the desperate fighting to establish a beachhead, being wounded by shrapnel, and the mass suicides of civilians and Japanese soldiers:

They called us, told us what our number was and we would report to the cargo net on a certain side of the ship. I never will forget, there was two cans of plums and I put them in my pack. We went aboard and got on the cargo net and we went down and got in the Higgins Boat. We made a big circle out in the ocean, humungous circle, I don't know how many boats, but there was hundreds of them and then they lined up all side-by-side to go into the beach. And the Higgins Boats got hung on the coral reef and the Japanese were able to drop mortars right in the boats with the men and in fact we were just sitting ducks really. So they pulled us out of there, took us off the Higgins Boats and put us on amphibious tanks and we went in and made the landing.

The first day and the first night we were on the beach I dug a foxhole in the sand and every time a wave would come in [water] would go in my foxhole, so I was continuously trying to get the foxhole a little bit deeper, pushing the sand out.

They sent the second wave in and for two or three days there it was just fierce fighting on the beach—we didn't move 40 yards out from the beach. That was as far as we could get, but as far as I could see to my right and far as I could see to my left there were dead Marines and Japs — Japanese piled up just like cordwood, bodies floating all over the water everywhere.

I don't know where this shell came from, but it was a humungous shell. There was three of us, we were staggered formation, one here, one here and one there like a diamond formation and the shell fell between the three of us and it blew the other two to smithereens, there was just nothing left of them at all. I got shrapnel, [one] on my leg and one on my arm. But I didn't leave the front lines at that time because I didn't feel like I was wounded bad enough, but I did get a Purple Heart for it.

[There was] a place called Suicide Cliff—the Japanese had told all the civilians on Saipan that if we captured them we were going to torture them something awful. When we got to this place called Suicide Cliff, it was probably close to 100 feet high, and they jumped down off this cliff on some rocks down in the ocean. I saw them jumping through the air. I was probably 200 or 300 yards from where they were jumping, women, children and Japanese soldiers also. I don't know, there was hundreds of them that jumped off and they were just piled up like animals down there. I went back to that place later and saw all the bones, the bones were still there.

Roberts was eventually evacuated for his wounds, and describes recuperating—and interacting with female nurses—aboard a hospital ship, where he would celebrate his birthday:

I had my squad book in my left pocket, [that's] where I got hit and it didn't tear the bones up too bad, but it sure did tear the flesh up pretty bad. I never will forget, they cut all my clothes off, they wouldn't let them come aboard ship because we had lice and fleas and everything on us.

So I was naked and I had a blanket over me. And this Navy nurse came—I never will forget, she came over and wanted to see where I was wounded and we had a fight over that blanket. They took me out [to] the surgical ward, the doctor says, "We're going to put you to sleep." And I said, "Doctor, I don't think you're going to put me to sleep." I'd been about 30 days without much sleep, all you do—you get in combat, you just kind of doze every once in a while. So I went off to sleep, didn't wake up 'til 3 or 4 o'clock in the afternoon. They had bandaged me up and all ready to go to the field hospital in Saipan. And I ask them, "What day is it?" I got hit on the 17th day of May and they said, "Today is the 19th." I said, "Today is my birthday, go get me some ice cream." I didn't know I was going to get some, but they did, they got me some ice cream for my birthday.

Raymond DeBarge, a medic in the Army's 88th Chemical Mortar Battalion, also recalls the horrific sight of women and children jumping to their deaths in Saipan. He also reports that men in his own unit forced captured Japanese soldiers off the cliffs:

The worst thing in Saipan is that part of the cliff, we got to see it, where [the Japanese] made the women just jump. They said we were red bearded devils with hate in our eyes [and] that if the Americans get you they're going to rape you and do all these horrible things.

After seeing some of the things that they had done to some of our guys, some of them were just torture, you get a guy with an ear cut off or his nose missing and part of his chin or something. You can't do too much for them, I mean, as a medic you can't. We were going through all the caves and stuff, clearing them out and we pretty much had that one secured and we took about 10, 15 Japs in the caves and brought them out and we had this old southern First Sergeant [who said] that you can't take pity because you're only ready to take care of number one, and so he would just say, "Well, we'll just march them," so we just marched them to the cliff up there. And we had that one Japanese interpreter, we didn't do a very good job of it, we were telling them that we wanted them to jump off and they were telling the kid, "No, no, no, no." And finally a couple of my guys got their point and they hit them with that bayonet in the rear end. Got them right to the cliff and they were going over there [and we'd say] in Japanese, "Bye, you flying home." But you'd go down and see these babies stuck on the rocks and stuff, I mean, I still have dreams about that. When you see little ones getting massacred and stuff [it's] a tough thing to take to sleep with you.

Herman Parker, an African-American, served as a steward's mate 1ˢᵗ class on the *USS Sumter*, an attack transport ship that supported the invasion of Saipan. He describes the fate of a Marine friend of his:

> We took troops into the invasion of Saipan. [There] was a fellow, a Marine, a white boy, but we was good friends, and he was making the invasion of Saipan. He left that morning about 5 o'clock. And I saw him maybe about 10 o'clock, and he was all shell-shocked and everything. I think they might have shot his leg off. The leg was gone or something. But I went in the room. He didn't know me from Adam because he was in shock, and I just looked at him and I cried. And I said, well, I'll be doggoned. I think he might have lived out that day, but he died and they buried him at sea. And I'll never forget him, because we were good friends.

Parker also recalls racially segregated life onboard the *Sumter*:

> We kept mostly to ourselves. [The] type of people that was around didn't want nothing to do with you nowhere. And you could just tell it. You could just look and see how they looked at you. So we just stayed mostly to ourselves.

More explicit racism appeared in the guise of a famous Hollywood actor, and Parker did what he could to resist it:

> One of my lieutenants junior grade was Douglas Fairbanks, Jr. He was nice. The funny thing [was] Doug never called you by your name. It was a throwback like the slavery time for the simple reason Doug would never say good morning, Parker. He would say good morning, Chocolate. What can you say? You'd better not say nothing. You had to endure that kind of abuse from Douglas Fairbanks, Jr.
>
> That was it, I couldn't hold my tongue. I cut loose on him one night. He was saying things, talking about [us black] boys. And I said, listen, Doug, I'm not going to take this. I confronted him right in front of some other officers who tell me, you shouldn't talk like that, that he was no good and all like that. And so it was during the time we was making the invasion of Saipan and they

gave me a summary court martial and 30 days in the brig on bread and water.

I did say something to him. It's hard when somebody's talking about you to your face and [they] care nothing about you. And I'm out there with my life on the line, just like he's got his on the line. Not that I wasn't proud to serve my country—I was very proud to serve my country.

While the battle of Saipan was continuing, the Navy was engaged in the Battle of the Philippine Sea (June 19-20, 1944), which severely damaged the Japanese Navy's fleet with the sinking of three of its carriers. Leroy Robinson flew a F6F Hellcat in the VF-2 Squadron off the *USS Hornet* (formerly the *USS Kearsage*, renamed after the 1942 sinking of the first *Hornet*) and notched his first kill during the battle, popularly known as the "Marianas Turkey Shoot" because of how poorly the Japanese fared in the engagement. Robinson compares the quality of Japanese planes and pilots to American, recounts his first kill, and then recalls barely surviving being hit in mid-flight by a torpedo launched from a Japanese plane attacking the *Hornet*:

They were better trained than we were at first. They had instrument readings and they were naval aviators, we were green compared to them, we got shot up a lot by Japanese and they had better airplanes, better everything.

We were in the Turkey Shoot. In fact, I flew with a guy who shot down five of them on one flight. His name was Webb, and he was trapped on the *Arizona* in Pearl Harbor. He was below deck when the bombs hit. He hated the Japanese as bad as I hated them.

The first one I got, I was [in the air] looking for a fella [who] had been shot down in the water, I had flaps down and low RPM. And so I looked up and said, "Hell, that's a damn Army airplane." About the time he banked up and I saw the red meatballs on him, I said, "hell, that ain't Army, that's Japanese." He came around shooting, I could see the smoke coming out of his wing and he was doing about 650 miles an hour. He fired and he had me and he was going so fast—I was going so slow that he decided to go under me. I was trying to pull up, full throttle, full RPM, full everything. And he missed, he came up right in front of me, all I had to do was sit there, oh, you damn fool you, you made a mistake and I had him like they do in the movies and parts of him went all around. I flew through parts of an airplane.

We was on patrol one time, I was senior officer. The [Japanese planes] were coming in through the ships and heading towards the *Hornet*, they were going to torpedo the *Hornet*. They were getting close and we intercepted them. They lowered their torpedoes, jettisoned was the word we used. And one of the torpedoes hit my airplane and I said, "Why didn't [it] explode?" because they had to be in the water, so many turns of their propeller before they were armed, they weren't armed yet. I was in flight. It dented [my plane], but it was quite an airplane, it kept flying.

Robinson would go on to fly 144 missions, becoming an ace (at least 5 confirmed kills) at age 19.

After the Saipan campaign, the Marines invaded the neighboring island of Tinian a few weeks later on July 24, 1944. Corporal Pat Roberts, veteran of Saipan, made the landing with the 2nd Division. He describes the difficulty in distinguishing local civilians from Japanese soldiers, and a rare night of celebration after the end of the campaign at the expense of an officer:

We had not taken very many Japanese prisoners up until Tinian and the reason why we hadn't taken very many prisoners is you couldn't depend on even the women and the children, they would kill you if they could, and a lot of times these Japanese soldiers would dress like women, so you really had to be careful about how you approached them. One time we had women that we were up on the frontlines and these women wanted to get back to their homes. Some of our troops picked up the fact that they were Japanese soldiers dressed up like women, they [would] pull all kinds of tricks and you just had to be awfully careful.

But on Tinian they kind of read the riot act to us and told us we were going to have to start taking more prisoners. So we probably had about 500 prisoners that we took on Tinian. We had them in a wire cage and that's the reason why I stayed there about two weeks because we were guarding those prisoners.

They found about 12 cases of Japanese rice whiskey and a lieutenant told me to have troops take them up to this house that he'd made his headquarters and put them under the floor. Well, I took him all but two cases and I gave [them] to the troops that night. The fighting was over and all the pup tents were out in the field. I passed those two cases of whiskey out and the next morning all those pup tents were laying on the ground and everybody was drunk.

Marion Brinkley was with the Navy's 107th Construction Battalion (the "Seabees") building roads and airstrips on Tinian after its capture and describes listening to the infamous Japanese propagandist Tokyo Rose:

She would tell us [the Japanese military is] going to the Marshall Islands. We're going to be in Kwajalein at such and such a time, but they never did raid us. When we got to Tinian and she said the same thing, we didn't pay too much attention to her. But [the Japanese] did show up at Tinian. They blew the siren and everybody stayed put. We was going to stay to watch a movie. And didn't a soul move 'til the first [Japanese] bomb hit the ground, and then they didn't have to tell them to move anymore. They was gone.

The conquests of Saipan and Tinian would prove immensely significant. Tinian became an airbase for the 20th Air Force, which would later conduct the destructive firebombing raids on the Japanese mainland and the atomic bombings of Hiroshima and Nagasaki. Jim Wetzel served as a B-29 navigator with the 20th Air Force and would make 23 bombing missions over Japan. Here he describes the pleasures of being stationed at Tinian:

The temperature was warm, we had a beach. I remember going swimming a couple of times, but it wasn't much of a beach because it was coral rock. We had an officer's club that was okay, [but] at the time I was a second lieutenant so I didn't really go there very often, except one of the benefits of being an officer was that once a month we got an allowance of three bottles of alcohol. I wasn't a drinking man at the time and on those occasions I was very popular. The regular brands that we got was Philadelphia and Four Feathers—I think, those are the only two

I really remember, but we'd get blends and then one time we got an American-made scotch thrown in and there was some vodka or gin or something like that—anyway, we got three bottles of booze, which I gave away, mostly to our crew. It was a pleasant experience. Anyway our pilot was half Indian from Florida and he had a capacity for alcohol, he lived up to his Indian traits. When you're giving booze away, you try to be fair to everyone, but I was always reluctant to give it to him.

While the Marines of the 2nd and 4th Divisions were busy securing Saipan and Tinian, the 3rd Division, together with the Army's 77th Division, fought a three-week battle for nearby Guam during July-August 1944. PFC Rufus Belding, veteran of the Bougainville and Guadalcanal campaigns, recalls the eerily quiet landing of his 3rd Marine Division on Guam and the difficulty of the ensuing fighting, during which he was seriously wounded:

[We] didn't hear a shot for six waves. They were hid in the caves and after [they'd] get out and start lobbing the shells all over, mortars and everything else. They had us zeroed in on the beach and they were smart, they killed a lot of Marines. But we started inland then, looking for those caves. And we used flamethrowers in the caves, we used hand grenades. And as we went we'd just mop them up.

I was there six days, and on the sixth day intelligence told us they were going to *banzai* attack the next morning, [but] we didn't know what time. And just about daybreak you could hear them coming, "Die! Die, Marine!" Boy I'm telling you they came through and we was fighting and all of the sudden I felt a sting. It went through and busted that big muscle in the back. I couldn't do nothing, this side was paralyzed. So I lost my rifle and the buddy in [my] foxhole said, "Take my pistol and go on back to the CP and they'll take care of you." When I got back to the CP there was no blood [for transfusions], there was nothing except some sulfa drugs. They put it on there and wrapped my arm up and it was midnight before I got on the hospital ship and got doctored on. When I got hit I reached up and stuck my finger in the hole to stop the bleeding. First time I ever prayed in my life. It taught me a lesson, when you need it, pray. And we got out of it. I asked the Lord, "Don't let me die on this island. I want to go home to Mom and Daddy." I was just 20 years old.

I went to the hospital ship that night and was operated on. I remember them cutting—they had a mirror up there—all that stuff that was dead.

Belding's wounds ended his combat duty but did not seriously disable him after the war: "I got 20 percent [disability] for that, but I still got well from it after I got out and worked at the telephone company 35 years."

The final battle in the Marianas campaign, but one of the toughest, was at Peleliu. It took the 1st Marine Division and the Army's 81st Division almost three months from September to November 1944 to secure the small coral island held by over 13,000 Japanese soldiers. The fighting on Peleliu is powerfully described in Eugene Sledge's Pacific combat memoir *With the Old Breed: At Peleliu and Okinawa*, and the National Museum of the Marine Corps has called it "the bitterest battle of the war for the Marines." Herman Boland, who had previously served in the Merchant Marine in the Atlantic, was now a PFC in the Marines' 1st Division. Boland describes the bloody landings, the tenacity of the Japanese, and the unforgiving conditions of battle:

They [brought] us in at 8 o'clock on September 15, 1944 and that was a horrible sight to see. These Marines never made it to the beach, they were floating in the water, they were lying there dead.

We fought with what we had and the Japanese had no mercy on us. They would come at night and there were batches of them hollering and shouting and screaming and shooting fireworks, just something to get our attention. These were the defenders on Peleliu, the same ones who murdered Chinese people in Nanking. They were several years older than we were. Most Marines at that time was 17 and 18, 19 years old. Men 22 years old, we'd call them Pop, that's facts. It was youth—youth is what makes the Marine Corps, their ability to not rest or give up hope—they don't know better. I know, I was one of them.

The terrain was terrible, terrible, terrible. Jagged, rugged, ragged. A terrible place to be. Coral that was torn up, [it would] cut you and eat you up on your legs and knees when you moved. Many dead Japs piled around there and many dead Marines, men were dead all over the place. We didn't have any water. We had left the ship with two canteens full of water, the Navy was going to dump us some water to wash ashore, but their water was tainted with gasoline. So it was two days before we got some fresh water.

Over the course of the campaign, Boland had several close calls, including hand-to-hand combat. But with the help of his fellow Marines, including one 'Yankee,' he survived:

> One boy I was with named Stony Stoneberg from New York State hollered at me, "Boland, look out." Well, I looked around and there was a big damn field tractor coming right on me. Well I just shut my eyes and rolled. Seemed like forever before that tank would get across me. I went down to get my rifle back after, it was bent like a figure S.

> I do remember another fella hollering at me, "Boland, look out." My goodness, I turned to see what was happening. A Japanese, I can see that fella right now, he had a big red star on his helmet, wrapped leggings and clean pants. But he was lunging at me with a bayonet. I tried to get out of the way, and when I did [one] knee went down and [the other] one came up and my bayonet went up in the air and he dived into my bayonet. He just squealed like a pig. I guessed he [wasn't] dead yet, but I remember a DI one time telling me at Parris Island, "If you ever get your rifle caught in a man's ribs or anywhere in him and you can't pull it out, fire the weapon." Well, this Japanese had my rifle in his ribs somewhere and I couldn't pull it—I pulled and I pulled and I pulled him three yards across the land and I finally pulled the trigger, but before I pulled that trigger I looked all around me and make sure there were no Marines present, I didn't want any friendly fire to kill any of my buddies.

"Bloody Nose Ridge" was one of the final, and most difficult, engagements in the struggle for Peleliu. Boland more than played his part, and his battle buddy Stoneberg was with him all the way:

> We went up Bloody Nose, the final pocket to fall. We were chased down off Bloody Nose by aircraft fire and firing over our heads and dropping these mortars. One boy named Archibald was on Bloody Nose Ridge and trying to get up there and walked

across a minefield and [a mine] blew him head over heels through the air, and he fell about ten feet from me. That man never got dirty. I was always amazed. But all his clothes were burnt off and his shoes and everything was gone and I got to see his chest swell one time.

Stoneberg, he was a BAR man. I had ammunition for him, I had ammunition for myself, I had hand grenades, he had hand grenades. We're not going to try and fire. The Japanese came out and I heard, "Corpsman, corpsman, corpsman." They weren't hit, they were trying to get our Navy medics to go out to them, that way they would murder them and try to make us fire rifles to give away our position. But we fought with hand grenades all night long.

Me and Stoneberg didn't last too long [one night] because he opened up a bottle of port wine and the little foxhole was not big enough for both of us, just piled up with coral rocks. He threw his feet on top of that, "ZZZZZZ," all night long, the loudest noise on that battlefield was this boy snoring, "ZZZZZZ," all because of that wine.

One time, we bypassed a Japanese pillbox and [a Japanese soldier] opened fire from our rear. We hit the ground, my shirt was off and I dived into the sand spurs, laying there and I heard, "pling." Bullet popped right [by] my head. I moved over a little bit anyhow, but deep into the sand spurs, "Bing." That same ricochet kicked up that dust the same distance from my head. I looked out from under my helmet as far as I could see and tried to find where this sniper was that had me pinpointed. I got another shot, I got seven shots in all, I think it was the same sniper. I couldn't stand it no longer, I just got up and ran to a tank that was about 80 yards away. I pick up this speaker on the back end and talk to the tank commander about the pillbox that had us pinned down. I said to him, "Watch out for those Marines." He said, "They'll get out of the way." I was following the tank with this telephone and he took that 75 millimeter, one shot's all it took to blow that thing from here to eternity. Japanese weapons and all—anything and everything went up.

Boland recalls that he actually met the tank gunner some years after the war: "I was back in Aiken many years after that and you know what the

227

man told me, he says, "I was on that tank. I was the gunner on that very tank that you're talking about, I remember that very well."

Sgt. Al Tewkesbury served as a stretcher bearer in the 1st Marine Division at Guadalcanal, Cape Gloucester (New Guinea), and at Peleliu. His comments offer a glimpse into the brutal nature of the Pacific War:

> For most of the boys like me in the Marine Corps, we had thought they were really stupid people because they always liked to attack just before dark or at night and they always loved to make a lot of noise. When they were coming at you across a field through the bushes or anything, you could hear them—their attitude was that if they made a lot of noise they would scare you to death. They're sadistic and very cunning, but as far as combat they didn't have a good attitude about protecting themselves.
>
> I went down this little two-rut road and halfway down it I met this young Japanese. He was half starved and he wasn't no big mean Jap. If I could have hit him with the butt of my rifle I could have done just as good, but I didn't have it. All I had was my .45 and I hadn't fired it since I left Parris Island. I figured all I got to do with this damn Jap is just pop him [on the] right side of the head and send him to glory. My God, he started running at me and I fired six shots and didn't even touch him. On the seventh shot he did a flip in the damn air and it surprised the hell out of me—and I figured, "Where did I hit this bastard." So I went up there while he was laying on the ground and I got a tooth off of him.

Gunner's Mate 2nd class Leonard Gunter, veteran of the Solomons campaign, was aboard LST 398 when it collided with a Merchant Marine ship en route from the Marianas to Hawaii:

> In Saipan, [we] headed for the Hawaiian Islands to pick up some mortars. About 100 miles [from] the Hawaiian Islands something hit. Sounded like torpedo or a freight train or something. I [thought] they torpedoed [us]. When we got topside [we saw a] ship. And then they hollered abandon ship. There wasn't anything left but your life jacket [when you] hit the water.

Soon Gunter was swimming in the Pacific Ocean with many of his shipmates, in the middle of the night. Luckily, the Merchant Marine ship sent out a lifeboat:

> They had to fish [us] out of the water and there were no flashlights. The fellow running the lifeboat off the Merchant Marine ship, he picked me up. He was drunk. And the skipper was, too. They couldn't even wake the skipper up, after all that [happened] on that ship.

Retaking the Philippines

At the same time as the Marines were heavily involved in major battles such as Saipan and Peleliu, the U.S. military was planning to retake the Philippines, from which it had retreated in the face of Japanese military superiority during the dark days of early 1942. In the late summer of 1944 the Army Air Force began raiding and bombing Japanese positions in preparation for an amphibious invasion.

Strategic desperation led Japan to a daring decision that nearly proved successful. American forces under General MacArthur began landing in the Philippine Islands in October 1944. The Japanese had 450,000 ground troops there, and a large battle fleet stationed nearby. They decided to throw everything into an attempt to destroy the American fleet of landing craft, using the remaining Japanese carriers as decoys to draw American naval air power away. Only the heroic actions by smaller American warships, and some good luck, prevented disaster. The Battle of Leyte Gulf was the last Imperial Navy fleet action; Japan still had warships, but hardly any fuel oil left.

First Lt. Jack Kendall, a B-24 Navigator with the 13th Air Force, flew on missions in support of the Philippines campaign, such as the raids on Yap Island. He would fly 24 missions in the Pacific, many of them long and dangerous. Here he describes the creative efforts of pilots to remain alert over the course of their missions:

> Some of the missions were extremely long, 12 to 13 hours and in fact [on] some of them we put extra tanks with gasoline in them and reduced the bomb load to maybe five bombs instead of the full load. We left at 3:00 in the morning so we'd be coming back at daylight and be able to find an island to land on. [On] those long missions, everybody was sleeping because it was late in the war and we did not encounter any enemy aircraft opposition, but over land we did encounter some anti-aircraft.

One mission I remember I looked up at the pilot and the copilot [were both] snoring away and they had it on automatic pilot. I reached up and tapped the pilot and said, "One of you guys have got to stay awake." So he punched the copilot and said, "You stay awake."

Tom Jackson also flew in a B-24 with the 13th Air Force, but as a ball-turret gunner. Here he describes the workings of the ball turret:

It was built by Sperry, and it had a gun sight that no other turret had. It had a gun sight where you could frame the plane and shoot, and then you'd go around. The Japanese knew that, and we were fortunate because they never hit us from the bottom. They'd hit us [at] a level and [on] top. They'd get ahead of you and come down on you and shoot you when you were coming down. But they never shot at me. I was at the bottom going around and around, just looking around. They gave me credit for one that was shot down.

Jackson flew 23 missions in the Pacific. Here he describes the importance of his unit's raids on Borneo from their base on the island of Espiritu Santo in the fall of 1944, for which it won a Distinguished Unit Citation:

Sixteen hours [round trip from base] traveling west was the island of Borneo and a town called Balikpapan. There were two refineries that were there before World War II. One was Shell and the other was Esso. And the thing is, we were not there to hit the pilots or the airport, we were to hit the tankers if they came in for petroleum. We were told that 15 percent of the petroleum the Japanese used at the beginning of World War II came from Borneo.

In between missions, in chow line Jackson found it was an advantage to be recognized as being from Georgia:

We were in line and sometimes there'd be a line of 2 or 300 people coming and going sort of like an airport. Anyway, I'm in line and going to eat there, this guy comes along and he looks me straight in the face and said, "You're from Valdosta, Georgia. I know your face but I don't know your name." I said, "Well, I don't know you." He said, "You don't remember me? I worked there at Walgreens and I used to sell you milkshakes. Get out of that line. I'm head of this thing here and I'll take care of you." I said, "Wait a minute, I've got this guy from North Carolina." He said "Bring him with you." And he took us to a room where they had a lunch room in the main place. And he said, "You don't go out there anymore, you come in here and order. They'll bring you what you want. We got all kind of steak, everything. All you got to do 24 hours a day is come in here and tell them you want to eat."

Stan Whitehead was a lieutenant in the Army's 11th Airborne Division and fought in the battle of Leyte in late 1944 as part of the Philippines campaign. Here he describes the soldierly comradeship that made the difficult conditions endurable:

[At] Leyte, our experiences were the first we had in combat and it was scary because we had nothing to do—except for what we've been told and of course at night you'd dig a foxhole, you'd sit in that foxhole and try to get sleep if you could. If it was raining you'd try to keep dry, foxhole would fill up with water, you were miserable. As we went through Leyte we gained a little bit more appreciation for things and we gained a knowhow of how to survive. Survival was the fact that we did have buddies and buddies looked after one another.

[I had] one sad experience in Leyte. We had gained the top of this ridge and had pushed forward, our two rifle companies were moving out and got stuck. They could not move forward. So we decided we'd take our wounded and try to get them back to headquarters. We're going off the mountain to get them back, and we [get] surrounded by Japanese, so we were stuck up here in this area for six days with rations for only one day. We drank foxhole water. We killed a Japanese. We'd try to get whatever food that he had and in doing this we were able to survive. Most of us lost much weight. Finally, the weather cleared. One reason they couldn't get food to us [was] the weather was so cloudy up in the mountains. But the weather cleared and they tried to drop boxes of C Rations from little L5s [small aircraft] and they did. Some of them rolled off the side of the mountain, but we were able to get enough food to regain our energy and we were able to push forward. This was when General Swing, our Division commander, came up and my particular squad was chosen to escort him from there out of the mountains. We got off of this situation without any more casualties. But it was a harrowing experience because a lot of men died, not necessarily from wounds, from exposure and from the fact that we could only treat them so much. But that was only a few, thank goodness.

Whitehead would later serve with the 101st and 82nd Airborne Divisions during the Vietnam War, eventually attaining the rank of Major.

Alvin Mays, Technical Sgt. in the Army's 24th Infantry Division, and veteran of the Pearl Harbor attack, was in the first wave of the Leyte invasion. Here he describes the initial calm of the amphibious landings, followed by a month of brutal fighting:

We invaded Leyte on October 21, 1944. There were approximately 125 ships in the convoy when we went to invade Leyte, just as far as you can see. I was right up on the number one in line. We went ahead and made the invasion with very little trouble, really, 'til we marched into the hills further up, possibly three miles inland. And from there on it was hell.

It's hard to think about, but there was approximately several thousand troops there that were slaughtered, both Japs and Americans. We had a bulldozer in the company there [which] trenched out places, pushed [them] in because the odor of it got to where it was unbearable.

The Imperial Japanese Division is what we ran into. They were all big people and they were tough eggs, let me tell you. They were well trained. We weren't taking prisoners. That invasion, I was on the front 28 days straight.

When Mays injured his shoulder in an accident on Leyte, he took extraordinary measures to return to his unit, even risking court martial. His actions attest to the powerful devotion soldiers felt toward the other men with whom they fought:

I fell off a truck and busted my shoulder and they sent me back to Saipan. I spent 11 weeks in the hospital there and they took the cast off on a Monday morning and assigned me to Okinawa that afternoon. I didn't go. I went over the hill. I went to the airport, got in [a plane, there was a] lieutenant down there flying supplies back to the Philippines. I asked was there any chance of boarding his plane. "No, we're loaded, can't get on." [But then] he said "if I turn my back I don't see you" and I hopped on that damn plane and it flew [me] back to the Philippines. AWOL. They didn't know where I was, approximately three months before I got back to the outfit. Reported there, I was told "We're going to court martial you." A colonel said "No, there ain't no way, you can't court martial a guy when he goes back to the front line." When I got back with [my] company, I was back at home then you might say.

Joseph (Tag) Sheppard had enlisted in the Navy in 1936, and was aboard the carrier *USS Franklin* (CV-13) in support of the Leyte invasion when the *Franklin* was attacked by kamikazes on October 30, 1944:

We were off the coast, and [the Japanese] had a place just above where we were and set up to send those planes out, kamikazes. And we got one and it was pretty bad. It made some damage there. [The kamikaze] hit right near the aft elevator. [When it] was coming and we had him spotted, our ships [shot] him all to pieces. But he held that thing as hard as he could and he did enough damage that we had to come back to the States [to] get fixed. About 55 or 60 [men were] killed, and I lost one of my best friends that I ever had. He was a big, nice fellow. I'd talked to him a whole lot, many times. And the first thing I knew, somebody told me that he was dead, and so that really upset me.

The *Franklin* did indeed return stateside for repairs, and was back in the fight off the coast of Japan by early 1945.

Leonard Lifsey, Army Sergeant 1st class, served on the hospital ship *USAHS Marigold*, which ferried wounded soldiers from Leyte to New Guinea:

As far as you could see, the beaches were strewn with Americans. They were on stretchers and LSTs brought them in and we could take about 100 of them each trip. Some of these patients was hurting. I'd get a hat or whatever you could get and lay [it] over their face, they were hollering the sun was killing them. It was hot in the Philippines, really hot. So we finally got loaded, between 700, 800, in that neighborhood, then we would leave Leyte and go to Hollandia, New Guinea. They had a general hospital there and we would unload these 600 or 700 people, then we would resupply and go back. Then we'd go back to the Philippines and we'd load with patients again and go back to New Guinea and unload and repeat, repeat, repeat—seven, eight, ten times, whatever that number was.

Lifsey saw quite a lot of the war. After serving stateside as a POW guard and in the Pacific caring for the wounded, he was aboard the *Marigold* when she was the first Allied ship to dock in Japan after the cessation of hostilities and witnessed the Japanese surrender that took place on the *USS Missouri* on September 2, 1945.

Boatswain's Mate 3rd class Emerald (Bill) Williams, aboard the hospital ship *USS Refuge*, had already seen service in the European theater. Here he describes the painful experience of caring for often grievously wounded men near Leyte, and a burial at sea:

We were so engrossed in what we were doing that [we had] so much urgency in getting them over to shelter—our only thoughts were to get these guys on the ship and to the hospital area to be treated as quick as we possibly could. And after it's all over, you sit there and look back at what you saw, the agony that some of these young men were in, and there were some very young [men]. You had this feeling of, "Oh my Lord, you know, what am I into?" It's sort of like when you're entering an emergency, you don't feel until it's all over and then you sit and watch what's happening and then you look at the men—they looked terrible, the wounds and all, and then you would see them later on laughing and talking. It was a good feeling, it was a good experience, but when it was actually happening you had no feeling or thoughts, it was just get these men in as carefully as you can with no more pain than they're already suffering.

We had picked up some troops that were burnt very bad with napalm. They was wrapped like mummies they were burnt so bad and they kept a solution on their bodies. We had one that was burnt so bad he couldn't make it. We even did some things to try to make him feel better because he wanted to get back to the States real bad. But he was really burnt so bad. That was our first burial at sea and that was very touching. He wasn't alone, he had almost 600 people honoring him when he went over the side.

234

Herman Parker, Steward's Mate 1st class, had seen service in the Saipan campaign and was now aboard the destroyer *USS Sands* in support of the Leyte invasion. He describes the rough seas that were almost too much for the *Sands*, and his friend's help in braving the storm:

> We were escorting some minesweepers because the invasion was going to be the next day. Us and all the aircraft carriers and the battleships and the cruisers, everything was coming in there. So we were sweeping the harbor with the minesweepers. The sky opened up. You couldn't see the sky for the water. We lost three of those minesweepers, they capsized. The water was so high over our ship, it would take it and run it up in the air maybe about 8 or 10 stories and run out from underneath it. That's when my friend Banks came in. I was looking for someplace to go, I didn't know where to go, but Banks was in the yeoman office. And I went in and Banks put his arms around me and said, "Parker, don't worry about nothing. Say nothing is going to happen to this ship." He said, "This ship was here before we was born and it will be here after we dead and gone, Parker." He said, "Don't worry about it. Just hold on Parker, hold on."

Unfortunately, the bonds between friends that helped men brave the rigors of sea duty could not save those who were washed overboard:

> As a matter of fact, that night on our ship we had an engineer working in the engine room and he came up that night to try to take a shower. Well, the shower was on the fantail, so the shower and the restroom and all that was exposed to anything coming over the top. And he got in there, the wave came over and took him out. We saw him, but was nothing we could do. [We] couldn't stop. He just washed away. You saw him one time when one of those big waves brought him up, then he went back down, that was all, couldn't see him anymore.

Hugh Bedingfield served as an ensign on the battleship *USS California*, which had been sunk in the attack on Pearl Harbor but was then restored to participate in the Marianas campaigns at Saipan, Tinian, and Guam. In the Philippines campaign, the *California* had supported the landings at Leyte, and was bombarding the Luzon peninsula in support of the landings at Lingayen Gulf when she was hit by two kamikazes on January 6, 1945. Bedingfield cogently describes the event:

The *California* became part of the operation at Lingayen Gulf in the northwest Philippines. In the course of the operation we were attacked by kamikaze planes. The first one that I recall was approaching the ship, just about to hit, but the anti-aircraft firing pretty much demolished it before it got to the *California*, so it did little or no damage. A little later we were hit by another kamikaze plane. That plane hit the *California* in the upper superstructure. There were about 50 people killed and maybe another 150 injured and the ship was damaged so much that we got orders back to the Navy yard at Bremerton, [Washington].

Bedingfield would go on to further service in the Pacific, rising to the rank of commander. The *California* would be repaired again, and supported the landings on Okinawa.

Hugh Alexander was an anti-aircraft gunner aboard the battleship *USS New Mexico*, another vessel that had already seen a lot of action in the Pacific. Likewise supporting the landings at Lingayen Gulf, it too was hit by kamikazes on January 6, 1945. Alexander describes his attempts to fend off the kamikazes, including a particularly close call:

They'd come out of the sun, you couldn't see them until they get on top of you. We had orders to fire at them until they hit whatever they were going to hit. There was usually about three of them that came at a time.

A guy [who] relieved me early told me to go to chow line, and while I was gone the suicide planes come in—two of them— they [shot] one of them down, but the other one went into the bridge and killed all the men on that 20mm I was on. Killed the skipper and all, except for one man.

[The first kamikaze] went down three decks, all the way through that 20mm I was on and then down another deck and exploded. [The second kamikaze] went all the way to the boiler rooms and they thought it was going to sink the ship, the magazines was going to go off, but they didn't. He knocked three [boilers] out of commission.

This attack on the *New Mexico* killed 30 and wounded 87, including the commanding officer, as Alexander notes. A high-ranking British general on board was also killed.

236

Tom Zwemer was a medic in the Army's 40th Infantry Division, and after having served at Cape Gloucester and New Guinea, spent three months in the Philippines campaign, beginning January 9, 1945, during the Battle of Luzon. As a medic, he worked close to the front lines; they tended the wounded as they were brought from the front, and as the line moved forward, his medical unit would pack up and follow. Here he describes going ashore during the Luzon invasion and being strafed by a Japanese Zero:

> The Japanese found that the beaches at Luzon were totally indefensible and so they retreated three or four miles, so our landing was a cakewalk, no problem. The interesting thing about it was the first time I made what we called an assault landing I was six feet tall and our major in our outfit, a physician, was just barely five feet tall, and so he said to me and to another guy that was six feet tall, "Do you mind when we hit the beach that I be between the two of you? In case the water is deep, you guys will be above water and you can pull me up." And so sure enough we hit a sandbar and they put the ramp down and we were the first three off the ramp and the water's up to here on me and I look and I can't find the major, and we go, "Where's the major?" We caught him, we pulled him up by the shoulder, he stutters and he says, "Thanks, fellas." And so we carried him about four or five paces until we hit the sand again. But I had one good major on my side.
>
> We get ashore and it's quiet, but the first thing after we got our hospital set up they said, "You've got to dig a foxhole perimeter." But who wants to dig a foxhole perimeter, nobody needs to, but the rule was to dig your foxhole. So I get out my little shovel and start digging, I get down about that far and I hit water. "Yeah, hey, Tom, scaredy cat, what are you going to do now?" I said, "Well, I guess instead of a foxhole, I'm going to build a slit trench down to water and I'm going to put up all the sand and muck towards the enemy and then I'll lay down—I'll be six feet long or where it needs to be and I think that much muck and sand will stop small arms fire if it should happen." "Ha-ha-ha." All of a sudden a Jap Zero comes over and of course I'm ready to dive into my slit trench and the guy that's ha-haing loudest is already in it and I'm lying on top of the dirt and he's lying down in the water and our faces—our noses are about this

close together, I said, "You know, if we live through this, I suggest you keep your mouth shut." "Yeah, okay." I said, "And dig your own hole."

This is not to say that Zwemer didn't take his work seriously; he was ready to challenge the authority of his superiors if the cause was just:

> We were at Clark Field and an ambulance came in with two Japanese soldiers that had been captured by Filipino guerillas and those guerillas had taken bamboo poles or sticks and beat them from one end to the other, they were black and blue, their eyes were closed, their noses were bleeding, wherever you could see it was bruised. And so this major starting examining, when he got to [their] legs he started twisting [them]. And even though these Japs were bruised, they were still conscious and you see them wince every time [he did that]. So I said, "Major, what in the world are you doing?" He said, "I'm checking for fractures." I said, "Well, Major, we don't check our men that way." And he says, "If it wasn't for these SOBs I'd be back in the Bronx making a damn good living." I said, "Well, Major, they're just as much victims of this war as you and I are." I said, "If you want to twist on somebody's leg get ahold of Tojo." He said, "You're out of order, soldier." And of course I shut up, but he quit.

Zwemer also relates some humorous incidents that occurred during his unit's down time:

> They gave us the job of carrying 105 shells up 100 yards or so up the bank making a cordwood pile. We started around 10:30 in the morning and around 8 or so the next morning we're still going and so we were pretty tired. The same major [who he had argued with about the Japanese wounded] came out onto a catwalk and saw us creeping along, at least according to his estimation, and yells at Chief. Chief was an Apache Indian-Mexican and he was 6 foot 2 or 3, weighed 240 pounds of muscle, he had been a professional wrestler. Chief looks up at the major and said, "Were you speaking to me, sir?" He said, "Yes, you." [Then] Chief said, "If you don't shut up, I'm coming up here with this 105 shell and sticking it up your ass." Just then our company commander, who was also a major, but out ranked him in time and service, came out. The major said to him, "I

238

want him court martialed, I want him court martialed." And of course the company commander knew how long we had been there and said, "That is your right, Major, that's absolutely your right. But if I were you and I didn't want a 105 shell up my ass," he said, "I'd get off this catwalk."

There was no shower or facilities or anything, our showers were a 50 gallon gasoline drum with a hole in the side, [with] a little piece of pipe coming out and a faucet, you'd turn that on and that was your shower. So I was assigned to set up the shower. I get the shower all set up and filled with water and I'm hot and sweaty and all, I said, "Well, I'm going to go try it and see how it works." So I get undressed and in order to save water I get wet enough to suds myself up and then I'm going to turn the sprinkler on to rinse off. Then the major shows, he says, "Soldier, what are you doing in here?" I said, "I'm taking a shower." "Yeah, I can see that, but why are you in this shower? This is the officers' shower." I said, "I was not told that, sir. I thought it was the enlisted men's shower." "Well, it's the officers' shower, now get out." I said, "It'll just take me 30 seconds to rinse off." He said, "Out, out, out, out." Well, out meant out, just outside. Outside of the shower area the soldiers were bartering with the women for one thing or another. Here I am totally naked. All I have is my helmet and there's a small pump there. I'm saying to the guys, "Help me pump my helmet full of water so I can dump it over," and they said, "nope." They all just stood there. Well, I'm six foot tall, but that's the only part of me that was of any impressive size. So there I was naked, trying to get rinsed off and everybody's standing around giving the he-haw.

They put me in charge of a prophylactic station and they had set up an ointment treatment that would prevent you from getting any kind of cooties or bugs, that would be wiped all over the genital area and then they would inject into the urethra a very dark brown iodine solution that was very mild, but that was to kill any kind of bacteria or bug of any sort. They wanted to keep those syringes sterile so they stored them in 70 percent alcohol. My job was to take each soldier that would come in for treatment and walk him through each stage [of the treatment]. Well, apparently some soldier in there, Louis, had put a syringe back in the alcohol without having taken all the brown iodine solution out of it, so the alcohol had turned a little brown and so this first sergeant—he had stripes [all] over, he had medals and was drunk as a lord and as big as an ox. And, I said, "May I help you, Sergeant?" He shoved me aside like I was a kid, "Where's the entrance?" "Right over there." So he goes in, he was all draped off with the cloth, it was private. He's in there about two or three minutes and he starts swearing. Oh, he's swearing up a stream. I said, "What seems to be the matter, Sergeant?" Now this iodine solution which was very mild and didn't burn at all was supposed to be held in the urethra canal before it was voided, that was the treatment, but he obviously had injected 70 percent alcohol, which would be 140 proof, and so he said, "There's not a man alive that can hold this for five minutes." I said, "Well, just do the best you can, Sergeant."

Zwemer moved to Georgia some years after the war to serve as vice president for academic affairs at the Medical College of Georgia. In 2009 Zwemer published *Do the Best You Can, Sergeant*, a series of often humorous reminisces that cover his life before, during, and after the war.

Dallas Bahm was a private equipped with the powerful Browning Automatic Rifle (BAR) in the Army's 41st Infantry Division. Here he describes a tense incident during the Battle of Mindanao in which he and his sergeant disagreed about how to treat Japanese prisoners:

I was a BAR man and I learned how to be pretty good with it. And we had a mean platoon sergeant, who later was killed in combat. However, we learned from this group of men where the Japanese was at and [the sergeant] broke us up into little [groups] and said, "Bahm, set your BAR right here. When we flush them out, you know what to do with them with that BAR, you're damn good with it." [We all] knew what he meant. He wanted me to waste them.

Meanwhile I had a little combat time behind me in Zamboanga [an earlier operation in the Philippines campaign] and even though I was just a private, I learned how to take orders and how not to take orders. So sure enough, after about 35 or 40 minutes, after I got my BAR set up and cleared, [the sergeant] says, "Okay, we're going to flush 'em out." And when they flushed out, they had their weapons, they come out three, four and five at a time. There would be a hesitation then they'd send some more out. Well, the first group [that] came out, there was four of them and they had their weapons in the air and they were just kind of walking and they had their weapons up. When they come out, I took my BAR and I zeroed in about 20 feet in front of them, and I went buh-buh-buh, buh-buh-buh, buh-buh-buh and shot the ground in front of them and it would kick up the dirt. The minute that old BAR is kicking up that dirt close to them, they threw their rifles up and give up. Threw their rifle down. Brought them over and sat them down. They sent four or five more, I did the same thing. I shoot at them, I could have killed them, cold blood, I could have killed every one of them. And that went on 'til 125 men come through there. We took every one of them prisoner and didn't kill one man.

I'm proud of that. That iron-ass platoon sergeant told me he wasn't too happy that I didn't kill them. He says, "You could have killed them slant-eyed son-of-a-bitches."

Bahm stayed in the Army after the war and was eventually promoted to sergeant first class, no doubt because of the kind of leadership capacity evidenced here.

James Eubanks, PFC in the Army's 32nd Division, describes the dangerously close quarters American soldiers had with the enemy:

They would sneak up on you and get you anyway they could. Nobody moved around too much at night. But [the Japanese] would if they knew where you were. That's the reason they would fire their guns, talk to you at night. I have laid out on the line and heard them talking all night. All they wanted you to do, get on your nerves and fire the gun and that's your position you're giving away.

[One day] we were following a trail in the jungle and we come out into a little clearing. And when we got out there we looked around and it was Japanese sitting around everywhere, eating their lunch, I guess. And, of course, we got outta there as fast as we could. They threw their food down and got their guns and started shooting, we went in a different direction. We had to run, turn, turn, zigzag. We went through some areas in the jungle that normally we would have avoided. I'm sure they sent out patrols looking for us, but they never did find us. After we got where we thought we were safe, we had to pull our clothes off, pick the leeches off each other before they ate us up. We made it back okay to our lines that time and reported the enemy back there.

This one time we had been moving through the jungle and had contacted the enemy several times that day. We was to stop that night. It was kinda on a hill. And I was gonna go out and have my flags placed where I was gonna put the outpost. And doing your outpost you usually tried to put something out front where there [would] be a noise made because when it's dark in the jungle, it's dark. I were out there trying to rig up some C-ration cans and let somebody trip over it. I had propped my rifle up against a tree. I must have sensed something or heard a little noise. When I stood up there were a gun barrel about 20 feet from me pointing right at me. Of course I fell over and run for my rifle. He fired two shots rapidly and I could feel them going by my head. Now I think that was one of God's miracles because it was unknown to miss that close with a rifle. That alerted my outfit, that gunfire. And I went back to the lines and we spent the night. And we did lose a couple of men that night.

Chapter 6
War in the Pacific, II: Iwo Jima to Japan

Iwo Jima

Japan could now only rely on defense-to-the-death and suicide tactics, such as the famous *kamikaze* air attacks and sending ships on one-way missions. In 1945 Americans experienced these desperate measures most prominently during the invasions of Iwo Jima and Okinawa; in the first invasion, made famous by the iconic photograph and subsequent monument of the Marines hoisting the flag, it took several weeks of fighting in February and March 1945 to conquer the eight square mile island. Almost the entire 21,000-man Japanese garrison perished, while nearly 7,000 American Marines were killed.

J. Stedman (Ted) Holladay served as Quartermaster on the *USS Abele*, a net-laying ship used to protect larger ships from torpedoes. Here he describes surviving an attack by Japanese fighter planes on the eve of the Iwo Jima campaign:

> We were about two days out from Iwo Jima when we had our first engagement. We went to General Quarters an hour and 45 minutes before sundown and 45 minutes before sunup, because the enemy would always come out of the sun, and you learned to look in that direction. You never approached a convoy at any time of sunrise/sunset from a specific direction because you knew that you were going to be shot. Well, at that particular time, they came out of our portside, and five planes — they were going for the bigger ships in the convoy, which was the LSTs. [They were] the biggest of the invasion boats, and they carried normally 200 men when just transporting them back and forth. But this was an entire fleet of these things. The guide ship was the *USS Keokuk*. They hit the *Keokuk*, killed 11 people, knocked the thing out of commission. They made a pass at the LST on our starboard flank. They came over us. We were the first ship in the line of fire. We had two 20-millimeters and one three-inch gun, which is worse than useless. Three inch [guns] couldn't hit anything, but the 20-millimeters were a very versatile piece. We opened fire on the plane, and by deflecting him, he missed his target and hit the LST, went in just above the water line, and it was like a cartoon. The tail of the airplane was sticking out the

side of the boat, and the boat was still floating. We lost five men on that [ship].

Finding Iwo Jima wasn't easy to begin with, and neither was building a pontoon bridge for the troop landings:

> Iwo Jima is like hitting a pin in a haystack. If your navigation isn't exactly right, you can miss the thing, because it is probably smaller than Hilton Head—maybe about the same size but very, very mountainous in terrain, so we had a bad time.

> In the North Pacific, you're like San Francisco. You've got the early morning fog that works in. So coming in we followed the sound of the cannon fire and the gunshots and the flares [so] we could see where we knew the land was. We were getting closer and closer to the shore. The fog broke just for an instant, and our ship's mast was under the 16-inch guns of the *West Virginia* and they were firing over our ship. Well, we got out of there in a hurry.

> So we went to the beach—our job was to put down the pontoon causeways. The division groups came in, went down the side of cargo nets and we'd take them in. They also brought in these large sections of pontoons, and we were to take these things and lash them together to make a causeway like they did at Normandy. Naval intelligence really fouled up on that one, because 20 feet off shore you could put down six fathoms of a 10-fathom chain and never hit bottom. There was no way that we could keep the pontoons anchored down. So then [we let] those things wash on the beach, and then we had to work with the LSTs that were going into shore, dropping these men off, and trying to back off but couldn't make it. We were trying to pull these [LSTs] off. That went on for eight days and they finally decided [it] was futile.

Boatswain's Mate 1st class Paul Harless, veteran of the Bougainville campaign, was still serving on the destroyer *USS John Rodgers* in preparation for the Iwo Jima landings:

> We would pound Iwo Jima, softening it up for future invasion, and then we would make a circle and go over to the Japanese' homeland and bomb them. Then we'd come down to Okinawa

and do the same thing and then back to Iwo Jima again. In fact, *The Saturday Evening Post* one time had the story of one trip that we made that lasted two months. And in that two months, we destroyed 2200 planes, 600 service craft and there was always mines floating. Everybody was destroying mines with 20- and 40-millimeter ammunition.

Naval combat was not the only danger at sea. Harless describes the *John Rogers* beset by Typhoon Cobra in December 1944:

One time we were clocking the wind at 162 miles an hour when the meter broke. And the waves were estimated over 100 feet high. One high observer that kept a diary said that he got scared when he looked up and saw the waves higher than our mast. We did lose power, we got water down in the engine room. We did have a stove break loose in the galley and it was going back and forth so much they wouldn't send someone in to try to secure it. It kind of tore things up to where it was three days before we were able to have a cooked meal. When a wave would come up, the top 50 or 60 feet of it would just take off in the air. We did lose two destroyers and a destroyer escort. We lost nearly 800 men in that.

If the preparations for the invasion were difficult, the landings themselves were extraordinarily bloody, to the extent that even today the necessity of taking Iwo Jima is still questioned. PFC Chester McCoy, veteran of the campaigns in the Marshall Islands and on Saipan (where he won the Purple Heart) was in the first wave of the 4th Marine Division's assault on Iwo Jima. Here he describes the well-prepared Japanese defenses and his company commander's efforts (along with his own, as radio operator) to counter enemy artillery:

Never heard of Iwo Jima, and no one knew anything about it. But as soon as we boarded ship, they brought out the maps and we started studying it. When we hit Iwo Jima, it was the 5th [and] 4th Marine Divisions, and we [landed] in the middle somewhere. The 5th Marine went to the left, [to] Mount Suribachi. They'd taken Mount Suribachi. The 4th Marine Division went to the right. We'd taken the other end of the island. Mount Suribachi was the roughest part to take because they had the big guns and they could aim them anywhere on that island they wanted, because they'd been there for years and they knew every inch.

245

And on the end [of the island] that we'd take, every time [our planes and ships] would quit bombing Mount Suribachi, they would bring the big guns out and start firing on us. They could pinpoint you, wherever you was at.

[The Japanese Army] lived underground. Nothing was above ground. A lot of times we would advance and they'd come up behind us and knock off some of our people. So the way we eliminated that, every time we would come to a cave or a hole, we would just dynamite it and fill it in. Seal it off. That way, they couldn't come in behind. I went in some of the caves. Then I went into the hospital they had, and it was all convenient, but everything was underground. Bunks and beds and everything.

Iwo Jima was a rough island. I think that was the roughest one I went through. I was the radio [operator] for my company commander. He was one of the bravest men I've ever met—Captain Eddy. He was our first lieutenant when I joined the company. In the meantime, he had [risen] through the ranks and made captain. [One time] we advanced a long ways, but they started bombarding us from Mount Suribachi, and bombs were falling everywhere. People were dropping like flies. But my captain, he never hesitated while the bombs was falling and the men all around him was falling. He stayed on the radio, told them where the bombs were coming from, and within 15 or 20 minutes, they bombed Mount Suribachi, and that stopped them from bombing us.

McCoy also recalls the particularly difficult terrain on Iwo Jima, and the kind of bombing mishap that is all too common in war:

The main thing that I remember, digging in black dirt, volcanic stuff, and you could only dig a little at a time because it was hot. The ground was hot. You could put your food in there and it would cook. If you had a can of beans or something you wanted to warm up, you could drop it in a hole and cover it. Dig it back up in a few minutes and it was hot, so I remember digging in.

When we'd advance, we'd lay out flags, and that way our bombers would come in, say the strafer would come in and fire. Well, we had our flags out and the planes come in strafing, dropping bombs. They wasn't supposed to come beyond [the] flags. But the tail end didn't get the word. They started firing too soon, and it knocked 14 of our people out. It didn't kill any of them, but it wounded 14. When you wound 14, you take 28 [more] out, because it takes two to take one back. One thing the Japanese believed in, they'd rather wound you than kill you. To kill you, you just take one, but if they wounded you, then you would have taken two more to get that one out.

Sgt. William (Sam) Carter, an Army radio repairman, landed on Iwo Jima with his Signals unit a few days behind the 5th Marine Division. By then the battle's horrendous toll was already evident:

> We were crouched on the beach praying for our lives. You look up, piles of dead Japanese. Can you imagine 20,000? We landed in blood and guts, and I mean red. We stayed on the beach for several days. Finally we moved up, maybe 20-40 yards, and that's moving behind stacks of dead bodies. They were bringing them in by the truckloads. There were big bulldozers bulldozing out trenches as long as they could and as deep as they could and cord-wooding the Japs in it.

Though his main task was technical, Carter still experienced the sharp end of war, especially the tenacity of the Japanese:

> [It was] my turn for frontline duty. I was on the outer perimeter. We had flares going up to cover us. You didn't get out of your emplacement to even take a leak. You stayed right there. About five o'clock all hell broke loose behind us. So we had to turn around and fight the Japanese banzai attack. You knew it was a banzai attack because [of] the smell of rice wine. They get drunk and the only weapons they had, that I remember, was hand grenades and a sword cutting holes in the tent. They sneaked around us and got back in the bivouac area. We lost the 21st fighter group, I know we lost a number of pilots because they hit their area. According to the *Army Times*, we got 426 Japanese. Dead. Didn't capture any. The banzai attack was the only time that my life was threatened and I had to do what you have to do. This is self-preservation. You will do whatever is necessary.

> Surrender? I can hardly spell it. And they don't even know what it is. They don't surrender. They'll cut their guts out. They have a harakiri kit with a flag and a little compass in it and a sharp

metal [knife] and rip their guts out when they know you've got them. Surrender is not in their language.

Seaman 1st class Carroll Scott, aboard Coast Guard vessel *USS Duval County* (LST-758) in support of the invasion of Iwo Jima, recalls the sickening carnage on the beaches, and his crew's contribution to the first flag raising atop Mount Suribachi:

> Bodies was floating by this [way], that way and another. You didn't have no taste for anything, it was a smell of death—like 100 funeral parlors thrown together. I said so many prayers I could fill a prayer book — to let this poor boy get back to Augusta, I'll never leave again.
>
> The first flag—when we was there and they run up the thing and they had an old rusted pump pipe, it was nothing but like the Marines and Ira Hayes and them. I mean it was a smaller flag, and the first raising they got from us and I guess they didn't have time to get the Navy vessels' flag, they couldn't find a bigger flag.

Navy Petty Officer 3rd class Hal Beman served in the Coast Guard aboard LST-795 during the Iwo Jima campaign, and had a small part to play in the second flag-raising on Mt. Suribachi. Joe Rosenthal's photograph of the event, published as a *Life* magazine cover, was one of the most famous pictures of the Second World War:

> A Marine officer wanted to know if we would build a flag pole on our LST. I came down off [my 40mm gun turret], it was way up, about second story. Now according to this officer that same flag pole was the second raising of the flag on Mount Suribachi. The first one was just an iron pole, but the second one was our flag pole—the flag came off of another LST, I don't remember which one. I can't think of that war correspondent's name at Iwo Jima [Joe Rosenthal], he staged that second one so he could film it, and that was our flag pole.

Navy Lt. Harry Kaplan, a supply officer on the attack transport ship *USS Talladega*, which took troops into the Iwo Jima landings beginning with the first day of the campaign, describes the frightened young men about to face enemy fire on the beaches:

248

These young Marines were assembled in order to get in the landing craft to go in, and some of them were 18, 19 years old, quite a few of them. I was about 25 or 26. I wasn't a lot older, but I felt like I was older than them. They had to see LCVPs [Landing Craft Vehicle, Personnel] with casualties coming in, because our wardroom was turned into an operating room, and they saw these young fellows who were broken up coming aboard ship. I had to remind them as they approached the debarkation that they were to loosen the chin strap on their helmet and loosen the strap on their rifle that they had over their shoulder, because if they had fallen off those ladders going into the LCVPs, they would have had a lot of problems. The young fellows were pretty frightened, but most of them were very good at what they did. They were well trained.

Four Marines who were in Rosenthal's photo came off the *Talladega*, including Ira Hayes and three other members of his platoon. Kaplan witnessed the second flag raising; though the event was cause for celebration, he did not lose sight of the battle's terrible costs:

An announcement came over the PA about a flag going up on Mount Suribachi. That was through all the smoke and haze and everything. I had a pair of field glasses as a debarkation officer, and I looked up and saw one of the flags going up. I don't know if it the first one or the second one, but I did see a flag going up on Mount Suribachi.

We had quite a celebration aboard ship when that occurred. It was quite an event—a milestone, to say the least. But the casualties were very heavy, and coming back from the first two or three waves going in, we had a large complement of medical officers and medical personnel aboard ship that were attached for the invasion, and there was a bloodbath going on there.

While the sailors supported the Marines on the ground, aviators had an essential role to play in the air. Navy Lt. JG Fred Langdon piloted a PB4Y-1 Liberator (a Navy version of the B-24 heavy bomber) with the VPB-116 patrol bomber squadron (the "Blue Raiders"). Here he describes his work supporting the invasion of Iwo Jima, fending off Japanese saboteurs, and his method for evading Japanese fighter planes:

It was February 19th [1945] and they had the whole fleet there. There must have been 70 or 80 ships, Navy ships, plus all the landing stuff, and our base operation was to keep the Japanese from resupplying, so we were looking for ships to sink and then we helped support the Marines by doing low-level bombing ahead of where they were positioned. That's kind of tricky because you've got your guys on this side and the other guys are the ones you're trying to shoot. [We] used ground control, and we were lucky, we didn't shoot any Marines. So it worked out pretty well.

We landed and they told us to park the planes along the side of the runway and I didn't think that was a good idea because when you line planes up, well they're subject to enemy action. I had four planes in this section—we taxied over onto a farm which was probably 500 or 700 feet from the runway. That night, the Japanese landed a plane on the runway, they got out, and they threw hand grenades up in the wheel wells of the planes that were along the runway. So at least we got our four planes back in one piece, but we were not stationed there long.

When they attack you [from the air], they come in usually above you. So the first thing you do with one plane against six, you drop down to the deck [to] about 50 feet. They can't get under you, so the only run they can make is what they call the high side, from either the right starboard or the left. And that way I've got four guns [to shoot at them], plus I can pull the nose up and squirt the 20 millimeters which I think I'd only scare them, but when you get [bullets] winking at you, you get a little unsettled. So I think that helped us. And then the plane was fast. A Liberator could probably make about 250, 275 knots, which is pretty good speed, on the water. We were protected and the gods were with us, so we got it home.

Langdon describes a 'typical' mission in the pre-electronic era, summarizes his combat experience in the Pacific, and reflects on the mental side of warfare:

Most times you fly at the wrong time of day, usually take off at 2:00 or 3:00 in the morning. So briefing is blurry-eyed [but] it doesn't take too long because the night before you go over what you really want to do and then they give you the weather in the morning and all that kind of stuff. You take off and you fly for 5.5 hours and look for something. By then the sun is up and you can look around and see what's going on. You're really out of communication. People don't realize that with today's communication you can talk to anybody anyplace, but 100 miles out we were out of radio communication and all we could do is Morse code. So you were on your own and the other thing is, you really didn't know where you were. You were navigating, but it's not like now with GPS [where] you can tell within feet where you are. So we'd make the run around the sector and then come back in and debrief with mostly if you've run into an enemy or if something big happened. Otherwise it was over to the O Club and have a couple beers.

I made 88 flights during the six months, of which I would say 30 were active combat. I'm talking about when we got shot at or shot at something. The rest of it we went out and looked and returned. And of course there was a lot of water out there and getting the [plane] out a thousand miles, getting it back is a job well done. We got credit for [sinking] 22 transport ships I think. Now some of these were small transports, 150, 200 feet long. Some of them were big, like 400 or 500 footers. What we needed to do was cut off the supply to the Japanese Islands and we shot at everything from fishing boats, you name it, we shot it.

You run scared a lot of the time. If you're not, well, you're lying. Let me put it that way. The main thing with being scared is not losing control. In other words, if you know the job and you think you can do the job, the scared thing is just something that you push in the background. You do your thing and usually you get through it. Most times you get through it. And I was lucky. You've got to be prepared, but you've also got to have a very stiff background, the backbone.

In early 1945, Langdon also flew missions near the Japanese mainland. Here he describes his role in rescuing a downed Army Air Force fighter pilot:

We got a call, we were [near] Tokyo Bay. With a P-51 Army fighter pilot in the water and they had a submarine net across the entrance to the bay, the Japanese, and he was on the inside of the net and there was an American submarine trying to get to him.

Submarine was outside the net. And this poor clown, the Army [pilot], he's in a rubber boat and having all kinds of trouble. There was another Liberator in the area and we kind of kept the enemy from coming down there [with] torpedo boats. We shot them up. I got a half a plane. There were two Japanese planes we shot down between the two of us. Then an Army B-17 came [with] a boat underneath it and they dropped the boat to the Army pilot. He got in the boat, got up to the net and the submarine surfaced again, picked him up and we got him out of there.

Flying wasn't Langdon's only talent:

There were three USO shows and I was a professional trumpet player when I was in high school and thereon, and I got to play with the band. It wasn't my tremendous ability but I was the only [trumpet-playing] Naval aviator in the Pacific. A guy like Bob Hope can play to the audience when you've got somebody up there with his [flight] goggles on, horn in hand. I played with Les Brown and a couple other ones. I didn't get in their way, let me put it that way.

Langdon would fly 88 missions in the Pacific War. After the war, he was instrumental in the founding of Aiken Technical College, and taught marketing and management there.

Okinawa

Soon after the battle of Iwo Jima, Okinawa was chosen as an invasion target because its location could provide excellent support for the planned invasion of Japan, and it was the one island in the region large enough to support airfields. At this late stage of the war, the weakened state of Japan's military led it to rely on suicidal tactics. American losses were high, totaling some 55,000 casualties, including 12,520 killed in action. Upwards of 100,000 Japanese soldiers died on Okinawa, as well as thousands of civilians. Fought between April 1-June 22, 1945, Okinawa was the last major American battle of the entire war.

Raymond DeBarge, medic in the Army's 88th Chemical Mortar Battalion, and already a veteran of Saipan when he arrived at Okinawa on April 1, the first day of the invasion, describes the brutal treatment meted out by the Japanese on wounded Americans, and the Americans' (including his own) understandable response:

[Okinawa] was the worst of all the battles. The Japanese were sadistic, we learned that on Saipan. I mean, chopping somebody [up], one guy they cut off his tongue. They'd capture somebody and they just torture him, anything, they'd end up chopping off fingers and that kind of stuff. I took care of more than my share of them. You'd hear them screaming and then somebody just wanted to get out there and get them. When you did get the opportunity [to fight the Japanese] it wasn't a lot of love lost. There was no prisoners taken, TNP, take no prisoners. As you think of the things that they did, first aid was to give them a shot of .45. Not to brag about it, but there's times that you did it.

Having survived a "banzai" attack ("they wanted to die, they were done, they're not going to get off the island," DeBarge says), DeBarge recalls a particularly painful incident where one of his best friends was killed on Okinawa:

We were up on FO, forward observation, and all of the houses would have a cement foundation, a typhoon or hurricane ain't going to blow it down. We were there directing fire, [my buddy] Doug had the radio going and was telling where the gun was firing, you're too long or too left or too right, come back, do this. They had a bomb, a buzz bomb, like three 50-gallon drums together, fired from a barrel-type thing and if you could look up and see it and hear it, you were all right. If you could look up and see it and not hear it, you better hunt [for] cover. I was there and the lieutenant and two riflemen there with us and the lieutenant said "We got to get off the hill." The buzz bomb come in [right on] Doug and I went hunting for him right off the bat. I knew it wasn't going to be good, but I knew I might be able to say a few words to Doug. We found the tip of his boot and part of the antenna from the radio, that's all we found.

Another painful aspect of his friend's death was that DeBarge was unable to inform Doug's family, because of wartime censorship:

We were like brothers really. We went through basic training, hung out together, went to church together and everything else. At the time they just said he's missing in action. He's missing in action until you had proof and the tip of the boot and the antenna didn't cover it. I was writing to his sister at the time and she got a letter saying Doug was missing in action. I wrote her a little letter [about what happened to Doug but] the company commander said, "No, you can't [write that]" They would just cut out anything they didn't want to be there. I never did get the opportunity to get [her a letter].

DeBarge recalls meeting Ernie Pyle, the most famous American correspondent of the war, and being impressed by his willingness to share in the risks of the troops:

We hit the beach, we had Ernie Pyle with us. It was like talking to your brother or father, he never pounded or tried to drag anything out of you. He was there with you. When he said this is the way it is, that's the way it was, he was there, he knows.

Pyle, having covered numerous campaigns in Europe and the Pacific, was killed April 18, 1945, on Ie Shima, a small island just northwest of Okinawa.

Corporal Pat Roberts, previously wounded at Saipan, was now a member of the Marines' 6th Division. He earned a third Purple Heart when his unit attempted to hold a position on Sugarloaf Mountain during the Okinawa campaign:

My squad and I went up Sugarloaf the first day. We went to the top in a wedge formation, but we could not establish a strong offensive line. So they sent Sherman tanks in and asked us to come out. Then we met some Japs right on the top—we had a little skirmish with them up and they fell back and we fell back and we tossed hand grenades on each other all afternoon. We got the order to move out. One of my men had just gotten hit and I was helping him and we were almost back to headquarters when I got hit with a Nambu machine gun.

Navy doctor Ernest Daniel, whose training at the Medical College of Georgia was temporarily interrupted by the attack at Pearl Harbor, was in charge of 29 corpsmen on Okinawa. He was allowed to carry a sidearm because the Japanese, unlike the Germans, had not signed the Geneva Convention, and so Daniel had occasion to use it when a Japanese soldier surprised him and a Marine buddy in their foxhole:

We had a pretty good moon out that night. We [would take] turns of about 15 or 20 minutes sleep. This [Japanese soldier] looked over that hole and me and the Marine both fired at about the same time, he said he didn't hit him because his hand hit the side of the foxhole. I fired the .45 and I hit him. Well, we spent the rest of the night wondering if he was dead or not or whether [he] was going to roll a grenade in on us, but he didn't.

Corporal Russell McClellan, a driver in the Marines' 1st Division, 3rd Battalion, describes an incident on Okinawa that illustrates the severe mental strain of combat that could break some men and their bond of trust with one another:

[Some men] would get under fire and kind of go whacky, but one of our men told me when I was on Peleliu and Guadalcanal that he wasn't going in [to fight]. I said, "Why not?" and he said, "I'm scared, it's gonna kill me if I go in." He told me that many a time. Well, everybody in the outfit knew it. But he did, he shot himself twice in the foot. Anyway, he had his carbine down on his foot and pulled the trigger. He didn't feel the first [shot], [so he] pulled [the trigger] again, shot himself twice in the foot. He ruined his foot.

They took him back to some islands and he wrote us a letter. "I'm back here, on the island, I'm having plenty to eat and everything." And he says, "How y'all doing?" One of the guys wrote him a letter and told him, "We walking on our own two feet."

Navy Quartermaster 2nd Class Jim Davis, aboard USS LCS-112 (Landing Craft Support), was impressed with the vast armada supporting the invasion of Okinawa. Kamikazes, however, could strike at any time:

The suicide planes were a frightening thing. They would come in with not only the sound of their engines and diving from about 10,000 feet, but they would attach sirens to their wing, a wind-activated siren that made it even louder, to instill fear. So, we got to Okinawa and we were put into the western side of the island first. And it was filled with ships. It was hard to imagine that many ships in one place. While we were there that afternoon, May the 6th, we were anchored just off the [USS] West Virginia. And a friend of mine was the ship's barber and while

255

he was giving me a haircut, a suicide plane came in and went right over the top of our ship into the *West Virginia,* and killed about 57 people there. And that was the first action that we saw.

Though kamikazes could be lethally effective, the "Baka bomb," a small but crude piloted aircraft, was less so:

> Baka was a Japanese word the Navy gave it for stupid. And the Baka bomb was a stupid bomb. It was about 13-feet long, like an aerial torpedo with little 6-foot wings and it would be carried on the bottom of a Betty bomber. It would be brought in at a height of about 25 or 30,000 feet then released. They had a rocket motor on it that would run for about 8 or 10 seconds. By that time, the pilot of that Baka bomb is supposed to have picked out a target and then go into it. Well, they were very ineffective because usually they didn't pick out the target in time and once they started the dive, they couldn't change. We saw a lot of them, heard a lot of them, but we never heard of any great damage being done by the Baka.

Even the quieter moments ashore could be interrupted by the enemy:

> We used to go to movies over on the beach—one of the bigger ships would send boats around to pick up everybody that wanted to go to the movie. And I remember one night we were watching a movie, probably one of those never to be remembered musicals, and somebody started shooting at us. All of us [were] watching the movie [when] somebody started shooting at us. It was a Japanese sniper up in the hills, shooting away at the people watching the movie.

After the war, Davis worked as a TV news anchor and news director in Augusta for 35 years, and wrote an online history of his ship LCS-112.

Ted Holladay, quartermaster on the *USS Abele* and veteran of the Iwo Jima campaign, describes fending off a Japanese suicide boat off the coast of Okinawa:

> I had just retired and hit my bunk and all of a sudden, General Quarters. We went topside. We didn't bother to dress, we just put on our skivvies and our shorts and put on our life jackets and

our helmets and reported. We could hear this noise coming from the distance, and all of a sudden a tremendous explosion.

You're in an area where airplanes are overhead, kamikazes are looking for a point of attack, so you don't show light. Everything on the ship is totally blacked out and we're operating with red lights so it can't be seen from afar. We could hear the explosion off our starboard side. Then we heard what sounded like an outboard motorboat and it began to get louder and louder. Well, after the explosion occurred, we could hear that the sound was coming towards us, so we had a decision to make. Do we turn on the lights and see what this thing is and run the possibility of having a kamikaze hit us, or do we hope that we can see him before whatever it is that's coming? Well, you don't make decisions like that. You make them in desperation, and the desperation was that you've got to stop the first point of danger. I was a quartermaster and my job was to use lights to transmit messages by Morse Code and blinker, but it also was a good searchlight. So we trained this light on the sound of it, and it was a boat, if you can call it a boat. If you can imagine a 16-foot fishing skiff with an air-cooled engine on the back of it. Whoever was running this boat was lying flat in the boat. There were two depth charges on the bow, and the motor was on the stern. We could see him coming at us.

Of course, he went to whatever Japanese heaven [there] was, and took the boat with him. When we hit him, he was probably half a football field away from us and he'd come into the range where we could see him. We used every fifth projectile we fired out of our 20-millimeters with a tracer, so you could manually train the arc [of gunfire] like taking a garden hose. The 20-millimeter was manned by a young boy from Maine. He loved firing that gun. His passion was to fire that gun, and he was good. We could see the arc going across and hit this boat, and when we hit it, it blew up and the splash from the depth charge came onto our deck. That's how close that we came to getting knocked out.

Boatswain's Mate 1st class Paul Harless, a veteran of the Bougainville and Iwo Jima campaigns, was serving as a gunner aboard the destroyer *USS John Rodgers* when he helped down two kamikazes during the Okinawa campaign:

He was headed straight for us…approximately 100 feet from us when we exploded whatever he was carrying. Just blew up in such small pieces that I received a small piece of aluminum from that plane. The propeller came on down and hit the deck and went over the side, no one could grab it. He was machine gunning as he came in.

Harless' accuracy did not only come from his military training. As he puts it, "I was quite a hunter when I was a little kid."

Navy doctor Ernest Daniel, serving on an attack troop transport, helped out a gunner when their ship was attacked by a kamikaze:

One was coming toward our ship. We had a black guy named Meeks, a 20 millimeter gunner. I had learned how to load the gun, but I had never fired one. But his loader got a wound, shrapnel, and I was out of the deck treating him, this kamikaze was coming for [us] and [Meeks] ran out of bullets, so I reached over and got a canister, slapped it into the gun and told him to cock and fire it and he did and he brought [the kamikaze] down about 800 yards off. From then on Meeks called that our—mine and doc's Jap. The whole time the Jap was coming at him he said, "Don't come at me, Jap. Don't come at me, mister Jap."

Aviation Machinist's Mate 3rd class Joe Vignati was on the carrier USS Bunker Hill when she was struck by kamikazes on May 11, 1945. He describes the chaos aboard the Bunker Hill, then jumping overboard and being rescued by a destroyer:

Maybe two, three 'o clock in the afternoon, I was up on top, in the back, my plane was back there. And the first [kamikaze] hit, seemed to me it skipped off, and the second [hit] the island [the ship's superstructure] and knocked out communications so we didn't know what was going on. We had no instructions, nobody to tell us what to do. Planes started burning, I went down and stayed there for a long time. There was a crew chief down there and I was talking to him. He said, "We gonna have to get out of here because there's [high] octane gas above us and it's burning up there."

There was smoke over here, planes was over here, gas was there. I imagine there [were] 50 or 60 of us back there. A bunch had gone [overboard] before I ever went. I kept looking around and the crowd got thinner and thinner. I says [to the crew chief], "Okay, you lead and I'll follow you." So I left with him. I took my shoes off and tied them around my neck so I'd have them.

[I was in the water about] three hours. Long enough to keep working my way towards the destroyer. They were picking up people all along. [I] swam over to a destroyer and the destroyer picked me up, brought us back the next day.

I never did see [the chief] anymore, so I don't know where he's at. And we had a couple hundred boys dead, that was down in the hole, smoke killed a lot of them.

Some 373 men were killed in the attack on the *Bunker Hill*, with 43 missing (never found) and 264 wounded. This was the worst kamikaze attack of the war. The *Bunker Hill* was then towed back to the United States for repairs. In the aftermath of the attack, a mass burial at sea followed. As witnessed by Vignati,

I remember probably somewhere around 40 or 50 boys laying out there covered up on the hanger deck when I came back aboard the next day. They'd wrap them in canvas, put a five inch shell in them. They had a boat set up on the side, they'd just put them on that boat and slide them over. One after the other because they had a preacher there doing the praying.

Vignati also recalls three incidents on the *Bunker Hill* that illustrate the ever-present danger, and mental strain, of naval warfare. In the first, a fellow mechanic accidentally falls into a running propeller; in the second and third, the strain of sea combat gets the better of two other sailors:

He just slipped on some oil on the deck, blew him right back into the next plane. Prop hit him. They shut it down, cleaned it up. We got the hell out of the way and after they cleaned it up we went on back in operation. He was trying to pass underneath one prop and he hit some oil and he was gone. The prop behind him caught him.

We had one boy [who] walked over the side one night, they never slowed down looking for him, it was dark. I don't know whether one of the destroyers stopped and looked for him, probably did, but we kept going. We had [another] boy hang himself on the fan tail. I don't know who he was, but gosh I guess his nerves got him and he hung himself.

Gunner's Mate 2nd class Richard Craig was a sailor on LSM-13, a medium-sized amphibious landing ship, which among its various duties would provide smoke screens to protect larger vessels from kamikaze attack. This tactic often left LSM-13 vulnerable:

> At sundown and sunrise is when [the kamikazes] would come in. One of our duties at Okinawa for several days was to go out on what the Navy referred to as the perimeter. The radar aboard the large ships could pick up air enemy, but they could not pick up surface enemy and the Japanese kamikazes would come in at water level. So [we] circled the island of Okinawa with ships, amphibious ships, smaller ships that had surface radar that could pick up the planes coming across the water and radio to the larger ships that they were on their way in. [This tactic] saved some lives.

> On Easter Sunday night, the 1st of April, one suicide plane came in, heading for us because the amphibious ships had smoke generators and we would generate smoke to cover up the larger ships, which left us exposed. Our smoke would cover the large ships and just before dark that day a suicide plane came in and without any doubt had picked us out, but the wind changed before he got to us, which exposed a troop carrier, the APA-91, with soldiers coming over the side, down the rope ladders to get in the small boats. He switched his course from crashing into us and went in the number three hole on the APA-91, and the report a couple of days later said that 347 Army personnel were killed.

When life at sea was quieter, Craig would write letters to his girlfriend back home. They invented a secret code to elude the censors:

> We worked out a code that in the first paragraph of a letter that I would sign Richard, because I was known as Dick. If I signed it Richard there was a message in the first paragraph, and the message was the first word in each sentence, whether it made sense or not, which spelled out where I was.

Seaman 1st class Reed Eubanks, on the attack transport *USS Barnett*, had already served in the Guadalcanal campaign when he arrived at Okinawa and faced the ubiquitous kamikazes, which, apart from the damage they could do themselves, sometimes created deadly confusion amidst the American ships. The incident Eubanks describes here, in which a US destroyer accidentally fired on the *Barnett*, occurred on April 6, 1945:

> A kamikaze slipped in out of the sun, their favorite trick, you couldn't see them late in the afternoon. Everybody started firing—there was a destroyer anchored next to us, one of those new super destroyers and they had electronic firing or whatever control on it and the kamikaze went on over us and the destroyer forgot to quit firing and shot a hole right through our ship. Shot all our booms and equipment away, booms are cranes which lifted boats in and out of the sea, load and unload equipment into the hull. Those booms were big, about 24 inches in diameter, and they shot them in two like a toothpick. And the whole deck, cables everywhere, booms everywhere, and we had five men wounded and they were all wounded in the butt, maybe we were running like hell. They all got the Purple Heart, but they were just flesh wounds from shrapnel.

Bombing the Japanese mainland

At the same time as the Battle of Okinawa, Japan was being subjected to immense air bombardments; its wooden cities were not able to withstand the growing American air fleets and Japan's air defenses were completely inadequate. One single bombardment of Tokyo killed more than two hundred thousand people.

Many soldiers and sailors expected to take part in what most assumed would be an extraordinarily bloody invasion of the Japanese homeland. The dread which infantrymen felt about the upcoming invasion of Japan is beyond imagination.

1st Lt. Jim Wetzel served as a radar operator on a B-29 in the 20th Air Force. Wetzel describes the complexity and danger of a 100-plane bombing run over Tokyo:

> My position on the plane was in the back in a windowless area with a radar scope in front of me. I really fought a virtual war, the only thing that I actually saw was on a radar screen. I was on

intercom and I could hear everything that was going on and could get as frightened and scared as anyone else, but I couldn't see what was going on.

[On one run] we were caught in lights when we hit the IP [Initial Point, the final point before dropping bombs] across Tokyo Bay. We flew individually into the target area, but as a lead crew we were ahead of everyone else anyway, so we started in and became a prime target for searchlights and antiaircraft and so forth.

So we started taking evasive action—Whitey [the pilot] started taking evasive action as soon as we got off the IP and Tokyo Bay had flak barges in the middle of it so—and antiaircraft searchlights also. So we were in searchlights and being shot at by antiaircraft, and Whitey was doing evasive action from the searchlights, so there wasn't really much to see on the radar. And this went on for a little while until we finally got to the stage where we were almost at the range of the target and it so happened that this was near the Imperial Palace, and we had to tell Whitey he had to flatten out, there was the bomb bay doors that had to be opened and away we go. So at that stage Tokyo was black and there were no incendiaries that preceded us, so we were doing visual and/or radar bombing at that stage and the bombardier took over—leveled [the plane], opened the bomb bay doors and let [the bombs] go. We were fortunate in that of the four planes that went in as lead planes, two got shot down, the third one got an engine knocked [out], but he made it back and fortunately for us we got flak holes, but nothing critical. And once you drop those bombs the bomb bay doors come open and the power goes and you get out of there. And you also have a flight path to get out, and the discipline in those night incendiary raids was that you had to fly a course because there may have been another B-29 a wing tip away from you on the run.

Wetzel would go on a total of 23 missions over Japan, earning the Distinguished Flying Cross.

Staff Sgt. Ed Ricketson flew 13 missions over Japan in 1945 as a B-29 gunner with the 20th Air Force. He recalls the emotional strain of flying dangerous missions and the powerful destructiveness of the United States' largest bomber:

[We'd fly] over there and get the target in line and miss it by a mile because of the winds. Then it's "Okay, boys, you're going in at 6,000 feet at night." So you can imagine what kind of news that was, that burned them out. It was a 12-hour trip, six hours and six back. You could see the target burning from a 100 miles away. That's all we did. They said burn it, burn it, that's it, just burn it, so that was what we [did]. Get over there safely, drop the bombs on a base, and get the hell home and hope we make it. You can imagine a city of 3 or 4 million people on fire, and they said, "Don't you ever get close enough to the smoke." It'll turn you upside down.

Joseph (Tag) Sheppard, aboard the *USS Franklin*, had already survived kamikaze attacks during the Battle of Leyte Gulf. While supporting airstrikes on Japan, the *Franklin* was hit by dive bombers and kamikazes on March 19, 1945. The attack ignited a massive fire on deck, and 807 U.S. sailors were killed, 487 wounded. The *Franklin* was the most heavily damaged US carrier that survived the war. Sheppard tells the harrowing story as well as any historian:

We must have had about 100 ships out there. We had plenty of help, and we was going in for the big push. We was getting ready to take over the country of Japan. And the first day, we were ahead of a string of ships. I guess it must have been about four or five carriers. And we had battleships, we had everything you could mention.

Two planes came in, and we were in a group and we thought we had everything covered. And these two planes somehow or another slipped in [through] some sort of a cloud. One of the planes spotted it and [reported], "You've got something coming in on you." We couldn't find it.

I was sitting on the pot. And that thing, it just knocked me almost off the pot, and I started getting ready to go to my battle station in the forward end. We were burning from one end to the other. Fire, fire everywhere, on the hangar deck and everything. I was down towards the aft end, and I had to get [to the forward end]. I started to run to get up there, and all of a sudden I was just swamped with everybody coming back. It was burning up there and blowing up. Our own ammunition started to blow up, fire

263

got into it. And so everybody was running and they were saying, "You can't get up there." So I ran aft as far as I could. I ran to the chief's quarters. That's where I was based, anyway, where I would've usually slept.

Man, that smoke came in there and it was just stifling. You couldn't go anywhere. It was burning down below and it was just staying in the ship, just drifting around, and everybody was choking. I was about choked to death. I picked up a big cloth off of the mess table where we had been eating and I wet it as good as I could and wrapped up my head to get away from that smoke. Then I got to thinking, well, I've got to do something. I can't stay here. Everybody else had the same idea, but we couldn't go anywhere. We were just jammed in there. We couldn't get out. It was burning and blowing up everywhere—2,000-pound bombs and everything else, our bombs blowing up. And so I'll tell you the truth, and I'm not ashamed of it. I looked up to the Master and I asked [that] if he would get me out of here, I would do better. That's what I said, I'll do better. And you know something? Just like that He said, go to the other side of the ship, and so I did. I went to the other side of the ship and I got up to the hangar deck and it was good air. It was air. That's what I wanted.

We had launched about four planes when we got hit, and the rest of them were up there [on deck] and loaded up with bombs, gasoline. Fire got in there, wiped out the whole thing, killed all the pilots.

And so I looked back [to] the aft part of the ship, there was a little shop back there, where people worked on the planes. So I ran back there and then I knew, too, that if I had to leave the ship, there was a door that went through that place and you could get out pretty easy. So I went back there and there was four people in there already. I didn't have on a life jacket. And so they said, "Come on, what are we going to do, Chief?" I told them, "I don't know, but let's just sit here for a minute and see what happens." And about that time, a 2,000-pound bomb went off on the other side of us, it just absolutely wiped that place out. It didn't bother us, but it just tore the whole back end of the ship.

We all looked up and I said, "Well, let's go." We didn't have any power, didn't have nothing. We just had ourselves. Five or six of us jumped over the side, and they gave me a life jacket. When we jumped out, this little seaman and me were drifting off by ourselves, and you don't want to do that because you could get left [behind]. It's hard to see a man's head out of the water. So I told him. He was a young fellow, wasn't over 18. He started to cry and I yelled at him, "You'd better shut your mouth or you'll get drowned out here." And he turned around and he saw me and he said, "Chief, what are we going to do?" And about that time I sort of kicked up on a swell, and I saw a life raft, and there was one man on [it], but it was about a mile from where we were. And so we started kicking and swimming. I said, "Let's make it to the raft." I knew if you could get on a raft, you'd get picked up a whole lot quicker. It took us about an hour to make it. We got to the life raft and the man was still sitting on there by himself, and so we got aboard. When we sat down, the little boy looked at me and he said, "Chief, let's you and me sing." "I don't want to sing, you can go ahead and sing if you want to, I don't feel like it." So he said, "Let's sing 'Give me land, lots of land and the starry skies above.'" And I said, "You go ahead" and he sang. We sat there until we got picked up by a destroyer. They sent a boat out and picked us up and took us over to their ship, and we came back to Ulithi [an atoll in the Carolina Islands].

No doubt because of his coolness under strain, and exceptional leadership abilities, Sheppard was subsequently promoted to officer.

Motor Machinist 1st Mate Bruce Wright, a veteran of the Pearl Harbor attack, was now aboard the submarine *USS Quillback* in the Pacific in mid-1945. On one particular patrol, the *Quillback* came across a Japanese submarine and a downed U.S. flier:

[We] went out to Japan, Guam, Saipan and what they call the Chosin Straits and chased an old Jap sub for three or four days. We had our torpedoes cocked on him but never could get a good shot. [Later we] picked up a downed flier. He was only a mile or two off the beach, paddling. I helped pull [him] in, got him down the [rear] battery hatch and put him to bed. He stayed in bed two or three days and they offered him a drink of whisky, but he declined.

Radioman 3rd class Robert Moore served on a submarine attached to Task Force 72 in the Pacific theater. Here he offers a glimpse into the experience of waiting through a depth charge attack:

> Under depth charge attack you had a certain assignment. It was just a business type atmosphere and later you might lose it, but during [an attack] you were steeled to do what you were supposed to do. That's the way I felt and that's what I remember about the other people.

This kind of stress would lead men to seek unorthodox outlets for their stress:

> The one thing that I remember more than anything else was a stowaway mouse. They could come across the lines from the dock and that mouse caused a lot of confusion. For instance, we had a man, Rothmale, from Maryland. His head sat right down on his shoulders, didn't have any neck. When he had his pea coat collar up, [it was] above his head. Rothmale came down off the bridge as a lookout and took off his coat. He had a .45 on and he was just about to take the belt off. I was in the next compartment and was laying on my stomach with my chin on my arms and all of a sudden he pulled [out] that .45 and emptied it. He was in the forward torpedo room so that caused a little bit of confusion.
>
> That .45 was ricocheting all over and the warheads were in place of course, not to mention every 12 feet in that submarine you had a device to scuttle the ship. One could have hit that and set them all off. The submarine was compartmentalized and had thick steel walls and big heavy doors and the skipper was in the compartment that I was in. He came by my bunk and went through the door and grabbed Rothmale. There wasn't anybody larger than this skipper, he was big. And he just grabbed Rothmale by the front of his shirt and he was standing there with a .45 in his hand. The old man says, "What the hell, Rothmale?" And he says, "That damn rat, sir." And [the skipper] said, "Did you hit him?" He said, "No, sir." And he smacked him right in the teeth, you know, the old man did, and Rothmale hit the deck.

Surrender

Whether the strategy of massive aerial bombardment would have

266

eventually convinced the hard line faction in Tokyo to surrender will never be known. But four days in August did. On August 6, 1945, an American B-29 (the most costly weapon system of the war) dropped the first atomic bomb on Hiroshima. On August 8, the Soviet Union declared war on Japan and sent 1.6 million soldiers into battle in Japanese-controlled Manchuria. On August 9, the second atomic bomb fell on Nagasaki. Which of these three events clinched the Japanese decision to surrender may never be known for certain, but on August 15, Japan agreed to end the war. On September 2, the official surrender document was signed in Tokyo Bay aboard the battleship *USS Missouri*.

Seaman 1st class Hugh Alexander witnessed the Japanese surrender. Both Alexander and his battleship, the *USS New Mexico*, had recovered from the kamikaze attacks of several months earlier during the Philippines campaign and arrived in Tokyo Bay on September 2. Though the war was nominally over, the scene was still tense with danger:

> [We were at the] signing of the peace treaty in Tokyo Bay. The [*USS*] *Missouri*—the Mighty Moe, didn't come in until after we got in there, they were laying 100 miles off. We were the second ship through the harbor. Admiral Spruance came on the PA system and said, "We don't have no idea what's going to happen, if they open fire on us our chances of getting out is going to be slim. Don't fire no guns until we're fired on." They had all the guns on the harbor flagged with white sheets. And boy they had the guns like you wouldn't believe.

The dropping of the atomic bombs has been debated ever since— but not by the infantrymen who would have been charged with invading Japan. The casualties would have been appalling, not to mention extraordinary loss of civilian life. Army Sergeant William (Sam) Carter, a signalman and veteran of Iwo Jima, describes the trepidation soldiers felt at the impending invasion of Japan and the immense sense of relief once the war had finally ended:

> Around July [1945], they [asked] us to fill out our wills and send them with all our personal items and a personal note [to our families] that our next stop would be the beaches of Japan and there would be approximate 250,000 fatalities before we could make a landing. Which I did. I didn't send it to my mother. I sent it to my uncle. And they started preparing us immediately to accept death. I mean you're already at the point that it's, you

know, it's going to happen. It might and it might not. You don't think about it.

August 6 the bomb was dropped. But what was amazing, what really touched you, from June to July you'd lay in your pup tents looking up at night and you'd see 200 B-29s headed to Japan. And hours later they returned to Iwo Jima. But every night it looked like a city up there and they were burning Japan block by block on purpose. So they dropped the bomb. We knew it was over because we knew how bad it was. And then when they dropped the second one, we knew it was over.

Boatswain's Mate 3rd class Emerald (Bill) Williams recalls feeling sympathy for the Japanese after the surrender:

[We] had an atomic bomb and it destroyed a city. We was like everybody else, "My gosh, one bomb destroyed a whole city, a huge city? What's going to happen next?" Then when we saw all the pictures, the Japanese didn't seem to be as terrible to us. If that could have happened in America, if they had got this bomb and dropped it on us before we dropped it on them, how horrible that would have been and then it sort of dawned on us and then compassion started building. There was a time when there was more hate for the Japanese people within us than there were compassion.

But for the most part, American servicemen felt an immense relief after the Japanese surrender. Sometimes, though, letting off steam could be dangerous. Russell McClellan of the 1st Marine Division and veteran of the bitter fighting on Okinawa recalls several servicemen being hit by celebratory gunfire:

We heard [about the atomic bomb] the night it dropped. We was watching a movie and all of a sudden all the guns on the island started firing and shrapnel was just falling everywhere. They was firing because they had heard before us and they stopped them right quick as [fast] as they could. They stopped the movie when the [guns] started firing, they thought planes was coming over. They was just shooting in joy because the war was over. And [that shell fire] killed, we heard, six people—I don't know whether it was all Marines or Army or not.

268

Tom Zwemer, medic in the 40th Army Division, realized the dangers and took cover:

> I had gotten through three assault landings and [on] VJ Day everybody that had a weapon was shooting in the air. So I got my cot and little bunk next to a concrete curb about 10 inches tall. I got down right next to that curb until the firing quieted down. I said, "I'm not going to go through this war and end being wounded or killed because somebody is too drunk and too exuberant."

Several other veterans remember the end of the war. Machine-gunner Henry Burch of the Army's 80th Division:

> We thought we was going [to invade Japan], yeah. And we heard that they'd dropped a bomb on Hiroshima. But we were told that you could hear General Patton cursing about two blocks because he knew the war would soon be over.

Naval aviator Fred Langdon:

> I lost some money on [V-J Day]. They were betting that the war would be over by August 6th or something like that. They were Air Force guys that had to make their money someway, so they were betting and we went ahead. At the time, my poker game was pretty good, so I had a few bucks and they dropped the bomb and kapoof, it was all over.

James Kauffmann, B-24 pilot in the 10th Air Force:

> The end of the war came through the rumor mill. It started I guess 10:00 in the morning, and it went from there. Sometime in the afternoon the base commander, Captain McAron, called us together and said that they had received a communiqué over the teletype that the Japanese had asked for unconditional surrender and it was confirmed at that point. And of course, everybody was very happy.
>
> After the war actually ended, the military did a good thing and I'm proud to have been a part of it. We took all of the ground personnel stationed there at the base to Agra [India] where they

could see the Taj Mahal. It was a beautiful place, a wonderful place to go. We carried every one of them.

Robert Scherer of the 11th Airborne Division:

[The major, our executive officer] said, "I've got some good news for you." He said, "The war is over." And he said, "But any man who fires his rifle or his pistol now will be court-martialed." And he said, "Open up the bars, drink all you want, drink it dry because the war is over." So they did.

The next morning the first sergeant came down and said to me, "Sergeant, get three men and go to the airstrip. Take a three-quarter ton truck." I went over there and reported to the warrant officer and he said, "I want to pile all these gliders up in the middle of the airfield." And we did, we piled the gliders all up, he threw gasoline on, they burned them up.

The extreme violence and terror of the war, and the clear Allied victory, brought to an end a half century of Japanese-American conflict and the two countries have been allies ever since. This attitude of forgiveness was not entirely universal and Americans who survived Japanese POW camps had great difficulties after the war coping with their experience. Life for American prisoners of war in Asia was far harder than in Europe. Almost 99% of the Americans held by the Reich would live to tell the tale; for those held by Japan, the survival rate was under 60%. Japanese culture was contemptuous of POWs and this was reflected in the brutality of the camps.

Army Lt. Bill Britton helped liberate American and other POWs from Camp Fukuoka 17 just after the Japanese surrender. As was the case at many other POW camps, conditions were deadly for the prisoners—malnutrition, physical abuse, and lack of medical care caused the death of thousands of men. Britton describes Japanese guards, alarmingly still armed, protecting his unit from hostile Japanese civilians (and, perhaps, the Japanese civilians from the American soldiers) while en route to a POW camp:

We boarded a train loaded with people and settled down. We noticed a Japanese guard at each end of the car with bayonets on their rifle. I asked an interpreter, "Why we got Japanese?" He said they are to protect us. They didn't want any [Japanese civilians] coming on this car and bothering us. So they're there to keep them out, not us in. I [thought], kinda feels funny, me sitting here with a Japanese with a bayonet and loaded rifle looking at me and I'm looking at him. I don't know if he lost his brother last week or something, mad with us or not. But I got a .45. He start anything up, I would shoot him, too.

As it turned out, we didn't have any need to worry. They were just there as guards. Later on we opened up C-rations or K-rations to eat. We noticed they looked hungry so I said "The war's over. Let's give them our rations." So we threw each one of them a box and had to show them what's in it and explain to them how to open it. And they just thought it was wonderful. Never seen anything like that. And what they really liked was three cigarettes in there. They would light one and take a few puffs and put it out and save it. They made those cigarettes stretch for a long time. They thanked us. *Arigato* is thank you in Japanese. *Arigato*, they'd bow clean down to the floor practically, thanking us for their food and everything. I told somebody I believed they'd join the American Army if we asked them to.

In these next excerpts, Britton describes the awful condition of the POWs, the lengths his unit went to notify the prisoners' families of their imminent return, and the brutal treatment meted out by the Japanese toward the prisoners, including dangerous mining work. The camp commandant, Asao Fukuhara, was later executed for war crimes.

The 13th of September is when we landed at [Camp] Fukuoka 17. The so-called hospital was just a barracks-type building with elevated straw mats for the men to lay on. It was not comfortable, it was not clean, and the men were in terrible condition. They were given little or no medical care by the Japanese. Our own doctors had to take care of them with little or no medicine. The stench in that building was horrible. It was so bad that we drew lots to see who would go get the information from each prisoner of war that we needed to get. I lost. So my team was given the job of going into the hospital area and processing those prisoners.

We had a questionnaire, what unit were you in, when you were captured, where were you captured, serial number and blah, blah, blah. Then 10 words that you want sent home to your family. This message will be sent immediately to Nagasaki and radioed to Manila and [then] the United States within 24 hours and your family would get this message. And they did. The next day people found out that their loved one was still alive. I think that's marvelous the way they did it.

We heard stories of the brutality that occurred. For instance, if a guard spoke, you came to attention and you bowed your head. If you failed to bow your head he'd knock you down. He'd knock your teeth out. If he was standing there and you walked by, you would immediately come to attention and bow your head to him as you passed. It didn't make any difference if you were an officer, a private, sergeant, whatever, they'd knock you down.

A lot of them took delight in tormenting the prisoners, particularly the ones that worked in the coal mine. It was a horrible situation. They needed the coal to run the defense establishment. The [guards] were peasant class people who'd always been at the bottom of the ladder all their life. They were mistreated themselves. They had a chance to get somebody one step below them and they took it out on them. And they were very, very brutal to our soldiers. Stuff happened down there in the mines that you just won't believe. A lot of them were killed in the mines. Cave-ins killed them or trucks ran off the track and pinned them to the wall and killed them. We lost a lot of people in the mines. The Japanese at this particular camp were horrible. I can't imagine being in a worse place. I really can't.

The [camp] clock was torn down by an Australian boy [whose] legs had to be amputated, due to the fact that Captain Fukuhara, for a very small crime like stealing a potato from the kitchen, had him beat severely and put on the parade ground with a bamboo rod behind his legs during the wintertime. [He] didn't have any very warm clothes on. All night long he was out in the weather with this bamboo rod behind his legs, which, of course, cut off the blood circulation to the lower part of his legs. Eventually they let him up, but the damage had been done. The legs began to turn blue and then gangrene set in. The American doctors, they had to amputate both his legs below the knee. He was an Australian and a very cheerful person. For someone that had gone through all that he seemed to keep his outlook good, cheerful, and accept it. [But] he didn't like that clock at all.

There's something about that clock, getting him up and doing things. He asked could he destroy the clock. So we gave him the clock and he threw it down on the ground and broke it all to pieces. And he just stood there and laughed like that was the biggest thing he could do was break that clock up.

In these next excerpts, Britton describes the ceremonial closing of the camp and the disposal of the remains of soldiers who had died at the camp:

I only wish it was possible for me to describe what actually happened when these men formed their ranks for the last time and moved up in front of the prison office for a prayer of thanks given by their padre, a great man. An honor guard had been at the gates and upon the conclusion of the prayer, the entire group snapped to attention, present arms was given, and the ashes of their deceased friends were moved out of the office through the gates. Each one of the four boxes of ashes [had] a national flag [for] each of the four nations [represented in the camp].

The truck took the ashes to the railroad station with the honor guard. Each unit then in turn executed right-face and marched out of the hell hole that had been their home for years. Their lines were straight, their step was perfect, and their heads were held high. At last, free men. It was one of the most stirring sights I have ever seen. The next day, 16th of September at 7:30 the Americans moved out and Camp 17 was closed. Gone was written in white paint on top of many of the buildings so the Air Force wouldn't drop any more food supplies. Supplies that wasn't needed were turned over to the Chinese camp. [We had] orders to maintain order between the Chinese and the Japanese. The Chinese wanted to go out and kill Japanese. We had to keep order in their camp. They were so mad. They got guns. They were ready to start a riot over there. We kept it down. It never happened.

Just as the prisoners showed their pride upon exiting the camp, they also showed their hunger for news of life back home and their appreciation for a humane Japanese commandant of another POW camp:

I walked over to an American camp about a half a mile away. They were glad to see us. Most of the men in the American camp were from the 200th Coast Artillery out of New Mexico and they'd been on Corregidor. And the 195th Tank Battalion from Illinois, National Guard Unit. They were captured on Bataan. But they'd been treated well at this camp. We drank beer and sang songs, and they asked me questions. They had no idea what had happened since they had been incarcerated. They didn't know about D-Day. They had heard rumors, but they didn't know what had happened in Europe. They didn't know that Roosevelt was dead. They didn't know that Truman was President. They didn't know anything about the B-29 bomber. They [looked up and] asked "what kind of plane is that? That is such a big plane." I told them it was a B-29. That's what dropped the atom bomb. "What's an atom bomb?" I explained to them that an atomic bomb destroyed Hiroshima, and one was dropped at Nagasaki. I went through that bomb area in Nagasaki and saw it. Anyhow, we were just flooded with questions. I stayed over there a long time at the American camp talking to them about what happened. They were all interested. We sat around sipping beer and talking. They knew they would be leaving the next day and they were so happy.

The next morning we moved them out. The camp commander stood at the gate and as each man came up he saluted that commander and he saluted him back and they shook hands. That's how they were treated. Every one of them went out, they saluted him. That's the respect they had for him for how he treated them—this was a good camp. This wasn't [Camp] 17. This camp commander had been a professor at university in Tokyo and he'd been to Harvard. He spoke fluent English. And he treated these men [humanely]. He complied with the Geneva Convention. I was amazed. [One American POW] said, "He's one of the finest gentlemen I've ever known."

Lastly, Britton describes a surprisingly festive parade as his unit finished its mission:

We stayed on for several days. I think it was the 5th of October when [members of] the 8th Marines came to recon the town. They couldn't believe we had a dining room where we were eating like kings and drinking beer when we wanted. They wanted to take over that place right away. The rest of their reinforced

274

company would come into Omuta in x-number of days. That's when we made plans to pack up and leave.

We decided to leave in style and we called in the [Japanese] chief of police. He could get anything done you wanted. I think he'd have shot his mama if we told him to. We had a conference with him with an interpreter. We told him we wanted to leave in style. We wanted him to lead the parade to the railroad station about two miles away. We wanted a Japanese Army band to play "Stars and Stripes Forever." We wanted rickshaws for the officers and the men could ride in the automobiles. Our trucks would bring our baggage and all the cold beer that we needed. He said, *hai*; that's yes, *hai*.

So the morning we got ready to leave, they were lined up. I went out in the street and there's that Japanese band out there in the street. We got in the rickshaws, the men loaded everything up, we pulled out, [the Japanese police chief] was directing traffic. He had a [motorcycle and a] driver. He sat in the sidecar. He got in front, pulled out his sword, banzai, and then took off, band playing. People lined the streets and the Marines were standing there with their mouth open. They couldn't believe it. Every once in a while Lt. Gibbs would pull his pistol out and go pow, pow, and shoot a couple in the air. We went around in those rickshaws with the band playing. I guess McArthur would have court martialed us if he could have seen us.

Anyhow, we got to the railroad station. They had all the geisha girls from the geisha house down there doing the dance for us while we were loading the train. The train had a big American flag on the front. We got onboard, and as we pulled out, the band struck up "Auld Lang Syne." That is a very popular song in Japan. They love that song. All of us on the train sang in English, they were singing in Japanese. The train took us down to a Japanese Air Force base some miles away.

The horror and celebration articulated here in Britton's experience in post-surrender Japan exemplifies the complex emotional mixture felt by many veterans as they gathered themselves, after several unforgiving years, to return home.

Chapter 7
Aftermath and Return

Postwar Occupation of Japan and China

The Japanese surrender led to a new and complicated phase: the occupation of Japan, and also of parts of China as the Japanese armies there surrendered. General George Marshall was even sent on a mission to mediate between the Chinese Nationalists and Communists to establish a unity government, but in this he could not succeed. Occupation duty in China could be hazardous, as shown by the death of three Marines in an ambush in July 1946. Japan was a different situation entirely. The Japanese government intended from the beginning to accommodate the 350,000-strong occupation force completely. These forces held an enormous collective power as General of the Army Douglas MacArthur had almost unlimited power to modernize and democratize Japan. This included trying and punishing select wartime Japanese leaders for war crimes.

Pat Roberts, Marine corporal, veteran of Saipan and Okinawa and recipient of three Purple Hearts, arrived with the 6th Division in China after the Japanese surrender to try to keep the peace between the Nationalists and the Communists. Roberts made some Chinese friends and enjoyed a hard-earned month's leave:

> This little Chinese fella, one night he appeared around the fire, and that began to be a nightly thing with us. He spoke Chinese and I spoke English and I finally started calling him Ding Ho, which means very good in Chinese. After several weeks I got him to go down to the compound and some of the fellas in my squad took some dungarees and cut them down and made him a little uniform. We got it okayed with the commanding officer and he became a runner. I never will forget—he hadn't had a bath in a long time, when we first took him down there he was rusty. Down in the bottom of this compound there was a pool that looked like what you'd put goldfish in and we took him down there and took his clothes off and got a scrub brush and scrubbed him and he was meanest little fella you ever heard in your life, he fussed and fussed and fussed. But he loved all of us and finally we met his friend up there, which we called Eight Ball, and they just became part of our organization [until] we left China.

One day I went to my commanding officer and said, "I've been in the Marine Corps now two and half, three years and I've never had a liberty or furlough. I want to take some time off here in China." He said, "Well, I don't know, what do you want, a week?" I said, "No, I want a month." He said, "A month? You're crazy." I said, "No, I've got more than that coming to me." After much to do he said, okay, I got a month's liberty. I went to Tientsin [now known as Tianjin, a major city in northern China]. I got a [hotel] suite and spent the whole month there. Every day I'd get a rickshaw and I'd go in a different direction. I went to Chinese dances, I went to Chinese funerals. A Chinese funeral is something like a wedding we have in this country, they really have a good time at a funeral, big, ringing bells and making noise and everything. I really got an education during that month, going to different places, seeing all these Buddha gardens and all that, it was quite an experience.

The 6th Division left China in April 1946.

Capt. W.G. (Curly) Watson was a medical officer with the 6th Division stationed in Yeosu, Korea at the end of 1945. His job was to care for U.S. personnel but found himself inundated with sick Korean civilians who had endured the privations of Japanese occupation:

[Our soldiers had] the usual respiratory diseases mostly. But we also took care of the Koreans with cholera and smallpox. We'd have a building, they'd bring the Koreans in there and we'd give them IV fluids. Thousands of them died, mainly from cholera. They would lose fluids so bad, nausea, vomiting, and diarrhea, and die from dehydration.

Watson was sent to a small island off the Korean mainland to attend to cholera victims; unfortunately, his party ran into boat trouble:

There was two islands off the southern tip of Korea in the East China Sea. Sorok was one island and Jeju-do was another island. One of those islands was the island of lepers and the other was Koreans. And we had some troops on this island with the Koreans. Cholera broke out in this island and since we had troops over there, General Hodge asked me to go over and check on them. I left Tuesday morning on a little 30-foot boat with three or four Koreans and two medics with me. 150 miles, said

I'd be there in about 12 hours. We got out in the East China Sea and the little boat broke down and we drifted and drifted.

Watson was adrift for 5 days, having packed food and water for only one meal. Luckily, they had calm seas and a small cabin to shelter from the sun:

> Finally on Friday, General Hodge called the island and asked if I was over there, [they] said we haven't seen him. So they sent airplanes out on Saturday morning. When the plane spotted us, they sent a ship to pick us up. That's the last ship I've been on.

Watson gained national recognition after the war as an obstetrician who oversaw the birth of over 15,000 babies in the CSRA. He continued his practice of medicine well into his 90s.

Thomas (Dick) Daniel was with the 8th Army during the postwar occupation of Japan. For two months he assisted with the Japanese people's difficult emergence from the war:

> My assignment was to work with a Japanese officer in coordinating the movement of the Japanese Army into a central location to be disarmed. He was Lt. Col. Ito, bright fellow, we had a good relationship and he and I met every morning. And one morning Colonel Ito wasn't there. A young captain was there and we went through our business and I said, "Colonel Ito be back tomorrow?" and he said, "Colonel Ito is dead." He had killed himself, he just couldn't handle the humiliation. That was the closest relation I had with any of the Japanese people.

> [In Japan] we were on C-rations, which is cans of hash and so on, and when [you] have that meal after meal you just can't handle it anymore and we would go down and empty what we had into a trash can. One day we looked down and there were Japanese children eating out of the trash can. That's something I'll never forget.

> We were in Yokohama and I was going into Tokyo for some reason. We crossed a bridge and a Japanese ex-soldier, I assume, was walking across the bridge toward us. I never saw such hatred as I saw in his eyes and his face as we passed by him very slowly. Some impressions stay with you forever.

Dallas Bahm, of the Army's 41st Division, describes occupation duty in Japan and especially the suffering of Japanese civilians:

> We was taught to kill or get killed. But let me tell you, the Japanese people, when we landed there, they was going through hell, believe me. And they treated us good. When we made our landing, the Emperor had ordered everybody out of the city into the country and he left a skeleton crew back to guard the city while we made our landing. The guards did not have weapons, they had club sticks on their side and as we would march in, they would be lined up on each side of the street, so many yards apart, with their backs to us. That was telling us that they was a conquered nation. They treated us good. We went in with full gear, full M1s, full BAR, full ammunition, full everything. But the Japanese people, we set up camp, they treated us good while we were doing that.
>
> The buildings that wasn't bombed out and burned out was still standing. [The Japanese people] had no medication, they had nothing to eat, they were starving to death and we'd feed them out of our mess gear. An old Japanese woman with a baby on her back was starving, we would give her food and she would feed the babies. All the GIs was treating the Japanese people like that and they appreciated it.
>
> My division, 41st Infantry Division, was the first division in Hiroshima, where the first bomb was dropped. When we got to Hiroshima, it was I guess 30 days elapsed, the buildings was still burning. The [Japanese] was dying from the effects of the bomb. We would ask them and they would tell us they was dying at the rate of 400 a day.
>
> We would go through and help them, we would feed them and we would find dead ones from time to time on the street. They just didn't have time to take care of them. They would be on the street and we'd pick them up and put them in ambulances and send them back to hospitals and so forth. I come along, there was a dead woman lying on her back with a small child and her breast was out. We looked at her close and it was obvious that she was dead, but the child was alive and the child was trying to nurse her mother's dead breast.

We picked the body up and the baby and put it into a three-quarter ton truck and the driver took the body and the child to God knows where. We don't know. I guess he took it to a hospital. But I hope they salvaged the baby, but the lady was dead already.

Navy Petty Officer Ed Prater witnessed the destructive effects of the atomic bombing on Nagasaki:

It was terrible, and it's sad to talk about. We would go over to the bomb site, and you'd see little Japanese children going around. Just about everybody had been affected by the radiation. They didn't know why. They didn't know what it was. The little kids running around, you'd see them decay, just actually going before your eyes. It was just a bad situation. They were trying to live and survive and they'd come around begging for food, chocolate, anything.

You'd see a warehouse that had been constructed of metal beams, I-beams, cross-beams, and the impact from the bomb. The bomb never actually hit the ground. It exploded up [in the air]. Everything was blown outward. And you could tell exactly where it had happened because all of the shrubbery, the trees, and everything was blackened and destroyed. I mean it was complete annihilation.

Navy Quartermaster Jim Davis witnessed the living conditions of the Japanese people on the main island of Honshu:

Our first experience was to go to Aomori, the main port on the northern end of Honshu. We were to go up there to support landings by the Marine Corps. That was our first time we set foot in Japan. We suddenly realized how destitute, how beat up, bombed out they were. Although that part of the city had never been bombed, they had suffered the ravages of war by what they didn't have. Their automobiles were not running on gasoline. They had devised a charcoal burner that ran their automobiles. They weren't very pleasant to look at, certainly no speed [limits] being broken, but they were managing.

Going home

Once the relief that accompanied the end of the war in Europe, and then three months later in the Pacific, died down, servicemen were impatient to get home. This would be no easy task: 12 million soldiers, Marines, sailors, and airmen were scattered all over the globe. The title of Andy Rooney's column on V-E Day captured this near-universal sentiment: "Good! When do we leave this hole and go home?"

To make the demobilization process fair, the military followed the principle of "first in, first out" by using a points system. Points were awarded for combat experience, overseas service, and marital status. One point was granted for each month of military service, with an additional point for each month overseas; 5 points were awarded for campaign stars or decorations, and 5 were awarded for each Purple Heart. Veterans with children received 12 points for each child under 18 (up to 3). A total of 85 points could send a GI home in the fall of 1945.

But as time dragged on, and the end of 1945 approached, servicemen and the folks back home became increasingly impatient. According to an Army survey conducted in 1945, two out of every three soldiers awaiting discharge thought the military was mishandling the process. Eventually the government changed the number of points needed for discharge: 60 points were needed by October, and 50 by the end of December. Redeployments home accelerated rapidly. By June 1947, the U.S. armed forces had been reduced to just 1.5 million men.

Capt. John Kristensen, veteran of Normandy and the Battle of the Bulge, didn't have enough points to go home at first but enjoyed his extra time on the French Riviera:

> You needed 85 points to get a ship home. Mine added up to 70, which meant two more months of loafing. I had a trip to the Riviera, to Cannes, and finally got on the USS *General Meigs* and returned to Camp Patrick Henry near Norfolk, Virginia. After a few days I was separated from the service at Fort Dix, New Jersey. As I was leaving, a major asked me if I would like to sign up with the National Guard or the Reserve. I shouted over my shoulder, "Not if it would take another minute here!"

Even veterans who had enough points were impatient to get home. 1st Lt. William Wells of the 112th Anti-Aircraft Gun Battalion was especially blunt about his situation:

After [V-E Day], I came back to the United States. They took me out of the 112th and put me in the 602nd. I asked, "What the heck is going on here?" They said the 602nd's going to fight the Japanese. I said, "Well, I ain't going to fight no Japanese." The colonel looked at me like, what the heck are you telling me all that for? I just wrote down 90. I said, "Do you know what 90 means?" The colonel says, yeah. I said, "It means that I can go home, and that's where I'm going."

Corporal Henry Windmuller recalls the relatively light duty of cooking for a general at Hickam Air Base in Hawaii just after the end of the war:

When the war wound down in the Pacific, this fellow who was cooking for that general, who was the Pacific commander of the air transport, he went out of the Army. He had enough time in the Army, and he went home. So that post was empty, so I got the job to cook for the general. That was okay by me, it was a nice job.

I only had to cook for him and his guests, his driver, and he had another couple of servants. If he had a party or something like that, sometimes there were a whole bunch of generals which he would host, then I had to work, but generally it wasn't too much of a demanding job, it was nice.

If I didn't have to work I could do whatever I felt like. [The general] had two cars and a jeep, if he didn't need his jeep I could use it. I would take the jeep and go to the beach.

Windmuller's war had been more complex than most. A Jew, he escaped Hitler's Germany to England via the *Kindertranport* at age 14. Interned as an enemy alien in England and Canada due to his German citizenship, he eventually enlisted in the U.S. Army Air Force.

Alvin Mays of the Army's 24th Division had joined up in 1940 and served in the Philippines and New Guinea campaigns. He had more than done his part:

I had 178 [points]. They asked me would I consider going on into the invasion of Japan. I said "I've had enough, let me go."

I had a pretty good offer, but I chose to go back. At that time, you didn't know how strong Japan might be and how long that thing would last over there. They had no idea, because they was still going quite strong. That was over there in their homeland and they wasn't ready to give up at that time. But the day that I got back to the United States, I noticed in the paper that Japan surrendered.

Wyndham Manning, B-24 pilot in the 14th Air Force, flew 99 missions in the China-Burma-India Theater. Manning was actually stateside when news of the surrender arrived:

They had lost my records. I thought I could get out early on what they called points, had certain decorations, if you were overseas, if you had so much combat, all of that amounted to a certain [number of points]. But they couldn't find that. They looked at my military records and said, "Lieutenant, you haven't even had any instrument training." Now I'd already flown over 50 times across "the hump." So they sent me out to Lubbock, Texas, and it just so by coincidence happened that I was on my final examination, 13,000 feet, when that news broke and we came on down then.

For most pilots and air crews, the return to the States was relatively easy: they could fly their plane home—but first they had to protect it from scavengers, as B-17 pilot Oscar Barney relates:

We were wondering, what's going to happen now the war is over? They told us the planes that are in good condition, we're going to send [you] back [on them] to the States. And they said, "If you have some [that] are nonoperational, if you can get them operational you can fly back to the States." Well that's when we [thought], if my plane doesn't work and I need a part, I know a plane I can get it from. So we had somebody by our plane all the time to be sure that nobody was messing with it.

With the salty language common to soldiers, Sgt. Charles Estes of the Army's 34th Division describes the rough Atlantic crossing:

We were aboard one of those old ships, I never will forget the name, it was called the *USS Bassett*, [but] we had another definition for her, we called it the B-A-S-T-A-R-D because the sea was so rough coming home, so that's what it felt like.

Ninth Air Force veteran Fairfield Goodale recalls the uncomfortably cramped accommodations aboard the retrofitted *Queen Mary*:

I was amazed at how quickly we came back across [from] France [on] the *Queen Mary*. We were bunked in cabins in which there were dozens of people all crammed together and the bunk next to mine had a man with crabs in it and I was about to be married, that made life awkward for me.

An 80th Division veteran of the Battle of the Bulge, Henry Burch recalls the rough crossing back to the States:

We [came back] on a converted tanker and the facilities there were very poor as far as luxury was concerned. We were in the North Atlantic heading for New York. They had violent weather. They had rope around banisters to keep from falling in. So many of the soldiers got seasick.

Some of those serving in Japan at war's end also had to negotiate bad weather during their return. Typhoon Louise hit Okinawa on October 24, destroying shore facilities of what had become a major military base for the invasion of Japan, and sinking 12 American ships or boats, killing 96, and leaving 47 missing. Jim Davis remembered the storm and the trip home afterwards.

[They] told us to make up a convoy for return to Pearl Harbor. Well, that was great, that was perfect. We were coming back. We came back almost to Tokyo Bay and we got caught in the big October typhoon and we were in that typhoon for four days. We couldn't get out of it.

On the way back, we had a boy onboard ship and we got a message from Naval Sea Headquarters in San Francisco for us to make contact with a certain troopship, [which] was going to be making San Francisco before we would make Seattle. This young man's mother was seriously ill in Cincinnati, Ohio, and they wanted us to put him on this troopship so he could get home to his mother. We finally made contact with them out in the middle of the Pacific, somewhere between Pearl Harbor and Seattle, a very rough day as I recall. We went alongside them as close as we could get, and they fired the breeches buoy [similar to a zip line] over and this young man, Jody Stich, said, "I'm not so sure I want to get home that fast." Because he was going to ride across about 75 yards of open sea in this breeches buoy. But we got him over there all right and he got home a lot sooner than we did.

Bill Britton describes the same dangerous typhoon that almost cut short his return home from Japan:

They said a typhoon was on the way. So we moved in to bomb shelters. Our planes had already come in, the C-48s [military versions of the DC-3]. Two for our baggage and one for us. I'll tell you that wind came up, that storm came up to 145 miles an hour. It blew the weather station off the airbase. We were in this big bomb shelter. Guess who was in there with us? Tyrone Power. He was a Marine pilot, and he'd flown up there for another matter. And he was playing poker with some men. Later on I went over and spoke to him, and he was very nice. He was a 1st lieutenant in the Marine Corps. We were down there about two days before we could get out of that bomb shelter. And [when] we came out, boy the hangers were shredded and debris was everywhere. We loaded up and got out of there and we went to Okinawa.

When we got to Okinawa it was the biggest mess you ever saw. There was ships up on the beach. There were big planes turned upside down. That tremendous typhoon had caused a lot of damage and some deaths. Buildings had collapsed on some of our people. We picked up this brigadier general who wanted to fly back to Manila. We got all his baggage aboard our plane and we took off for Manila. We hadn't been about two hours out of Okinawa when the right engine started cutting out. The crew chief came back and told us "We're having engine trouble. They hope it'll straighten out. If it don't we may have to try to get back on one engine." I said isn't this a heck of a note. The war is over. I'm out in the middle of the ocean and the plane's losing an engine. I mean what's going on, you know? Well, it went out. Before it went out, the crew chief came back and said, "Open the door. We're going to throw everything out we don't need. All the fire extinguishers, all the tools, equipment, seats, anything that's heavy, and that general's baggage, we gotta throw it out, too." So we threw everything out and went back and got his footlocker. It was heavy as lead. He's standing there watching. We took his footlocker and threw it out the door. He came over and took his hat off and threw his hat out the door. But he smiled when he did it. He said "Might as well let that go, too." He threw his hat out. We went down about 20 or 30 feet off the water. Wasn't high. You could look out and see the waves. We made it all the way back to the Philippines right above the water with one engine in that C-48. We landed about 9 o'clock that night at Nichols Field and ran off the end of the runway. He couldn't reverse the prop, so we had to keep going and went into a rice paddy. But it didn't hurt us. The only thing is, [when] we got off we was all up to our knees in goo. But we were so happy to be back. And that ended our journey up there.

Arrival

Arrival in the States anywhere was a joyful occasion. But coming into New York Harbor was a special thrill. Ray Hitt's reaction was pretty typical:

> We landed in New York. When I got off the ship, I saw the Statue of Liberty and I got down and kissed the ground. I was so glad to be on American soil.

When Wayne Jolley's transport sailed into New York Harbor, a special welcoming party from Radio City Music Hall was there to greet the returning GIs:

> When the sunlight lifted so a harbor ship could carry us in, the Rockettes, all of them, came out on two huge barges [with] a full orchestra behind each group and they circled us all the way around, at high-speed, the girls dancing all the time. And as we went up into the harbor all the fireboats in the harbor [were] throwing water into the air. We had been welcomed home. It was some greeting.

Lou Brissie, his legs shattered in Italy, saw New York Harbor from the air as he returned to the States in a plane carrying the badly wounded.

286

The pilot saw to it that his wounded passengers were welcomed home by the lady with the torch:

> When we got to New York, the nurse announced to us, says, "There's a welcoming home committee, and the pilot wants everybody to be properly welcomed." And she says, "We're going to circle to the right for two trips. On the first trip, we want you fellas on the lower stretchers to look out the window. On the second trip, you lie down so the guys in the upper stretchers on the opposite side can look down and see what you saw. And then we will reverse it and fly the other way twice so that everybody can be welcomed home."
>
> And he flew around the Statue of Liberty four times, two each way, and to me, that was a thoughtfulness. Every one of us was from a different town, from a different sized community, from a different state. Most of us had never been anywhere or done much. We didn't know anything about people from New York or Texas normally, the average guy, those of us particularly that were younger. But that statue represented what life in America meant to each one of us, regardless of where we were from or what we did, and I've never forgotten that. But I want to tell you, when he started circling, you could hear a pin drop. There was no conversation, no "how about that!" or "look, man, look what he's doing!" – not a word, not a sound. Absolute, total quiet both ways, and there were some tears. But it meant an awful lot, because it meant basically you're home and that's what you'd been talking about, and some of those fellas had been overseas two and three years.

Homecomings in other places might be less dramatic, but they were no less memorable. For some soldiers, it was American food served by American women that welcomed them home. Stan Whitehead returned to San Pedro, California, from his duty with the 11th Airborne Division in New Guinea and the Philippines:

> We had Red Cross ladies at the gangplank who offered a cup of milk. Would you be surprised, we didn't care for anything else, just good old milk. Then they took us in and processed us, gave us clean clothes if we needed them and took us to a mess hall that was just overloaded with all kinds of goodies. We had steak,

milk, ice cream – we hadn't had ice cream in I don't when and it was just so good.

Bill Britton, returned from repatriating POWs in Japan to San Francisco, sought out stronger drink and enjoyed the generous gratitude of his fellow Americans:

> A bunch of us went ashore where they had all the good restaurants—Joe DiMaggio had a restaurant there called the Sea Food Grotto. We went down there and sat down at a table and, oh, we had the best seafood and salad, we hadn't had any fresh lettuce. Had wonderful food and cold beer, everything. We got ready to go, we asked for the check, and they said, "You don't get a check." "Why don't we get a check?" "Because somebody's already paid your check." "Well, who did?" "They don't want you to know." Well, we want to pay our check. We're officers. We got the money." "Well, [it's] no good in here." That's what they told us. So we went back to the ship, and boy, I slept like a baby that night.

> We stayed at the pier about five or six days before they took us out and moved us to Camp Stoneman [an Army base just inland from San Francisco]. I went into the Fairmont Hotel, myself and two other guys and we rented a suite. It had two bedrooms in it. The Fairmont is one of the best hotels in San Francisco. We went down to the bar, and this friend of mine sat down at the bar. "What will you all have?" He says, "You got any Jack Daniels?" Guy says "Yeah." He says "I want one bottle of Jack Daniels, three glasses of ice, and a bottle of ginger ale." The bartender said "Okay" and brought a bottle of Jack Daniels and set it in front of him and bottle of ginger ale, three glasses of ice. We poured a few drinks. Got ready to go. Bartender said no charge whatsoever. I liked to fall off the seat. That's the way they treated you.

And finally, after years and miles and sometimes unspeakable horrors, the veterans returned to their home towns and families. Pat Roberts of the 6th Marine Division was on his way home aboard a troop train when he lost several souvenirs of the brutal Pacific campaigns he fought in:

I had a lot of souvenirs, I planned on selling some when I got back to the States. It's not nice to say but I had a lot of Japanese gold teeth. Each Japanese soldier wore a flag around his body, like a belt, but it was inside of his pants – and I had numerous flags. I had sabers, binoculars, Japanese rifles. That was all stolen from me after I got back to the States. I was on my way to New River, North Carolina, and somebody cut my sea bag open and got all my souvenirs.

Soon after, Roberts' train was scheduled to pass through his hometown of Elberton, Georgia. He wanted his mother to know he'd be passing through so he could at least wave to her at the station. He used ingenuity and a $10 bill to get word to her:

I had not seen my mother since I'd left home in '43. So I wrote a note, "Whoever finds this note, please call my mother and tell her that I'm coming through Elberton on the troop train." And I put a $10 bill in there. As we went through Athens, Georgia, there was a woman standing out there and I opened the window and hollered at her and threw the note to her. I saw her pick it up, not knowing if she would do what I asked her to do. I thought maybe she'd take the $10, but she called my mother. The train was going right through Elberton and the conductor told me, "Well, we're not gonna stop, we're going through Elberton wide open."

But when we got to Elberton there was a little black man who I had known before that sold papers down there and he got in the way of the train and the train ran over him and killed him and they had to stop the train. The diner was set up and we were getting ready to eat. When they hit [the] airbrakes, the soup and everything was on top of the ceiling. They stopped the train for an hour or more for the coroner to come down there. My mother and the black woman who helped raise me were there waiting on me and I got to see them.

William (Sam) Carter, after service in the Army on Iwo Jima and five other Pacific islands, returned like Lazarus. Due to confusion over his name, the Army had mistakenly informed his family in Springfield, South Carolina, that their son had been killed:

The first thing I saw was that gold [star] flag in the window. The gold flag was for families with dead soldiers. The blue flag was for the families that had people serving. And as it turned out, [my mother] didn't know because nobody at Springfield knew. Nobody knew William H. Carter.

Everyone knew him as Sam. "I was named after an old gray mule, I believe it was." But the Army reported that William H. Carter had been killed. When Sam showed up at home, his parents couldn't believe it. "They went crazy when I walked up the steps."

James Wicker, who had spent months as a POW after being shot down on D-Day, lived outside of Monticello, Georgia. Upon arrival back in the States, Wicker spent a month in Miami Beach on R-and-R, where with the help of a friend from back home he met his future wife:

A friend from Monticello drove his car down and his two sisters had a girlfriend and she came to Miami Beach with him and they introduced me to her and I got to know Adele a little bit. Then later on I used to come and see her every weekend and I married her in June of the next year. So I got a wife out of that too. I've always kidded with her that she got me because she knew I had a lot of back POW pay.

Wicker recalls his eventual arrival home:

My parents lived in the country and didn't have a telephone. They didn't know I was coming home. We went into town to eat at a restaurant, me and this boy, and there happened to be a person from my hometown in the restaurant and he knew all about me being a POW, he knew my parents and he said he would gladly give me a ride home. So he took me home that same afternoon, which was wonderful.

Albert Shaw's welcoming party when he got off the bus in Augusta reveals a lot about the complexities of domestic intimacy in the segregated South:

When I got there, my mother was there at the bus station waiting. And this black maid that we'd had for 30-some years walked right up to me and put her arms around me and said, "Boy, you'd better come here and give me a hug" in front of all my buddies.

She says, "I was the first one to change your diapers, don't you remember that?" I said, "No, ma'am, I don't remember that, but I'll give you a hug."

By the war's end, about 1,200,000 military personnel were African-American. All the services were segregated. As historian Stephen Ambrose points out, "the world's greatest democracy fought the world's greatest racist with a segregated army." Charles Estes saw segregation at work on the troop train carrying soldiers to Camp Gordon:

> I never will forget, when we boarded the train there were a lot of black troops with our unit that was coming south and officer George said, "All you black GIs, you go down this way, the rest of you follow me." That was segregation at its height. And the black soldiers, most of whom did a wonderful job during World War II—especially the 92nd, it was aerial combat overseas—they looked [like] somebody hit them with a laser, they were shocked, as if to say, "Well, we came over here and served our country, why are you separating us?" Well, anyway, that's the way it was back then as we all know.

PFC Jesse Scott, with the 4455th Quartermasters, experienced the Army's treatment of blacks as second-class soldiers temporarily relaxed in the camaraderie of combat:

> We had white commissioned officers. Noncommissioned was black. We didn't have no privates to come in that were white, we was all black. But you still was lieutenant this," "lieutenant that" and "yes sir, no sir." But when we went overseas, that's when we broke out of it. I don't know who started it, but they [were] calling you "private so and so," "yeah," "no" and "sure enough."

But back in the States, black veterans found that not much had really changed. Though the Veterans Administration offered unprecedented benefits to World War II veterans, including the GI Bill, southern state officials often refused to administer these benefits to black veterans, and the federal government refused to intervene. For example, in Columbus, Georgia, African-American veterans were required to use the rear entrance of the U.S. Employment Service branch office. And while black veterans often resisted the resumption of their second-class status, whites often violently resisted this change. In February 1946, Sgt. Isaac

Woodard was beaten and blinded by the sheriff of Batesburg, South Carolina. In July 1946, a black veteran named Maceo Snipes was abducted and murdered by four white men after voting in the primary election in Taylor County, Georgia.

When black troops returned to the States, they felt they had earned something like respect. Jesse Scott tells another story, wherein the intervention of a high-ranking officer was necessary to calm tensions between whites and blacks waiting to collect their overseas pay:

> When I come from overseas and got in the pay line, that's when it told the big story. They lined you up company by company and we must have had about six, eight companies of us and about that many white.

> [We were all] on the same ship coming back [and] we went in to Newport [News, a Navy base in Virginia]. They called the roll [to give us our overseas pay]. They called it for a while and sent some of the blacks back. We kept wondering what's going wrong. All I'm trying to do [is] walk home and they didn't want to let me go home. Finally, a big old tall fellow from Charleston said, "Oh, look what they're doing, look what they're doing."

> And then we went to noticing. Because we all got live ammunition, hand grenades and everything. I was a little surprised that they let us come from Europe that way. But we ready, and boy, you talk about carbines and all that, we're going to stop this. They wouldn't let [them] pay us.

> And then when we was up close, they didn't want [us] putting the pressure on, so then they haul in the Colonel, the man with the chicken, and he come down, and he's running up on the stage and they said something to him. He told them, "Call the roll like it comes." So then they went to call the roll and the black one would go up there as well as the white.

Herman Parker, an African-American who had joined the Navy at age 14, participated in seven Pacific invasions, and was highly decorated, was proud of his country despite its flaws, and was also aware that his view of whites, and his expectations for postwar life, were changing:

> In America you're happy. If you're not happy, you're crazy. Because you're coming to the greatest country in the world,

regardless [of] its faults. We don't enjoy the things that were done to us, but man, when you step foot on America, on terra firma, you're home, man, you're home.

And so after we was in World War II, we learned a lot about race relations. When we were in the war, we were kind of halfway scared of white people. But I guess by being around them and seeing them, they were nothing but another man. Then you kind of lost that fear. The only fear that you would have then was their ganging up [on you] because we felt that one of them wouldn't fight you by himself for nothing in the world. That's why when you take the Ku Klux Klan, they sent a hundred people to get one or two.

So then we learned a little different about the white man, that he wasn't nothing but a man, just like we were. And I still say the change that the Civil Rights movement brought was from the fellows from World War II. It was what they were telling their sons and their daughters. They were telling them, "He ain't nothing but a man just like you. If you hit him, try to take his head off." We came back with a different attitude and a different feeling.

As Parker notes, black veterans were key to the Civil Rights movement of the 1950s and 1960s. Indeed, between 1940 and 1946, NAACP membership increased from 50,000 to 450,000. And the most rapid growth appeared in the South: nearly 80% of the new local branches chartered between 1946-1950 were below the Mason-Dixon line.

For many veterans, white and black, the color of the shared uniform was more important than the color of one's complexion. When a fellow soldier or sailor was in trouble, you did what you could to help, regardless of race. More than ten years after the war ended Jack Sloan, who had served on the destroyer *USS Swanson* during the war, was the commanding officer of the Naval Reserve Training Center in Augusta in the late 1950s. Admiral Daniels called him and told him that a black sailor had been arrested south of Waynesboro, Georgia, for speeding and had been seriously injured in police custody:

The Admiral wanted me to find out the man's condition and ask the sheriff to release him to my custody, and the Admiral said he'd also notified University Hospital if the man needed hospitalization.

I got down there and the old sheriff refused to let me see the man first. But I was insisting, and then I said, "I want the man released into my custody." And the sheriff said, "No. We're going to try him in two or three weeks" and I said, "I want a doctor to look at him." Admiral Daniels had given me a phone number. He said, "If you have no cooperation from the sheriff, you call this number and then ask the sheriff to talk to the man on the other end of the phone."

So I dialed that number. I told him what was happening and I told the sheriff "This man wants to talk to you." I never found out his name. So I handed him the phone and almost instantly the sheriff became very cooperative. And when I got in to see this black man laying up in the bunk, he was bleeding from [both] sides of his head. He was in terrible condition. The doctor said he had compound fractures, both sides of the head and I wanted an ambulance right away and the doctor to go with him to University Hospital in Augusta. The sheriff arranged it and we got him on down there. They operated on him [and] saved him. His parents arrived and thanked me and all, and I never did see him again.

Chapter 8
Moving On and Looking Back

Postwar Life

When the men came home after the war ended, everything looked the same: in Augusta, the cadets still drilled at Richmond Academy, cars and shoppers still clogged up Broad Street, the looms at area mills still turned cotton into textiles. If black veterans' status in a still-segregated world was in flux, the transition of all veterans was difficult and complex. After years of service overseas—during which their connections to home were strained and their bonds with fellow soldiers strengthened—many veterans were unsure how they would fit back into civilian society. An Army survey recorded that 48% of returning GIs worried whether they would be able to settle down and return to civilian life.

One important aspect of veterans' transition to civilian life was psychological. Many who came home were still fighting the war in their minds. Luckily, however, during World War II it became widely accepted—with the notable exception of General Patton—that no matter what his level of bravery might be, almost any soldier would begin to break down after enough time in combat. "Combat fatigue," as it was then called, was caused by combat, not by weakness.

Robert Jones had flown 59 missions with the Army Air Force's 22nd Bomb Group in its Pacific operations. Jones testifies to the enormous stress faced by combat aircrews that temporarily got the better of him:

> I did not perform well. I was up to here. They decided I'd best go back to the States. I couldn't hold my temper, I wasn't thinking straight. I was an old-timer. Well, you feel defeated when you do that. But I went home on a ship, had 21 days between New Guinea and San Francisco. I must have put on 15 pounds. By the time I got home, I was pretty normal.

Leonard Gunter had participated in several invasions in the Pacific aboard an LST. He couldn't bring himself to talk about the things he had experienced. Eventually he got psychological help:

> When [I got back from the war I didn't] talk about it, unless I was at a ship's reunion and talked to somebody. It stayed bottled up. I was very nervous when I come back, very nervous. You

could shoot a firecracker or [have] a car backfire, I'd jump eight or ten feet. It just wouldn't come out for a long time. Still today, I don't like to get mad. My stomach will get to churning.

And the reason I got out of that, they sent to me a psychiatrist after I come back. I wasn't the only one. And he told me there's a hospital in Asheville, North Carolina. He says "I can send you down there now." He said, "The shape you're in, you'll be able to go home on the weekend." I says, "Will I have to go?" He says "No, you don't." I says, "Well, if I don't have to go, I'll stay." He says "You are the only person that can help you." And he said "[You can have a] drink or two," but he said "don't get smoking drunk." He says "It'll take a long time," and today I still don't like no firecrackers.

Stan Whitehead, of the 11th Airborne Division, needed time for his nerves to adjust from wartime high alert to peacetime mode:

For the longest time I would not sleep with my back to an open door. Finally, I got to the point where I could do it, but for a long time I would not. My mother even mentioned that to me, "You seem awful jumpy." And I said, "Well, I'll get over it." I did, but it wasn't easy. You live in a foxhole, you live in dirt, you live in filth, it's hard to come home.

Whitehead stayed in the Army and later served in the Airborne during the Vietnam War.

Normandy veteran Johnny Ware recalls the gradual buildup of hopelessness experienced by many combatants who had been long overseas:

I lay awake at night a lot of times thinking about all the different things that happened over the years, but that was a fast 33 months. I did get to the point over in Europe where I didn't think I ever was going to be coming back home.

Jay Pearlstein, veteran of D-Day and the Hürtgen Forest, felt strangely alienated when he returned to Augusta:

We were discharged and sent back to Augusta. VJ Day happened when we were in Augusta, I remember the celebration. I couldn't go down on Broad Street to participate because I just felt peculiar. I felt after being in the Army for five years, I just felt the civilians were— I don't know who they were. I think something was wrong with me.

Slamming the door shut on his military experience, B-24 gunner Julian Proctor refused service in the postwar Reserves, even with the financial incentive:

After I come back from overseas I quit flying. I had a chance to—they would pay me half pay if I flew four hours a month and I could go down on the flight lines where I was stationed. But I quit. "I'm through flying," I said. Really, after going through all of that, I figured that if God had expected me to fly he'd give me wings.

But whatever wounds they carried, physical or psychological, veterans soon assumed new roles in the postwar years. After James Wisenbaker returned home from his service with the 106th Division in Germany, he didn't feel much like doing anything. Then an old family friend gave him some advice that epitomizes the "get on with it" attitude that enabled his generation to be the "greatest":

I stayed at home a little bit. The doctor that assisted my mother in the birth of all of us was our dear friend and he lived about four houses down the same street. His son was my age and we were friends. Dr. Quarterman called and said, "James, when you have a moment come by my office, I want to talk with you." So I found the time and I went down and talked to him. He said, "James, I know that you've had it rough." He says, "I care about you and I want to give you some advice. Get busy and get this stuff off of your mind. You can't change it. Make your life because there's a good life ahead."

And he said, "Don't the railroad want you back?" I said, "Yeah, they called and they're very nice about it. They said they're not rushing me, that my job is available anytime I'm ready." He said "Go to work and put this behind you." I tried my best to put it behind me.

Wisenbaker ended up working for the railroad for more than 40 years. Early on in his career he met a college girl:

I was working for the railroad and I ended up on a job in Pelham, Georgia. Pelham is a small town and I was boarding with a lady that had sold a farm to a Mr. Joiner and she thought the world of the Joiners. She kept telling me, "James, I've got a girl I want you to meet." Well, I never did like somebody to fix me up, but finally it worked out. She had a picnic for us on a 4th of July. [My future wife] was with somebody else and I was with somebody else. [But] I finally met Betty Dean and I decided she had enough college. She was attending Shorter University. I said "I'll give you an MRS degree." We married that November.

The Oscar winner for Best Picture of 1946, *The Best Years of Our Lives*, sensitively depicted the physical, psychological, and economic difficulties veterans and their families faced in the immediate postwar era. And the fact that the film was the box-office hit of the year indicates that it was in line with popular sentiment.

But when veterans returned in 1945, the booming wartime economy had fallen into a postwar slump as production orders for military related products disappeared and workers were laid off in the thousands. In the 10 days after V-J Day, 1.8 million workers lost their jobs. And for the next couple of years, jobs were hard to come by. According to a June 1945 survey, 21% of GIs said they worried "a lot" about what kind of work they'd get once they returned home; 49% said they worried "a little."

Cliff Cherry was reluctant to leave the Army. It had provided a dependable paycheck:

That's one reason I didn't want to come back home, there was no employment. I mean, I couldn't make a living. When I did get out I went to work at a power company, they paid me 25 cents an hour. I couldn't support a child and a wife [on that salary]. We had to live with her parents.

Pearl Harbor veteran Alvin Mays was lucky to find construction work in Jackson, South Carolina. The pay and the hours were terrible. Eventually he started his own business:

I was driving from Augusta to Jackson. [After doing] that for 15 days, I went up to the superintendent, Charles Gomps, [and] said "I got a sick young'un, I need a job." And he says, "I don't need you." I said "I've got to have a job, sir." And he said, "Well, go

298

on out there to Jackson, tell them to put you on the payroll." Went to work there for 75 cents an hour at 12 hours a day, 7 days a week. I worked that 53 weeks at 84 hours a week. With time and a half, I was able to save. I jumped from there, I had to join the union, from 75 cents an hour to $2.40 an hour, by golly overnight.

After that job I went to Cedartown, Georgia, and went to work on a power plant. And [I] like to starved to death up there because it rained every day, and operating a rubber tire tractor, you could not get no time in. So I left there and came back here and went in business [in Augusta] ever since, Mays Nursery and Landscaping, 44 years.

Willard Blankenship, former member of Merrill's Marauders, recalls the difficulty many veterans faced in the postwar job market in which those who had stayed home had an advantage over those who went to war:

I went to work in a Delco plant, Dayton, Ohio. They laid me off because I didn't have no seniority. I had four jobs in a year's time. Every one of [them] laid [me] off for lack of seniority. People [said we veterans were] coming back from the war [and] took their jobs, [but that] was nothing but right.

John Taylor did not want to go back to work in the mills. With all the competition for jobs, he was happy to get one with the highway department:

I came home and of course I wasn't the only [one] trying to get a job. I didn't want to go back to the cotton mill, so I got a job with the South Carolina Highway Department as an instrument man, taking these dirt roads and surveying them to be paved. Back then they didn't have many paved roads, and our job was to survey these dirt roads and get them ready to turn over to a contractor to get paved. We did roads all over, Aiken County, Barnwell County, Allendale County, Hampton County, up into Greenwood, Edgefield and even to Greenville, and I did that for almost three years.

Next, Taylor got a job with Sears in downtown Augusta. He left Sears over an incident that demonstrates the continuing tensions between the races:

> A job came up at Sears in the plumbing department on Broad Street and I worked there a while. One day [in] the housewares department these two black women came in, about 40 years old, and said they wanted a washtub. Back then very few people had washing machines. They wanted a washtub. So I picked one up and carried [it] to the register and told her, "That's $2.95." She reached in her pocket book and brought out a wad of money and peeled off three or four $1 bills and let [them] float to the floor. I told her again, "That's $2.95." She said, "There's your money on the floor, if you want it, pick it up." I said, "Did you throw it down there or did you drop it?" She says, "It don't matter how it got down there, if you want it, you pick it up." I said, "Well, I saw you throw it down there and I'm not going to pick it up."
>
> So I took the washtub and put it back on the rack. She said, "Where is the manager?" I says, "He's down on the mezzanine." She went down there and reported me that I treated a customer wrong. Everybody in the plumbing department saw what happened and tried to defend me. [The manager] wouldn't listen. He said, "Well, you're a hothead, I'm going to either have to put you up in the [stock] room or you can't work here." I said, "Well, I just won't work here." I had my pride and I walked out and I don't regret it.

Ex-infantryman Ray Hitt came home with his heart set on playing professional baseball. That never quite worked out:

> I did get to play for the old Augusta Tigers back in 1947. They was affiliated with the New York Yankees. [After that I played] Class A ball and I really wasn't ready for Class A ball, so I was sent to Miami, Florida. And that's where I met my wife of 61 years. I went several places in Florida, and I finally hurt my arm and I had to give up baseball completely. So I came on home, but I was able to play in a city league, and I played there for a number of years. And then children started coming along, so that was about the end of the baseball season.

Hitt ended up working for the railroad.

300

There wasn't much for ex-machine gunner Henry Burch to do in Lincolnton, Georgia, but help his brother with his mail route. Eventually he moved to Atlanta and found a job with Sherwin-Williams:

> I was fortunate. That was a good company and I stayed with them for 39 years. Moved three times, but it was all in the Atlanta area and that was good. I had an opportunity to go to Chicago if I had pushed for it, but I didn't push. I'd rather stay right where I was because I still had my family, my mom and my brother and his family and [they] all were in Lincolnton at that time.

Army Capt. George Leitner managed to parlay his military experience into an ROTC job at Wofford College before being called back to active duty in Korea:

> My wife was living in Spartanburg at that time, so I thought I'll go out to Wofford College and see about an ROTC job. Well, the guy was very nice, [but] he says, "I'm sorry, but I've got a full staff."
>
> In the meantime, my wife had given birth to twins. The day after I talked to this man, I took the twins to the pediatrician. While we were in the office, the nurse came out and said, "A man from Wofford College wants to talk to you."
>
> The night before, the Vice President of Wofford College had seen one of the instructors come out of a beer parlor. He called the PMS [Professor of Military Science] and said, "He's not to be brought back on campus." And so the PMS had remembered that I'd been there the day before and he ran me down in the doctor's office. So I taught ROTC at Wofford College.
>
> I stayed there for about a year and a half. The ex-artillery officer and myself got a letter from the Army wanting to know if we wanted to come back on active duty. We both said no, because you don't give up an ROTC assignment. About three months later, we got another letter asking us the same thing and we said no. Thirty days later, they didn't give us a choice. They just gave us an order to come back on active duty.

Bruce Wright, who had been a machinist's mate in the Navy, bought a tractor trailer with his brother-in-law and started hauling freight up and down the east coast. He then found a job at the new Savannah River Site:

> [My brother-in-law] went to work at Oak Ridge and I was in Charleston. I like it down here better. I found out about this plant being built and I come up and got me a job at the Savannah River Nuclear Plant, doing the same thing I did in the Navy, diesels, boilers, turbines.

Charles Beason of the 4th Infantry Division struggled for a while when he returned to Aiken until his determination and energy got him out of a failing service station and into a lucrative business:

> I bought a Gulf service station on the corner of Park Avenue and Short Street. First month I was there I pumped 300 gallons of gas and I told my wife, I said "Honey, I'm going to have to get out of that service station, we ain't gonna make it in the service station." She said, "I'll tell you what to do. I'll go down to the mill to get me a job and I'll run the house, you run that service station." I ran that service station for two years, paid off everything I owed, wound up with a little bit of money in the bank, sold it and opened me up a wheel alignment business, went to Rock Island, Illinois, to wheel alignment school and learned how to do that, it was technical. I was the best wheel alignment man that ever hit South Carolina, in fact, I probably opened up the first wheel alignment shop in South Carolina in 1946. I stayed in it 40 years and sold it to a guy and financed it for him and got a job at Western Auto and worked there a little while, sold tires, man, I could sell tires, and retired out of that, went to the Sheriff's Office, got me a job, got 15 years retirement out of that and then I opened my grandson a paint and body [shop].

Gertie Parille, an Austrian Jew who had fled Hitler's Europe and arrived in Augusta in 1940, took business courses after the war and started a long career at Fort Gordon:

> I went to work at Davison's [a department store] in the office for a short period. In the meantime, I went to night school and took a business course and took my exam out at Fort Gordon. [The people at Fort Gordon] called and asked me if I would come for a 30 day appointment – they [would] pay $3,000 a year and I

was making $32 a week. So I grabbed it. [This was] 1950. I stayed there 30 days and then they asked me if I would stay another 30 days, and I said yes, and then they said, "How would you like to be permanent out here?" I stayed there 30 years.

Instead of trying to find work, thousands of returning servicemen in the area and millions across the nation decided to take advantage of the GI Bill and attend schools and colleges. The bill had been signed by President Roosevelt in June 1944. As thousands of men stormed the Normandy beaches, a grateful nation prepared for their life after the war. The bill provided veterans with college tuition, unemployment insurance for one year ($20 per week), and loan assistance for homes, farms, and small businesses. Any veteran with at least 90 days service and a non-dishonorable discharge could qualify. The GI Bill allowed millions of veterans to provide their families with a middle-class life. The postwar boom that lasted until the 1970s was directly fueled by federal legislation and the hard work of ex-servicemen.

Whereas in 1930 only 1 million people attended college (2% of the total population), at the start of the 1947 school year, 1.1 million veterans—nearly 50% of all students—were enrolled in college courses. By 1956, 2.2 million veterans used the GI Bill to attend college, and over 5 million others used it for vocational training. (Just as with other benefits for veterans, many African-Americans were effectively excluded).

The Junior College of Augusta, then housed in Richmond Academy, responded to the surge in enrollment from returning servicemen and women by establishing an evening division, but the crowding was so severe that students had to be turned away. The University of South Carolina opened a new branch in Aiken in 1961.

Oscar Barney stayed in the Air Force after his days as a B-17 pilot ended and served as a guidance counselor to ex-servicemen:

There were many airmen and officers getting out of the service, so they assigned me to [be] a counselor. I was counseling these folks as to what they planned to do with their life, what the opportunities were and where they wanted to go. It was real interesting. I remember one fellow I talked to that had five degrees. I asked him what his plan was and he said, "I have no idea." He had a lot of smarts, but didn't know what to do with it. We tried to encourage a lot of them to go back to college under the GI Bill. That's one of the reasons that I didn't get out of the service. Everybody was going back to college and it seemed like

303

it was going to be flooded with people going back to college, so I decided I would stay in awhile.

Ray Lundquist, a B-24 navigator, was one of the millions who returned to school:

> I went to the University of Iowa with the G.I. Bill, which is one of the greatest things that the United States government has ever done. Millions of individuals that would have never have had a chance to go to school got that privilege.

Jack Kendall, also a B-24 navigator, returned to college for an engineering degree and worked on the Clarks Hill dam on the Savannah River, a federally funded project in flood control and hydroelectric power that created a 100,000-acre reservoir and recreational area north of Augusta. The project was completed in 1954:

> I went back to school, to Georgia Tech, and got a degree in civil engineering. From that, I came back to Augusta on Clarks Hill Dam. I was on that job for four years. [During] that time I met a girl in North Augusta and we ended up getting married in 1950. I spent 51 married years with her and she died in 2001.

Not everyone ended up with degrees, of course. Pat Roberts tried majoring in business, but he ended up leaving the University of Georgia to get into the poultry business:

> Well, I came home and of course I didn't do a whole lot of anything for a while, just kind of enjoyed being home and having an automobile to drive and eating good food and all that. Finally some of my friends decided that they were going to University of Georgia under the [GI] Bill of Rights. So I decided that I would do that. When I got over to Georgia I decided to major in business administration. I wasn't doing [badly], I had probably B or C average or something, but I wasn't doing as well as I wanted to do.

> A friend of my brother and I was building a poultry place in Athens, his name was Doyle Terry. This was in the very beginning, when they built the plant and start dressing poultry in quantities. He wanted my brother and [me] to take the distributorship for South Carolina and most of Georgia. Well, I

304

was in school and I had to make a decision. Did I want to be in the poultry business? If I wanted to be in there, then I had to leave school because I couldn't wait until I graduated to get involved in this.

So my brother and I took this distributorship. We started off just delivering chickens from his plant. Anyway, for years my brother and I in Elberton, Georgia, we had this distributorship. We distributed chickens; here in Augusta was a big account. We brought a lot of chickens down.

Carl Sanders, who grew up in Augusta, is a virtual poster child for the benefits of service in the Army determining a path and the GI Bill making that path possible. Sanders had trained as a B-17 pilot. When he returned to the University of Georgia on the GI Bill, he used his pilot's training to make a little extra money flying at air shows on weekends:

We would fly over to Mr. Jones' pasture, we'd take people up. I never got over a thousand feet and I'd do a slow roll, a snap roll, or a loop, a split air, come back down on the ground. And he would charge, I've forgotten how much, $5 or $6, $7 a ride. I would land the aircraft with a crazy Irishman who would sit out on the wing. Then we'd do a parachute jump at 500 feet, I'd cut the throttle, he'd climb out on the wing and pull the ripcord and float down.

At the insistence of his wife-to-be, Sanders quit stunt flying and finished law school. Eventually he bought his own plane, and it helped him get elected Governor of Georgia in 1963:

I bought a small single engine Comanche aircraft, 250 horsepower. I campaigned for Governor, no one else to my knowledge has ever campaigned for Governor in an aircraft, but I did. And I landed on cow pastures, I landed on little strips that had been cut off the top of mountains. I learned how to fly that aircraft with my eyes closed, in any and all kind of weather. I was successful in the Governor's race.

That experience revealed to Sanders the need for more airports in rural Georgia to attract industry. During his term, he had 42 new community airports built.

Within a few years of the war's end, the Central Savannah River Area became the site of several huge federal projects and the economic benefits they brought. Already mentioned was the massive Clarks Hill Dam project, begun in 1946 and completed in 1954. As the conflict in Korea threatened to turn the Cold War hot, plans for a nuclear bomb plant along the Savannah River below Augusta were announced. Construction began in 1951. In the next couple of years, thousands of farmers and other residents around Ellenton, South Carolina, would be displaced to create the vast 300 square-mile Savannah River Plant, producing nuclear materials for the hydrogen bomb. Physical plant construction was complete in 1956.

These projects turned Augusta and Aiken into boomtowns, creating thousands of jobs and bringing thousands of new residents to Augusta and Aiken. In 1940 the population of Richmond County was 81,863. In 1950 it was 108,876. Then the metropolitan population exploded as the "Bomb Plant" was built, increasing by 46,000 in the early 1950s. Aiken County's population grew by almost 53 percent in the 1950s. At about the same time, Camp Gordon became a permanent base, and the Army's Oliver General Hospital became a VA facility; the state of Georgia's investments in Augusta's Medical College of Georgia with the opening of Talmadge Hospital in 1956 would help make the healthcare industry one of the area's chief employers. "It is as if Scarlett O'Hara came home from the ball, wriggled out of her satin gown, and put on a space suit," Dorothy Kilgallen wrote in *Good Housekeeping* in 1953. Today, the CSRA is home to more than half a million people.

Looking Back

Especially for the World War II generation, talking about their war experiences—experiences that often don't decrease in intensity with the passage of time—is not something most veterans feel comfortable doing. Much of this tendency derives from their natural reticence and humility—it is the present generation that has grown up with talk shows and YouTube—but it also derives from the age-old difficulty veterans have communicating their extreme experiences to others, especially non-veterans. Hence the importance for most veterans of maintaining the comradely connections with their own "band of brothers" forged in wartime.

These bonds were, for many vets, irreplaceable. As B-29 gunner Ed Ricketson put it, "Fighting like that, you got a camaraderie there, nothing can take the place." For years his crew had periodic reunions in places ranging from rural Georgia to New York City. "You don't forget people like that," he said.

B-25 pilot Ferrell Holley felt the same kind of bond with his aircrew after the war:

> All of them are dead except my best friend [who] was my navigator, and we traveled the United States together by car after the war. I think we went through every state. He died at about age 65. My little tail gunner was only 19 years old when he went over. He was a boy from Kentucky. He had a damn good education for a Kentucky boy [from] the mountains. Read books all the time, kept notes on where we were, he's still living. I call him every Sunday or he calls me every Sunday. He was a fine little fellow and we keep in touch. All the rest that I knew, we had reunion meetings and things like that all over the United States, went to a whole lot of those, we called it the 57th Bomb Wing. But my little tail gunner still calls me or I call him every Sunday.

Charles Estes, veteran of the Army's Italian campaign, wept at a reunion in 1994 when he heard the voice of an officer he had respected during the war:

> The best officer I ever had I still remember, Captain John S. Thomas from Norristown, Pennsylvania. He was my company commander at the ASTP [Army Specialized Training Program] at Fort Benning. I went to Valley Forge [Pennsylvania] for a reunion in 1994 and I had the privilege of speaking with him a few minutes. To hear the voice and speak to him I actually broke down and cried because I really loved the man, he was just a wonderful officer. The others were just casual, you couldn't call them a friend or they were just somebody you respected and saluted, but I just really had a love for Captain Thomas. He was an A1 soldier.

The crew of Richard Craig's ship had its first reunion in 1983; 13 of the 17 surviving crew members (the ship's crew had numbered about 58) attended, including the ship's cook, who came in spite of extraordinary physical and emotional obstacles:

> Our ship's cook was at that reunion in 1983. His mother had died that morning and he was not going to come, but his family knew

he wanted to come so bad that he flew down from Providence, Rhode Island, and attended our reunion. He was totally blind at the time. He had run an Italian restaurant in Providence and he died a couple of years after that reunion himself.

Of the 13 at that reunion, there's about six still living. We have to give credit to the wives of these sailors because they put up with us for a long time. Since then, we have met at Washington, D.C., Williamsburg, a couple of times at Annapolis, one time at Nashville, Tennessee, for a national reunion and one time at Charleston for a national reunion. And this year [2008] our national reunion is going to be in Savannah, Georgia. I haven't been to one since 1998, but I'm going to be in Savannah.

Reunions bring back floods of memories and a painful awareness of those who never returned from the war. Herman Boland's closest Marine buddies were killed on Pacific islands or were lost in the years since:

They're dead, they're dead. I have very few people. I knew a boy, he won the Congressional Medal of Honor on Okinawa, his name was Dane Reinhardt and he lived in New Hampshire. I went up there to see him one time and nobody knew him, nobody knew where he was, didn't know who he was. That's a disgrace. I mean that's a shame.

My close friends, like Bill Bennett, Sergeant Mills, Don Cooney, Don Melons, they [are] left on Peleliu. Don Melons was shot – he was a flamethrower man. We had a tank attack on Peleliu. Stony Stoneberg knocked out one of these tanks with a BAR and set it afire. But that's where my friends are, that's where they are.

I don't know what happened to Pete Belts, I don't know what happened to Don Cooney. I know one thing, Don Cooney—the last time I saw him he was sitting up on a bunker singing one of his songs, "I've Got a Wife and Fourteen Dollars," and the Japanese opened fire, that's the last time I saw him, and he was from Anderson, South Carolina. People have never heard of him in Anderson.

Rufus Belding remembers both his pride as a Marine in the Pacific and the emotional pain of watching his buddies die:

The Marines taught us we were the best fighting people in all the world and nobody could kill us. And of course we were. But at the same time, I'm going to tell you, when I went into the service in 1940 there wasn't a patriotic bone in my body. I didn't think about it.

As I trained for it and as the war started, I got patriotic and let's go get them. In fact I was in New Zealand and they were going to barbeque a bunch of pigs and they were doing it wrong and I had barbequed pigs with my daddy all my life. I barbequed those pigs for them and the captain said, "Do you want to be a cook?" I said, "No, sir. I want to fight." And I didn't go in to be a cook. I was really wanting to get in a fight. I thought it would be fun, but it wasn't as much fun as it was pain. Especially when you see your buddies dying on the field and in the foxhole and you hold them in your arms. I was just, I don't like to think about it.

For many veterans, dreams of the glories of war were shattered by the realities of modern warfare. Cliff Cherry, having fought through France and into Germany with the Army's 70th Division, worries that such a lesson has been forgotten:

The man that said "war is hell" knew what he was talking about. When we went to war, we were glorified just to get in a uniform. When you get out of combat, you see people blown apart, dead and all, it don't take long to make you change your mind about that thing.

I'm not sure we can learn. I think we make the same mistakes over and over. It bothers me that we get involved in everybody's wars. I wish it wasn't that way, but that's the way it is. Good old United States, we'll protect you. Very naïve.

Roosevelt Brooks thinks Americans tend to glorify war because most of them have never experienced it:

People here in the States—they wave the flag and cheer. [But] the Italians, the Germans, the Japanese, they know what war is, this country don't know what war really is. To suffer the slaughter, it's a terrible thing, terrible thing. They don't know what war is. If they did they wouldn't be so quick to be, "Charge!

Charge!" Pushing some of us to go and do the work, but if they had to do it you wouldn't be so quick to start no wars in the first place. If they really knew what war is they just wouldn't do it.

Airborne veteran Robert Scherer's war experiences taught him the hard lesson that war is often futile:

You don't know how bad things [are] until you're in something like a war and see dead people for no reason whatsoever as we're seeing now in Iraq and Afghanistan. I'm not trying to be political, I'm just trying to tell you how I feel. We're wasting our time and money there. All we're doing is breaking up a lot of rocks and killing a lot of people for no reason whatsoever. Just keep going to school and get smart, that's the only thing I can say.

Former POW James Wisenbaker considers the popular label "The Greatest Generation":

A news commentator said [we are] America's greatest generation. I appreciate that. But we were because we had the chance to be. Our young people today are just as fine as we could ever be. If the chance is there for them to do their job, they'd do it. I'm not a hero. Never thought about being one. I just have had some experience and now that I've lived through it, I am a better person. I assure you that I am. I may not be as good as I should be, but I'm a better person because of what I went through. The greatest generation met their responsibility. I agree with it. I'm proud and honored to be a part of that. But I don't want to sell [out] the young people we have now. If they get the leadership and the opportunities to show what they got, they'll make it better.

On the other hand, Charles Estes feels a contrast between his generation and the current one:

I enjoyed my military service. I was glad to be able to give part of my effort to keeping our country free and would do the same again today if I had the opportunity, as most GIs would. Of course I have the utmost respect for all the men and women who have served.

310

During the Depression and following the Depression, our country was unified. It's not the same today. We didn't have any of these pleasures and frills [that] we have today, but all the way from Rosie the Riveter down to Kilroy, it was a concerted effort. That was the way World War II was won. Not demeaning the GIs that were in Korea, Vietnam, the Gulf War, Afghanistan, Iraq, because they do a marvelous service—I appreciate everything they do every day because I know if it weren't for them, we wouldn't be as free and we wouldn't be the country we are. But back in those days, we worked together, families had Victory gardens and the women worked in factories, it was just a whole different concept, the world was different back then.

Willard Blankenship finds the discipline and comradeship he knew in his days as one of Merrill's Marauders in Burma lacking in today's military:

They don't have the discipline we had. I actually believe when I was a young soldier, if my platoon sergeant told me to climb the barracks and walk off the end of that son of a bitch, you know what I would have done? I would have walked off the end of it because I'd've figured he wouldn't have told me to walk off that if he hadn't had a way figured out for me to land. That's the trust we had in one another. The soldiers today—don't get me wrong, they're great and I go see them three or four times a year at Fort Campbell—but I don't think [they] have got what we had then. As far as the dedication I guess they've got that, but I don't think they've got the comradeship amongst themselves.

Fifth Air Force pilot Bob Jones says that a sense of morality permeated the World War II experience: all were making sacrifices for the common good:

I think there were an awful lot of people in World War II who did what was right. They didn't do it for themselves. There are people out there that are after themselves. But for the most part, I felt everybody that I ran into was in there to serve.

Lessons learned while serving in the military lasted a lifetime. Far from being brutalized by his experience in the Pacific theater, Tom Zwemer, who was later to serve on the dental school faculty at the

Medical College of Georgia, thinks he became a better man during his time as a medic. It's one of two things he is sure of about the war:

> I believe that the dropping of the atomic bomb saved my life. The other thing I'm sure of is that the war and Army made a man out of me. I was discharged in March and entered dental school in September. I believe that I became a better dental student, a better dentist, and a better man [for] having served in World War II. So I don't regret it at all. It really opened my eyes to what the world was like and I think it made me more kind and generous about people.

Julian Proctor experienced a very different side of Germany—the country he had bombed during the war—when he returned to visit much later in life:

> We dropped our bombs from about three miles in the air, I never did get to see any of those people. Well, I got the chance to go back over in 1970 and I got to see some of them—I found out that they were friends—and not enemy.

Aerial combat taught P-51 pilot Fairfield Goodale to stay calm in stressful situations, but it was an experience on the ground—a visit to the Buchenwald concentration camp—that determined the direction his life was to take:

> When I left that prison camp, I was not able to eat or sleep for three or four days afterwards because of the profound effect that camp had on me and I knew that at the end of three or four days that I was definitely headed for medical school because I knew, among other things, that after that experience I had to somehow aid and abet the healing system in the future. [Buchenwald] was a mind—I mean, it was a life-changing episode for me.

After his return to the States, Goodale went to medical school at Case Western Reserve University. In a long and distinguished career as a pathologist and teacher, he served as dean at the Medical College of Georgia.

Naval aviator Fred Langdon developed a "can-do" attitude that characterized a whole generation of those who returned to the area after

312

the war. Langdon himself became one of the founders of Aiken Technical College:

> When you're 18 years old and you accomplish something as big as what I was fortunate enough to do, it gives you self-confidence and you get what I call a can-do attitude. It carried with me all my life. It's changed my life completely. Anybody that goes into the product development business knows what I'm talking about. You're not afraid to go into something that you may not have done before. That's helped me all along, even after I retired.

> This World War II thing, there were a bunch of fellows who weren't military and they went in the service. They were trained, they believed in what they were doing and they went over there and they won the war. And they came home and built the economy. That is can-do attitude.

> I just hope we have more of those kinds of people coming up. I'm sure they're out there. I just hope that they have the same will and drive to do what has been done.

FURTHER READING

Berkow, Ira. *The Corporal Was a Pitcher: The Courage of Lou Brissie.* Chicago: Triumph Books, 2009.

Brokaw, Tom. *The Greatest Generation.* New York: Random House, 1998.

Craven, W.W. and J. L. Cate. *Army Air Forces in World War II*: Volume 6: *Men and Planes.* Chicago: University of Chicago Press, 1955.

Dear, I.C.B. ed. *The Oxford Guide to World War II.* New York: Oxford University Press, 1995.

Ellis, John. *On the Front Lines: The Experience of War through the Eyes of the Allied Soldiers of World War II.* Hoboken, NJ: Wiley, 1991.

Fussell, Paul. *Wartime: Understanding and Behavior in the Second World War.* New York: Oxford University Press, 1989.

Gambone, Michael D. *The Greatest Generation Comes Home: The Veteran in American Society.* College Station, TX: Texas A&M University Press, 2005.

Gawne, Jonathan. *Finding Your Father's War.* Philadelphia: Casemate, 2006.

Goodale, Fairfield. *The Absolute Truth and Other Uncertainties - a Remembrance.* Lincoln, Nebraska: iUniverse, 2005.

Hynes, Samuel, Roger Spiller, Nancy Sorel, and Anne Matthews, eds. *Reporting World War II, Part Two - American Journalism, 1944-1946.* New York: The Library of America - Penguin Books, 1995.

Kagan, Neil and Stephen G. Hyslop. *Eye Witness to World War II.* Washington, DC: National Geographic Society, 2012.

Kennedy, David M. ed. *The Library of Congress World War II Companion.* New York: Simon & Schuster, 2007.

Kennett, Lee. *GI: The American Soldier in World War II.* New York: Scribners, 1987.

Miller, Donald L. *The Story of World War II.* (Revised/updated from original text by Henry Steele Commager, 1945.) New York, Simon & Schuster, 2001.

Overy, Richard. *Why the Allies Won.* New York: W. W. Norton, 1995.

Palmer, Robert R., Bell. I. Wiley, and William R. Keast. *The Procurement and Training of Ground Combat Troops.* Washington, DC: Historical Division, Department of the Army, 1948.

Smith, Perry. *Courage, Compassion, Marine: The Unique Story of Jimmie Dyess.* Lincoln, Nebraska: iUniverse, 2015.

Terkel, Studs. *"The Good War" - An Oral History of World War Two.* New York: Pantheon Books, 1984.

Weinberg, Gerhard. *A World at Arms: A Global History of World War II.* New York and Cambridge (UK): Cambridge University Press, 1994.

Zwemer, Tom. *Do the Best You Can, Sergeant: If You Insist on Learning the Hard Way – Learn to Laugh.* Scotts Valley, CA: CreateSpace, 2009.

ACKNOWLEDGMENTS

My sincere thanks are extended for the work of the three editor/writers for their commitment to produce a book that includes selective recollections of qualified CSRA veterans of World War II from interviews conducted during the national Veterans History Project that covered events of 70 or more years ago:

> Dr. James Garvey, Professor Emeritus of Communications and English, Augusta University, and current President of the Augusta Richmond County Historical Society

> Dr. Douglas Higbee, Associate Professor of English, University of South Carolina, Aiken, South Carolina

> Dr. Hubert van Tuyll, Professor of History, Augusta University, and past chairman - Department of History, Anthropology and Philosophy, Augusta University

We certainly appreciate being given free access to many principal interview sites for conducting the video interviews, foremost to Augusta University and Aiken Technical College. Many were also conducted at the homes of the veterans; other sites included the Georgia War Veterans Home, Brandon Wilde, Augusta Preparatory High School, a number of area churches, Augusta Technical College, etc.

Many thanks are also extended to the 75 volunteer interviewers for their time in preparing for and then guiding each veteran during the interview. After production of each DVD, the volunteer reviewed the veteran's comments on the required Video Recording Log and posted noteworthy statements for inclusion with other information sent to the Library of Congress. Uncounted hours were necessary for the volunteers to complete a total of better than 800 separate interviews.

Although there is no room available to list all 75 volunteer interviewers, our top three producers were:

> Retired Major General Janet Hicks, former Commanding General, Fort Gordon
> Retired Major Bill Tilt, Vietnam era
> Retired Lt. Colonel Stanley Schrader, Vietnam era

Appreciation is also extended for behind the scenes support provided by numerous video camera operators; to Rick Kelly for producing the majority of individual DVDs of each interview—over 500 in total; to Donald Patterson for technical support and labelling sets of 4 or more DVDs, each veteran interview; and to Steve Rauch, Signal Corps Historian, Fort Gordon, for initial counsel on interview procedures.

I would also like to extend my personal thanks to all who gave their time as volunteers and support persons:

To the office support staff of Judy McAlhany, Molly Montgomery and Elaine Benton for numerous hours producing forms and necessary support documents sent to the Library of Congress in Washington, D.C.

To volunteer reviewers for identifying qualified CSRA veterans for transcription and inclusion, for use by the editor/writers to be included in the book.

To Doug Hastings, outstanding leader of the Vets to Washington bus trips, who conducted the very first interview in November 2007. To date, he has taken over 1500 veterans and guests to Washington, D.C., and other World War II sites in the U.S. over the past 10 years; expenses have been covered by generous donations from businesses and individuals in support of Doug's unique project.

To Roy Walsh, who willingly served as camera operator and DVD reviewer in the later stages of the Veterans History Project.

To retired General Perry Smith for writing the Foreword to the book and for advice on publishing sources as well as conducting preliminary review of the initial drafts by the editor/writers.

To my wife, Jane, for continuous technical support on our home computer to provide out-going and in-coming communications. She is now happy to have our dining room no longer inundated with files and papers that prevented use of the room for dinners for better than nine years!

Finally, to the more than 800 participants of the Veterans History Project for telling their stories of past wartime experiences so that current and future generations will know what they endured during the Second World War. We stand in awe and admiration of these CSRA citizens for their commitment and sacrifices made during those tumultuous and historic years.

F.P. Gehle

I would like to add a special note of thanks to my wife, Debra van Tuyll, who designed and prepared the appendix of veterans' biographies.

Hubert van Tuyll

CONTRIBUTIONS, DONATIONS AND GRANTS TO THE PUBLICATION

Many thanks are extended to the following Foundations, business organizations, financial institutions, civic/social groups, veterans organizations, universities, special event and individuals for their generous pre-publication support to the Publication Project.

1. **Foundations**
   Augusta State University Foundation
   Community Foundation of the CSRA
   Creel – Harrison Foundation
   Georgia Humanities Council
   Porter Fleming Foundation
   Storey Foundation, Inc.

2. **Business Organizations**
   ADP (Automatic Data Processing, Inc.)
   Augusta Computer Exchange
   GIW (Georgia Iron Works Industries, Inc.)
   Howard Lumber Company
   MAU Workforce Solutions
   Savannah River Remediation
   Solvay Specialty Polymers USA
   Zaxby's Restaurant

3. **Financial Institutions**
   Augusta First Bank & Trust
   Bank of America
   First Bank of Georgia
   Georgia Bank & Trust Company
   Savannah River Banking Company
   Wells Fargo

4. **Civic/Social Groups**
   National Hill Lions Club
   Sage Valley Golf Club
   Scottish Rites

5. **Veterans Organizations**
   American Legion Post No. 71
   Greater Augusta Chapter – American X – POW's

6. Academic Institutions
University of South Carolina, Aiken—Office of the Executive Vice-Chancellor
Augusta University
Augusta University Foundation

7. Special Event
Concerts with a Cause (St. John United Methodist Church)

8. Individuals
Cornell Angleman
  Vicki Bolton
  Ralph G. Busbee
  Albert F. Cheatham
  Bobbye Cobb
  William F. Force, Jr.
  Patrick J. Garvey
  Bonnie Given
  Lyle & Shirley Glascock
  Dr. & Mrs. Joseph Griffin
  Gould B. Hagler
  Judy Howard
  Jack Kendall
  Bates McCutcheon
  Ann Marie McManus
  E. G. Meybohn
  Charles W. Moye
  Brian Mulherin
  Sara W. Newton
  Perry Smith, Maj. Gen., USAF (ret.)
  Charles W. Whitworth

-FPG

EDITORS

Dr. James Garvey taught English and journalism for almost 40 years, first at the State University of New York at Geneseo, and since 1979 at Augusta University, where he was also director of the Honors Program and founding chair of the Department of Communication. He retired in 2009. He has written nine plays based on local history, served as writing coach at *The Augusta Chronicle* for 20 years, and writes for *Augusta Magazine*.

Dr. Douglas Higbee is Associate Professor of English and Anonymous Endowed Chair in the Humanities at the University of South Carolina, Aiken. He edits *The Oswald Review*, an undergraduate journal of literary criticism. He is also editor of *Military Culture and Education* (Ashgate, 2010), and co-editor of *Teaching Representations of the First World War* (Modern Language Association, 2017) and the forthcoming *Hunting and the Ivory Tower* (University of South Carolina Press).

Dr. Hubert van Tuyll is Professor of History and former department chair at Augusta University. A native of the Netherlands, he is a specialist in military history. He has written six books, most recently *Castles, Battles, and Bombs* (2008: with Jurgen Brauer), and *Small Countries in a Big Power World* (2017). He is currently working on a study of civil war in the Anglo-Celtic world.

Appendix:
Thumbnail biographies of veterans included in the book

ALEXANDER, Hugh: Navy Seaman on flagship of Admiral Spruance, *U.S.S. New Mexico*. On board at Iwo Jima when 25 kamikazes were shot down; in 7 major Pacific sea battles. Retired after 31 years, Savannah River Plant.

ASHHURST, Fred: Joined Army before Pearl Harbor; with artillery unit from France to end of war in Germany at Elbe River. Saw capture of Heinrich Himmler. Tennis professional in New York City after the war.

BAHM, Dallas: Army veteran during Philippine campaign at Leyte and other island locations. Helped with Japanese POWs and clean-up at Hiroshima after the A-bomb. Retired from the military after 26 years.

BALLAS, Charles (Chuck): Infantry Sergeant with Army's 28th Division in Europe from D-Day, liberation of Paris, Huertgen Forest to Aachen. After war, worked on hydrogen bomb development, then moved to Augusta as owner of Luigi's Restaurant.

BARNARD, Doug: Served in financial support unit with Army in France before transfer to infantry MP in Belgium during the Battle of the Bulge. With Georgia Railroad Bank 25 years before serving 4 terms in the U.S. Congress.

BARNEY, Oscar: Pilot of B-17 Flying Fortress with 8th Air Force; flew 5 missions near war's end including raid over Berlin. In service with U. S. Air Force through 1964, including Berlin Airlift/Bay of Pigs. Worked for the state of Georgia 20 years.

BARRETT, Olander (Jack): Saw combat with 80th Infantry Division, Third Army in Europe. Recipient of 5 Purple Hearts. Cast on legs for 18 months after discharge. In construction industry after the war.

BELDING, Rufus: Combat veteran in the Pacific with 3rd Marine Division at Guadalcanal and Bougainville. On first wave, invasion of Guam. Purple Heart recipient. A native of Augusta, returned home to work for Southern Bell 35 years.

BEASLEY, Charles: Served in Army combat engineers, Europe. D-Day in Huertgen Forest. Served 1939 to 1963. Worked with clergy and in business after war.

BEMAN, Hal: Served on Coast Guard LST in the Pacific during invasions of Iwo Jima and Okinawa; survived two typhoons. Flagpole for second flag raising on Mt. Suribachi constructed on his boat. Worked for Southern Railroad after war, then Savannah River Plant 28 years.

BEASON, Charles: After work in the Civil Conservation Corps, joined Army in 1940. Landed on Utah Beach with 4th Infantry Division, D-Day plus 1. Combat in Europe lasted "one year, 8 months 10 days." After war with car dealer, started own auto service business, finally retiring at age 90.

BLANKENSHIP, Willard: Joined Army in 1939; served in North Africa then "Special Units" assignment in Burma with Merrill's Marauders. Served in the Airborne until 1962.

BEDINGFIELD, Hugh: Officer in Navy on battleship U.S.S. California at the Battle of Leyte Gulf. After the war became a CPA.

BOLAND, Herman: Wounded in combat with 1st Marine Division at Peleliu; Purple Heart. Back to sea as a rigger after the war, tretired from Du-Pont/Savannah River.

BOWEN, Charles: Born in 1933, he was too young to serve but grew up in Augusta during the war. Richmond Academy graduate. Worked in real estate and financial services.

BRENNAN, Jim: Army Air Corps transport pilot; 20 trips over the Atlantic; flew Dutch POWs out of Japan at war's end. Worked for Southern Bell 46 years in Augusta.

BRINKLEY, Marion: Navy Seabee; served on Kwajalein and other Pacific islands. Stationed on Tinian when the Enola Gay left and returned after bombing Hiroshima. After war, worked at father's grocery store in Ellenton, GA.

BRISSIE, Lou: Squad leader with 88th Infantry in Italy. Despite serious leg wound, became Major League All-Star pitcher after war. Brissie's biography, *The Corporal Was a Pitcher*, published in 2009. After, war, United Merchants and Manufacturers as Personnel Manager, served as national head of American Legion Baseball.

BRITTON, Bill: Army service, mostly in Philippines, included recovering POWs held captive by Japanese and mop-up on Luzon. Long military service until 1971.

BROOKS, Roosevelt: Sent into combat "raw" as replacement in northern Italy with the 92nd Infantry Division (Buffalo Soldiers). After war, served as police officer in New York City. Moved to Augusta in 1996.

BURCH, Henry: Survived severe leg wound on Christmas morning during Battle of the Bulge; hospitalized 3 months. Awarded Purple Heart and Bronze Star. After discharge, worked for Sherwin-Williams 39 years.

BUSBEE, George: Army artillery veteran of campaigns in North Africa, Sicily, and Italy. Received Purple Heart for wound received at Monte Cassino. Employed 42 years at Graniteville Company after war.

323

CARROLL, Charles (C.Q.): As Navy hospital corpsman, saved several from drowning when ship sank during North African invasion. After invasion of Sicily, sent to Pacific and served in several island invasions, including Makin and Roi Namur. Retired from Navy after 20 years and became landowner of over 1000 acres in central Georgia.

CARSTARPHEN, Robert (Sarge): Infantryman, 94th Infantry Division. Cleared 3 German machine gun nests in France; later fought in Battle of the Bulge. Awarded 2 Bronze Stars, 4 Battle Stars. Returned to family wholesale grocery business.

CARTER, W. Broadus: Frostbitten and wounded during Battle of the Bulge with Army's 99th Division. Witnessed many fellow soldiers wounded during initial arrival at the front. Re-enlisted twice, employed at Keller Industries in Waynesboro, GA., until retirement.

CARTER, William H. (Sam): Army Signal Corps communications specialist with 5th Marine Division in Pacific, 6 different island battles. Remembered Japanese fighting out of caves on Iwo Jima after its conquest. Following 12 years military service, went into missile industry in Florida.

CASEY, Gail (Gene): During Battle of the Bulge, deployed in anti-aircraft artillery to protect airfields in Belgium from German attack. Retired after 40 years at Savannah River Plant.

CHERRY, Cliff: With 70th Infantry Division in France, last year of war. Engaged in Vosges Mountains, Colmar, and advances into Germany. Retired from Savannah River Plant after 37 years.

CHITTY, Wes: Army Air Corps pilot with Ninth Air Force in Europe; flew 14 bombing missions in Douglas A-20 Havoc, and 40 missions in A-26 Invader. Wounded during mission over Germany; awarded Purple Heart and Distinguished Flying Cross. Opened a flying school after the war.

CHURCH, Bill: Extensive combat with 3rd Infantry Division in Sicily, Salerno, Anzio, Cassino, Rome, southern France, Rhine River, where captured (POW). Awarded 2 Purple Hearts, 5 Battle Stars. Retired after 28 years at Savannah River Plant.

324

CLEMENTS, John: With 2nd Armored Division in 6 major battles including North Africa, Sicily, D-Day to war's end in Germany. After serving 21 years in the Army, worked for 20 years at Augusta Post Office.

COCKRELL, Rufus: Machinist Mate in Navy on troop transport sunk in North Africa; then, on Attack Cargo vessel in Pacific, shot down Japanese aircraft at Okinawa. Employed by Georgia Power 40 years after war.

COLEMAN, Billy: Commanded Higgins boats as Navy officer during invasions of Sicily, Italy and Utah Beach on D-Day. After war, practiced law beyond age 90 as oldest practicing lawyer in South Carolina.

CONNELL, Jack: Flew 79 missions with Army Air Corps as Bombardier/Navigator on B-26 medium bomber, including low-level mission over Normandy on D-Day. Ran several businesses after war, served 34 years in Georgia State Legislature, including 26 years as Speaker Pro-Tem, longest in U.S. political history.

COURSEY, Marvin: Combat veteran with 30th Infantry Division from Normandy to war's end in Germany. While at Battle of the Bulge, was close to Malmedy massacre. After war, served over the years as choir director, 4 different churches.

CRAIG, Richard: Gunner's Mate on amphibious troop carrier ship at New Guinea, Bougainville, Philippines, and Okinawa. On one of first ships in Tokyo Bay at end of war. After the war, returned to Augusta to finish high school. Post-war career in consumer finance, vice-president at C & S Bank before retirement.

CRAWFORD, Mabel: Navy WAVE stationed in Washington working with top secret code breakers on German code. Returned to family farm after war.

DANIEL, Dick: Officer with Eighth Army in New Guinea and Philippines. During late stages of war in the Pacific, on the G-3 staff planning invasion of Japan. After discharge, returned to his father's Augusta wholesale business before going into insurance industry.

325

DANIEL, Dr. Ernest: After medical school and joining Navy, served as doctor in the Pacific at Peleliéu, Iwo Jima, and Okinawa. During one engagement, the arm of a wounded soldier he was trying to help became detached. After war, had family practice in Carroll County, GA, then went into neurosurgery.

DAVIS, David: Trained with 101st Airborne Division in Europe to fly gliders. Transfer to Pacific postponed when A-bomb ended war. Stayed in Army 29 years.

DAVIS, Jim: On landing craft support vessel during Okinawa invasion. Eight months with occupation forces in Japan. After war became respected TV newsman in the CSRA.

DeBARGE, Ray: Army medic in the Pacific at Saipan, Guam, Philippines. On Okinawa, saw his best friend blown to pieces. Stayed in service until 1962 but released on 100% disability because of heart attack. Worked at Masters Tournament 30 years.

DeLORME, Hank: With 9th Infantry Division on initial invasion of North Africa, where he was shot at by the French. Received Purple Heart for permanent injury to hand. Retired after 28 years with U.S. Postal Service.

DICKEY, Clifford: Petty Officer in Navy "island hopping" in the Pacific. During last major air battle over Guadalcanal, saw many Japanese aircraft shot down. Retired after 33 years at Savannah River Plant.

DONNER, Don: Captured while in combat with 103rd Division in France, POW for 6 months at 4 different German prison camps, escaping briefly one time. Returned to Iowa after war before returning to military service.

ESTES, Charles: With 85th Infantry Division in northern Italy, wounded third day on line. After war, spent 42 years with U. S. Postal Service.

EUBANKS, James: With 32nd Infantry Division; on patrol in jungles of New Guinea, experienced several face-to-face encounters with the Japanese. Awarded Purple Heart. Employed post-war for 37 years at Milliken Textiles.

FREEMAN, Galen: Performed aircraft maintenance work with the Army Air Corps on B-24's and C-47's in China. After war, worked as a self-employed accountant for more than 50 years.

EUBANKS, Reed: Left high school early to join Navy, last full year of war. Served on board an Assault Personnel Attack transport ship during invasion of Okinawa. Returned after war to finish high school at Richmond Academy. After business college and early varied employment, worked for 37 years with wholesale industrial equipment company.

FULGHUM, Kasper: Joined Augusta National Guard in 1939 before entering Army after Pearl Harbor. Platoon leader, Combat Engineers, during entire Italian campaign, earning 6 Bronze Stars. Owned hardware store in Greenville, S.C., after war.

FIVEASH, Charles: Landed at Utah Beach, D-Day plus 1, with 4th Infantry Division. Worked with "Red Ball Express" transport system across France before winding up behind the lines during Battle of the Bulge. Earned engineering degree at Georgia Tech on GI Bill; worked for DuPont 30 years.

GIBSON, Dr. Henry: Flew 25 missions as pilot of B-24 Liberator with 8th Air Force in Europe. Despite a direct hit by a German 88, plane did not go down. After war and medical school, had family practice of 57 years in Barnwell, S.C.

GLISSON, Lloyd: Served in Army in European campaign as Platoon Sergeant in Normandy, Battle of the Bulge and end of war in Austria. Worked at Augusta's Merry Brothers Brick for 30 years, rising to plant manager.

GOOD, Joe: With 28th Infantry Division in Huertgen Forest, Battle of the Bulge. Captured by Germans, freed by Russians near war's end. Owned small restaurant in Augusta after war.

GOODALE, Dr. Fairfield: Flew P-51 Mustang with Army Air Corps in Europe; tactical air support reconnaissance squadron during Patton's drive into Germany. In autobiography, *The Absolute Truth…*, wrote went into medicine: seeing horrors of Buchenwald. Became Dean, Medical College of Georgia.

GUNTER, Leonard: Served during naval war in Pacific as Gunner's Mate on LST. On board during invasions at Bougainville, Munda, Rendova, etc. After war, employed by South Carolina Electric and Gas for 32 years.

HADDOCK, Julian: Combat soldier with 89th Infantry Division during last months of war, from crossing Rhine River to end of hostilities in Czechoslovakia. After military service, worked at paper mill, north Florida.

HAGLER, Gould: Served in artillery battalion with the Third Army in central Europe. Involved in 5 major battles, including Battle of the Bulge. Received Bronze Star for event when shot at by German tank. Practiced law in Augusta for 40 years.

HARLESS, Paul: Entered Navy in 1939 with early assignment on President Roosevelt's private yacht "Potomac," which carried FDR to meeting with Churchill on the *U.S.S. Augusta* off Newfoundland. When war began, assigned to destroyer in the Pacific which received 12 Battle Stars. Employed 27 years after war at Savannah River Plant.

HITT, Ray: Served with a heavy weapons company of the 65th Infantry Division in Europe through the Siegfried line to the Danube River into Germany, last months of war. Played professional baseball after war and then worked at Merry Brothers Brick in Augusta.

HOLLADAY, J. Stedman (Ted): Assigned to auxiliary ships doing anti-submarine work at Guam, Leyte, Iwo Jima, and Okinawa. Survived kamikaze attacks; awarded 3 Bronze Stars. Earned engineering degree from University of South Carolina after war, then worked as Consulting Engineer.

HOLLEY, Ferrell: Pilot of a B-25 Mitchell medium bomber with 12th Air Force. Flew 65 bombing missions in the Mediterranean, most without fighter escort. Returned to work in family business after war.

HOWARD, Roy: With Army's 35th Infantry Division as gunner on a tank destroyer during combat at Saint-Lo and Battle of the Bulge, where he saw General Patton. 32 years in military, including Korea and Vietnam.

HUIET, James (Fritz): In the Navy on LST at Omaha Beach on D-Day. Later served in the Pacific on destroyer escort. After war, worked on construction of the Savannah River Plant before becoming Postmaster, Trenton, S.C.

JACKSON, Clarence: With the 3rd Armored Division, received slight leg wound during Battle of the Bulge. Fought against SS troops and Tiger tanks. After war, became a pharmacist in Augusta.

JACKSON, Tom: Flew 23 bombing missions with the 13th Air Force in the Pacific as a 6'2" ball turret gunner on a B-24 Liberator. 16 hour-plus bombing runs to oil refineries in Borneo, originally owned by major U. S. companies. After war, worked for a distributor of petroleum products in Williston, S.C.

JARRELL, Tom: Pilot of B-26 Marauder medium bomber on 37 missions over Europe. Primary targets included German positions at Battle of the Bulge and the Rhine River. After war, worked at family owned Bailey's Art Center 55 years.

JOLLEY, Wayne: With 30th Infantry Division in Europe during Battle of the Bulge and Rhine River crossing. Remembered 22,000 paratroops dropping over Rhine and attacks by 12 German tank divisions during Battle of the Bulge. Employed at Savannah River Plant after the war.

 JONES, Robert: Pilot with 5th Air Force in South Pacific on B-26, B-25 and B-24 aircraft on total of 59 missions, based primarily in Australia. On one mission, plane hit by shell on bomb bay but no one killed. Owned land-development company after the war.

 KAPLAN, Harry: Navy Supply Officer on an Assault Personnel Attack transport carrying up to 2,000 troops on invasions of the Philippines, Iwo Jima and Okinawa. After war, went back into family dry cleaning business in Florida for 40 years.

 KAUFFMANN, James: Pilot in 10th Air Force on B-24 Liberator in the China-Burma-India theater with combat photo mapping reconnaissance squadron. Based in India, flew the Hump on many missions. After war, went into auto repair business at Fort Gordon then to Florida with an auto dealer 40 years.

 KEMP, Harry: Combat infantryman in Europe with 14th Armored Division. Only PFC promoted to 2nd Lieutenant in WWII. Led platoon on attack at Siegfried Line; was one of 15 who survived out of 48. Twin brother died in combat. Met wife when treated for leg wound in Augusta. After college, went into citrus industry in Florida, then into teaching.

 KENDALL, Jack: Navigator on 24 missions in a B-24 Liberator with 13th Air Force in the Pacific. Several long missions required 12-14 hours flight time. After war, returned to Georgia Tech for civil engineering degree and then worked on the Clark Hill Dam project.

KRISTENSEN, John: Army Quartermaster officer with platoon of 30 working in a semi-mobile laundry unit throughout the European campaign. Trapped during Battle of the Bulge near Malmedy, site of the massacre. Went into retail industry after service, retiring from J. B. White's as a buyer.

LEITNER, George: 23 years in Army, beginning in 1935. After Officer's Candidate School in 1943, rose to Captain with 5th Infantry Division in the Normandy break-out to the Rhine. Wounded before battle at Metz, fought at Battle of the Bulge. After service, became high school ROTC teacher, Anderson, S.C.

LANDRETH, Evelyn: 1st Lieutenant in the Pacific with Army Nurse Corps serving in New Guinea and then Manila, Philippines. Officers were not supposed to fraternize, she met enlisted man; they were married for 45 years before he died. Worked for 30 years after war at V.A. Hospital in Augusta

LEOPARD, John (Bob): Joined Army before Pearl Harbor, resigned, then joined Navy. Served on 4 different ships and crossed Atlantic 14 times, once with 8,000 on board when attacked by U-boats. After working 40 years with Greenwood Mills, started own trucking company.

LANGDON, Fred: Flew in the Pacific with the Navy on PB 4Y-1 Liberators. Based on Tinian, experience included patrol and bombing missions at Peleliu, Iwo Jima and Okinawa. To college after war on GI Bill, then worked for Milliken before self-employment. Later became one of the founders of Aiken Tech.

LIPSEY, Leonard: Army service included guarding enemy POWs in Georgia before serving on a hospital ship in the Pacific at Leyte and the Philippines. After war, became a night club owner and real estate developer in Augusta.

LUNDQUIST, Dr. Donald: Artillery veteran, European campaign. During Battle of the Bulge, saw bodies removed following Malmedy Massacre. Crossed Rhine River at Remagen. Following war and training in dentistry, on staff at Dental School in Augusta.

LUNDQUIST, Raymond: B-24 Liberator navigator, 15th Air Force in Italy. Flew 50 missions, including 4 over Ploesti in Romania. College degree in engineering, retired after 20 years at Kimberly Clark, Beech Island, S.C.

MANNING, Wyndham: B-24 Liberator pilot with 14th Air Force in China-Burma-India Theater. Flew nearly 100 flights, many on bombing missions over China. Missing-in-action two weeks after bail-out before plane crashed. Varied career after war: farming, construction, sales, real estate.

MAYS, Alvin: Entered Army in 1940; stationed at Pearl Harbor during Japanese attack. Technical Sgt. with Army's 24th Division; on 3 invasions in New Guinea and Philippines, with 2 long engagements in combat at Leyte and Mindanao. Established successful nursery business in Augusta after war.

McCLELLAN, Russell: Served as driver with artillery battalion, 1st Marine Division on Okinawa. Brief experience after Japanese surrender with Marines in China. Returned home to farming before working 33 years at Savannah River Plant.

McCOLLUM, Thomas: In Europe with Patton's 5th Infantry Division. Injured when blown off tank near Metz, in hospital 116 days; Purple Heart. Foreman at Savannah River Plant after war; volunteer wood worker for local area churches.

McCOY, Chester: With the 4th Marine Division on Saipan where he was wounded; also fought on Tinian, Iwo Jima and Roi-Namur, where he served under Medal of Honor recipient Jimmie Dyess, also from Augusta. Following the war worked at Borden's 40 years.

McDONALD, Richard: Bombardier on B-24 Liberator with 15th Air Force in Europe. Shot down on 20th mission over Germany, 9 months as POW at Stalag Luft 3. After war and brief employment with VA in Texas, went into construction industry in New Mexico.

McLAIN, Ralph: Assigned to technical classified work in the Army Air Corps as a radio operator during development of radar. Flew number of classified missions, one of which resulted in surviving ditching on British Mosquito aircraft in the North Sea. Returned to the military after the war, retiring in 1966.

MENGER, Bill: Flew 49 missions as captain/bombardier of a B-17 Flying Fortress with 8th Air Force, including 6 over Berlin and once landing in Russia. Following 21 years in military, worked at Davison's Department Store and then Montgomery Ward in Augusta.

MOORE, Robert: Radioman on 3 different submarines which sank several Japanese ships. On board submarine when ammunition ship USS Mount Hood exploded nearby, largest U.S. ship explosion of war. After service, taught communications at Fort Gordon 28 years.

MURRAY, Marie: With Army Nurse Corps at Normandy after D-Day, helped set up field hospital near Utah Beach where she was slightly wounded. She later treated Senator Bob Dole, wounded in Italy, after war. Returning to Augusta, employed at St. Joseph's Hospital 28 years.

MURRY, Jim: Served in Pacific with 5th Air Force as B-24 Liberator bombardier. On night flight over water, survived near crash with war nearly over. Studied at University of Georgia; television pioneer in Atlanta before starting own public relations/financial planning firm.

NEWMAN, Lewis (Pop): B-17 Flying Fortress pilot in Army Air Corps, flew missions over North Africa, Italy and Sicily; trained B-17 pilots in Louisiana. Managed dry cleaning business after war; served as Augusta mayor.

OWENS, W. Milwee: Officer with 45th Infantry Division, Europe. Awarded Bronze Star, Purple Heart, Combat Infantry Badge and 3 Battle Stars. Slept in Hitler's bed in Munich at end of war! Hardware store owner in Augusta after war.

PAGE, Weldon: With 87th Infantry Division during Battle of the Bulge. German artillery shell killed buddy next to him; another landed as a dud or he would have been killed. After war, worked as roofer/gardener before becoming self-employed.

PARILLE, Gertie: Austrian Jew who left family as a young woman and escaped Nazis through sponsorship by a Quaker family in Pennsylvania. Eventually came to Augusta through relative Judge Nathan Jollies. Employed in Civil Service at Fort Gordon 30 years.

PARISH, Reeves: With 35th Infantry Division in France. Survived face-to-face combat with German soldier; awarded 2 Purple Hearts, one from wounds at Metz. Stayed in Army 20 years then became EMT and Fire Chief in Wrens, GA.

PARKER, Herman: Joined Navy at age 14, served as Steward's Mate in the invasion of Sicily, then in the Pacific on 7 separate invasions, including Iwo Jima and Okinawa. Describes segregated conditions aboard ship. To New York after war, then back south to return to school in ninth grade.

334

PAULK, Gerald: Paratrooper of the famous 101ˢᵗ Airborne Division, he fought at Normandy, Holland, and Battle of the Bulge at Bastogne, when it was surrounded. Following college, he became a chiropractor for a total of 50 years.

PEARLSTEIN, Jay: Trained in Augusta with 4ᵗʰ Infantry Division, then landed on Utah Beach on D-Day. Fought through France to Battle of the Bulge. Served with JAG unit after V-E Day, although not a lawyer. Upon return to Augusta, started Key Wholesalers.

PRATER, Ed: "Land-lubber" in Navy unloading ships at Okinawa and Japan after V-J Day. Twice a cancer survivor after exposure to radiation at Nagasaki. Postwar career involved sales of heavy construction equipment.

PROCTOR, Julian: Flew 32 missions as B-24 Liberator gunner with 8ᵗʰ Air Force. Aircraft was shot up on bombing runs over Europe on several occasions. Returned home to work at family grocery store before spending 30 years with A & P.

PROUT, Bill: Served on PT Boat 191, Squadron 12, in the Solomon Islands that downed 6 Japanese planes, sank 2 ships, 48 barges and one 2-man submarine. After war earned Ph.D. in chemistry, worked at DuPont laboratory, Savannah River Plant 30 years. Scorer for 43 years at the Masters and had a hole-in-one on the 12ᵗʰ hole (Amen Corner).

RABORN, Leland (Roy): Army Signal Corps communications specialist, landed on Omaha Beach at "H" Hour (6:30 AM) on D-Day. Continued through France to Battle of the Bulge and into Germany to war's end. Awarded Silver Star for D-Day operations. After war, worked at clothing store in Greenwood, S.C., 40 years.

RICKETSON, Ed: Gunner on B-29 Superfortress in the Pacific, flew 13 missions over Japan, including 6 aborted missions requiring emergency landings on Iwo Jima. Graduate of Emory University then went into insurance business.

335

RILEY, Tom: Army infantry officer, Europe, following ROTC at University of Georgia. Lost most of his hearing when wounded in Germany; Purple Heart. After war, became college professor at University of South Carolina and Augusta College.

ROBBINS, Jim: With Army anti-aircraft artillery battalion at Guadalcanal, Bougainville and the Philippines. During invasion of Luzon, saw 3 Kamikazes hit three different ships. Worked for Texaco Oil 35 years.

ROBERTS, Robert (Pat): With 6th Marine Division at Saipan, Tinian, and Okinawa, earning 3 Purple Hearts. After Japanese surrender, processed freed prisoners in northern China. Became a distributor of poultry products then built a processing plant in Athens, GA.

ROBINSON, Leroy: Navy Hellcat fighter pilot off carrier *USS Hornet* in the Pacific. Became Ace after credit for shooting down 5 Japanese planes. Involved in sea battles at Leyte Gulf and Philippine Sea. Pilot with Delta Airlines 32 years.

RUCKER, Joseph T.: With 9th Infantry Division in Europe, second wave on Utah Beach, D-Day. In combat to war's end, received Purple Heart, Bronze and Silver Stars as well as 7 campaign medals. Worked for textile companies after war, including Lowenstein and Owens Corning.

SABINE, George: Rifleman in Darby's 3rd Ranger Battalion from North Africa to Sicily and Italy, where he was wounded near Cassino. Later served in southern France to war's end in Germany. Postwar career in sales management.

SANDERS, Carl: Trained as B-17 Flying Fortress pilot late in war but never sent overseas. Bombing practice over town in Tennessee resulted in complaint by mayor after event. University of Georgia and UGA Law School, eventually went into politics and rose to become Governor of Georgia.

SCHERER, Robert: Observer with Army Airborne Artillery unit in combined operations with infantry and paratroopers for liberation of prisoners at Los Baños Prison Philippines. Served briefly during Korean War; worked in metals manufacturing industry.

SCHUTTE, Carl: 66th Infantry officer in Europe. Saw ship sunk alongside his ship with losses of over 200 in frigid waters of the English Channel. Worked for VA in Alabama, then at Savannah River for 33 years.

SCOTT, Carroll: Served on Coast Guard LST; at Iwo Jima, saw flag raising on Mount Suribachi and shelling during invasion by USS Augusta. Employed by Pure Oil Petroleum Company for 39 years.

SCOTT, Jesse: With Army Quartermasters in Europe on non-combat activities with motor pool maintenance, ammunition/food distribution. With advances into Germany, served as back-up to combat troops. After war wored as service station operator in Langley, S.C.

SHAW, Albert: Mortar specialist in Europe, landing in Normandy on D-Day plus 1. Fought at Battle of the Bulge, crossed the Rhine River at Remagen, then met Russians at the Elbe. After service, became Senior Executive VP at Pennzoil, later Exxon Oil Company.

SHEPPARD, Joseph F. (Tag): Joined Navy at age 17 in 1936. On board carrier USS Franklin in the Pacific when attacked by kamikazes, 832 crewmen killed—the most decorated ship in U.S. Navy history. After war, rural mail carrier for 41 years.

SHIVERS, Quentin: Marine stationed on battleship USS Pennsylvania (Admiral Kimmel's Flag ship) at Pearl Harbor on December 7, 1941—his 21st birthday. Later sent to Guam in anticipation of invasion of Japan. Following war, worked in field engineering 35 years with IBM.

337

SLOAN, Jack D.: Navy career over 20 years beginning in 1935. In action one year before Pearl Harbor in the Atlantic; wrote book about his ship, destroyer *USS Swanson*, which participated in 9 invasions. Also worked on LORAN (Long Range Navigation), a secret project relating to radar. After war, worked in personnel administration in textile manufacturing.

SMITH, Clarence: Navigator on PBY Catalina Flying Boat in the Pacific. Aircraft were painted black for night flights on reconnaissance missions with PT Boats, therefore named "Black Cat Squadron." Engineering degree at University of Michigan after war; retired as Technical Sales Manager at Tranter in Edgefield, S.C.

SMITH, Curby L.: Served on aircraft carrier *USS Hornet* when Doolittle's Raiders attacked Tokyo in April 1942 and when the *Hornet* was sunk by the Japanese in October 1942 near Guadalcanal. Went into milk industry with Borden's in Augusta following war, 35 years.

TARVER, Chuck: Flew 50 missions with 15th Air Force in Italy on B-24 Liberator. Significant flights included 5 times over Ploesti oil fields, bombing aircraft factory and submarine pens in France. After serving 20 years in the military, participated as volunteer church worker.

TAYLOR, John W.: Entered Army during last year of war; with only 13 weeks training, joined 106th Infantry Division during Battle of the Bulge. Grew up as one of 10 children during the Depression. After war, became a Manager with Prudential Insurance Company.

TEWKSBURY, Al: With 1st Marine Division at Guadalcanal, Cape Gloucester and Peleliu. As stretcher bearer carrying wounded Marines on Peleliu, partner was shot and killed. Engineering degree at Clemson, helped build Clarks Hill Dam and then worked 33 years at J. M. Huber in Langley, S.C.

THOMPSON, Bennie: Rifleman with 34th Infantry Division in North Africa and Italy; awarded Bronze Star and 3 Purple Hearts for wounds in combat. Captured by Germans in the Po Valley in 1944, sent to Germany and forced to work as POW in labor gangs until end of war. After the war he worked building houses, became tool and die worker for 29 years at Savannah River Plant.

TILLER, Traylor A.: On battleship USS New York in the Atlantic before transfer to carrier USS Yorktown in the Pacific. As a gunner, credited with shooting down many Japanese planes; also wounded by an explosion of a plane landing on the carrier. Participation in 11 separate sea battles. Worked after war at Augusta Arsenal then the Corps of Engineers for 22 years.

TRUDEAU, Dennis: Born in U.S. but served in Canadian Army as paratrooper when family moved to Canada. Jumped into Normandy night before D-Day; wounded and captured on June 6. As POW in Germany, forced to work in coal mine until end of war. After war, served 21 years in U. S. Army. Served several years as mayor of Grovetown.

VIGNATI, Joe: Aviation machinist on carrier USS Bunker Hill and survived deadliest kamikaze attack of the war. On board during Battle of Philippine Sea and invasion of Okinawa. Worked 30 years in HVAC business with brother-in-law after war.

WADDELL, George: Flew 18 missions over Central Europe as B-24 Liberator tail gunner with 15th Air Force based in Italy . On one mission, returned to base with 3 engines out and nearly 300 holes from enemy gunfire. Returned to farming after war, then employed 31 years as pipefitter, Savannah River Plant.

WARE, Johnny: Served with Army Signal Corps construction battalion in France, then Germany, where he was fired on by enemy 88s while on telephone pole. Ended war on Okinawa preparing for invasion of Japan. After working 22 years with railroad, retired from Kimberly Clark.

WARREN, Richard: Landed on Omaha Beach with 29th Division on D-Day. Attached to different divisions throughout European campaign with military police. In Belgium when Germans first attacked in Battle of the Bulge. After war, managed an LP gas company.

WATERS, John Roland: Crewmember on Coast Guard icebreaker in North Atlantic that captured a German trawler near Greenland. After schooling in plumbing and electrical trades, ordained as minister.

WATKINS, George D.: With 8th Armored Division on a Tank Destroyer at Battle of the Bulge. Liberated Sudetenland, German speaking sector of Czechoslovakia. Optician for 39 years after war.

WATSON, Joe: Captain, 75th Infantry Division, over Mortar Platoon of 3 officers and 80 enlisted men throughout campaign in Europe, including Bulge, Rhineland, Ruhr Pocket. Awarded Purple Heart and Bronze Star. Returned to farming after war.

WATSON, Dr. W. G. (Curley): Served in Army Medical Corps late in war in Philippines, then briefly in Korea after Japanese surrender. Practice of medicine continued well into his 90's and gained national fame as obstetrician birthing over 15,000 babies in the CSRA.

WELLS, William T.: Served with artillery units of the 7th and 3rd Armies in North Africa and invasion of southern France. Advanced to Battle of the Bulge and then to Austria at war's end. After college, began career in retail when he bought a grocery store.

WETZEL, Jim: Flew 23 missions over Japan as navigator/radar operator of B-29 Superfortress, 20th Air Force. One of 4 Pathfinders during incendiary raid on Tokyo, entire crew awarded Distinguished Flying Cross when two planes were shot down. Practiced patent law until retirement.

WHITEHEAD, Stan: Paratrooper with Army's 11th Airborne Division. During Philippine Liberation, made jumps at Leyte and Luzon. Joined Marines after war, then went into Air Force—finishing with 26 years in military.

WILLIAMS, Emerald (Bill): Served on hospital ship with Navy in Mediterranean, picking up wounded from southern France. Transferred to Pacific for similar duties at Leyte and China. Went back into Navy during Korean War for long career in military.

WICKER, James E.: Flew modified P-38 Lightning on photo reconnaissance mission when shot down over Normandy on D-Day. POW in Germany until end of war, initially at Stalag Luft 3. Following 24-year career in Air Force, employed as Airport Manager at Bush Field.

WINDMULLER, Henry: Left Germany as a 14-year-old Jewish boy as part of the Kindertransport program in England. Sent to Canada then to U.S. where he joined Army Air Forces near end of war as cook. Became a hotel cook after war before becoming a toolmaker.

WILLIAMS, A. L. (Coach): Assistant radio operator on B-24 Liberator with 8th Air Force. Shot down on 10th mission over Germany; several in crew were killed. Captured by Germans, POW for 16 months at Stalag 17. At Richmond Academy, coached 7 consecutive State Championship baseball teams and rose to become school's principal.

WISENBAKER, James: With Army's 106th Infantry Division, captured at Battle of the Bulge. Spent 4 months as POW in Germany. Following military service, worked for railroad 40 years.

WOODHURST, Stan: B-26 Marauder pilot with 12th Air Force in the Mediterranean. Flew 60 missions to support land operations in Sicily, in Italy at Anzio and Monte Cassino, and then France. Captured by German SS near war's end. Entered service after degree from Clemson, then established successful architectural firm in Augusta after war.

WRIGHT, Bruce: Joined Navy in 1939, stationed on a destroyer at Pearl Harbor during Japanese attack. Served on two different submarines, chasing and sinking Japanese shipping until end of war. After war, worked with brother in coal business; served 2 more years during Korean War.

ZWEMER, Dr. Tom: Served in Medical Battalion with Army's 40th Infantry Division in the South Pacific. Participated in 3 invasions in the Philippines: Luzon, Panay Island, and Los Negros. After the war, helped to establish the dental school at Medical College of Georgia.

342

INDEX

To Carl Waddell

Life is all about Love

Love your Loard

Love your family.

Love your freedom + country

Love your friends and Neighbor.

Love your enemys

I Love you,
Dad
Sgt George Waddell
8/2/17

CPSIA information can be obtained
at www.ICGtesting.com
Printed in the USA
LVOW10*0409190717

541293LV00006B/10/P

9 780937 044049